CONSUMER GUIDE

1991 EDITION

CONSUMER BUYING GUIDE

Cover Photo Credits: Commodore Business
Machines; Chrysler Motor Corporation;
JVC Company of America; Mitsubishi
Electric Sales; Sunbeam Appliance
Company; White Consolidated
Industries.

Contents

Introduction

If you have ever gone shopping for a car, a major appliance, a television set, or stereo components, you know that buying wisely is more than a matter of luck. It takes experience and expert knowledge. This is especially true today when rapid advances in technology and shifts in the world's economy can quickly change the price, availability, and long-term usefulness of a product.

No person can ever know everything about every available product; there is simply too much to know. CONSUMER GUIDE® recognizes that it's a challenge to pick a "best buy," which meets your requirements for quality, performance, and value. Our experts in the major product fields have done the research, testing, and comparison shopping for you. We have taken the guesswork out of making major purchases. CONSUMER GUIDE® has no ties to manufacturers or retailers, we accept no advertising, and we are not interested in selling products. Our sole purpose is to provide you with the information you need to make intelligent purchases.

We have tried to review a wide variety of products in this publication, ranging from small personal items, such as hair dryers and small-capacity automatic drip coffee makers, to major purchases, such as refrigerators and stereo systems. We have not limited ourselves to lower-priced products or top-of-the-line products. A product is a best buy only if it meets your needs, so we have selected products in a variety of sizes and prices to match the requirements of many kinds of shoppers.

Beyond simple supply and demand, many factors influence the prices of products. This year's prices reflect two opposing economic trends. Some products cost less because they incorporate microchips or other modular electronic devices, while other products have higher prices because of the decline in the value of the U.S. dollar and increased production costs. Many products such as CD players, personal cassette players, computers, and food processors are much less expensive today than they were when they first came on the market. But some products, including stereo equipment, major appliances, and camcorders, have become more expensive over the last year.

To make the best use of this publication, first review the introductory material at the beginning of each chapter. This introduction contains important information about the product, describes its features, and explains the terminology you need to know when you shop. Once you are acquainted with the criteria we use to select products, go on to our Best Buy selections. These products were chosen for their usefulness, high quality, and overall value. A Best Buy isn't necessarily the least expensive model; it's the highest-quality product available at a reasonable price. Recommended selections are also good products, but for one reason or another, they do not measure up to our Best Buy standards. Such a product may carry a high price tag, it may have limited appeal, or it could be so new on the market that we don't yet know how it will perform over time.

When you shop, compare prices and models. If a dealer quotes a price close to the Approximate Low Price in this publication, then you know that you are getting first-rate value for your money. All the prices listed were accurate at the time of printing, but due to currency fluctuations and manufacturers' price adjustments, both retail and low prices may change. In some cases, prices were not available. All products were checked to make sure that they would be available to consumers in 1991, but product manufacture and distribution is beyond our control, and manufacturers may discontinue models in the future without notice.

Cars, Vans, and 4-Wheel-Drive Vehicles

The Auto Editors of CONSUMER GUIDE® have selected Best Buy and Recommended vehicles in ten categories of passenger cars, compact vans, and 4-wheel-drive vehicles. A vehicle is assigned to one of these categories based on its size, price, and market position.

At least one Best Buy has been selected in each category. Some categories also include models labeled Recommended, which are also worthy of attention. Road-test results play a major role in the selections. Some new models, such as the Acura Legend, were not available for road testing in time to be considered for this issue. Other factors used to select Best Buys among cars include cost of ownership, warranties, reputation for reliability and durability, and safety record.

SUBCOMPACTS

HONDA CIVIC ✓ BEST BUY

The Honda Civic is a Best Buy among small cars because of its good fuel economy, high quality, and commendable durability. Civic's prices start at less than $7,000 for a base 3-door hatchback, climb to nearly $12,000 for a loaded sedan, and top out at $13,140 for a 4-wheel-drive station wagon. The mid-level DX models offer the most value, with prices ranging from $8,745 for a 3-door hatchback to $10,420 for a 4-door with automatic transmission. Another $1,000 or so should be added for air conditioning and a stereo, which are dealer-installed options that don't carry manufacturer's suggested retail prices (dealers are free to set their own prices). Civics are among the most expensive subcompacts, but they're also among the most dependable, and they have exceptionally high resale value. One way to save money on a Civic is to buy one with manual transmission instead of the more popular—and more expensive—automatic.

MAZDA 323/PROTEGE, FORD ESCORT, AND MERCURY TRACER

RECOMMENDED

The Mazda 323/Protege, Ford Escort, and Mercury Tracer are the collaborative effort of Ford Motor Company and Mazda Motor Corporation. The Mazda models, built in Japan, arrived in the U.S. last year: the 323 is a 3-door hatchback, and the Protege is a 4-door sedan. Ford's versions arrived last spring as early 1991 models. The Escort and Tracer are built in the U.S. and Mexico. Though most of their parts are also built in North America, all of their transmissions and some of their engines are supplied by Mazda. The Escort comes in three body styles: 3- and 5-door hatchbacks and a 5-door wagon. The Tracer comes as a 4-door sedan and a 5-door wagon. All models have above-average acceleration, good fuel economy, and spacious interiors with rear seats that fold down for extra cargo room. In addition, dealers should be willing to discount prices, no matter which brand you choose.

TOYOTA COROLLA AND GEO PRIZM

RECOMMENDED

The Toyota Corolla and Geo Prizm are similar cars that promise commendable reliability, low maintenance costs, and

Prices are accurate at time of printing; subject to manufacturer's change.

high fuel economy. The Prizm is built from the same design as the Corolla, but has different exterior styling and is sold through Chevrolet dealers with Geo franchises. Prizms and some Corolla 4-door sedans are built at a General Motors-Toyota plant in California. We don't see any difference in quality between U.S.-built Corollas and those imported from Japan. Since Corollas and Prizms share mechanical components, they should be equally reliable and durable. The only advantage to buying a Corolla might be higher resale value; the Toyota brand name is much better known than the Geo. Base prices for both models are *lower* this year. Corollas start at about $9,000 and Prizms at about $9,700. Because today's car market is so competitive, you should be able to buy either a Corolla or a Prizm for less than suggested retail price, with bigger discounts available on Prizm. You can save even more money on a leftover 1990 model; they differ little from the 1991s.

COMPACT CARS

DODGE SPIRIT AND PLYMOUTH ACCLAIM

The Dodge Spirit and Plymouth Acclaim are nearly identical front-drive 4-door sedans that have ample passenger space and roomy trunks that can be expanded by folding the rear seats. Three engines are available: two Chrysler 4-cylinders (one with a turbocharger, one without) and a Mitsubishi 3.0-liter V-6. We like the V-6 best because it's the quietest and smoothest, but could live with either of the available 4-cylinder engines. A driver's airbag is standard and anti-lock brakes are a new option for all models. A loaded Spirit or Acclaim with anti-lock brakes, V-6, air conditioning, power locks and windows, stereo with cassette player, and other extras will be around $15,500 at suggested retail price. A basic 4-cylinder model with fewer features runs about $13,000. Actual selling prices should be hundreds of dollars lower because of factory and dealer discounts. Chrysler's 7-year warranties make the deals even better.

Prices are accurate at time of printing; subject to manufacturer's change.

TOYOTA CAMRY

The Toyota Camry is a roomy, economical, and reliable compact that offers buyers much to choose from: front-wheel or 4-wheel drive, 4-door sedan or 5-door wagon body styles, 4-cylinder or V-6 engines, and optional anti-lock brakes. Some Camrys are imported from Japan, but Toyota also builds 200,000 Camry sedans a year at its Kentucky plant. Toyota has been giving its dealers incentives to discount prices on Camrys to boost sales and to keep the Kentucky plant running. Quality on the U.S.-built models appears to match that of the Japanese-built models. A top-line Camry LE sedan can be quite expensive—over $20,000 with the V-6, anti-lock brakes, leather upholstery, and a few other options. However, a deluxe 4-door with the standard 115-horsepower 4-cylinder engine, automatic transmission, air conditioning, power windows and door locks, stereo, and cruise control is around $15,000.

HYUNDAI SONATA

RECOMMENDED

The Hyundai Sonata is a Korean-built 4-door sedan with a roomy interior, a fairly peppy 2.4-liter 4-cylinder engine, and a low price. A Mitsubishi-designed V-6 engine (the same one used in the Dodge Spirit and Plymouth Acclaim) is optional. The base Sonata with automatic transmission starts at around $11,400; a top-line GLS with automatic transmission is under $14,000, including air conditioning, power door locks and windows, cruise control, and stereo with cassette player. That's considerably less than a comparably equipped Toyota Camry LE. Sonata's assembly quality and interior materials don't match Camry's, but Hyundai's attractive prices make this car a good value among compact family sedans.

MID-SIZE CARS

FORD TAURUS AND MERCURY SABLE

The Ford Taurus and Mercury Sable are in their sixth model year, yet they still rank as Best Buys among mid-size, mod-

---

erately priced family cars because of their capable handling, roomy interiors, sound ergonomics, and reasonable prices. In addition, they have two safety features we recommend: a standard driver's airbag and optional anti-lock brakes. We recommend the 3.0-liter V-6 that's standard on all Sables and most Tauruses, or the 3.8-liter V-6 that's optional on both. The 4-cylinder engine, which is standard in lower-priced Taurus models, is more economical than the V-6, but it doesn't have enough power for a car this heavy. The front-drive Taurus and Sable are functionally the same and are similarly priced, from a minimum of $14,000 to over $20,000, depending on model and equipment. The best deals are on a Taurus GL or Sable GS through one of Ford's "preferred equipment" packages, which lump popular options into groups at discount prices. For example, a Taurus GL 4-door with the 3.0 V-6, anti-lock brakes, and Preferred Package 204A comes to $17,372, including the destination charge—a reasonable price for such a well-equipped car. In addition, Ford and Mercury are offering rebates and other sales incentives on these cars.

HONDA ACCORD

The Honda Accord is a front-drive vehicle redesigned for 1990, growing from a compact to a mid-size car available in 4-door sedan and 2-door coupe styling. This year, there are two major developments. One is that anti-lock brakes are standard on the SE 4-door sedan; the other is that a 5-door station wagon will be added to the roster (prices have not been announced for the wagon). We're glad to see anti-lock brakes, an important safety feature, on the Accord, but we wish it were also available on other models, not just the $20,000 SE. The Accord has several other good points: ample room for four people and their luggage, solid construction, a comfortable ride, competent handling, peppy acceleration, high resale value, and impressive quality. Apparently, a lot of other people agree; it's the best-selling car in America, and there are no cash rebates on the Accord. Honda has increased prices by only $200 for 1991, and you should be able to buy an Accord for less than suggested retail price in most areas. The mid-level LX models, at about $15,000 to $16,000, offer the most value.

Prices are accurate at time of printing; subject to manufacturer's change.

FULL-SIZE CARS

BUICK LE SABRE, OLDSMOBILE EIGHTY-EIGHT, AND PONTIAC BONNEVILLE

The Buick LeSabre, Oldsmobile Eighty-Eight, and Pontiac Bonneville are built from the same design and share their front-drive chassis, engines, and transmissions. They differ mainly in exterior styling and interior features. For the past two years, LeSabre has scored the highest among domestic cars in the J.D. Power initial quality survey. Anti-lock brakes are available as a $925 option on all three, while a driver's airbag is optional on the Eighty-Eight for $850. Anti-lock brakes can help you avoid an accident, while an airbag reduces the chances of injury in case of an accident. All three models use a 165-horsepower 3.8-liter V-6 engine that delivers strong acceleration and better fuel economy than V-8-powered full-size cars. Their front-wheel drive design gives them better traction in snow than rear-drive rivals. All three have abundant passenger and cargo space, and they're built with corrosion-resistant galvanized steel, eliminating the need for extra-cost rustproofing. The sticker price on these cars is at least $18,000 and will be more than $20,000 for plush versions, but dealers should be offering substantial discounts.

PREMIUM COUPES

CADILLAC ELDORADO

The Cadillac Eldorado coupe is scheduled to be redesigned for 1992, but it is also significantly changed for its final season in this form. The Eldorado's V-8 engine grows from 4.5 liters to 4.9, boosting horsepower from 180 to 200, and is teamed with General Motor's new smooth-shifting, electronically controlled, 4-speed automatic transmission. Also new this year is Computer Command Ride (CCR), Cadillac's new speed-dependent damping system. With CCR, shock-absorber firmness increases with vehicle speed to maintain a stable ride. Anti-lock brakes, previously optional, are now standard. A driver's airbag is also standard. Fuel economy wasn't great with the old engine and probably won't improve with the new one, and since it requires expensive premium unleaded gasoline. The price has also increased about $2,400 this year to $31,245. However, Cadillac dealers were offering big discounts on 1990s, and should be doing the same on 1991s.

LINCOLN MARK VII

RECOMMENDED

The Lincoln Mark VII is a rear-drive luxury coupe with substantial power, a full load of luxury equipment, and fine quality. A driver's airbag and anti-lock brakes are standard. The Mark VII comes two ways: the Bill Blass Designer Series and the sportier LSC. Both use a 225-horsepower 5.0-liter V-8 engine that delivers strong acceleration and a smooth, steady power flow. This year, both models also have a firm sport suspension and high-performance tires; previously, only the LSC had those features. Some may find the ride too firm, so we strongly suggest you try it before you buy. Base price for both is nearly $31,000 and, since most everything is standard, there are only a few big-ticket options. The Mark VII hasn't been a hot seller recently, so you'll probably be able to buy one at a large discount.

PREMIUM SEDANS

LEXUS LS 400

 ✔ BEST BUY

The Lexus LS 400 is the top model in Toyota's Lexus Division. Its 1991 base price is $38,000—$3,000 more than a year ago. Even at the current price, this car is an excellent buy. The LS 400 is a rear-drive sedan with a 250-horsepower 4.0-liter V-8 engine and a 4-speed automatic transmission. Standard equipment includes anti-lock disc brakes and a driver's-side airbag; a traction-control system is optional. The LS 400 is one of the quietest cars we've driven and its powerful V-8 engine is incredibly smooth, even when the throttle pedal is pressed to the floor. The ride is stable at high speed yet absorbent over tar strips and bumps, and the anti-lock brakes are strong and provide excellent control. The interior is elegant, comfortable, and generally accommodating. The overall quality is exceptional. The LS 400 is an extremely rewarding car that we rate higher than competing models—BMW, Mercedes-Benz, and Infiniti—in the same price range.

NISSAN MAXIMA ✔ BEST BUY

The Nissan Maxima is a front-drive 4-door that is competent, pleasant, and a bargain among premium sedans. The Maxima's base prices run from $18,399 for the GXE to $19,499 for the sportier SE, handily undercutting most rivals. Both use a 160-horsepower V-6 engine that provides smooth, brisk acceleration. We prefer the SE for its better handling and 4-wheel disc brakes; you also have to buy the SE to get the optional anti-lock brakes, which we highly recommend. Maxima has a clean, modern design, more than adequate room, and quality workmanship. It isn't in the same league as the Lexus LS 400, but it costs only half as much.

CADILLAC DE VILLE AND FLEETWOOD RECOMMENDED

The Cadillac De Ville and Fleetwood are both full-size front-drive sedans. The only difference is in the Fleetwood's more lavish standard features and higher prices. This year, they both have a new 200-horsepower 4.9-liter V-8 engine connected to a new electronically controlled 4-speed automatic transmission. Computer Command Ride (CCR), which varies shock-absorber damping based on vehicle speed, is standard this year on the Fleetwood and optional on the lower-priced De Ville. Anti-lock brakes and a driver's airbag are standard on all models. The new engine, transmission, and CCR improve the performance of these cars, but Cadillac has also improved in other ways in recent years. Overall quality—fit and finish, reliability, and durability—seems to get better each year. Unfortunately, this year's bigger engine will probably use more gas than the previous V-8, and prices are up sharply for 1991—about $2,900 for the De Ville and $1,900 for the Fleetwood sedan. Some of the increases are due to additional standard

Prices are accurate at time of printing; subject to manufacturer's change.

features, but Cadillac is boldly boosting its prices in a highly competitive market. Because there's so much competition, you should be able to negotiate a big discount.

TOYOTA CRESSIDA `RECOMMENDED`

The Toyota Cressida is a rear-drive sedan with a long list of standard features, a smooth, refined 6-cylinder engine, and a commendable reputation for reliability. The Cressida was nearly invisible in the marketplace last year until it scored the highest among all new cars covered in the 1990 J.D. Power initial quality survey. That sparked more interest in the Cressida and encouraged Toyota to raise the base price for 1991 by a modest $700, which is the first increase in two years. At just over $22,000, this is a good buy. Anti-lock brakes are a $1,130 option we recommend. The Cressida isn't as roomy as the Lexus LS 400 or the Cadillac De Ville/Fleetwood, and it lacks the style and verve of the Nissan Maxima. However, the Cressida compensates with dependable performance and low maintenance costs.

SPORTS COUPES

ACURA INTEGRA   **BEST BUY**

The Acura Integra is a front-wheel drive coupe that comes in two body styles: a 3-door hatchback coupe and a 4-door sedan with a longer wheelbase and roomier interior. The sportier hatchback is by far the more popular, so it usually sells at higher prices than the 4-door. Both have a 130-horsepower 1.8-liter 4-cylinder engine that delivers spirited acceleration and high fuel economy. This engine is much livelier and a little more economical with the 5-speed manual transmission than the optional 4-speed automatic. Since most buyers prefer automatic transmissions, the best deals are on manual-shift Integras. Anti-lock brakes are standard on the top-line GS models. With any Integra, you get a refined, well-made sporty car that should be reliable and have good resale value. Base models start in the $12,000 to $13,000 range, and the GS models top out at around $18,000.

Prices are accurate at time of printing; subject to manufacturer's change.

MITSUBISHI ECLIPSE, EAGLE TALON, AND PLYMOUTH LASER

The Mitsubishi Eclipse, Eagle Talon, and Plymouth Laser are sold under three different brand names, but there are only minor differences among them. All three offer sporty performance at reasonable prices. And, they are all built in Illinois by Diamond-Star Motors, a partnership between Mitsubishi and Chrysler. Front-wheel-drive models are sold under all three brands; in addition, the Eclipse and Talon are available with permanently engaged all-wheel drive. The AWD Talon TSi and Eclipse GSX models have outstanding traction, sticking like glue even to wet roads. The AWD versions come with a powerful turbocharged engine that is available with automatic transmission this year. In addition, anti-lock brakes are now available on certain models in each line. Prices start at around $12,000 to $13,000, while fully equipped front-drive models climb to the $15,000 to $17,000 range. The AWD versions get up to $20,000 or so, but even that isn't excessive considering the performance.

SPORTS AND GT CARS

MAZDA MIATA

The Mazda Miata is a classic sports car—a 2-seat convertible with racy styling, spirited performance, and road-hugging handling. The base price is a modest $13,800 for 1991 (unchanged from last year). The rear-drive Miata comes with a 116-horsepower, dual-cam 1.6-liter engine and a 5-speed manual transmission. A 4-speed automatic transmission is a $720 option, but Miata is quicker and more economical with the slick-shifting manual. Also available this year are anti-lock brakes, a $900 option we recommend. Standard features include a driver's airbag and a manual folding top that can be raised or lowered by one person from inside the car. Perhaps the best news this year is that price gouging by Mazda dealers has subsided, so you should be able to buy a Miata for suggested retail price—instead of thousands more, which was the case a year ago.

TOYOTA MR2 `RECOMMENDED`

The Toyota MR2 was redesigned for 1991 and sports new styling, larger dimensions, and more power. Two engines are offered in the rear-drive MR2: a base 130-horsepower 2.2-liter 4-cylinder and a turbocharged 200-horsepower 2.0-liter four. Both have a standard 5-speed manual transmission; a 4-speed automatic is optional on the base engine only. A driver's airbag is standard and anti-lock brakes are a $1,130 option. With either engine, this is a terrific little sports car. The least-expensive model starts at $15,148, while a Turbo with the T-bar roof and all the options zooms to nearly $25,000. Even though the MR2 is a much costlier proposition than Miata, it is the more mature sports car of the two. Save money and buy one with the base engine. It will be more economical than the Turbo and just as much fun.

COMPACT VANS

DODGE CARAVAN AND PLYMOTH VOYAGER

The Dodge Caravan and Plymouth Voyager are Chrysler's nearly identical minivans that are substantially revised for 1991. They again rank at the top of this class, despite new rivals from domestic and Japanese companies. Both models return in standard and long wheelbase sizes with seats for five to seven people, but the exterior has been restyled and the interior redesigned. All-wheel-drive (AWD) models and optional anti-lock brakes have been added. The front-drive Caravan/ Voyager already had better traction than rear-drive vans; the AWD models have even better grip, with little apparent loss in acceleration or ride quality due to their additional weight. The interior is much improved, with controls placed much closer to the driver, where they're easier to operate on the road. A revised suspension shows up in reduced body roll in turns, making Caravan and Voyager feel even more carlike. One 4-cylinder and two V-6 engines are available, and either V-6 engine is preferable to the underpowered 4-cylinder. Chrysler has reasserted its minivan leadership with this year's changes. Unfortunately, prices are higher this year. Base prices are up from about $700 on the long wheelbase Grand Caravan/ Voyager to $1,600 on the regular-length versions. AWD adds about $3,000. A luxury version of the Caravan/Voyager is sold as the Chrysler Town & Country (base price is $23,905), but since it offers no substantive advantages we don't list it as a Best Buy.

MAZDA MPV RECOMMENDED

The Mazda MPV (Multi-Purpose Vehicle) is a good choice in a compact passenger van. Unlike most other rear-drive compact vans, the MPV is quite carlike to drive, similar to the Caravan/ Voyager. A 4-wheel-drive model with a convenient on-demand 4WD system is also available. The MPV's most unusual feature is its swing-out rear side door, instead of the sliding type found on most vans. A 121-horsepower 2.6-liter 4-cylinder engine is standard on rear-drive MPVs. We prefer the optional 150-horsepower 3.0-liter V-6, which generates sufficient power for the rear-drive MPV to safely merge with traffic and haul a full load of people and cargo. The V-6 is standard on the 4WD model, which weighs nearly 500 pounds more than the rear-drive version. That extra weight slows down acceleration and hurts fuel economy, so opt for 4WD only if you really need it. Seats for five are standard, and seats for seven are optional. A rear-drive MPV with the V-6 should cost between $17,000 to $19,000, while a 4WD model will run $20,000 to $22,000.

TOYOTA PREVIA RECOMMENDED

The Toyota Previa arrived as an early 1991 model to replace the Toyota Van. Like its predecessor, the Previa's engine is placed almost directly over the front wheels, and it is available in rear-drive and all-wheel-drive versions (called All-Trac). Most everything else is new on the Previa. All versions use a 138-horsepower 2.4-liter 4-cylinder engine. Standard on all Previas are two front bucket seats and a 3-place rear bench.

Prices are accurate at time of printing; subject to manufacturer's change.

Optional arrangements provide seats for seven people. The Previa is as versatile as any minivan and has more passenger and cargo room than most. It's not as carlike as the popular front-drive Chrysler products or Mazda's MPV, but it's not a truck by any means. While the Previa lacks the V-6 power and front-drive traction of the Chrysler minivans, its biggest advantage over the Caravan/Voyager is superior assembly quality, which was very impressive on models we've tested.

4WD VEHICLES

FORD EXPLORER

The Ford Explorer succeeds the Bronco II for 1991 as Ford's compact 4WD vehicle and comes in 3- and 5-door body styles (Bronco II came only as a 3-door). The 5-door has a 112-inch wheelbase, one of the longest among compact 4-wheel-drive vehicles. The 3-door has a 102-inch wheelbase. Ford positions the 5-door Explorer as a 4WD family wagon, while the 3-door is designed to appeal to a younger crowd that's more interested in sport than utility. Both models hit the mark, especially the 5-door, which is a roomy, versatile vehicle with a carlike interior. A 155-horsepower 4.0-liter V-6 teams with either a standard 5-speed manual or optional 4-speed overdrive automatic transmission. Both body styles are available with on-demand 4-wheel drive or rear-wheel drive. Standard on 4WD Explorers is Touch-Drive, which engages or disengages 4WD by pushing a dashboard button (whether the vehicle is moving or stationary). Anti-lock rear brakes are standard on all Explorers. A low ride height helps entry and exit, and the 5-door's rear wheels are pushed back far enough so that they hardly intrude into the rear doorways. The 5-door Explorer moves Ford to the head of the class with its spacious, well-designed interior, convenient 4WD system, and strong engine. Mazda sells a similar version of the 3-door as the Navajo.

JEEP CHEROKEE

The Jeep Cherokee remains a Best Buy in this class because it does so many things so well. The Cherokee has come in 3- and

5-door body styles since 1984, while Ford and General Motors just added 5-door models for 1991. Jeep still has the most horsepower in this class; its 4.0-liter 6-cylinder engine gains 13 horsepower this year to 190. The Cherokee offers two 4WD systems, both with full shift-on-the-fly that allows changing in and out of 4WD at any road speed (some Japanese rivals still don't offer that feature). And, the optional Selec-Trac 4WD system can be left permanently engaged. Anti-lock brakes are optional; this system works on all four wheels and in 2WD and 4WD (most rivals have rear anti-lock brakes that work only in 2WD). Jeep charges a high price for those features, so $20,000 for a Cherokee is about average. However, intense competition has forced Jeep to actually *lower* some prices this year. Dealers are giving bigger discounts on the slower-selling 3-door models, but cash rebates and other incentives also apply to the more-popular 5-door versions.

CHEVROLET S10 BLAZER, GMC S15 JIMMY, AND OLDSMOBILE BRAVADA

RECOMMENDED

The Chevrolet S10 Blazer and GMC S15 Jimmy now have 5-door versions as early 1991 models. They have been joined by a new luxury model, the Oldsmobile Bravada. While the Blazer and Jimmy have an on-demand 4WD system, engaged by shifting a transfer-case lever, the Bravada's system is always engaged. All three versions use a 160-horsepower 4.3-liter V-6 engine. While the Bravada comes only in the 5-door style, the Blazer and Jimmy also come as a 3-door. Rear-seat legroom is identical in either body style, but the 5-door's longer wheelbase allows the back seat to be fitted ahead of the rear wheels for 15 inches more hiproom than the 3-door. All 5-door models have 4-wheel anti-lock brakes; only the rear wheels have the anti-lock feature on the 3-door. While the 5-door's longer wheelbase improves ride quality, the Blazer/Jimmy suspension is still among the least compliant in the class (the Bravada has somewhat better ride quality). These aren't the best in their class, but the strong engine, convenient 4WD systems, and new 5-door body style make GM's compact 4WDs competitive.

Prices are accurate at time of printing; subject to manufacturer's change.

PRICES FOR CARS, VANS, AND 4-WHEEL DRIVE VEHICLES

Acura Integra

	Retail Price	Dealer Invoice	Low Price
RS 3-door hatchback, 5-speed	$11950	—	—
RS 3-door hatchback, automatic	12675	—	—
LS 3-door hatchback, 5-speed	13825	—	—
LS 3-door hatchback, automatic	14550	—	—
GS 3-door hatchback, 5-speed	15925	—	—
GS 3-door hatchback, automatic	16650	—	—
GS 3-door, 5-speed, leather interior	16425	—	—
GS 3-door, automatic, leather interior	17150	—	—
RS 4-door notchback, 5-speed	12850	—	—
RS 4-door notchback, automatic	13575	—	—
LS 4-door notchback, 5-speed	14545	—	—
LS 4-door notchback, automatic	15270	—	—
GS 4-door notchback, 5-speed	16450	—	—
GS 4-door notchback, automatic	17175	—	—
GS 4-door, 5-speed, leather interior	16950	—	—
GS 4-door, automatic, leather interior	17675	—	—
Destination charge	295	295	295

Dealer invoice and low price not available at time of publication.

Standard equipment:

RS: 1.8-liter DOHC 16-valve PFI 4-cylinder engine, 5- speed manual or 4-speed automatic transmission, power steering, 4-wheel disc brakes, motorized front shoulder belts, cloth reclining front bucket seats, split folding rear seat, tinted glass, remote fuel door and hatch releases, dual manual mirrors, fog lights, rear defogger, rear wiper/washer (hatchback), tachometer, coolant temperature gauge, tilt steering column, intermittent wipers, door pockets, cargo cover (hatchback), 195/60R14 tires. **LS** adds: power mirrors, power locks (4-door), power sunroof (hatchback), AM/FM cassette with power antenna, driver's seat lumbar support adjustment, cruise control, map lights (hatchback). **GS** adds: anti-lock braking system, power windows, map lights, adjustable side bolsters on driver's seat, power sunroof, alloy wheels.

OPTIONS are available as dealer-installed accessories.

Buick LeSabre

2-door notchback	$17180	$14826	$15451
Custom 4-door notchback	17080	14740	15365
Limited 4-door notchback	18430	15905	16530
Limited 2-door notchback	18330	15819	16444
Destination charge	535	535	535

Prices are accurate at time of printing; subject to manufacturer's change.

Standard equipment:

Base and Custom: 3.8-liter PFI V-6, 4-speed automatic transmission, power steering, air conditioning, door-mounted automatic front seatbelts, cloth bench seat with armrest, tinted glass, AM/FM radio, tilt steering column, trip odometer, 205/75R14 tires. **Limited** adds: 55/45 front seat with recliners and storage armrest, upgraded exterior moldings.

Optional equipment:	Retail Price	Dealer Invoice	Low Price
Anti-lock brakes	925	786	833
Pkg. SA	STD	STD	STD
Popular Pkg. SB, base & Custom	729	620	656
Intermittent wipers, cruise control, rear defogger, white-stripe tires, 55/45 front seat with storage armrest, floormats.			
Premium Pkg. SC, base	1274	1083	1147
Custom	1314	1117	1183
Pkg. SB plus power locks, cassette player, wire wheel covers.			
Luxury Pkg. SD, base	1914	1627	1723
Custom	2029	1725	1826
Pkg. SC plus power windows, power driver's seat, front seatback recliners, door edge guards.			
Prestige Pkg. SE, base	2260	1921	2034
Custom	2375	2019	2138
Pkg. SD plus remote decklid release, lighted right visor mirror, power antenna, power mirrors, Concert Sound speakers.			
Popular Pkg. SB, Ltd 2-door	1411	1199	1270
Ltd 4-door	1516	1289	1364
Intermittent wipers, cruise contol, rear defogger, white-stripe tires, floormats, power windows and locks, cassette player, power driver's seat.			
Premium Pkg. SC, Ltd 2-door	1824	1550	1642
Ltd 4-door	1939	1648	1745
Pkg. SB plus wire wheel covers, remote decklid release, lighted right visor mirror, power antenna, door edge guards.			
Luxury Pkg. SD, Ltd 2-door	2303	1958	2073
Ltd 4-door	2418	2055	2176
Pkg. SC plus power mirrors, power passenger seatback recliner, deluxe trunk trim, automatic climate control, front and rear reading lamps, front door courtesy lamps.			
Prestige Pkg. SE, Ltd 2-door	2828	2404	2545
Ltd 4-door	2943	2502	2649
Pkg. SD plus power passenger seat, upgraded audio system (UX1) with AM stereo, EQ, and Concert Sound speakers.			
Gran Touring Pkg., w/Pkg. SA	738	627	664
w/SB	662	563	596
w/SC/SD/SE	447	380	402
Gran Touring suspension, 215/65R15 tires on alloy wheels, 2.97 axle ratio, HD cooling, leather-wrapped steering wheel, automatic level control.			
2.97 axle ratio	NC	NC	NC
Requires HD cooling.			
HD cooling	40	34	36

Prices are accurate at time of printing; subject to manufacturer's change.

	Retail Price	Dealer Invoice	Low Price
Power locks, 2-doors	190	162	171
4-doors	230	196	207
Gauges & tachometer	110	94	99

Includes coolant temperature and oil pressure gauges, voltmeter; deletes trip odometer.

Decklid luggage rack	115	98	104
Cassette player, Custom w/SA	140	119	126
UX1 audio system, Custom w/SB, others w/SA	375	319	338
Custom w/SC/SD, Ltd w/SB/SC/SD	235	200	212
Custom w/SE	150	128	135

Includes tape search/repeat, EQ, and Concert Sound speakers.

Power antenna	75	64	68
Bodyside stripes	45	38	41
Automatic level control	175	149	158
Full vinyl top, 4-doors	200	170	180
55/45 seat w/storage armrest, base & Custom	183	156	165
Leather/vinyl 55/45 seat, Ltd	450	383	405
Alloy wheels, w/SA/SB	270	230	243
w/SC/SD/SE	55	47	50
Wire wheel covers, w/SA/SB	215	183	194
Power windows, 2-doors w/SB/SC	245	208	221
4-doors w/SA/SB/SC	310	264	279

Cadillac De Ville/Fleetwood

Coupe de Ville 2-door notchback	$30205	$25765	$26680
Sedan de Ville 4-door notchback	30455	25978	26893
Fleetwood 2-door notchback	34695	29595	30510
Fleetwood 4-door notchback	34945	29808	30723
Fleetwood Sixty Special 4-door notchback	38345	32708	33623
Destination charge	580	580	580

Standard equipment:

De Ville: 4.9-liter PFI V-8, 4-speed automatic transmission, anti-lock brakes, power steering, driver's-side airbag, 45/55 cloth reclining front seat with storage armrest, automatic climate control, outside temperature readout, power windows, automatic power locks, heated power mirrors, cruise control, AM/FM cassette with EQ, power antenna, automatic level control, automatic parking brake release, Twilight Sentinel, solar-control glass, intermittent wipers, trip odometer, tilt steering column, remote decklid release, rear defogger, Fuel Data Center, PASS-Key theft-deterrent system, seatback pockets, door edge guards, litter receptacle, 205/70R15 whitewall tires on alloy wheels. **Fleetwood** adds: Computer Command Ride System, power passenger seat, vinyl roof (4-door), cabriolet roof (2-door), fender skirts, remote fuel door release, automatic day/night mirror, front and rear lighted visor mirrors, floormats. **Sixty Special** adds: Ultrasoft leather upholstery, 22-way power heated front seats (includes 2-position memory, adjustable lumbar and side bolsters, and power head restraints).

Prices are accurate at time of printing; subject to manufacturer's change.

Optional equipment:	Retail Price	Dealer Invoice	Low Price
Option Pkg. B, De Ville	320	269	285
Power passenger seat, floormats.			
Option Pkg. C, De Ville	586	492	522
Pkg. B plus lighted visor mirrors, power decklid pulldown, trunk mat.			
Option Pkg. D, De Ville	1045	878	930
Pkg. C plus remote fuel door release, digital instruments, automatic day/night mirror, trumpet horn.			
Security Pkg., De Ville	385	323	343
Fleetwood	295	248	263
Remote keyless entry, theft-deterrent system, illuminated entry (std. Fleetwood).			
Cold Weather Pkg.	369	310	328
Engine block heater, heated windshield system.			
Custom Seating Pkg., Fleetwood	425	357	378
Driver's seat memory, power recliners.			
Astroroof	1355	1138	1206
Coachbuilder Pkg., Sedan de Ville	1000	840	890
Computer Command Ride System, De Ville	380	319	338
Gold Ornamentation Pkg.	395	332	352
HD Livery Pkg., Sedan de Ville	1000	840	890
Leather seating area (std. Sixty)	570	479	507
Firemist paint	240	202	214
Delco-Bose audio system	576	484	513
w/CD player	872	732	776
Formal cabriolet roof, Coupe de Ville	825	693	734
Padded vinyl roof, Sedan de Ville	825	693	734
Full cabriolet roof, Coupe de Ville	1095	920	975
Phaeton roof, Sedan de Ville	1095	920	975
Wire wheel discs, De Ville	235	197	209
Fleetwood	NC	NC	NC
Lace alloy wheels, De Ville	235	197	209
California emissions pkg.	100	84	89

Cadillac Eldorado

	Retail Price	Dealer Invoice	Low Price
2-door notchback	$31245	$26652	$27402
Destination charge	580	580	580

Standard equipment:

4.9-liter PFI V-8, 4-speed automatic transmission, anti-lock 4-wheel disc brakes, power steering, driver's-side airbag, Computer Command Ride System, automatic level control, cloth and leather power front seats with manual recliners, center console with armrest and storage bins, automatic climate control, power windows and locks, cruise control, heated power mirrors, rear defogger, AM/FM cassette with EQ, power antenna, remote fuel door and decklid releases, power decklid pulldown, illuminated entry, Driver Information Center, lighted visor mirrors, intermittent wipers, floormats, PASS-Key theft-deterrent

Prices are accurate at time of printing; subject to manufacturer's change.

system, tinted glass, leather-wrapped steering wheel, tilt steering column, Twilight Sentinel, 205/70R15 whitewall tires on snowflake alloy wheels.

Optional equipment:

	Retail Price	Dealer Invoice	Low Price
Touring Coupe Pkg.	2050	1722	1825
Uprated suspension, 215/60R16 Goodyear Eagle GT + 4 tires on forged alloy wheels, 3.33 final-drive ratio, Ultrasoft leather upholstery, sport seats with power recliners and lumbar support adjusters, rear head restraints, added birdseye maple trim, automatic day/night mirror.			
Biarritz Pkg.	3180	2671	2830
Leather upholstery, power front recliners and lumbar support adjusters, seatback pockets, walnut trim, cabriolet roof with opera lamps, two-tone paint, closed-in backlight treatment, wire wheel discs.			
Option Pkg. 1SB	NC	NC	NC
Choice of full vinyl roof or full cabriolet roof; not available with Touring Coupe or Biarritz.			
Option Pkg. 1SC	NC	NC	NC
Leather seating areas, Delco-Bose audio system with choice of cassette or CD player; not available with Touring Coupe or Biarritz.			
Option Pkg. 1SD	NC	NC	NC
Delco-Bose audio system with choice of cassette or CD player.			
Biarritz & Touring Coupe Pkg. 1SE	NC	NC	NC
Includes Astroroof.			
Biarritz & Touring Coupe Pkg. 1SF	NC	NC	NC
Security Pkg., Delco-Bose audio system with choice of cassette or CD player.			
Security Pkg.	480	403	427
Automatic locks with central door unlocking and remote keyless entry, theft-deterrent system.			
Birdseye maple wood appliques	245	206	218
Astroroof	1355	1138	1206
Gold Ornamentation Pkg.	395	332	352
Heated windshield system	309	260	275
Leather seating area	555	466	494
Automatic day/night mirror	99	83	88
Monotone Firemist paint	240	202	214
Primary Firemist paint	190	160	169
Secondary Firemist paint	50	42	45
White diamond paint	240	202	214
Delco-Bose audio system, w/cassette	576	484	513
w/CD player	872	732	776
Full vinyl roof	1095	920	975
Full cabriolet roof	1095	920	975
215/65R15 tires, w/Touring Suspension	76	64	68
Touring Suspension	155	130	138
Wire wheel discs	235	197	209
PW8 alloy wheels	115	97	102
California emissions pkg.	100	84	89

Prices are accurate at time of printing; subject to manufacturer's change.

1991 Chevrolet S10 Blazer/ GMC S15 Jimmy

	Retail Price	Dealer Invoice	Low Price
Chevrolet			
3-door wagon, 2WD	$12966	$11578	$11928
5-door wagon, 2WD	15272	13638	13988
3-door wagon, 4WD	14631	13065	13415
5-door wagon, 4WD	16905	15096	15446
GMC			
3-door wagon, 2WD	13159	11751	12101
5-door wagon, 2WD	15637	13964	14314
3-door wagon, 4WD	14845	13257	13607
5-door wagon, 4WD	17291	15440	15790
Destination charge	435	435	435

Standard equipment:

4.3-liter TBI V-6, 5-speed manual transmission, anti-lock rear brakes (3-door), 4-wheel anti-lock brakes (5-door), power steering, tinted glass, coolant temperature and oil pressure gauges, voltmeter, AM radio (Chevrolet) AM/FM radio (GMC), tow hooks (4WD), dual outside mirrors, front armrests, rubber floor covering, highback vinyl front bucket seats, 205/75R15 tires with full-size spare.

Optional equipment:

4-speed automatic transmission	860	731	774
Optional axle ratio	38	32	34
Locking differential	252	214	227
Air conditioning	755	642	680
w/engine oil cooler	699	594	629
Tahoe/Sierra Classic (SC) Pkg., 2WD	841	715	757
4WD	809	688	728
Reclining seatbacks, bright wheel opening moldings, black bodyside and quarter window moldings, upgraded door panels with pockets, console, floormats, visor mirror, reading lamp, special body insulation, engine compartment lamp, rally wheels (2WD), black steel wheels (4WD), trim rings.			
Sport/Gypsy Pkg., 3-door	1038	882	934
Tahoe/SC Pkg. plus black wheel opening moldings, Sport two-tone paint, alloy wheels.			
Deluxe cloth seats, 3-door w/rear seat	26	22	23
Leather bucket seats, 3-door w/o rear seat	312	265	281
3-door w/rear seat	412	350	371
Air dam w/fog lamps	115	98	104
HD battery	56	48	50
OS spare tire carrier w/cover	159	135	143
Cold-Climate Pkg., 5-door	146	124	131
3-door	189	161	170
3-door w/Tahoe/SC or Sport/Gypsy	146	124	131
HD battery, engine block heater, special insulation.			
Console, 3-door	135	115	122
HD radiator	56	48	50

Prices are accurate at time of printing; subject to manufacturer's change.

	Retail Price	Dealer Invoice	Low Price
HD radiator & transmission oil cooler	118	100	106
w/A/C or LD Trailering Pkg.	63	54	57
Engine oil cooler	135	115	122
Driver Convenience Pkg. ZM7	180	153	162
Intermittent wipers, tilt steering column.			
Driver Convenience Pkg. ZM8	197	167	177
Rear defogger, remote tailgate release.			
Front floormats, 3-door	20	17	18
Rear floormats, 3-door	16	14	14
Deep-tinted glass	225	191	203
w/light-tinted rear window	144	122	130
Electronic instrumentation	296	252	266
Luggage carrier & air deflector	169	144	152
Lighted visor mirrors, 5-door	68	58	61
3-door	75	64	68
3-door w/Tahoe/SC or Sport/Gypsy	68	58	61
Black wheel opening moldings, 5-door	13	11	12
3-door	43	37	39
3-door w/Tahoe/SC	13	11	12
Operating Convenience Pkg., 5-door	519	441	467
3-door	344	292	310
Power windows and locks.			
AM/FM radio, Chevrolet	131	111	118
AM/FM cassette, Chevrolet	253	215	228
AM/FM cassette w/EQ, Chevrolet	403	343	363
AM radio delete (credit), Chevrolet	(95)	(81)	(81)
Folding rear bench seat	409	348	368
Shield Pkg., 4WD	75	64	68
Shields for transfer case, front differential, fuel tank, and steering linkage.			
HD front shock absorbers	40	34	36
Cruise control	225	191	203
Bodyside striping	55	47	50
Manual glass sunroof	250	213	225
HD front suspension, 5-door	23	20	21
3-door	63	54	57
Off-Road Suspension Pkg., 5-door	122	104	110
3-door	182	155	164
3-door w/Tahoe/SC or Sport/Gypsy	122	104	110
HD Trailering Special Pkg.	211	179	190
LD Trailering Special Pkg.	165	140	149
w/engine oil cooler	109	93	98
Trim rings, 3-door	60	51	54
Rally wheels	92	78	83
Alloy wheels, 5-door 4WD	269	229	242
3-door 4WD	325	276	293
3-door 4WD w/Tahoe/SC or Off-Road Suspension	269	229	242
5-door 2WD	233	198	210

Prices are accurate at time of printing; subject to manufacturer's change.

	Retail Price	Dealer Invoice	Low Price
3-door 2WD	325	276	293
3-door 2WD w/Tahoe/SC	233	198	210
Sliding rear quarter window	257	218	231
Rear wiper/washer	125	106	113
P205/75R15 on/off-road WL tires	170	145	153
P205/75R15 WL tires	121	103	109
P205/75R15 on/off-road tires	49	42	44
P235/75R15 on/off-road WL tires	345	293	311
Special two-tone paint	218	185	196
Deluxe two-tone paint	177	150	159

Dodge Caravan/ Plymouth Voyager

	Retail Price	Dealer Invoice	Low Price
Base SWB	$13215	$11859	$12537
SE SWB	14345	12854	13600
LE SWB	17645	15758	16702
ES SWB	19140	17073	18107
Grand SE	16095	14394	15245
Grand LE	19255	17174	18215
SE SWB AWD	17240	15401	NA
LE SWB AWD	20535	18301	NA
Caravan ES/ Voyager LX SWB AWD	21049	18753	NA
Grand SE AWD	17945	16022	NA
Grand LE AWD	21105	18802	NA
Destination charge	520	520	520

SWB denotes short wheelbase; AWD denotes All Wheel Drive.

Standard equipment:

2.5-liter TBI 4-cylinder engine, 3-speed automatic transmission, power steering, 5-passenger seating (front bucket seats, 3-passenger middle bench seat), tinted glass, trip odometer, coolant temperature gauge, dual outside mirrors, visor mirrors, AM/FM radio, intermittent wipers, rear wiper/washer, 195/75R14 tires. **SE** adds: 7-passenger seating (2-passenger middle and 3-passenger rear bench seats), dual-note horn, remote liftgate release, rear trim panel storage and cupholders, sport wheel covers. **LE** adds: front air conditioning, front storage console, overhead console with outside temperature readout and mini trip computer, rear defogger, power front windows, power quarter vent windows, remote fuel door release, tachometer, oil pressure gauge, voltmeter, illuminated entry, headlamp delay system, heated power mirrors, lighted visor mirrors, bodyside moldings, cruise control, tilt steering column, sport steering wheel, storage drawer under front passenger seat, two-tone paint, floormats; ES/LX has fascia with fog lamps, bodyside and sill appliques, alloy wheels. **Grand** models have 3.3-liter PFI V-6, 4-speed automatic transmission, 205/70R15 tires. **All Wheel Drive** models have 3.3-liter V-6, 4-speed automatic transmission, 7-passenger seating, power mirrors (SE), heated power mirrors (LE), 205/75R15 tires.

Prices are accurate at time of printing; subject to manufacturer's change.

Optional equipment:

	Retail Price	Dealer Invoice	Low Price
3.0-liter V-6, 2WD SWB	694	590	638
3.3-liter V-6, SE/LE 2WD SWB	796	677	732
4-speed automatic transmission, SE/LE w/V-6	173	147	159
Anti-lock brakes, SE & LE	799	679	735
2WD SWB requires 3.3-liter V-6.			
Front air conditioning, base & SE	857	728	788
Rear air conditioning, Grand LE 2WD	466	396	429
Grand SE 2WD	571	485	525
Grand SE 2WD w/Family, Popular, or Luxury Pkg. . . .	466	396	429
Grand SE 2WD w/Trailer Tow Pkg.	509	433	468
Grand SE 2WD w/Trailer Tow Pkg. and			
Family, Popular, or Luxury Pkg.	404	343	372
Grand SE 2WD requires front air conditioning, rear defogger, and Storage Convenience Pkg.			
Quad Command Seating (NA base)	597	507	549
Two front and two middle bucket seats, 3-passenger rear bench seat.			
Converta-Bed 7-pass. seating, SE	553	470	509
Leather trim, LE	865	735	796
Requires Luxury Pkg.			
Popular Value Pkg., base	1431	1216	1317
Base w/Family Pkg.	1054	896	970
SE	1059	900	974
SE SWB w/Family Pkg.	743	632	684
7-passenger seating, Light Pkg., Deluxe Convenience Pkg., oil pressure gauge, voltmeter, dual-note horns, added sound insulation, remote liftgate release, lighted visor mirrors, speed-sensitive power locks, floormats.			
Luxury Value Pkg., SE	2321	1973	2135
SE w/Family Pkg.	1837	1561	1690
LE	232	197	213
Popular Pkg., Storage Convenience Pkg., overhead console, rear defogger, headlamp delay system, heated power mirrors, Infinity I audio system w/cassette, power driver's seat, power front windows, power quarter vent windows.			
Family Value Pkg., base w/2.5	1102	937	1014
Base w/V-6	1402	1192	1290
SE	1041	885	958
Front air conditioning, rear defogger, dual-note horn, remote liftgate release, Light Pkg.			
HD Trailer Tow Pkg., SE 2WD	557	473	512
LE 2WD	443	377	408
AWD	265	225	244
HD alternator, battery, flasher, radiator, and transmission oil cooler, trailer wiring harness, HD suspension (2WD), sport wheel covers, 205/70R15 tires with conventional spare.			
Storage Convenience Pkg., SE	149	127	137
Forward storage console, storage drawer under passenger seat.			
Deluxe Convenience Pkg., base & SE	404	343	372
Cruise control, tilt steering column, sport steering wheel.			
Power Convenience Pkg., SE	490	417	451

Prices are accurate at time of printing; subject to manufacturer's change.

	Retail Price	Dealer Invoice	Low Price
SE w/Popular Pkg.	250	213	230
Power front windows, power locks.			
Sport Handling Pkg., SE/LE SWB	138	117	127
Grand SE/LE	24	20	22
HD brakes, rear sway bar, sport wheel covers, 205/70R15 tires.			
Rear defogger, base	217	184	200
SE	168	143	155
Base includes remote liftgate release.			
Speed-sensitive power locks, base & SE	240	204	221
Sunscreen glass	414	352	381
Luggage rack, 2WD	143	122	132
Cassette player	155	132	143
Infinity I audio system, SE/LE	461	392	424
Infinity II system, SE/LE w/Popular Pkg.	675	574	621
LE/SE w/Luxury Pkg.	214	182	197
HD suspension	69	59	63
205/70R14 whitewall tires, 2WD SWB	143	122	132
205/70R15 whitewall tires, SE/LE	69	59	63
Conventional spare tire, 2WD	109	93	100
15" alloy wheels, SE/LE	363	309	334
Wire wheel covers, 2WD LE SWB	245	208	225
Requires 14" whitewall tires and Luxury Pkg.			
Extra-cost paint	77	65	71
Two-tone paint, SE	296	252	272
California emissions pkg.	102	87	94

Dodge Spirit

4-door notchback	$10925	$9784	$10069
LE 4-door notchback	12925	11544	11829
ES 4-door notchback	13709	12234	12619
R/T 4-door notchback	17820	15851	NA
Destination charge	465	465	465

Standard equipment:

2.5-liter TBI 4-cylinder engine, 5-speed manual transmission, power steering, driver's-side airbag, cloth reclining front bucket seats, tachometer, coolant temperature and oil pressure gauges, tinted backlight, remote mirrors, left visor mirror, narrow bodyside moldings, AM/FM radio with two speakers, remote decklid release, intermittent wipers, 195/70R14 tires. **LE** adds: 3-speed automatic transmission, rear defogger, fog lamps, tinted glass, Message Center, four speakers, cruise control, tilt steering column, wide bodyside moldings, floormats. **ES** adds: 2.5-liter turbocharged PFI engine, 5-speed manual transmission, 4-wheel disc brakes, cassette player, trip computer, 205/60R15 tires on alloy wheels. **R/T** adds: 2.2-liter DOHC 16-valve turbocharged engine, rear spoiler, heated power mirrors, 205/60VR15 tires.

Prices are accurate at time of printing; subject to manufacturer's change.

Optional equipment:

	Retail Price	Dealer Invoice	Low Price
2.5-liter turbo engine, LE	694	590	611
3.0-liter V-6, base & LE	694	590	611
ES	NC	NC	NC
3-speed automatic transmission, base & ES	547	465	481
4-speed automatic transmission, base & ES	640	544	563
LE	93	79	82
Available only with V-6.			
Anti-lock 4-wheel disc brakes	899	764	791
Air conditioning, LE & ES	821	698	722
Super Discount Pkg. A, base	915	778	805
Air conditioning, tinted glass, rear defogger, four speakers, cruise control, tilt steering column, floormats.			
Super Discount Pkg. B, base	1491	1267	1312
Pkg. A plus power windows and locks, heated power mirrors.			
Super Discount Pkg. C, LE & ES	972	826	855
Air conditioning, power windows and locks, heated power mirrors.			
Premium Equipment Pkg., base	241	205	212
Split folding rear seat, added sound insulation, misc. lights, Message Center.			
Deluxe Convenience Pkg., base	359	305	316
Cruise control, tilt steering column, floormats.			
Power Equipment Pkg., R/T	533	453	469
Power windows and locks, heated power mirrors.			
Overhead Convenience Pkg., LE & ES	333	283	293
Overhead console (with outside temperature readout, compass, reading lamps, and storage for sunglasses and garage door transmitter), lighted visor mirrors.			
Center armrest, base w/5-speed	81	69	71
Console w/armrest, base	155	132	136
Rear defogger, base	163	139	143
Power locks	245	208	216
Cassette player & 4 speakers, base	205	174	180
Base w/Super Discount Pkg.	155	132	136
w/seek/scan, base w/Super Discount, LE	430	366	378
w/seek/scan, ES & R/T	275	234	242
Cassette player w/Infinity speakers, LE	645	548	568
ES & R/T	490	417	431
Power driver's seat	296	252	260
Base requires Super Discount Pkg.			
Front bench seat, base	102	87	90
w/split folding rear seat, base & LE	61	52	54
Split folding rear seat requires Premium Pkg. on base.			
Removable glass sunroof, LE & ES	405	344	356
Whitewall tires, base	73	62	64
205/60R15 tires, base & LE w/alloy wheels	145	123	128
Alloy wheels, base & LE	328	279	289
Conventional spare tire (14") , base & LE	95	81	84
Extra-cost paint	77	65	68
California emissions pkg.	102	87	90

Prices are accurate at time of printing; subject to manufacturer's change.

Eagle Talon	Retail Price	Dealer Invoice	Low Price
3-door hatchback (5-speed)	$12990	$11911	$12297
w/Pkg. 23B (5-speed)	13801	12600	13038
w/Pkg. 24B (automatic)	14489	13185	13666
B Pkgs. add: air conditioning.			
w/Pkg. 23C (5-speed)	14578	13261	13748
w/Pkg. 24C (automatic)	15266	13846	14376
C Pkgs. add to B: cruise control, rear wiper/washer, power windows and locks.			
w/Pkg. 23D (5-speed)	15097	13702	14222
w/Pkg. 24D (automatic)	15785	14287	14850
D Pkgs. add to C: premium audio system with EQ, alloy wheels.			
TSi 3-door hatchback (5-speed)	14609	13368	13816
TSi 3-door hatchback (automatic)	15432	14068	14568
w/Pkg. 25F (5-speed)	16197	14718	15267
w/Pkg. 26F (automatic)	17020	15417	16018
F Pkgs. add: air conditioning, cruise control, rear wiper/washer, power windows and locks.			
w/Pkg. 25G (5-speed)	16716	15159	15741
w/Pkg. 26G (automatic)	17539	15859	16493
G Pkgs. add to F: premium audio system with EQ, alloy wheels.			
TSi AWD 3-door hatchback (5-speed)	16513	15082	15602
TSi AWD 3-door hatchback (automatic)	17336	15781	16354
w/Pkg. 25J (5-speed)	18101	16432	17053
w/Pkg. 26J (automatic)	18924	17131	17805
J Pkgs. add: air conditioning, cruise control, rear wiper/washer, power windows and locks.			
Destination charge	328	328	328

Standard equipment:

2.0-liter DOHC 16-valve PFI 4-cylinder engine, 5-speed manual or 4-speed automatic transmission, 4-wheel disc brakes, power steering, motorized front shoulder belts, cloth reclining front bucket seats, driver's-seat lumbar support adjustment, folding rear seat, console (with armrest, storage, and cupholders), rear defogger, tinted glass, tachometer, coolant temperature and oil pressure gauges, trip odometer, map lights, power mirrors, visor mirrors, AM/FM cassette, remote fuel door and hatch releases, tilt steering column, tonneau cover, intermittent wipers, floormats, 205/55HR16 tires. **TSi** adds: turbocharged engine, sill extensions and specific fascias, driving lamps, performance seats, turbo boost gauge, leather-wrapped steering wheel and shift handle, 205/55VR16 tires. **TSi AWD** adds: permanent 4-wheel drive, limited-slip differential, uprated suspension, alloy wheels.

Optional equipment:

Anti-lock brakes	925	786	814
Requires security alarm on TSi & AWD; deletes limited-slip differential from AWD.			
Security alarm, TSi & AWD	163	139	143
Requires anti-lock brakes.			
Premium audio system, AWD	241	205	212

Prices are accurate at time of printing; subject to manufacturer's change.

	Retail Price	Dealer Invoice	Low Price
Pop-up sunroof	366	311	322
Leather upholstery, TSi & AWD	427	363	376
Alloy wheels, base & TSi	278	236	245

Ford Escort

Pony 3-door hatchback	$7976	$7393	$7693
LX 3-door hatchback	8667	7849	8149
GT 3-door hatchback	11484	10356	10656
LX 5-door hatchback	9095	8230	8530
LX 5-door wagon	9680	8750	9050
Destination charge	365	365	365

Standard equipment:

Pony: 1.9-liter PFI 4-cylinder engine, 5-speed manual transmission, motorized front shoulder belts, cloth and vinyl reclining bucket seats, one-piece folding rear seatback, tinted glass, coolant temperature gauge, trip odometer, intermittent wipers, cargo cover, door pockets, right visor mirror, 175/70R13 tires. **LX** adds: upgraded upholstery, 60/40 split rear seatback, console storage bin and cupholders, AM/FM radio, bodyside molding, full wheel covers. **GT** adds: 1.8-liter DOHC 16-valve engine, power steering, 4-wheel disc brakes, sport suspension, tachometer, cloth sport seats, AM/FM cassette, Light Group, lighted visor mirrors, removable cupholder tray, remote fuel door and hatch releases, power mirrors, variable intermittent wipers, fog lights, rear spoiler, rocker panel cladding, 185/60HR15 tires on alloy wheels.

Optional equipment:

4-speed automatic transmission	732	622	641
Power steering, LX	235	200	206
Preferred Pkg. 320A, LX	185	157	162
Power steering, Light/Convenience Group, rear defogger.			
Preferred Pkg. 330A, GT	496	422	434
Air conditioning, rear defogger, Luxury Convenience Group.			
Air conditioning, LX & GT	744	632	651
Rear defogger	160	136	140
Light/Convenience Group, LX	290	246	254
Light Group, power mirrors, remote fuel door and hatch releases, removable tray with cup holders.			
Luxury Convenience Group, LX 3-door	251	213	220
LX 5-door & wagon	334	284	292
GT	336	286	294
Tilt steering column, cruise control, tachometer, power locks.			
Power moonroof, LX & GT	549	466	480
AM/FM radio, Pony & LX	245	208	214
AM/FM cassette, Pony	400	340	350
LX	155	132	136

Prices are accurate at time of printing; subject to manufacturer's change.

	Retail Price	Dealer Invoice	Low Price
Premium sound system	138	117	121
Wagon Group	241	204	211
Luggage rack, rear wiper/washer.			
Clearcoat paint	91	78	80
California emissions pkg.	70	59	61

Ford Explorer

	Retail Price	Dealer Invoice	Low Price
XL 3-door wagon, 2WD	$14451	$12958	$13308
XL 3-door wagon, 4WD	16240	14532	14882
Sport 3-door wagon, 2WD	15494	13876	14226
Sport 3-door wagon, 4WD	17225	15399	15749
Eddie Bauer 3-door wagon, 2WD	18668	16669	17019
Eddie Bauer 3-door wagon, 4WD	20399	18192	18542
XL 5-door wagon, 2WD	15406	13798	14548
XL 5-door wagon, 4WD	17219	15394	16144
XLT 5-door wagon, 2WD	17151	15334	16084
XLT 5-door wagon, 4WD	18905	16877	17627
Eddie Bauer 5-door wagon, 2WD	19811	17674	18424
Eddie Bauer 5-door wagon, 4WD	21566	19219	19969
Destination charge	475	475	475

Standard equipment:

XL: 4.0-liter PFI V-6, 5-speed manual transmission, anti-lock rear brakes, power steering, Touch Drive electronic shift (4WD), knitted vinyl front bucket seats, split folding rear seat, tinted glass, flip-open opera windows (3-door), intermittent wipers, dual outside mirrors, carpet, load floor tiedown hooks, rear seat heat duct, tachometer, coolant temperature gauge, trip odometer, AM/FM radio, 225/70R15 tires with full-size spare. **Sport** adds: rear quarter privacy glass, Light Group, map light, load floor tiedown net, leather-wrapped steering wheel, lighted visor mirrors, alloy wheels. **XLT** adds: cloth captain's chairs, floor console, power mirrors, cargo cover, upgraded door panels with pockets, power windows and locks, cruise control, tilt steering column. **Eddie Bauer** adds to Sport: premium captain's chairs, floor console, power mirrors, power windows and locks, cruise control, tilt steering column, roof rack, rear defogger and wiper/washer, cargo cover, upgraded door panels with pockets, floormats, garment bag, duffle bag, Ford Care maintenance and warranty program.

Optional equipment:

4-speed automatic transmission	870	739	770
Limited-slip rear axle	252	215	223
Air conditioning	755	642	668
Preferred Pkg. 931G, Sport	516	438	457
Preferred Pkg. 932F, Eddie Bauer 3-door	105	89	93
942F, Eddie Bauer 5-door	605	514	535

Prices are accurate at time of printing; subject to manufacturer's change.

	Retail Price	Dealer Invoice	Low Price
Preferred Pkg. 941F, XLT w/automatic	410	348	363
XLT w/5-speed	NC	NC	NC
Cloth captain's chairs, XL, Sport	265	225	235
Cloth 60/40 split bench seat, XL 5-door	232	197	205
XLT (credit)	(33)	(28)	(28)
Cloth sport bucket seats, Sport	805	684	712
XLT, Sport w/captain's chairs	540	459	478
Leather sport seats, XL	1217	1035	1077
XLT, Sport w/captain's chairs	952	810	843
Eddie Bauer	412	350	365
Super engine cooling	56	48	50
Rear quarter privacy glass, XL 3-door	144	122	127
Manual locking hubs, 4WD (credit)	(104)	(88)	(88)
Light Group	29	25	26
Bodyside molding	121	103	107
Power Equipment Group, Sport	568	483	503
Luggage rack	126	107	112
Tilt-up sunroof	250	213	221
Cruise control & tilt steering column	348	295	308
Trailer Towing Pkg., w/A/C	106	90	94
Alloy wheels, XL 2WD	326	277	289
XL 4WD	265	225	235
Deluxe wheels w/trim rings, 2WD	61	52	54
Rear defogger & wiper/washer	279	237	247
AM/FM cassette	122	104	108
Premium AM/FM cassette	200	170	177
Ford JBL Audio System	688	585	609
Upgrade from premium cassette	488	415	432
Ford JBL Audio System w/CD player	983	835	870
Upgrade from premium cassette	783	665	693
Engine block heater	33	28	29
Deluxe tape stripe, 5-door	55	47	49
Deluxe two-tone paint	122	104	108
California emissions pkg.	100	85	89

Ford Taurus

	Retail Price	Dealer Invoice	Low Price
L 4-door notchback	$13352	$11548	$11923
GL 4-door notchback	13582	11742	12117
LX 4-door notchback	17373	14965	15340
SHO 4-door notchback	22071	18958	19333
L 5-door wagon	14784	12765	13140
GL 5-door wagon	14990	12940	13315
LX 5-door wagon	18963	16317	16692
Destination charge	480	480	480

Prices are accurate at time of printing; subject to manufacturer's change.

Standard equipment:

L: 2.5-liter PFI 4-cylinder engine (4-door; 3.0-liter PFI V-6 on wagon), 4-speed automatic transmission, power steering, driver's-side airbag, cloth reclining split bench seat with dual center armrests, tilt steering column, remote mirrors, tinted glass, intermittent wipers, cup/coin holder, door pockets, AM/FM radio, 205/70R14 tires. **GL** adds: rear armrest, cargo tiedown net, visor mirrors, seatback pockets. **LX** adds: 3.0-liter V-6 (4-door; 3.8-liter V-6 on wagon), air conditioning, power windows and locks, power driver's seat, power front lumbar supports, remote fuel door and decklid releases, tachometer, diagnostic alert lights, automatic parking brake release, cornering lamps, bodyside cladding, Convenience Kit (vinyl pouch with fluorescent lantern, tire pressure gauge, gloves, poncho, shop towel, distress flag, headlamp bulb), Light Group. **SHO** deletes automatic parking brake release and remote fuel door and decklid releases and adds: 3.0-liter DOHC 24-valve V-6 with dual exhaust, anti-lock 4-wheel disc brakes, foglamps, front bucket seats with console, cassette player, leather-wrapped steering wheel, rear defogger, cruise control, 215/60R16 tires on alloy wheels.

Optional equipment:	Retail Price	Dealer Invoice	Low Price
3.0-liter V-6, L & GL 4-doors	521	443	458
3.8-liter V-6 (std. LX wgn), L & GL 4-doors	1076	914	947
Others	555	472	488
Anti-lock brakes (std. SHO)	985	838	867
Manual air conditioning, L & GL	817	695	719
Automatic air conditioning, GL	1000	850	880
LX, SHO, or w/Pkg. 204A	183	155	161
Preferred Pkg. 203A (L Plus), L	964	820	848
Air conditioning, power locks, rear defogger, paint stripe.			
Preferred Pkg. 204A, GL 4-door	1804	1544	1588
GL wagon	1754	1491	1544
Air conditioning, rear defogger, power windows and locks, power driver's seat, remote fuel door release, remote decklid release (4-door), Light Group, rocker panel moldings, cassette player, cruise control, finned wheel covers, paint stripe.			
Preferred Pkg. 207A, LX	795	674	700
Rear defogger, cassette player with premium sound, cruise control, Autolamp system, leather-wrapped steering wheel, illuminated entry, alloy wheels, floormats, paint stripe.			
Preferred Pkg. 208A, LX 4-door	2350	1998	2068
LX wagon	1795	1526	1580
Pkg. 207A plus 3.8-liter engine (standard on wagon), anti-lock brakes, automatic climate control, high-level audio system, power antenna, keyless entry, power front seats, electronic instruments, speed-sensitive power steering; deletes premium sound.			
Preferred Pkg. 211A, SHO	724	615	637
Autolamp system, automatic climate control, high-level audio system, power antenna, keyless entry, power front seats, floormats.			
Bucket seats w/console, L Plus & GL	NC	NC	NC
Leather bucket seats w/console, GL	593	504	522
Leather upholstery, LX & SHO	489	416	430
Vinyl seat trim, L & GL	37	31	33
AM/FM cassette (std. SHO)	155	132	136

Prices are accurate at time of printing; subject to manufacturer's change.

	Retail Price	Dealer Invoice	Low Price
Premium sound, L Plus, GL, & LX	168	143	148
Power antenna	82	69	72
High-level audio system, L Plus, GL, & LX w/Pkg. 208A	490	417	431
GL w/204A, SHO w/211A	335	285	295
LX w/Pkg. 207A	167	142	147
CD player, L Plus, GL, LX, & SHO	491	418	432
Ford JBL audio system, L Plus, GL, LX & SHO	526	447	463
Autolamp system, LX & SHO	73	62	64
Cargo area cover, wagons	66	56	58
Convenience Group, GL	830	706	730
L	540	459	475
L w/Pkg. 203A	315	267	277
Power windows and locks, power driver's seat.			
Cornering lamps, L Plus & GL	68	58	60
Rear defogger	160	136	141
Extended-range fuel tank (std. SHO)	46	39	40
Remote fuel door & decklid release, 4-doors	91	78	80
Remote fuel door release, wagons	41	35	36
Illuminated entry (NA L)	82	69	72
Keyless entry, GL & LX	218	186	192
LX w/208A, SHO w/211A	137	116	121
Electronic instruments, GL	351	288	309
LX	239	196	210
Light Group, L & GL	59	50	52
Picnic table load floor extension, wagons	90	77	79
Power locks, L Plus	226	192	199
Lighted visor mirrors, L Plus & GL	100	85	88
Rocker panel moldings, L Plus & GL	55	47	48
Power moonroof, GL, LX, & SHO	776	659	683
Automatic parking brake release, L, Plus, & GL	12	10	11
Rear-facing third seat, wagons	155	132	136
Power seats, each	290	247	255
Cruise control	210	178	185
Speed-sensitive power steering (NA SHO)	104	88	92
Leather-wrapped steering wheel	63	54	55
HD suspension (NA SHO)	26	22	23
Rear wiper/washer, wagons	126	107	111
Styled road wheels, L Plus & GL	193	164	170
LX	128	109	113
Finned wheel covers	65	55	57
Alloy wheels, L Plus & GL	344	292	303
LX	279	237	246
Insta-Clear heated windshield (NA L & SHO)	305	259	268
205/70R14 whitewall tires (NA SHO)	82	69	72
Conventional spare tire (NA SHO)	73	62	64
HD battery (NA SHO)	27	23	24
Engine block heater	20	17	18

Prices are accurate at time of printing; subject to manufacturer's change.

	Retail Price	Dealer Invoice	Low Price
Floormats	43	36	38
Clearcoat paint	188	160	165
Paint stripe	61	52	54
California emissions pkg.	100	85	88

Geo Prizm

	Retail Price	Dealer Invoice	Low Price
4-door notchback	$9680	$8906	$9106
5-door hatchback	10295	9741	9891
GSi 4-door notchback	12195	11219	11419
GSi 5-door hatchback	12695	11679	11829
Destination charge	345	345	345

Standard equipment:

1.6-liter DOHC PFI 4-cylinder engine, 5-speed manual transmission, cloth reclining front bucket seats, tinted glass, door pockets, cup holders, left remote mirror, folding rear seat (hatchbacks), remote fuel door release, bodyside molding, 175/70R13 tires (notchback), 175/70R13 tires (hatchback). **GSi** adds: higher-output engine, 4-wheel disc brakes, power steering, uprated suspension, driver's-seat height adjustment, tachometer and oil pressure gauge, rear spoiler, rear wiper/washer (hatchback), left remote and right manual mirrors, AM/FM radio, 185/60HR14 tires on alloy wheels.

Optional equipment:

Air conditioning	690	587	604
Preferred Group 1, base 4-door	840	714	735

Rear defogger, AM/FM radio, power steering, left remote and right manual mirrors, full wheel covers, 175/70R13 tires.

Preferred Group 2, base 4-door	1305	1109	1142

Group 1 items but with 3-speed automatic transmission.

Preferred Group 3, base 4-door	1785	1517	1562

Group 1 plus air conditioning, power locks, remote decklid release.

Preferred Group 4, base 4-door	2250	1913	1969

Group 3 items but with 3-speed automatic transmission.

Preferred Group 1, base 5-door	662	563	579

Rear defogger, AM/FM radio, power steering, left remote and right manual mirrors.

Preferred Group 2, base 5-door	1127	958	986

Group 1 items but with 3-speed automatic transmission.

Preferred Group 3, base 5-door	1607	1366	1406

Group 1 plus air conditioning, power locks, remote hatch release.

Preferred Group 4, base 5-door	2072	1761	1813

Group 3 items but with 3-speed automatic transmission.

LSi Preferred Group 1, base 4-door	2502	2127	2189

Air conditioning, AM/FM radio, power steering, power locks, tilt steering column, remote decklid release, rear defogger, cargo area lamp, chrome and black bodyside moldings, full wheel covers.

Prices are accurate at time of printing; subject to manufacturer's change.

	Retail Price	Dealer Invoice	Low Price
LSi Preferred Group 2, base 4-door	2967	2522	2596
Group 1 items but with 3-speed automatic transmission.			
LSi Preferred Group 3, base 4-door	3467	2947	3034
Group 2 plus power windows, cruise control, intermittent wipers.			
Preferred Group 1, GSi 4-door	1059	900	927
GSi 5-door	909	773	795
Air conditioning, split folding rear seat, tilt steering column, remote decklid/hatch release, visor mirrors, floormats.			
Preferred Group 2, GSi 4-door	1834	1559	1605
GSi 5-door	1684	1431	1474
Group 1 items but with 4-speed automatic transmission.			
Preferred Group 3, GSi 4-door	1764	1499	1544
GSi 5-door	1614	1372	1412
Group 1 plus power windows and locks, cruise control, intermittent wipers.			
Preferred Group 4, GSi 4-door	2539	2158	2222
GSi 5-door	2389	2031	2090
Rear defogger	105	89	92
Power sunroof	530	451	464
Tachometer, LSi	60	51	53
AM/FM cassette	140	119	123

Honda Accord

	Retail Price	Dealer Invoice	Low Price
DX 2-door notchback, 5-speed	$12345	$10370	$11595
DX 2-door notchback, automatic	13095	11000	12345
LX 2-door notchback, 5-speed	14895	12512	14145
LX 2-door notchback, automatic	15645	13142	14895
EX 2-door notchback, 5-speed	16595	13940	15845
EX 2-door notchback, automatic	17345	14570	16595
DX 4-door notchback, 5-speed	12545	10538	11795
DX 4-door notchback, automatic	13295	11168	12545
LX 4-door notchback, 5-speed	15095	12680	14345
LX 4-door notchback, automatic	15845	13310	15095
EX 4-door notchback, 5-speed	16795	14108	16045
EX 4-door notchback, automatic	17545	14738	16795
SE 4-door notchback, automatic	19545	16418	18795
Destination charge	260	260	260

Standard equipment:

DX: 2.2-liter SOHC 16-valve PFI 4-cylinder engine, 5-speed manual or 4-speed automatic transmission, power steering, motorized front shoulder belts, cloth reclining front bucket seats, folding rear seatback, tachometer, coolant temperature gauge, trip odometer, tinted glass, tilt steering column, intermittent wipers, rear defogger, remote fuel door and decklid releases, door pockets, maintenance interval indicator, 185/70R14 tires. LX adds: air conditioning, cruise control, power windows and locks, power mirrors, AM/FM

Prices are accurate at time of printing; subject to manufacturer's change.

cassette, power antenna, rear armrest, beverage holder. **EX** adds: 130-horsepower engine, driver's seat lumbar support adjuster, front spoiler, power sunroof, sport suspension, upgraded audio system, 195/60R15 Michelin MXV3 tires on alloy wheels. **SE** adds: 140-horsepower engine, anti-lock 4-wheel disc brakes, leather on seats and door panels, leather-wrapped steering wheel.

OPTIONS are available as dealer-installed accessories.

Honda Civic	Retail Price	Dealer Invoice	Low Price
3-door hatchback, 4-speed	$6895	$6206	$6551
DX 3-door hatchback, 5-speed	8745	7433	7892
DX 3-door hatchback, automatic	9625	8181	8686
Si 3-door hatchback, 5-speed	10295	8751	9291
DX 4-door notchback, 5-speed	9490	8067	8890
DX 4-door notchback, automatic	10420	8857	9820
LX 4-door notchback, 5-speed	10500	8925	9900
LX 4-door notchback, automatic	11200	9520	10600
EX 4-door notchback, 5-speed	11195	9516	10595
EX 4-door notchback, automatic	11895	10111	11295
2WD 5-door wagon, 5-speed	10325	8776	9318
2WD 5-door wagon, automatic	11370	9664	10260
4WD 5-door wagon, 6-speed	12410	10548	11199
4WD 5-door wagon, automatic	13140	11169	11858
Destination charge	260	260	260

Standard equipment:

1.5-liter TBI 16-valve 70-bhp 4-cylinder engine, 4-speed manual transmission, door-mounted automatic front seatbelts, reclining front bucket seats, 50/50 split folding rear seatback, remote fuel door and hatch releases, tinted glass, rear defogger, 165/70R13 tires. **DX** adds: 92-bhp engine, 5-speed manual or 4-speed automatic transmission, power steering (with automatic transmission), motorized front shoulder belts (4-door), rear wiper/washer (hatchback), tilt steering column, cargo cover (hatchback), intermittent wipers, 175/70R14 tires. **Si** adds: 108-bhp PFI engine, power steering, dual manual mirrors, power moonroof, digital clock, tachometer, sport seats, 185/60R14 tires. **LX** adds to DX 4-door: power mirrors, power windows and locks, cruise control, digital clock, tachometer. **EX** adds: 108-bhp PFI engine, upgraded interior trim, 175/65HR14 tires. 2WD wagon has DX equipment plus digital clock, tachometer; 4WD wagon has 108-bhp PFI engine, 6-speed manual or 4-speed automatic transmission, permanent 4WD.

OPTIONS are available as dealer-installed accessories.

Hyundai Sonata

4-door notchback, 5-speed	$10700	—	—
4-door notchback, automatic	11420	—	—

Prices are accurate at time of printing; subject to manufacturer's change.

CAR PRICES

	Retail Price	Dealer Invoice	Low Price
4-door notchback w/V-6, automatic	12170	—	—
GLS 4-door notchback, 5-speed	13250	—	—
GLS 4-door notchback, automatic	13970	—	—
GLS 4-door notchback w/V-6, automatic	14720	—	—
Destination charge	NA	NA	NA

Dealer invoice and low price not available at time of publication.

Standard equipment:

2.4-liter PFI 4-cylinder or 3.0-liter PFI V-6 engine, 5-speed manual or 4-speed automatic transmission, power steering, motorized front shoulder belts, cloth reclining front bucket seats, driver's-seat height adjustment, center console, tachometer, trip odometer, AM/FM cassette, tilt steering column, digital clock, remote fuel door and decklid releases, rear defogger, door pockets, remote outside mirrors, bodyside molding, tinted glass, intermittent wipers, visor mirrors, 195/70R14 tires. **GLS** adds: air conditioning, power windows and locks, cruise control, upgraded audio system, power antenna, 6-way driver's seat, oil pressure gauge, voltmeter, power mirrors, 60/40 folding rear seatback, console with storage, lighted right visor mirror, seatback pockets.

Optional equipment:

Option Pkg. 1, base	825	—	—
Air conditioning.			
Option Pkg. 2, base	945	—	—
Pkg. 1 plus upgraded audio system.			
Option Pkg. 3, base	1740	—	—
Pkg. 2 plus power windows and locks, cruise control, power mirrors, power antenna.			
Option Pkg. 4, base	1440	—	—
Pkg. 2 plus sunroof.			
Option Pkg. 5, base	2235	—	—
Pkg. 3 plus sunroof.			
Option Pkg. 12, base	3010	—	—
Air conditioning, Hyundai/Polk Audio AM/FM cassette, power windows and locks, cruise control, power mirrors, power antenna, sunroof, 205/60HR15 tires on alloy wheels.			
Option Pkg. 15, base	120	—	—
Upgraded audio system.			
Option Pkg. 6, GLS	495	—	—
Sunroof.			
Option Pkg. 7, GLS	920	—	—
Hyundai/Polk Audio cassette system, Leather Pkg.			
Option Pkg. 8, GLS	945	—	—
Sunroof and 205/60HR15 tires on alloy wheels.			
Option Pkg. 9, GLS V-6	2855	—	—
Hyundai/Polk Audio CD system, sunroof, Leather Pkg., 205/60HR15 tires on alloy wheels.			
Option Pkg. 10, GLS	1270	—	—
Hyundai/Polk cassette system, sunroof, 205/60HR15 tires on alloy wheels.			

Prices are accurate at time of printing; subject to manufacturer's change.

	Retail Price	Dealer Invoice	Low Price
Option Pkg. 11, GLS V-6	2260	—	—
Pkg. 10 but with Hyundai/Polk Audio CD system.			
Option Pkg. 13, GLS	1865	—	—
Hyundai/Polk Audio cassette system, Leather Pkg., sunroof, 205/60HR15 tires on alloy wheels.			
Option Pkg. 14, GLS V-6	1765	—	—
Hyundai/Polk Audio CD system, 205/60HR15 tires on alloy wheels.			

Jeep Cherokee

	Retail Price	Dealer Invoice	Low Price
3-door 2WD, Pkg. 23A (2.5/5-speed)	$13822	$12448	$12698
3-door 2WD, 25A (4.0/5-speed)	13634	12289	12539
3-door 2WD, 26A (4.0/automatic)	14511	13034	13284
3-door 2WD, 25B (4.0/5-speed)	15534	13904	14154
3-door 2WD, 26B (4.0/automatic)	16411	14649	14899
3-door 4WD, 23A (2.5/5-speed)	15267	13720	13970
3-door 4WD, 25A (4.0/5-speed)	15379	13815	14065
3-door 4WD, 26A (4.0/automatic)	16256	14561	14811
3-door 4WD, 25B (4.0/5-speed)	17279	15430	15680
3-door 4WD, 26B (4.0/automatic)	18156	16176	16426
5-door 2WD, 23A (2.5/5-speed)	14699	13220	13670
5-door 2WD, 25A (4.0/5-speed)	14511	13060	13510
5-door 2WD, 26A (4.0/automatic)	15388	13806	14256
5-door 2WD, 25B (4.0/5-speed)	16411	14675	15125
5-door 2WD, 26B (4.0/automatic)	17288	15421	15871
5-door 4WD, 23A (2.5/5-speed)	16144	14492	14942
5-door 4WD, 25A (4.0/5-speed)	16256	14587	15037
5-door 4WD, 26A (4.0/automatic)	17133	15332	15782
5-door 4WD, 25B (4.0/5-speed)	18156	16202	16652
5-door 4WD, 26B (4.0/automatic)	19033	16947	17397
Pkg. 25B/26B: air conditioning, carpet, console with armrest, rear wiper/washer, roof rack, spare tire cover, tilt steering column, dual remote mirrors, intermittent wipers, wheel trim rings, 205/75R15 tires.			
Sport 3-door 2WD, 25C (5-speed)	13986	12588	12838
Sport 3-door 2WD, 26C (automatic)	14863	13333	13583
Sport 3-door 2WD, 25D (5-speed)	15639	13993	14243
Sport 3-door 2WD, 26D (automatic)	16516	14738	14988
Sport 3-door 4WD, 25C (5-speed)	15731	14114	14364
Sport 3-door 4WD, 26C (automatic)	16608	14860	15110
Sport 3-door 4WD, 25D (5-speed)	17384	15731	15981
Sport 3-door 4WD, 26D (automatic)	18261	16265	16515
Sport 5-door 2WD, 25C (5-speed)	14863	13360	13810
Sport 5-door 2WD, 26C (automatic)	15740	14105	14555
Sport 5-door 2WD, 25D (5-speed)	16516	14765	15215
Sport 5-door 2WD, 26D (automatic)	17393	15510	15960
Sport 5-door 4WD, 25C (5-speed)	16608	14886	15336

Prices are accurate at time of printing; subject to manufacturer's change.

CAR PRICES

	Retail Price	Dealer Invoice	Low Price
Sport 5-door 4WD, 26C (automatic)	17485	15632	16082
Sport 5-door 4WD, 25D (5-speed)	18261	16291	16741
Sport 5-door 4WD, 26D (automatic)	19138	17037	17487

Pkg. 25D/26D: air conditioning, cassette player, console with armrest, tachometer and gauges, spare tire cover, tilt steering column, dual remote mirrors, intermittent wipers.

	Retail Price	Dealer Invoice	Low Price
Laredo 5-door 2WD, 25J (5-speed)	16166	14467	14917
Laredo 5-door 2WD, 26J (automatic)	17043	15213	15663
Laredo 5-door 2WD, 25K (5-speed)	18321	16299	16749
Laredo 5-door 2WD, 26K (automatic)	19198	17044	17494
Laredo 3-door 4WD, 25J (5-speed)	17034	15222	15472
Laredo 3-door 4WD, 26J (automatic)	17911	15967	16217
Laredo 5-door 4WD, 25J (5-speed)	17911	15994	16444
Laredo 5-door 4WD, 26J (automatic)	18788	16739	17189
Laredo 5-door 4WD, 25K (5-speed)	20066	17825	18275
Laredo 5-door 4WD, 26K (automatic)	20943	18571	19021

Pkg. 25K/26K: air conditioning, power windows, power locks with keyless entry, cassette player with premium speakers, cruise control, tilt steering column.

	Retail Price	Dealer Invoice	Low Price
Limited 5-door 4WD	25231	22536	22986
Briarwood 5-door 4WD	24710	22078	22528
Destination charge	465	465	465

Standard equipment:

2.5-liter PFI 4-cylinder or 4.0-liter PFI 6-cylinder engine, 5-speed manual or 4-speed automatic transmission, power steering, vinyl front bucket seats, folding rear seat, mini console, AM/FM radio, vinyl floor covering, tinted glass, 195/75R15 tires; 4WD system is Command-Trac part-time. **Sport** adds: 4.0-liter 6-cylinder engine, carpet, hockey-stick-style armrests, cargo tiedown hooks, 225/75R15 outlined white letter all-terrain tires on alloy wheels. **Laredo** adds: reclining front bucket seats, fabric upholstery, cargo cover, skid strips, console with armrest and storage, rear defogger, upgraded sound insulation, tachometer, coolant temperature and oil pressure gauges, voltmeter, trip odometer, deep-tinted rear quarter windows (3-door), swing-out rear quarter windows (3-door), dual-note horn, headlamp delay system, misc. lights, dual outside mirrors, roof rack, spare tire cover, leather-wrapped steering wheel, intermittent wipers, rear wiper/washer, 215/75R15 outlined white letter tires. **Limited** adds: 4-speed automatic transmission, Selec-Trac transfer case, air conditioning, leather upholstery, power front seats, power windows, power locks with keyless entry, overhead console (with outside temperature readout, compass, bins, map lights), cruise control, fog lamps, deep-tinted glass, illuminated entry, power mirrors, cassette player, power antenna, tilt steering column, 225/70R15 Eagle GT+4 tires. **Briarwood** adds: bright trim, woodgrain exterior applique, 215/75R15 tires.

Optional equipment:

Anti-lock brakes	799	679	699
Available only on 4WD models with 4.0-liter engine and Selec-Trac.			
Air conditioning, base, Sport, & Laredo	836	711	732
Selec-Trac, base, Sport, & Laredo 4WD	394	335	345

Prices are accurate at time of printing; subject to manufacturer's change.

CONSUMER GUIDE®

	Retail Price	Dealer Invoice	Low Price
Carpet, base	209	178	183
Fabric seats, base & Sport	137	116	120
Console w/armrest, base & Sport	142	121	124
Rear defogger, base & Sport	161	137	141
Cassette player, base, Sport & Laredo	201	171	176
Premium speakers, Laredo	174	148	152
Roof rack, base & Sport	139	118	122
Tilt steering column, base, Sport & Laredo	132	112	116
Base & Sport require Visibility Group.			
Spare tire cover, Sport	46	39	40
Visibility Group, base & Sport	138	117	121
Dual outside mirrors, intermittent wipers.			
Rear wiper/washer, base & Sport	147	125	129
Deep-tinted glass, base & Sport 3-door	333	283	291
Tachometer & gauges, Sport	158	134	138
Front vent windows	91	77	80
Rear quarter vent windows, 3-doors	161	137	141
HD Alternator & Battery Group, base, Sport & Laredo	135	115	118
Base, Sport & Laredo w/A/C	72	61	63
Fog lamps, Laredo	110	94	96
Overhead console, Laredo	203	173	178
Illuminated entry, Laredo	78	66	68
Requires Power Window & Lock Group.			
Power Window & Lock Group, Sport & Laredo 3-door	437	371	382
Sport & Laredo 5-door	582	495	509
Power windows, power locks with keyless entry.			
Power mirrors, Laredo	100	85	88
Power front seats, Laredo	416	354	364
Security alarm, Laredo	226	192	198
Includes illuminated entry; requires Power Window & Lock Group.			
Skid Plate Group, 4WD models	144	122	126
Cruise control, base, Sport, & Laredo	230	196	201
Tilt steering column, Laredo	132	112	116
Trailer Tow Pkg. B	358	304	313
4WD models w/Off-Road Pkg.	242	206	212
Off-Road Pkg. (4WD only), base	982	835	859
Sport	552	469	483
Laredo	579	492	507
Manual sunroof, Laredo	357	303	312
Limited & Briarwood	154	131	135
Protection Group, base & Sport	164	139	144
Front bumper guards, cargo skid strips, floormats, bodyside moldings.			
205/75R15 tires, base 2WD	46	39	40
215/75R15 OWL tires, base	359	305	314
Base 4WD w/Pkg. 25B/26B	313	266	274
Laredo	46	39	40
225/75R15 tires, base 4WD	405	344	354
Base 4WD w/Pkg. 25B/26B	359	305	314

Prices are accurate at time of printing; subject to manufacturer's change.

	Retail Price	Dealer Invoice	Low Price
Spare tire cover, base	46	39	40
Outside spare tire carrier, base & Sport	173	147	151
Laredo	101	86	88
4 styled steel wheels, base	103	88	90
5 styled steel wheels, base	129	110	113
4 alloy wheels, base	348	296	305
Base w/Pkg. 25B/26B	283	241	248
5 alloy wheels, base	432	367	378
Base w/Pkg. 25B/26B	367	312	321
Leather-wrapped steering wheel, Sport	48	41	42
Metallic paint	173	147	151
California emissions pkg.	124	105	109

Lexus LS 400

4-door notchback	$38000	$30400	$36000
Destination charge	350	350	350

Standard equipment:

4.0-liter DOHC 32-valve PFI V-8, 4-speed automatic transmission, anti-lock braking system, 4-wheel disc brakes, power steering, driver's-side airbag, automatic climate control, cloth reclining front bucket seats, power windows and locks, remote entry, cruise control, power mirrors, tachometer, trip odometer, coolant temperature gauge, tilt/telescopic steering column, AM/FM cassette, intermittent wipers, toolkit, first aid kit, 205/65VR15 tires on alloy wheels.

Optional equipment:

Leather Pkg.	1400	1120	1292
Moonroof	900	720	831
Traction control & heated front seats	1600	1280	1477
Electronic air suspension	1500	1200	1385
Requires Leather Pkg., moonroof and memory system.			
Memory system	800	640	738
Lexus/Nakamichi audio system	1000	750	897
Requires CD changer.			
Remote 6-CD auto-changer	900	675	808

Lincoln Mark VII

Bill Blass 2-door notchback	$30238	$25781	$26631
LSC 2-door notchback	30362	25885	26735
Destination charge	580	580	580

Prices are accurate at time of printing; subject to manufacturer's change.

Standard equipment:

Bill Blass: 5.0-liter PFI V-8, 4-speed automatic transmission, anti-lock 4-wheel disc brakes, power steering, driver's side airbag, automatic climate control, power front bucket seats, leather upholstery (cloth may be substituted at no cost), keyless illuminated entry, power windows and locks, heated power mirrors, overhead console with compass and thermometer, cruise control, power decklid pulldown, Autolamp system, automatic dimmer, rear defogger, tinted glass, AM/FM cassette, power antenna, remote fuel door and decklid releases, cornering lamps, electronic instruments, trip odometer, intermittent wipers, tilt steering column, trip computer, center console with armrest, storage, and cupholder, lighted visor mirrors, 225/60R16 tires on alloy wheels. **LSC** adds: articulated sport seats, analog instruments including tachometer and coolant temperature gauge, fog lights.

Optional equipment:	Retail Price	Dealer Invoice	Low Price
Anti-theft alarm system	295	248	258
Traction-Lok axle	101	85	88
LSC Special Edition	680	571	595
Includes unique BBS wheels with dark titanium wheel spiders.			
Automatic day/night mirror	111	93	97
Power moonroof	1540	1293	1348
CD player	299	251	262
Requires Ford JBL audio system.			
Ford JBL audio system	575	483	503
Cellular telephone	799	671	699
Engine block heater	26	22	23
California emissions pkg.	100	84	88

Mazda 323/Protege

	Retail Price	Dealer Invoice	Low Price
323 3-door hatchback	$6899	$6471	$6750
323 SE 3-door hatchback	7849	7154	7319
Protege DX 4-door notchback	9359	8430	8678
Protege LX 4-door notchback	10999	9779	10136
Protege 4WD 4-door notchback	11239	9985	10353
Destination charge	279	279	279

Standard equipment:

323: 1.6-liter PFI 4-cylinder engine, 5-speed manual transmission, motorized front shoulder belts, vinyl reclining front bucket seats, one-piece folding rear seat, left remote mirror, coolant temperature gauge, trip odometer, cargo cover, console with storage, rear defogger, 155SR13 tires. **SE** adds: cloth upholstery, 60/40 split rear seat, dual remote mirrors, tinted glass, door pockets, bodyside moldings, wheel covers. **Protege DX:** 1.8-liter SOHC 16-valve 4-cylinder engine, 5-speed manual transmission, motorized front shoulder belts, cloth reclining front bucket seats, 60/40 folding rear seat, remote mirrors, coolant temperature gauge, trip odometer, console with storage, tinted glass, bodyside moldings, door pockets, remote fuel door and decklid releases, righte visor mirror, digital clock,

Prices are accurate at time of printing; subject to manufacturer's change.

rear defogger, 175/70R14 tires; 4WD has permanent 4-wheel drive, 4-wheel disc brakes, power steering, intermittent wipers, 185/65R14 tires. **LX** adds to DX: DOHC 16-valve engine, 4-wheel disc brakes, power steering, velour upholstery, power windows and locks, cruise control, AM/FM cassette, power mirrors, intermittent wipers, tachometer, cupholder, left visor mirror, 185/60R14 tires.

Optional equipment:

	Retail Price	Dealer Invoice	Low Price
4-speed automatic transmission	700	630	649
Protege 4WD	750	675	695
Power steering, 323	250	213	226
Air conditioning	795	636	698
Value Pkg., Protege DX	270	238	248
Power steering, AM/FM cassette, tilt steering column, intermittent wipers.			
Value Pkg., Protege LX	1160	1009	1058
Air conditioning, power sunroof, alloy wheels.			
AM/FM cassette, 323 SE, Protege DX & 4WD	450	342	386
Power sunroof, Protege LX	555	444	487
Floormats	59	43	50

Mazda MPV Wagon

Wagon, 5-pass., 2.6, 5-speed	$13715	$11932	$12974
Wagon, 5-pass., 2.6, automatic	14415	12541	13628
Wagon, 7-pass., 2.6, 5-speed	14985	13037	14161
Wagon, 7-pass., 2.6, automatic	15685	13646	14816
Wagon, 7-pass., 3.0, automatic	16435	14298	15517
4WD wagon, 7-pass., 3.0, automatic	19435	16908	18322
Destination charge	279	279	279

Standard equipment:

5-passenger: 2.6-liter PFI 4-cylinder engine, 5-speed manual or 4-speed automatic transmission, anti-lock rear brakes, power steering, reclining front bucket seats, 3-passenger middle bench seat, remote mirrors, tachometer, coolant temperature gauge, trip odometer, intermittent wipers, rear defogger and wiper/washer, tinted glass, door pockets, remote fuel door release, tilt steering column, AM/FM cassette, 205/70R14 tires. **7-passenger:** 2.6-liter 4-cylinder or 3.0-liter PFI V-6, 4-speed automatic transmission (with V-6), two-passenger middle and 3-passenger rear bench seats, power mirrors. **4WD** has selectable full-time 4WD, 215/65R15 tires on alloy wheels.

Optional equipment:

Single air conditioning	849	696	782
Dual air conditioning (3.0 req.)	1497	1228	1380
Cold Pkg.	298	256	281
HD battery, larger windshield washer solvent reservoir, rear heater.			
Value Pkg. A, 2WD w/7-pass. seating	498	428	469
Power windows and locks, cruise control, privacy glass.			

Prices are accurate at time of printing; subject to manufacturer's change.

	Retail Price	Dealer Invoice	Low Price
Value Pkg. B, 2WD w/7-pass. seating	895	770	843
Pkg. A plus 215/65R15 tires on alloy wheels, color-keyed exterior treatment, pushbutton heater controls.			
Value Pkg. C, 4WD	695	598	655
Pkg. A plus color-keyed exterior treatment, pushbutton heater controls.			
Luxury Pkg. (Option Pkg. D), 2WD	3883	3223	3598
4WD	3423	2841	3172
Value Pkg. B (2WD), Value Pkg. C (4WD), leather seating, leather-wrapped steering wheel, color-keyed bodyside moldings, two-tone paint, lace alloy wheels.			
CD player	699	559	637
Requires Value Pkg. B or C, or Luxury Pkg.			
Two-tone paint	251	206	231
Towing Pkg., 2WD w/3.0	498	428	469
4WD automatic	398	342	375
Transmission oil cooler, HD radiator and fan, conventional spare, automatic load leveling (2WD).			
Floormats, w/5-pass. seating	59	42	51
w/7-pass. seating	84	59	72

Mazda Miata

2-door convertible	$13800	$12101	$13800
Destination charge	279	279	279

Standard equipment:

1.6-liter DOHC 16-valve PFI 4-cylinder engine, 5-speed manual transmission, 4-wheel disc brakes, driver's-side airbag, cloth reclining bucket seats, tachometer, coolant temperature gauge, trip odometer, intermittent wipers, 185/60R14 tires.

Optional equipment:

4-speed automatic transmission	720	634	720
Anti-lock brakes	900	765	900
Requires Pkg. B; not available with CD player.			
Air conditioning	795	636	795
Detachable hardtop	1400	1134	1400
Requires Option Pkg. A or B.			
Option Pkg. A	1370	1151	1370
Power steering, alloy wheels, leather-wrapped steering wheel, AM/FM cassette.			
Option Pkg. B	1965	1651	1965
Pkg. A plus power windows, cruise control, headrest speakers.			
Limited-slip differential	250	200	250
CD player	600	480	600
Requires Option Pkg. A or B.			
Floormats	59	43	59

Prices are accurate at time of printing; subject to manufacturer's change.

Mercury Sable

	Retail Price	Dealer Invoice	Low Price
GS 4-door notchback	$15311	$13224	$13599
LS 4-door notchback	16154	13941	14316
GS 5-door wagon	16256	14028	14403
LS 5-door wagon	17124	14766	15141
Destination charge	480	480	480

Standard equipment:

3.0-liter PFI V-6, 4-speed automatic transmission, power steering, driver's-side airbag, air conditioning, cloth reclining 50/50 front seat with armrests, tinted glass, intermittent wipers, tachometer, coolant temperature gauge, trip odometer, power mirrors, tilt steering column, AM/FM radio, slide-out cupholders and coin holder, front door pockets, rear armrest (4-door), covered package tray storage bin (4-door), visor mirrors, cargo net, 205/70R14 tires; wagon has 60/40 folding rear seat, tiedown hooks, luggage rack. **LS** adds: power windows, automatic parking brake release, remote fuel door and decklid releases, Light Group, bodyside cladding, power lumbar supports, seatback pockets, lighted visor mirrors.

Optional equipment:

3.8-liter V-6	555	472	488
Anti-lock 4-wheel disc brakes	985	838	867
Luxury Touring Pkg., LS 4-door	2050	1743	1804
Anti-lock brakes, leather bucket seats, power moonroof.			
Variable-assist power steering	104	88	92
Automatic climate control	183	155	161
Preferred Pkg. 450A, GS 4-door	802	681	706
GS wagon	752	638	662
Power windows and locks, remote decklid and fuel door releases, cruise control, rear defogger.			
Preferred Pkg. 451A, GS 4-door	1138	967	1001
GS wagon	1088	924	957
Pkg. 450A plus power driver's seat, cassette player, Light Group, floormats, 205/65R15 tires on alloy wheels.			
Preferred Pkg. 461A, LS	1502	1277	1322
3.8-liter V-6, power driver's seat, leather-wrapped steering wheel, cruise control, rear defogger, cassette player with premium sound, power antenna, power locks, remote fuel door and decklid releases, floormats, 205/65R15 tires on alloy wheels.			
Preferred Pkg. 462A, LS	2294	1951	2019
Pkg. 461A plus keyless entry, electronic instruments, Autolamp system, automatic climate control, High Level Audio System.			
Autolamp system	73	62	64
Rear defogger	160	136	141
Extended-range fuel tank	46	39	40
Electronic instruments	351	299	309
Includes extended-range fuel tank.			
Keyless entry	218	186	192
Includes illuminated entry; requires Power Lock Group.			

Prices are accurate at time of printing; subject to manufacturer's change.

	Retail Price	Dealer Invoice	Low Price
Light Group, GS	59	50	52
Power Lock Group, GS 4-door	317	270	279
GS wagon	267	227	235
LS	226	192	199
Power locks, remote fuel door and decklid releases.			
Luxury Trim Option, LS 4-door	600	510	528
Cloth and leather trim, upgraded carpet and floormats, two-tone paint, alloy wheels.			
Lighted visor mirrors, GS	100	85	88
Power moonroof	776	659	683
Cassette player	155	132	136
High Level Audio System	490	417	431
GS w/Pkg. 451A	335	285	295
LS w/Pkg. 461A	167	142	147
CD player	491	418	432
Requires High Level Audio System.			
Ford JBL sound system, 4-doors	526	447	463
High Level Audio System or CD player.			
Premium sound system	168	143	148
Power antenna	82	69	72
AM/FM radio delete (credit)	(206)	(175)	(175)
Rear-facing third seat, wagons	155	132	136
Power front seats, each	290	247	255
Bucket seats w/console	NC	NC	NC
Leather seat trim	489	416	430
Vinyl seat trim, GS wagon	37	31	33
Cruise control	210	178	185
Leather-wrapped steering wheel	63		55
Requires cruise control.			
HD suspension	26	22	23
Rear wiper/washer, wagons	126	107	111
Requires rear defogger.			
Power windows, GS	315	267	277
Insta-Clear heated windshield	305	259	268
Requires rear defogger.			
Clearcoat paint	188	160	165
Picnic tray, wagons	90	77	79
205/70R14 whitewall tires	82	69	72
205/65R15 tires	65	55	57
205/65R15 whitewall tires	146	124	128
Includes deluxe wheel covers.			
Conventional spare tire	73	62	64
Polycast wheels, GS	138	117	121
Alloy wheels, GS	224	191	197
Requires 205/65R15 tires.			
Bodyside accent stripes	61	52	54
Engine block heater	20	17	18
Floormats	43	36	38

Prices are accurate at time of printing; subject to manufacturer's change.

	Retail Price	Dealer Invoice	Low Price
HD battery	27	23	24
California emissions pkg.	100	85	88

Mercury Tracer

4-door notchback	$9386	$8503	$8803
5-door wagon	10407	9411	9711
LTS 4-door notchback	11636	10505	10705
Destination charge	355	355	355

Standard equipment:

1.9-liter PFI 4-cylinder engine, 5-speed manual transmission, motorized front shoulder belts, cloth reclining front bucket seats, 60/40 split rear seatback, AM/FM radio, tachometer, coolant temperature gauge, right seatback pocket, tinted glass, 175/70R13 tires. **Wagon** adds: power steering, variable intermittent wipers, remote fuel door release, power mirrors, rear defogger, cargo cover, rear wiper/washer, 175/65R14 tires, full wheel covers. **LTS** adds: 1.8-liter DOHC 16-valve engine, 4-wheel disc brakes, sport suspension, tilt steering column, AM/FM cassette, remote decklid release, Light Group, driver's seat tilt adjustment, cruise control, center console with removable tray, leather-wrapped steering wheel, 185/60HR14 tires on alloy wheels.

Optional equipment:

4-speed automatic transmission	732	622	641
Requires power steering.			
Power steering, base 4-door	235	200	206
Air conditioning	744	632	651
Requires power steering.			
Preferred Pkg. 572B, base 4-door	470	399	411
Power steering, intermittent wipers, remote fuel door and decklid releases, power mirrors, rear defogger, Light Group, 175/65R14 tires, full wheel covers.			
Preferred Pkg. 573B, base 4-door	1136	964	994
Wagon	632	536	553
Pkg. 573A plus air conditioning, driver's seat tilt adjustment, tilt steering column.			
Rear defogger, base	160	136	140
Remote fuel door release, base	24	21	21
Remote decklid release, base	50	42	44
Driver's seat tilt adjustment, base	37	31	32
Light Group, base	116	98	102
Tilt steering column, base	135	115	118
Cruise control, base	201	171	176
Power windows	306	260	268
Power mirrors, base 4-door	98	83	86
Power locks	205	174	179
Intermittent wipers, base 4-door	55	47	48
Luggage rack, wagon	115	97	101

Prices are accurate at time of printing; subject to manufacturer's change.

	Retail Price	Dealer Invoice	Low Price
Cassette player, base	155	132	136
Premium sound system	138	117	121
Requires cassette player.			
Power moonroof (NA wagon)	549	466	480
AM/FM delete, base (credit)	(245)	(208)	(208)
AM/FM cassette delete, LTS (credit)	(400)	(340)	(340)
175/65R14 tires, base 4-door	132	112	116
California emissions pkg.	70	59	61

Mitsubishi Eclipse

3-door hatchback, 5-speed	$10859	—	—
3-door hatchback, automatic	11499	—	—
GS 1.8 3-door hatchback, 5-speed	11899	—	—
GS 1.8 3-door hatchback, automatic	12539	—	—
GS DOHC 3-door hatchback, 5-speed	12789	—	—
GS DOHC 3-door hatchback, automatic . . .	13439	—	—
GS Turbo 3-door hatchback, 5-speed	15099	—	—
GS Turbo 3-door hatchback, automatic . . .	15879	—	—
GSX 3-door hatchback, 5-speed	16759	—	—
GSX 3-door hatchback, automatic	17529	—	—
Destination charge	328	328	328

Dealer invoice and low price not available at time of publication.

Standard equipment:

1.8-liter PFI 4-cylinder engine, 5-speed manual or 4-speed automatic transmission, 4-wheel disc brakes, motorized front shoulder belts, cloth reclining front bucket seats, split folding rear seat, tilt steering column, map lights, remote fuel door and hatch releases, visor mirrors, tachometer, coolant temperature gauge, dual trip odometers, intermittent wipers, automatic-off headlamp feature, AM/FM radio, tinted glass, remote mirrors, 185/70R14 tires. **GS adds:** power steering, 3-way driver's seat, upgraded door panels, power mirrors, rear defogger, cargo cover, center console with coin and cup holders, AM/FM cassette, full wheel covers. **GS DOHC adds:** 2.0-liter DOHC 16-valve engine, sport suspension, 205/55R16 tires. **GS DOHC Turbo adds:** turbocharged engine, rear wiper/washer, air dam and rear spoiler, sill extensions, 6-way front sport seats, cruise control, power antenna, alloy wheels. **GSX adds:** permanent 4-wheel drive, cruise control, 6-way driver's seat, driving lamps.

Optional equipment:

Anti-lock brakes, GS Turbo	924	—	—
GSX	680	—	—
Power steering, base	262	—	—
Air conditioning	811	—	—
AM/FM cassette, base	170	—	—
AM/FM cassette w/EQ, exc. 1.8	209	—	—

Prices are accurate at time of printing; subject to manufacturer's change.

CAR PRICES

	Retail Price	Dealer Invoice	Low Price
AM/FM cassette w/CD player, exc. 1.8	704	—	—
Power Pkg., exc. base	444	—	—
Power windows and locks.			
Leather front seating surfaces, GSX	427	—	—
Security alarm, GSX	163	—	—
Alloy wheels, GS DOHC	315	—	—
Rear wiper/washer (std. GSX)	129	—	—
Cruise control (std. GSX)	210	—	—
Sunroof (NA base)	366	—	—
Rear defogger, base	119	—	—
Wheel covers, base	100	—	—
RS Pkg., GS DOHC	305	—	—
Front air dam, rear spoiler, fog lamps, etc.			

Nissan Maxima

	Retail Price	Dealer Invoice	Low Price
GXE 4-door notchback	$18399	—	—
SE 4-door notchback	19499	—	—
Destination charge	275	275	275

Dealer invoice and low price not available at time of publication.

Standard equipment:

3.0-liter PFI V-6, 4-speed automatic transmission, power steering, motorized front shoulder belts, air conditioning, power windows and locks with keyless entry, velour reclining front bucket seats, driver's seat height and lumbar adjustments, split folding rear seat, power mirrors, cruise control, tinted glass, AM/FM cassette with diversity antenna, theft deterrent system, tilt steering column, variable intermittent wipers, rear defogger, remote fuel door and decklid releases, illuminated entry, tachometer, dual trip odometers, coolant temperature gauge, digital clock, 195/60R16 tires on alloy wheels. **SE** adds: 5-speed manual or 4-speed automatic transmission, 4-wheel disc brakes, Nissan-Bose audio system, leather-wrapped steering wheel and shift knob, power glass sunroof, fog lights.

OPTIONS prices not available at time of publication.

Oldsmobile Bravada

	Retail Price	Dealer Invoice	Low Price
5-door 4WD wagon	$23795	$21249	—
Destination charge	455	455	455

Low price not available at time of publication.

Standard equipment:

4.3-liter TBI V-6, 4-speed automatic transmission, permanent 4-wheel drive, anti-lock brakes, power steering, air conditioning, cloth reclining front bucket seats, center console

Prices are accurate at time of printing; subject to manufacturer's change.

with cupholders and electrical outlets, folding rear seat with armrest, cruise control, power windows, power locks with remote, power mirrors, rear wiper/washer, intermittent wipers, rear defogger, coolant temperature and oil pressure gauges, voltmeter, trip odometer, fog lights, lighted visor mirrors, remote tailgate release, roof luggage rack, AM/FM cassette w/EQ, leather-wrapped steering wheel, floormats, 235/75R15 tires on alloy wheels.

Optional equipment:	Retail Price	Dealer Invoice	Low Price
Custom leather trim	650	553	—
HD Towing Pkg.	409	348	—
Cold Climate Pkg.	90	77	—
Electronic instruments	296	252	—
Mud & snow tires	182	155	—
California emissions pkg.	100	85	—

Oldsmobile Eighty Eight

Royale 2-door notchback	$17095	$14753	$15103
Royale 4-door notchback	17195	14839	15189
Brougham 2-door notchback	18695	16134	16484
Brougham 4-door notchback	18795	16220	16570
Destination charge	535	535	535

Standard equipment:

Royale: 3.8-liter PFI V-6, 4-speed automatic transmission, power steering, door-mounted automatic front seatbelts, air conditioning, front bench seat with armrest, left remote and right manual mirrors, tinted glass, AM/FM radio, intermittent wipers, tilt steering column, trip odometer, 205/75R14 tires. **Brougham** adds: 55/45 reclining front seat with storage armrest, remote mirrors, visor mirror, cassette player, remote decklid release, whitewall tires.

Optional equipment:

Anti-lock brakes	925	786	819
Inflatable Retraint System (airbag), 4-doors	850	723	752
Option Pkg. 1SA	STD	STD	STD
Option Pkg. 1SB, Royale	549	467	486
55/45 reclining front seat with storage armrest, cruise control, visor mirror, misc. lights, floormats.			
Option Pkg. 1SC, Royale 2-door	1374	1168	1216
Royale 4-door	1489	1266	1318
Pkg. 1SB plus power windows and locks, power driver's seat, power antenna, door edge guards.			
Option Pkg. 1SD, Royale 2-door	1620	1377	1434
Royale 4-door	1735	1475	1535
Pkg. 1SC plus Remote Lock Control Pkg., Reminder Pkg.			
Option Pkg. 1SB, Brougham 2-door	1005	854	889

Prices are accurate at time of printing; subject to manufacturer's change.

	Retail Price	Dealer Invoice	Low Price
Brougham 4-door	1120	952	991

Power windows and locks, cruise control, power driver's seat, door edge guards, floormats.

Option Pkg. 1SC, Brougham 2-door	1151	978	1019
Brougham 4-door	1266	1076	1120

Pkg. 1SB plus power antenna, Reminder Pkg.

Option Pkg. 1SD, Brougham 2-door	1606	1365	1421
Brougham 4-door	1721	1463	1523

Pkg. 1SC plus automatic climate control, Driver Information System, Remote Lock Control Pkg.

Power passenger seat, Royale	290	247	257
Power locks, Royale 2-door	190	162	168
Royale 4-door	230	196	204
Power windows, Royale 2-door	255	217	226
Royale 4-door	320	272	283
Vinyl roof covering, Brougham 4-door	200	170	177
Rear defogger	160	136	142
FE3 Touring Car suspension, Royale	779	662	689
Brougham	713	606	631

Sport suspension, automatic leveling, leather-wrapped steering wheel, high-capacity cooling, 2.97 axle ratio, 215/65R15 tires on alloy wheels.

Wire wheel covers, Royale	291	247	258
Brougham	215	183	190
Alloy wheels, Royale	368	313	326
Brougham	320	272	283
Convenience Value Group, Royale	317	269	281
Brougham	287	244	254

Power mirrors, lighted right visor mirror, misc. lights.

Cassette player, Royale	140	119	124
w/EQ, Brougham	235	200	208
CD player, Brougham	359	305	318
Instrument panel gauge cluster	66	56	58
Towing Pkg.	271	230	240
Decklid luggage rack	115	98	102
Whitewall tires, Royale	76	65	67
High-capacity cooling	66	56	58
Accent stripe	45	38	40
Engine block heater	18	15	16
California emissions pkg.	100	85	89

Plymouth Acclaim

4-door notchback	$10825	$9696	$9981
LE 4-door notchback	12880	11504	11789
LX 4-door notchback	14380	12824	13109
Destination charge	465	465	465

Prices are accurate at time of printing; subject to manufacturer's change.

Standard equipment:

2.5-liter TBI 4-cylinder engine, 5-speed manual transmission, power steering, driver's-side airbag, cloth reclining front bucket seats, coolant temperature gauge, voltmeter, trip odometer, dual remote mirrors, AM/FM radio with two speakers, remote decklid release, intermittent wipers, narrow bodyside moldings. **LE** adds: 3-speed automatic transmission, rear defogger, tilt steering column, tinted glass, four speakers, misc. lights, Message Center, floormats, grooved bodyside molding, 195/70R14 tires. **LX** adds: 3.0-liter PFI V-6, 4-speed automatic transmission, air dam with fog lamps, decklid luggage rack, cassette player, leather-wrapped steering wheel, trip computer, 205/60R15 tires on alloy wheels.

Optional equipment:	Retail Price	Dealer Invoice	Low Price
3.0-liter V-6, base & LE	694	590	611
Requires 4-speed automatic transmission; base requires 195/70R14 tires.			
3-speed automatic transmission, base	547	465	481
4-speed automatic transmission, base	640	544	563
LE	93	79	82
Available only with V-6.			
Anti-lock brakes	899	764	791
Air conditioning, LE & LX	821	698	722
Super Discount Pkg. A, base	915	778	805
Air conditioning, rear defogger, tinted glass, four speakers, cruise control, tilt steering column, floormats.			
Super Discount Pkg. B, base	1491	1267	1312
Pkg. A plus power windows and locks, heated power mirrors.			
Super Discount Pkg. C, LE & LX	972	826	855
Air conditioning, power windows and locks, heated power mirrors.			
Premium Equipment Pkg., base	241	205	212
Split folding rear seat, misc. lights, Message Center, upgraded sound insulation.			
Deluxe Convenience Pkg., base	359	305	316
Cruise control, tilt steering column, floormats.			
Overhead Convenience Pkg., LE & LX	333	283	293
Overhead console (with outside temperature readout, compass, reading lamps, and storage for sunglasses and garage door transmitter), lighted visor mirrors.			
Front bench seat, base	102	87	90
w/55/45 split rear seat, base	61	52	54
Requires Premium Equipment Pkg.			
Premium bench seat w/55/45 rear seat, LE & LX	61	52	54
Console & armrest, base	155	132	136
Rear defogger, base	163	139	143
Power locks	245	208	216
Cassette player w/4 speakers, base	205	174	180
LE, base w/Super Discount Pkg.	155	132	136
Cassette player w/Infinity speakers, base & LE	430	366	378
LX	275	234	242
Base requires Super Discount Pkg.			
Cassette player w/EQ & 4 speakers, LE	645	548	568
LX	490	417	431

Prices are accurate at time of printing; subject to manufacturer's change.
CONSUMER GUIDE®

CAR PRICES

	Retail Price	Dealer Invoice	Low Price
Power driver's seat	296	252	260
Pop-up sunroof, LE & LX	405	344	356
Tachometer, base	107	91	94
195/70R14 tires, base	31	26	27
195/70R14 whitewall tires, base	104	88	92
LE	73	62	64
Conventional spare tire, base	85	72	75
Base w/195/70R14, LE	95	81	84
Alloy wheels, base & LE	328	279	289
Base requires 195/70R14 tires.			

Plymouth Laser

	Retail Price	Dealer Invoice	Low Price
3-door hatchback (5-speed)	$10864	$10012	$10412
w/Pkg. 21B (5-speed)	11439	10501	10901
w/Pkg. 22B (automatic)	12127	11085	11485
B Pkgs. add: power steering, rear defogger, tonneau cover, console cupholder, wheel covers, floormats.			
w/Pkg. 21C (5-speed)	12250	11190	11590
w/Pkg. 22C (automatic)	12938	11774	12174
C Pkgs. add to B: air conditioning.			
w/Pkg. 21D (5-speed)	12630	11513	11913
w/Pkg. 22D (automatic)	13318	12098	12498
D Pkgs. add to C: cassette player, cruise control.			
RS 3-door hatchback (5-speed)	12770	11673	12073
w/Pkg. 23F (5-speed)	13581	12362	12762
w/Pkg. 24F (automatic)	14269	12947	13347
F Pkgs. add: air conditioning.			
w/Pkg. 23G (5-speed)	14200	12889	13289
w/Pkg. 24G (automatic)	14888	13474	13874
G Pkgs. add to F: cassette player w/EQ, console cupholder, cruise control, rear wiper/ washer, floormats.			
w/Pkg. 23H (5-speed)	14638	13261	13661
w/Pkg. 24H (automatic)	15326	13846	14246
H Pkgs. add to G: power windows and locks.			
w/Pkg. 23J (5-speed)	15266	13795	14195
w/Pkg. 24J (automatic)	15954	14379	14779
J Pkgs. add to H: CD player.			
RS Turbo 3-door hatchback (5-speed)	13954	12739	13139
w/Pkg. 25F (5-speed)	14765	13428	13828
w/Pkg. 26F (automatic)	15588	14128	14528
F Pkgs. add: air conditioning.			
w/Pkg. 25G (5-speed)	15384	13954	14354
w/Pkg. 26G (automatic)	16207	14653	15053
G Pkgs. add to F: cassette player with EQ, console cupholder, cruise control, rear wiper/ washer, floormats.			

Prices are accurate at time of printing; subject to manufacturer's change.

	Retail Price	Dealer Invoice	Low Price
w/Pkg. 25K (5-speed)	15822	14326	14726
w/Pkg. 26K (automatic)	16645	15026	15426
K Pkgs. add to G: power windows and locks.			
w/Pkg. 25L (5-speed)	16450	14860	15260
w/Pkg. 26L (automatic)	17273	15560	15960
L Pkgs. add to K: CD player.			
Destination charge	328	328	328

Standard equipment:

1.8-liter PFI 4-cylinder engine, 5-speed manual or 4-speed automatic transmission, motorized front shoulder belts, cloth reclining front bucket seats, one-piece folding rear seatback, center console, tachometer, coolant temperature and oil pressure gauges, trip odometer, tinted glass, remote fuel door and hatch releases, dual remote mirrors, visor mirrors, AM/FM radio, tilt steering column, intermittent wipers, 185/70R14 tires. **RS** adds: 2.0-liter DOHC PFI 4-cylinder engine, power steering, driver's-seat lumbar support adjustment, rear defogger, center armrest, power mirrors, cassette player, tonneau cover, dual-note horn, 205/55HR16 tires. **RS Turbo** adds: turbocharged, intercooled engine, performance suspension, leather-wrapped steering wheel, 205/55VR16 tires.

Optional equipment:

Anti-lock brakes, RS & RS Turbo	925	786	833
RS requires Pkg. H or J; RS Turbo requires Pkg. K or L and security alarm.			
Cassette player, base w/Pkg. B or C	170	145	153
Rear defogger, base	123	105	111
Sunroof	366	311	329
Security alarm, RS Turbo	163	139	147
Requires anti-lock brakes.			
Alloy wheels, RS & RS Turbo	315	268	284
RS requires Pkg. G, H, or J; RS Turbo requires Pkg. G, K, or L.			

Pontiac Bonneville

LE 4-door notchback	$16834	$14528	$14878
SE 4-door notchback	20464	17660	18010
SSE 4-door notchback	25264	21803	22153
Destination charge	525	525	525

LE: 3.8-liter PFI V-6, 4-speed automatic transmission, power steering, door-mounted automatic front seatbelts, air conditioning, cloth 45/45 front seat with armrest, AM/FM radio, 215/65R15 tires. **SE** adds: 2.97 axle ratio, power driver's seat, upgraded upholstery, storage armrest, power windows and locks, remote decklid release, intermittent wipers, cruise control, tilt steering column, tachometer, coolant temperature and oil pressure gauge, voltmeter, rear defogger, leather-wrapped steering wheel, 215/60R16 tires on alloy wheels. **SSE** adds: anti-lock brakes, 3.33 axle ratio, sport suspension with Electronic Ride Control, automatic climate control, articulating bucket seats, upgraded audio system

Prices are accurate at time of printing; subject to manufacturer's change.

with EQ and Touch Control, remote keyless illuminated entry, cruise control, accessory kit (light sticks, raincoat, first aid kit, gloves, spotlight), Twilight Sentinel, headlamp washers, misc. lights, heated power mirrors, lighted visor mirrors.

Optional equipment:

	Retail Price	Dealer Invoice	Low Price
Anti-lock brakes, LE & SE	925	786	819
LE requires Pkg. 1SD or 1SE.			
Option Pkg. 1SB, LE	269	229	238
Tilt steering column, intermittent wipers, Lamp Group.			
Option Pkg. 1SC, LE	629	535	557
Pkg. 1SB plus cruise control, remote decklid release, tachometer, coolant temperature and oil pressure gauges, voltmeter.			
Option Pkg. 1SD, LE	1039	898	936
Pkg. 1SC plus power windows and locks, power driver's seat.			
Option Pkg. 1SE, LE	1354	1166	1215
Pkg. 1SD plus illuminated entry, power mirrors, lighted visor mirrors, Twilight Sentinel.			
Value Option Pkg. R6A, LE	408	351	366
Cassette player, 215/60R16 tires on alloy wheels.			
Option Pkg. 1SB, SE	255	217	226
Illuminated entry, power mirrors, lighted visor mirrors.			
Option Pkg. 1SC, SE	315	268	279
Pkg. 1SB plus Twilight Sentinel.			
Value Option Pkg. R6A, SE	610	523	545
Upgraded audio system with EQ, two-tone paint.			
Option Pkg. 1SB, SSE	1259	1093	1139
Power glass sunroof, leather trim.			
Value Option Pkg. R6A, SSE	1080	918	957
Power glass sunroof, theft-deterrent system.			
Rear defogger, LE	160	136	142
Power locks, LE	230	196	204
Power windows, LE	390	332	345
Remote keyless entry, LE & SE	125	106	111
Convenience Pkg., LE	315	268	279
Illuminated entry, power mirrors, lighted visor mirrors, Twilight Sentinel.			
Power antenna, LE	75	64	66
Cassette player, LE	140	119	124
UX1 audio system, LE	805	684	713
LE w/Pkg. R6A	665	565	589
SE	615	523	545
Includes cassette player, EQ, performance sound system, power antenna, Touch Control, leather-wrapped steering wheel, anti-theft feature, automatic climate control.			
U1A audio system w/CD player, LE	1031	876	913
LE w/Pkg. R6A	891	757	789
SE	841	715	745
SE w/Pkg. R6A, SSE	226	192	200
Includes performance sound system, EQ, Touch Control, leather-wrapped steering wheel, power antenna, anti-theft feature, automatic climate control; LE requires cruise control, tilt steering column, intermittent wipers, and power windows.			

Prices are accurate at time of printing; subject to manufacturer's change.

	Retail Price	Dealer Invoice	Low Price
Bucket seats with console, LE & SE	235	200	208
Leather trim, SSE	779	662	690
Custom interior trim, LE w/Pkg. 1SC	620	527	549
LE w/Pkg. 1SD or 1SE	130	111	115
Power glass sunroof, SE & SSE	1230	1046	1089
215/65R15 whitewall tires, LE	70	60	62
215/60R16 tires, LE	88	75	78
15" alloy wheels, LE	296	252	262
16" alloy wheels, LE	330	281	292
Theft-deterrent system, SSE	150	128	133
Two-tone paint, LE & SE	105	89	93
Warranty enhancements for New York	65	55	58

Toyota Camry

4-door notchback, 5-speed	$11948	$10275	$10947
4-door notchback, automatic	12618	10851	11561
Deluxe 4-door notchback, 5-speed	12588	10785	11514
Deluxe 4-door notchback, automatic	13378	11371	12192
LE 4-door notchback, automatic	15028	12624	13622
Deluxe All-Trac 4-door, automatic	15358	13054	13996
LE All-Trac 4-door, automatic	17018	14295	15425
Deluxe V6 4-door notchback, 5-speed	13968	11873	12730
Deluxe V6 4-door notchback, automatic	14658	12459	13358
LE V6 4-door notchback, automatic	17418	14631	15788
Deluxe 5-door wagon, automatic	14158	12034	12902
LE V6 5-door wagon, automatic	18208	15295	16504

Dealer invoice and destination charge may vary by region.

Standard equipment:

2.0-liter DOHC 16-valve PFI 4-cylinder engine, 5-speed manual or 4-speed automatic transmission, power steering, motorized front shoulder belts, coolant temperature gauge, trip odometer, cloth reclining front bucket seats, remote fuel door and trunk releases, rear defogger, front door pockets, intermittent wipers, tinted glass, 185/70SR14 tires. **Deluxe** adds: driver's-seat height adjustment, tilt steering column, rear wiper/washer (wagon), right visor mirror, All Weather Guard Pkg.; V6 has 2.5-liter DOHC 24-valve V-6, 4-wheel disc brakes, 195/60HR15 tires. **LE** adds: power mirrors, tachometer, split folding rear seat, multi-adjustable driver's seat, folding rear armrest, cargo cover (wagon), illuminated entry with fadeout, AM/FM radio with power antenna; V6 has air conditioning, cruise control, power windows and locks, cassette player, floormats. **All-Trac** models have permanent 4-wheel drive and 4-wheel disc brakes.

Optional equipment:

Anti-lock brakes, LE V6	1130	904	1002
LE All-Trac	1280	1024	1135

Prices are accurate at time of printing; subject to manufacturer's change.

CAR PRICES

	Retail Price	Dealer Invoice	Low Price
Air conditioning (std. LE V6)	825	660	732
Leather trim, LE 4-doors	1080	864	958
Includes power driver's seat.			
Alloy wheels, LE 4-door 4-cyl.	360	288	319
LE V6 4-door	380	304	337
CQ Convenience Pkg., base	120	96	106
Full-size spare tire, digital clock.			
Power Pkg. Deluxe 4-doors	640	512	567
Deluxe wagon	590	473	524
LE 4-door 4-cyl.	585	468	519
Power windows and locks, split folding rear seat (std. LE), lighted visor mirrors (LE).			
Sunroof, Deluxe & LE	700	560	621
Power Seat Pkg., LE	230	184	204
Requires Power Pkg. or Value Pkg.			
Cruise control, base	315	258	282
Includes tilt steering column.			
AM/FM radio, base & Deluxe 4-doors	330	247	284
Deluxe wagon	360	270	310
w/cassette player, base & Deluxe 4-doors	480	360	414
Deluxe wagon	510	382	439
Premium AM/FM cassette, LE	320	240	276
Deluxe wagon	170	136	151
Value Pkg., Deluxe	1474	1327	1380
Deluxe wagon	1404	1264	1314
LE 4-cyl.	939	845	879
Air conditioning, cruise control, power windows and locks, split folding rear seat (std. on LE and wagons), AM/FM cassette, floormats.			
Split folding rear seat, Deluxe 4-doors	100	80	89

Toyota Corolla

	Retail Price	Dealer Invoice	Low Price
4-door notchback, 5-speed	$8998	$8008	$8398
4-door notchback, automatic	9468	8427	8837
Deluxe 4-door notchback, 5-speed	9998	8597	9183
Deluxe 4-door notchback, automatic	10468	9001	9614
LE 4-door notchback, 5-speed	11478	9837	10526
LE 4-door notchback, automatic	12148	10411	11140
Deluxe 5-door wagon, 5-speed	10668	9173	9798
Deluxe 5-door wagon, automatic	11138	9579	10231
Deluxe All-Trac wagon, 5-speed	12368	10635	11360
Deluxe All-Trac wagon, automatic	13138	11297	12067

Dealer invoice and destination charge may vary by region.

Standard equipment:

1.6-liter DOHC 16-valve PFI 4-cylinder engine, 5-speed manual or 3-speed automatic transmission, door-mounted automatic front shoulder belts, cloth reclining front bucket

Prices are accurate at time of printing; subject to manufacturer's change.

seats, console with storage, coolant temperature gauge, trip odometer, door pockets, 155SR13 tires. **Deluxe** adds: rear defogger, remote fuel door and decklid releases, intermittent wipers, split folding rear seat (wagon); All-Trac wagon has permanent 4-wheel drive, 5-speed manual or 4-speed automatic transmission, mud guards, rear wiper, 165SR13 tires. **LE** adds: 5-speed manual or 4-speed automatic transmission, power steering, dual remote mirrors, AM/FM radio, 6-way driver's seat with lumbar support adjustment, split folding rear seatback, tachometer, tilt steering column, full wheel covers, 175/70SR13 tires.

Optional equipment:	Retail Price	Dealer Invoice	Low Price
Air conditioning	775	620	689
Power steering, base & Deluxe	250	214	229
Alloy wheels, LE	370	296	329
Exterior Appearance Pkg., Deluxe 4-door	85	68	76
Tilt steering column, Deluxe	85	73	78
Sunroof, Deluxe & LE (NA 2WD wagon)	530	424	471
Fabric seats, wagons	70	60	64
Rear wiper, 2WD wagon	135	111	121
Audio Accommodation Pkg., All-Trac wagon	115	92	102
AM/FM radio w/2 speakers, base & Deluxe 4-doors . . .	210	157	181
All-Trac wagon	330	247	285
AM/FM radio w/4 speakers, base & Deluxe 4-doors . . .	330	247	285
AM/FM cassette w/2 speakers, 2WD wagon	380	285	328
All-Trac wagon	480	360	415
w/4 speakers, base & Deluxe 4-doors	480	360	415
w/4 speakers, LE	150	112	129
Power Pkg., LE	530	424	471
Power windows and locks.			
Tachometer, Deluxe w/5-speed	60	48	53
Cruise control, Deluxe & LE	210	168	187
Value Pkg., Deluxe 4-door	544	490	511
Deluxe 2WD wagon	514	463	482
Deluxe All-Trac wagon	564	508	529
LE	724	652	680

Deluxe: power steering, AM/FM cassette with 4 speakers (4-door; 2 speakers on wagon), digital clock, split folding rear seat, floormats, fabric seats (wagon). LE adds: air conditioning, power locks, cruise control, variable intermittent wipers.

Toyota Cressida

4-door notchback	$22198	$18202	$19707

Dealer invoice and destination charge may vary by region.

Standard equipment:

3.0-liter DOHC 24-valve PFI 6-cylinder engine, 4-speed automatic transmission, power steering, 4-wheel disc brakes, motorized front shoulder belts, automatic climate control,

Prices are accurate at time of printing; subject to manufacturer's change.

reclining front bucket seats, cruise control, variable intermittent wipers, trip odometer, coolant temperature gauge, tachometer, AM/FM cassette with EQ, diversity power antenna, power windows and locks, heated power mirrors, tilt/telescopic steering column, theft-deterrent system, 205/60R15 tires.

Optional equipment:	Retail Price	Dealer Invoice	Low Price
Anti-lock brakes	1130	904	992
Power glass sunroof	810	648	711
Power Seat Pkg.	880	704	773
w/leather trim	1585	1268	1392
CD player	700	525	598

Toyota MR2

	Retail Price	Dealer Invoice	Low Price
2-door notchback, 5-speed	$15148	$12800	$13974
2-door notchback, automatic	15898	13434	14666
2-door notchback w/T-bar roof, 5-speed	16098	13603	14851
Turbo 2-door notchback, 5-speed	18478	15614	17046
Turbo w/T-bar roof, 5-speed	19378	16374	17876

Dealer invoice and destination charge may vary by region.

Standard equipment:

2.2-liter DOHC 16-valve PFI 4-cylinder engine, 5-speed manual or 4-speed automatic transmission, 4-wheel disc brakes, driver's-side airbag, cloth reclining bucket seats, tilt steering column, AM/FM radio, tachometer, coolant temperature gauge, trip odometer, 195/60HR14 front and 205/60HR14 rear tires on alloy wheels. **Turbo** adds: 2.0-liter turbocharged engine, AM/FM cassette, power mirrors, rear spoiler, V-rated tires.

Optional equipment:

	Retail Price	Dealer Invoice	Low Price
Anti-lock brakes	1130	904	1017
Electro-hydraulic power steering	600	513	557
Air conditioning	825	660	743
Pop-up/removable sunroof	380	304	342
Power Pkg., base	535	428	482
Turbo	425	340	383
Power windows and locks, power mirrors (std. Turbo).			
Cruise control & intermittent wipers	245	196	221
Rear spoiler, base	225	180	203
Theft deterrent system	165	132	149
Alloy wheels, base	360	288	324
Leather Trim Pkg., base	1710	1368	1539
Turbo	1235	988	1112
Seven-way leather seats, leather interior trim, power windows and locks, power mirrors, center storage box.			
AM/FM cassette, base	250	187	219
Premium AM/FM cassette, base	655	491	573

Prices are accurate at time of printing; subject to manufacturer's change.

Base w/T-bar roof	590	442	516
Turbo	340	255	298
Includes seven speakers, biamplified woofer, power antenna.			
Premium AM/FM cassette w/CD player, base	1355	1016	1186
Base w/T-bar roof	1290	967	1129
Turbo	1040	780	910

Toyota Previa

Deluxe 2WD, 5-speed	$14398	$12310	$13354
Deluxe 2WD, automatic	15148	12952	14050
LE 2WD, automatic	19298	16403	17851
Deluxe All-Trac, 5-speed	17008	14457	15733
Deluxe All-Trac, automatic	17848	15171	16510
LE All-Trac, automatic	21908	18622	20265

Dealer invoice and destination charge may vary by region.

Standard equipment:

Deluxe: 2.4-liter DOHC 16-valve PFI 4-cylinder engine, 5-speed manual or 4-speed automatic transmission, power steering, cloth reclining front bucket seats, 3-passenger middle seat, tinted glass, digital clock, dual outside mirrors, bodyside moldings, full carpet, full wheel covers, P205/75R14 tires. **LE** adds: dual air conditioning, 4-wheel disc brakes, fold-down third seat, cruise control, rear defogger, power locks, privacy glass, AM/FM radio, tilt steering column, intermittent wipers, P215/65R15 tires with full-size spare.

Optional equipment:

Anti-lock brakes, LE	1130	904	1017
Dual air conditioning, Deluxe	1420	1136	1278
Convenience Pkg., Deluxe w/5-speed	805	649	727
Deluxe w/automatic	745	601	673
Tilt steering column, rear defogger, fold-down third seat, tachometer (with 5-speed).			
Power Pkg., Deluxe	615	482	549
LE	390	312	351
Power windows, power locks (std. LE), power mirrors.			
Cruise control & intermittent front wipers, Deluxe	240	192	216
Cruise control & intermittent front & rear wipers, Deluxe .	395	319	357
AM/FM radio, Deluxe	330	247	289
AM/FM cassette, Deluxe	520	390	455
LE	190	142	166
Premium AM/FM cassette, LE	530	397	464
Premium AM/FM cassette w/CD, LE	1260	945	1103
Dual sunroofs, LE	1370	1096	1233
Captain's chairs w/armrests, LE	620	496	558
Fold-down third seat, Deluxe	550	440	495

Prices are accurate at time of printing; subject to manufacturer's change.

Television Sets and TV/VCR Combinations

You can expect that the television set you buy this year will not become outmoded by advances in technology for at least the next ten years. Big TV tubes are now readily available so that prices on 30- to 35-inch sets may be more competitive. However, the price of making and selling these large TVs is still significantly higher than those of 27-inch picture tubes. A bargain-minded shopper will find sets with superior pictures and every possible feature in 27-inch sets for far less money than would be required for a 30-inch or larger set.

A major change in television that seems likely to occur in the not-so-distant future is HDTV (high-definition television). This is a method for delivering TV signals that promises to provide pictures that are nearly twice as clear as current U.S. television and images that are as high and wide as those shown in movie theaters. It will also offer digital audio similar to that supplied by CD players. International agreement on the compatibility of HDTV and other existing television technologies is pending, but it's the high cost to broadcasters that will impede the onset of HDTV in the United States.

Digital TV

Digital televisions with built-in microchips have a much clearer, sharper picture than traditional televisions. In most new TV sets, everything but the final picture is digital. The most expensive sets may use digital processing to improve the picture and eliminate scan lines as well as providing Picture-in-Picture (PIP), strobe, and mosaic effects. But the benefits of digital technology are more than "special effects." Integrated chips (ICs) provide better pictures and better performance. They add to the initial cost of television sets, but they offer good value for the money. Because chips do not wear out as rapidly as vacuum tubes and transistors, digital TVs are virtually maintenance-free during the life of the set.

Top-of-the-line 27-inch and larger TV sets may employ a variety of digital processing chips, ranging from comb filters to fuzzy logic to enhance the picture. While these almost always make a dramatic (and initially attractive) difference, care must be taken to do serious comparative shopping. Make sure you check out the range of adjustments so that you can modify the picture to your tastes and preferences.

Digital TV Effects

Here are some of the terms you should know before you shop for a television:

Biphonic is an alternate term for Carver's Sonic Holography. It overlaps the right and left stereo signals, extracts common information, and reinforces the differences to provide a much clearer sonic perspective and imagery.

Comb filters provide better edges and definition of a picture.

Dynamic sound enhancement uses a computer chip (or chips) to expand the sound signal to increase dynamic range, which is the difference between the loudest and softest sounds in any musical selection. Some dynamic sound enhancers may expand the sense of stereo field as well.

Express tuning allows the viewer to scan channels quickly.

Freezing allows the viewer to fix a video image digitally on the screen.

Fuzzy logic is a digital process that makes delicate adjustments on picture quality.

On-screen displays can be channel numbers, time of day, or guides to all the adjustments that can be made from the TV screen to improve the picture and sound. They are controlled by the remote and appear on the TV screen.

Picture enhancement may involve a special computer chip, which will sample the electronic signal and enhance it to provide better color or to overlap two pictures to eliminate scan lines. Remember that the TV image consists of 270 to 800 or more lines swept across the screen from top to bottom with space between each line. The next picture consists of another set of lines swept into the spaces between the previous lines. Even though our eyes compensate for these scan lines, computer chips do it better.

Panning allows the viewer to select a part of a frozen picture in order to examine it more closely.

Picture-In-Picture (PIP) permits the user to view an alternate video image from another channel or video source in a box on the main screen.

Stereo decoder chips extract stereo from the MTS (multi-channel television sound) signal. Some of these chips provide matrix (electronically stimulated) stereo from monaural sources. Others can decode Dolby surround-sound signals and provide sound for rear speakers that fill the room with sound as clear as that at the movies.

S-Video separates luminance (brightness portion of color TV signal) and chrominance (color portion of color TV signal) to significantly sharpen any picture when the S output is available.

Video noise-reduction chips clean out most of the white streaks and ghosts that can intrude from off-the-air or cable signals.

Zooming allows the viewer to enlarge a frozen picture for closer inspection.

Stereo

When you shop for a new television set be sure that you understand how stereo TV works. The MTS (multichannel television sound) decoder built into the TV set receives the stereo signal. Stereo-ready or stereo-capable televisions can receive stereo signals from broadcasts made in stereo only with the addition of a separate adapter. While some adapters must be installed by a trained technician, CONSUMER GUIDE® recommends those adapters that can be easily attached by the TV owner. With these adapters, installation is as easy as plugging the converter into a jack in the back of the TV set.

If you are satisfied with your monaural TV set but would like to enjoy stereo sound, consider purchasing a stand-alone stereo decoder. This is essentially a radio that is capable of receiving stereo-TV broadcasts and is connected to an external pair of speakers to produce two-channel sound.

Satellite Television

Satellite broadcasts are no longer free for the taking. For years, satellite dish owners had their pick of hundreds of channels because program distributors, such as HBO and Showtime, did not scramble the signals they bounced off satellites in order to send them to local cable companies. Recently, distributors have begun scrambling the signals so the broadcast received by the dish is an unwatchable garble. But dish owners can still use their systems; distributors now rent converter boxes like those used to receive cable service. A satellite dish is still a good buy for consumers who live in areas where they cannot receive good quality broadcasts.

New Tube Shapes and Sizes

Most manufacturers have replaced their round-cornered screens with squarer, flatter tubes. Although they function in exactly the same way as tubes with rounded corners, the flat tubes eliminate much of the distortion that occurs along the edges of concave screens, while adding extra viewing area.

Projection TV offers viewers a much larger picture than conventional television sets. Rear-projection TVs have improved considerably this year. These sets have a brighter picture, a wider viewing angle, and enhanced pictures. They use picture processing, comb filters, and S-Video connections to refine and clarify the video signal. Although these sets compete directly with the 30-inch and larger direct-view TV sets, they are still very large and have fairly big price tags.

Evaluating a Television Set

Since differences in major-brand televisions are slight, manufacturers have added all sorts of special features to their sets in an attempt to differentiate them. Deciding which television to buy is a matter of matching a set's features with your needs. For example, some TVs offer a feature called *channel block* that allows parents to program the set so their small children cannot tune in certain stations, such as cable channels that offer "adult" programming. If you do not have children, you will have little use for a set with this feature and will not want to pay extra to buy one.

TVs are becoming more automated. Many sets now have a sleep-timer function that lets you nod off to late-night television and sleep securely in the knowledge that the set will automatically turn itself off, usually at a preselected 30-, 60-, 90-, or 120-minute interval. Other sets can be programmed to turn themselves on and off at preselected times either as a security measure or as a way to make sure you do not miss your favorite program.

The most popular TV feature is remote control, which has now sprouted many new functions of its own. Today, more than half of all TVs come equipped with "remotes." CONSUMER GUIDE® recommends a set with a digital remote because it is more versatile and less prone to interference than other types of remote control. You may also want to consider other convenience features, such as random access, channel memory, and sound mute. Many manufacturers have conveniently designed their sets with either a slot or a spring-loaded holder for the remote, reducing the chance of misplacing it.

If you have more than one remote-controlled piece of equipment, you may want to buy a programmable remote that can "learn" the infrared control codes of a number of different products, such as VCRs, disc players, and cable boxes, made by different manufacturers.

Cable Terminology

A major cause of confusion for television shoppers is the term "cable ready." Many people incorrectly believe a cable-ready TV set will let them receive cable programming, such as

HBO and Showtime, for free. A cable-ready set only eliminates the need for a converter box. You still have to pay the initial cable hookup costs and monthly fees. If you want any of the premium services for which the cable company charges extra, you will need the converter box to unscramble the signal.

Because the converter box may render a TV's remote control useless, some cable companies offer boxes that have their own remotes. CONSUMER GUIDE® suggests that you call your local cable company before buying a cable-ready set. If you plan to subscribe to a premium service, you may not need a cable-ready set.

Best Buys '91

Our Best Buy and Recommended television sets follow. The unit we consider the best of the Best Buys is first, followed by our second choice, and so on. The picture quality of most of the major-brand televisions varies only slightly, and differences are highly subjective. Some of this year's choices are included because they offer a particularly good picture, but most sets were chosen because they offer packages of desirable features. While features and styling change from model to model, TV technology is often carried through a company's entire line. This means that many of the TVs from the same manufacturer offer the same quality picture, but the combination of features in addition to the price of the set is the basis for our choice of one TV over another as a Best Buy. For this reason, the Best Buy and Recommended designations apply only to the model listed and not necessarily to other models from the same manufacturer.

31/32-INCH COLOR TV SETS

JVC AV-3150S

The JVC AV-3150S is a 31-inch square-tube receiver with a fine picture and an artificial intelligence that provides a three-page on-screen menu to adjust for picture, sound, and user interfaces. It includes a child timer, which will turn off the set when the child's allotted viewing time is over. Only a fixed user code

Prices are accurate at time of printing; subject to manufacturer's change.

can reverse the shutdown. It is possible to extract MTS stereo sound, matrix stereo sound, and biphonic sound from the very respectable audio side of this set. The artificial intelligence really makes this an extremely attractive model with readily accessible features. Although this model does not have zoom or pan, the balance of features, sound, and price makes this a Best Buy.

Specifications: height, 26"; **width,** 29⅝"; **depth,** 27⅞"; **weight,** 122¹⁄₁₀ pounds. **Warranty: parts and labor,** one year; **picture tube,** two years.

Approx. retail price	Approx. low price
$1,600	not available

RCA F31400SB COLORTRAK 2000

RECOMMENDED

The RCA F31400SB ColorTrak 2000 is a 31-inch stereo monitor/receiver with a number of interesting digital features. It can provide zoom and pan effects to look at details of a given picture that has been frozen. There is PIP (Picture-in-Picture) and a 12-channel "snapshot" that provides a quick visual peek at what's available without random channel switching. It even has a commercial-skip feature built in. This unit with its audio/video monitor panel makes a good foundation for a serious audio/visual system. RCA maintains a 24-hour customer hotline for customer questions and problems.

Specifications: height, 26¾"; **width,** 32"; **depth,** 20¾"; **weight,** not available. **Warranty: parts,** two years; **labor,** 90 days; **picture tube,** two years.

Approx. retail price	Approx. low price
$2,000	$1,850

TOSHIBA CF3275K

RECOMMENDED

The Toshiba CF3275K is a 32-inch monitor/receiver that combines a superior picture with particularly fine sound. The Carver Sonic Holographic System makes this a serious high-fidelity sound system as well as a great television set. The on-screen displays in English, French, and Spanish are a nice

Prices are accurate at time of printing; subject to manufacturer's change.

touch, even though not much use in a one-language household. Channel captioning, which allows you to assign captions to specific channels so that you can find them quickly if the cable jumbles your channels, is a useful feature when scanning with the remote control. The precognition matrix and vocal zoom circuitries make maximum use of the Carver Holographic Sonic System even with monaural signals. This is a TV set that must be both seen and heard.

Specifications: height, $40\frac{33}{64}$"; **width,** $33\frac{35}{64}$"; **depth,** $25\frac{15}{16}$"; **weight,** $122\frac{1}{10}$ pounds. **Warranty: parts and labor,** one year; **picture tube,** two years.

Approx. retail price	Approx. low price
$2,400	$1,533

27-INCH COLOR TV SETS

PANASONIC CTM-2776S

 ✔BEST BUY

The Panasonic CTM-2776S is an impressive 27-inch television with a very modest price and a full complement of features. Thanks to rear-mounted front-firing dome speakers that send out the sound through slim slots, the CTM-2776S is a very attractive unit. While this TV doesn't have PIP, zoom, or freeze, it has fine on-screen graphics to control all the picture and sound adjustments with the remote control. There is a sleep timer and an "on" timer so that you can wake up to your favorite morning program.

Specifications: height, $22\frac{4}{5}$"; **width,** $27\frac{7}{10}$"; **depth,** $19\frac{4}{5}$"; **weight,** 214 pounds. **Warranty: parts,** one year; **labor,** 90 days; **picture tube, parts,** two years; **labor,** 90 days.

Approx. retail price	Approx. low price
$730	$648

SONY KV-27XBR50

RECOMMENDED

The Sony KV-27XBR50 has fuzzy logic. This feature uses computer chips to evaluate many areas of the picture simultaneously and then to adjust the picture. The results are subtle

and worth seeing. With its detachable speakers and super woofer, this 27-inch set has excellent sound as well. Sony's microblack picture tube with one pan-focus gun remains a model for the industry. Sony's XBR on-screen window control lets the viewer be in control of this very sophisticated and feature-laden set. The KV-27XBR50 has enough inputs and outputs to serve as the monitor for a studio or home A/V center.
Specifications: height, 22¼"; **width,** 26⅛"; **depth,** 21⅝"; **weight,** 105⅝ pounds. **Warranty: parts,** one year; **labor,** 90 days; **picture tube,** two years.

Approx. retail price	**Approx. low price**
$1,350	$1,144

RCA F27196BT

RECOMMENDED

The RCA F27196BT is a 27-inch television loaded with top-of-the-line features like advanced color Picture-In-Picture (PIP), zoom, pan, and freeze. This set decodes Dolby surround-sound with optional rear-channel speakers. The Invar picture tube delivers an excellent picture. Channel Guide provides a "snapshot" of 12 channels at one time, and the zoom and pan features allow you to take a closer look at whatever catches your fancy. You can tweak the sound to your taste with an on-screen graphic equalizer. You can also assign captions to specific channels so that you can find them quickly if the cable jumbles your channels. This model is loaded; the price is fair given all the features.
Specifications: height, 23¼"; **width,** 35¼"; **depth,** 19⅛"; **weight,** not available. **Warranty: parts,** one year; **labor,** 90 days; **picture tube,** two years.

Approx. retail price	**Approx. low price**
$1,099	$866

EMERSON TS2750D

RECOMMENDED

The Emerson TS2750D is a serious contender for consideration as the center of a home A/V system. This 27-inch television has inputs for audio, video, and S-Video. There are outputs for audio, video, and external speakers. The 500 lines of resolution provide a very crisp video image, and the on-screen displays make it easy to tailor the picture and sound to individual preferences. The remote control handles a generous range of functions. Emerson also has a very strong service network in the unlikely event that any problems develop.

Specifications: height, 27⅗"; **width**, 25"; **depth**, 17⁹⁄₁₀"; **weight**, 79⅕ pounds. **Warranty: parts**, two years; **labor**, one year; **picture tube**, four years.

Approx. retail price	Approx. low price
$900	$470

TERA 629B `RECOMMENDED`

The Tera 629B is a 27-inch television that shows how fine current TV signals can look on a set that has been carefully tweaked to provide an optimum picture. This set uses a special circuit that continuously evaluates the video signal and then electronically enhances it to produce significantly improved outline and edge definition. It has a unique compensation feature that optimizes high-frequency signals to yield a picture of maximum detail with minimal video noise, and it uses nonlinear compensation to improve the gradations of the gray scale for a more accurate contrast range and improved color saturation. It is worth checking this set out if only as a reference guide to real quality video images.

Specifications: height, 23¾"; **width**, 27¼"; **depth**, 21½"; **weight**, 103 pounds. **Warranty: parts and labor**, one year; **picture tube**, two years.

Approx. retail price	Approx. low price
$1,500	$1,050

19/20-INCH COLOR TV SETS

MITSUBISHI CS-2015R   ✓ BEST BUY

The Mitsubishi CS-2015R is a 20-inch television that can function as a monitor/receiver and has all the necessary inputs and outputs. The lack of an S-Video input shouldn't be critical with a 20-inch set. There are speaker outputs since the cabinet doesn't allow for true stereo separation. It is interesting to note that Mitsubishi makes a nonstereo model in the same size at the same price. This may be taken as an indication that stereo TV has become the norm. With its stereo and on-screen displays, this is a remarkable set for the money.

Specifications: height, 18⅛"; **width**, 19⅞"; **depth**, 19¼"; **weight**, 46 pounds. **Warranty: parts and labor**, one year; **picture tube**, two years (in-home service).

Approx. retail price	Approx. low price
$399	$371

RCA F20343WN RECOMMENDED

The RCA F20343WN (also known as the XL-100 Stereo TV) is a 20-inch square-corner set with stereo sound, a channel lock, and a 19-button remote control that provides direct access to channel, volume, mute, and power. There are on-screen displays for operating and status reports and on-screen channel numbers for ready reference.

Specifications: height, 18"; **width**, 24½"; **depth**, 19 1/18"; **weight**, 57 pounds. **Warranty: parts**, one year; **labor**, 90 days; **picture tube**, two years.

Approx. retail price	Approx. low price
$369	$322

SAMSUNG TC9865TB RECOMMENDED

The Samsung TC9865TB is a good basic TV without inputs and outputs. It provides a very good picture with its 19-inch black matrix tube. The 270 lines of horizontal resolution (compared to 550 for some 20-inch sets) are sufficient. On sets of 20 inches or less, the horizontal lines do not really intrude that much. You get on-screen channel display and a sleep timer. There is a good service network.

Specifications: height, 18"; **width**, 19⅝"; **depth**, 18⅛"; **weight**, 41 pounds. **Warranty: parts**, one year; **labor**, 90 days; **picture tube**, two years.

Approx. retail price	Approx. low price
$340	$257

SONY KV-20EXR10 RECOMMENDED

The Sony KV-20EXR10 is a loaded 20-inch set that offers a full complement of inputs and outputs including S-Video. This set has 550 lines of resolution for a very impressive picture. While this may seem more than most people need in a 20-inch model, it is wonderful for those who want the fullest possible range of features in a modest size. The KV-20EXR10 could serve as the foundation of a first class A/V system and truly deserves the designation "monitor/receiver." Moreover, the audio options are as complete as the video. The microblack Trinitron tube is enhanced with dynamic picture processing.

Specifications: height, 23½"; **width,** 26"; **depth,** 20⅛"; **weight,** 108 pounds. **Warranty: parts,** one year; **labor,** 90 days; **picture tube,** two years.

Approx. retail price	**Approx. low price**
$600	$479

TERA 621B RECOMMENDED

The Tera 621B is a 20-inch monitor/receiver with an excellent picture. Special circuitry is incorporated in the 621B to provide a crisp, clear picture with saturated colors and sharp edges. This 20-inch set has a powerful stereo amplifier and speaker outputs to permit full enjoyment of MTS stereo with or without SAP. The Tera 621B's picture is very intense and has an almost three-dimensional quality.

Specifications: height, 20⅝"; **width,** 21¾"; **depth,** 19⅜"; **weight,** 62 pounds. **Warranty: parts,** one year; **labor,** 90 days; **picture tube,** two years.

Approx. retail price	**Approx. low price**
$999	not available

PORTABLE COLOR TV SETS

SAMSUNG TC3833TB

The Samsung TC3833TB is a very reasonably priced 13-inch set with a very good picture. Market forces make it possible for

---

Prices are accurate at time of printing; subject to manufacturer's change.

Samsung to offer this set with a 21-key remote control, direct access tuning, on-screen channel display, programmable scan, and an on-screen sleep timer. This model comes in black; alternate wood grain veneer is available in the TC3833T to fit into formal decorating schemes. Samsung also provides a good service network nationwide.

Specifications: height, 13¾"; **width**, 14¼"; **depth**, 15"; **weight**, 22¼ pounds. **Warranty: parts**, one year; **labor**, 90 days; **picture tube**, two years.

Approx. retail price	Approx. low price
$280	$189

RCA EO9435GB

RECOMMENDED

The RCA EO9435GB ColorTrak is a petite 9-inch set that concentrates on delivering a good picture. While putting major emphasis on the picture, this set has a 24-button remote control, which makes it useful for anyone who is immobilized or confined to bed. The on-screen displays are very useful for people who do not like to read manuals. The sleep timer is a nice feature for late-night TV watchers. This set even offers an on-screen automatic demonstration to enable viewers to fully use its features without having to read manuals.

Specifications: height, 10"; **width**, 11"; **depth**, 12½"; **weight**, 21½ pounds. **Warranty: parts**, one year; **labor**, 90 days; **picture tube**, two years.

Approx. retail price	Approx. low price
$289	$279

PANASONIC CTM-134OR/ CTM-134I2

RECOMMENDED

The Panasonic CTM-134OR/CTM-134I2 is a simple, sturdy, and serious 13-inch portable TV set. It offers on-screen display, an auto program scan, rapid tune, and a sleep timer. If you are using this as a kitchen set, the 24-function remote control is handy when you don't want to interrupt your domestic tasks. This 13-inch set offers a bright, crisp picture and is ideal for the bedroom and cottage as well as the kitchen. The CTM-

134OR is white; the CTM-134IR is the exact same model in black.

Specifications: height, 13⅖"; **width,** 14¹/₁₀"; **depth,** 15⅕"; **weight,** 21 pounds. **Warranty: parts,** one year; **labor,** 90 days; **picture tube, parts,** two years; **labor,** 90 days.

Approx. retail price	Approx. low price
$350	$263

SONY KV-13TR24 RECOMMENDED

The Sony KV-13TR24 is a petite monitor/receiver that is also a very attractive 13-inch TV set with a brilliant picture. Sony's A/V on-screen window display is a well-thought-out system of menus and prompts that enable the user to get the full range of options and adjustments from this set. The high-contrast mirror-black picture tube comes alive with color and detail when it receives a signal. The picture on this set can put some larger sets to shame.

Specifications: height, 13⅛"; **width,** 14⅛"; **depth,** 16⅛"; **weight,** 23 pounds. **Warranty, parts,** one year; **labor,** 90 days; **picture tube,** two years.

Approx. retail price	Approx. low price
$400	$286

MITSUBISHI CS-1348R RECOMMENDED

The Mitsubishi CS-1348R is a very attractive 13-inch set that could add real sparkle to a kitchen, bedroom, or den. The black matrix tube delivers a fine color picture, and you can adjust tint, color, brightness, contrast, and sharpness using the 23-key remote and the on-screen displays. The built-in clock with its on-screen display is handy for viewers who like to watch TV at breakfast. The price is relatively modest, and the picture is very good.

Specifications: height, 12⅝"; **width,** 13⅞"; **depth,** 15⅛"; **weight,** 21 pounds. **Warranty: parts and labor,** one year; **picture tube,** two years.

Approx. retail price	Approx. low price
$329	$248

Prices are accurate at time of printing; subject to manufacturer's change.

EMERSON TC4253

The Emerson TC4253 is a serious and sensible 13-inch set. You get a sleep timer, a 26-key remote control, on-screen picture control, automatic channel programming, and memory erase/write (this feature allows the user to add or subtract channels from the automatic channel programming). Moreover, the memory erase/write feature can be used as a channel lock to control children's viewing. The warranty is very generous.

Specifications: height, 14⅖"; **width,** 14³⁄₁₀"; **depth,** 14⅕"; **weight,** 23 pounds. **Warranty: parts,** two years; **labor,** one year; **picture tube,** four years.

Approx. retail price	Approx. low price
$350	$203

MINI TV SETS

CASIO TV-430

The Casio TV-430 offers a high-resolution liquid crystal display (LCD) with a high luminance backlight. You can operate this latest mini TV from Casio with four AA batteries, an AC adapter (supplied), or an optional 12-volt DC adapter. For the best possible picture, you should connect an external antenna. (The rod antenna is good, but not that good.) If you want a mini color TV, the Casio TV-430 is an economical option.

Specifications: height, 5⅛"; **width,** 3³⁄₁₆"; **depth,** 1¼"; **weight,** 8½ ounces. **Warranty: parts,** 90 days; **labor,** one year.

Approx. retail price	Approx. low price
$200	$168

SONY WATCHMAN FD-555

The Sony Watchman FD-555 provides a crisp black-and-white picture. This is a generous-size mini TV with an AM/FM radio, a cassette player, surprisingly smooth 4-inch speakers, and a

4½-inch black-and-white screen. This is an interesting combination portable unit that provides both a clear picture and good sound. It's almost a TV boom box. You can have TV, radio, or cassette sources and alternate between batteries, AC, or 12-volt DC. This set even has a sleep timer.

Specifications: height, 8⅜"; **width**, 13¼"; **depth**, 7¼"; **weight**, 9¼ pounds. **Warranty: parts**, one year; **labor**, 90 days; **picture tube**, one year.

Approx. retail price	Approx. low price
$200	$146

SONY WATCHMAN FD-250 `RECOMMENDED`

The Sony Watchman FD-250 has a generous 2⁷⁄₁₀-inch black-and-white picture and 1⅛-inch speakers. The rugged and fashionable case with its circular top makes a serious fashion statement. A prejudice in favor of big screens even in mini TVs leads to this set's failure to secure top ranking.

Specifications: height, 7⅜"; **width**, 4¼"; **depth**, 2⅛"; **weight**, 17 ounces. **Warranty: parts**, one year; **labor**, 90 days; **picture tube**, one year.

Approx. retail price	Approx. low price
$170	$119

CASIO TV-7500 `RECOMMENDED`

The Casio TV-7500 can serve as a color monitor for a camcorder as well as a personal portable color TV set. The 3³⁄₁₀-inch screen is much bigger than a 2-inch screen, since the added area is exponentially increased. Keep in mind that you can't take this unit (or any similar set) to Europe and get over-the-air programming. We use the NTSC format and Europe favors the PAL format. Still, this is a very portable unit and only the price keeps it from Best Buy status.

Specifications: height, 3⅝"; **width**, 3⅝"; **depth**, 1⅞"; **weight**, 15½ ounces with batteries. **Warranty: parts**, 90 days; **labor**, one year.

Approx. retail price	Approx. low price
$400	$334

Prices are accurate at time of printing; subject to manufacturer's change.

REAR-PROJECTION TV SETS

MITSUBISHI VS-50VX1

The Mitsubishi VS-50VX1 demonstrates the maturation of rear-projection TV with a picture that is bright and crisp enough to rival direct-view sets. Moreover, this set can be viewed from an oblique angle with little loss of quality. The availability of front and rear connectors is especially handy with a set this big. No one wants to move these units in and out any more than is absolutely necessary. The seven-element all-glass lens system delivers the carefully optimized picture to the 50-inch screen. Even though the price is high, there is no faulting the quality or the value.

Specifications: height, 49¾"; **width,** 44¼"; **depth,** 32⅞"; **weight,** 277 pounds. **Warranty: parts and labor,** one year; **screen,** three months.

Approx. retail price	**Approx. low price**
$5,399	$2,766

HITACHI CU-4601B/K

The Hitachi CU-4601B/K is typical of the best that high technology can produce in a rear-projection TV. The Insight 2001 on-screen displays are models of clarity and make it easy to extract the many nuances of performance that this set provides. Hitachi is justly proud of the new green phosphor, which provides a more balanced 46-inch color picture. Hitachi uses time-compressed picture enhancement to deliver a picture with 825 lines of resolution. These special processors require complex large-scale integrated chips, and Hitachi not only makes their own chips but gives them a very generous ten-year guarantee. This set offers premium features at an economical price.

Specifications: height, 48⅜"; **weight,** 42⁷⁄₁₆"; **depth,** 26⁷⁄₁₆"; **weight,** 220 pounds. **Warranty: parts,** two years; **labor,** one year; **transistors,** ten years.

Approx. retail price	**Approx. low price**
$2,999	$2,116

Prices are accurate at time of printing; subject to manufacturer's change.

PIONEER SD-P5043 RECOMMENDED

The Pioneer SD-P5043 is a feature-laden rear-projection TV that includes Picture-In-Picture (PIP) with two video sources. Its picture is enhanced with a dynamic picture optimizer. The video noise-reduction chip is much appreciated when the picture is expanded to 50 inches. There is a 96-function remote control, and the on-screen display helps you enjoy all the features on this set. As might be expected from a corporation that pioneered the laser videodisc, this set has an especially effective laser videodisc interface. Pioneer has designed the basic SD-P504 so that the owner can order custom design finishes and/or the features to fit his or her budget, tastes, and decor. **Specifications: height,** 52¾"; **width,** 47"; **depth,** 27¹¹⁄₁₆"; **weight,** 246¹⁵⁄₁₆ pounds. **Warranty: parts and labor,** one year; **picture tube, parts and labor,** two years.

Approx. retail price	Approx. low price
$3,900	$2,166

FRONT-PROJECTION TV SETS

SHARPVISION XV-100

SharpVision XV-100 is a new technology for front-projection TV using three LCDs (liquid crystal displays) to provide the color image. This image is projected through a single-lens system that permits the viewer to project images from 20 to 100 inches. This technology keeps the weight of the unit to less than 31 pounds and makes this the most versatile and portable projection TV on the market. It can serve for domestic, outdoor, and professional applications and can be used effectively by educators, businesspersons, and families. While a screen is optional, SharpVision XV-100 can be projected on alternate surfaces. (SharpVision XV-101 can be mounted on a ceiling or wall and used with remote control.) While three-tube projection systems can have problems with fuzzy convergence, this set uses only one lens system to eliminate the problem. **Specifications: height,** 9⅞"; **width,** 9³¹⁄₃₂"; **depth,** 23⅜"; **weight,**

30⁹⁄₁₀ pounds. **Warranty: parts and labor**, one year; **projector lamp**, 90 days or 2,000 hours (whichever comes first).

Approx. retail price	**Approx. low price**
$3,999	$2,665

HARMAN JBL RSVP II

✔**BEST BUY**

The Harman JBL RSVP II is a classic front-projection TV with up to 600 lines of resolution depending on the source. It will give rear-projection TV makers a standard to shoot for. Compared to SharpVision, this is a fairly conventional three-tube model, but the brightness and sharpness of the projected image clearly mark this as an exceptional set. The optional high-brightness tubes provide an even brighter picture that can be used with considerable ambient light. The oak cabinet serves as a very handsome coffee table. This model has a lower price and a brighter picture than last year's model, Convergence. All adjustments can be made very quickly using the 40-function remote control. Anyone shopping for this set either has the necessary speakers for an A/V system or will have to purchase them.

Specifications: height, 17½"; **width**, 42"; **depth**, 28"; **weight**, 128 pounds. **Warranty: parts and labor**, one year; **picture tubes**, two years.

Approx. retail price	**Approx. low price**
$4,295	$4,000

TV/VCR COMBINATIONS

TV/VCR combinations save space and avoid the tangle of wires and sometimes complicated connections that you encounter when you attempt to unite your television with a videocassette recorder (VCR). If you often show videotapes to groups of people, you may find that a TV/VCR combination is more portable and easier to set up and operate than separate units. The smallest TV/VCR combinations have LCD (liquid crystal display) screens. This makes the minis highly portable, but you may find that the features on the smaller sets are too limited.

Prices are accurate at time of printing; subject to manufacturer's change.

Best Buys '91

Our Best Buy TV/VCR combinations are listed below in order of decreasing value. The set we consider to be the Best Buy is listed first, followed by our second choice. Remember that a Best Buy rating applies only to the model listed; it does not necessarily apply to other models made by the same manufacturer.

PANASONIC PV-M1328/ PV-M1328A

✔**BEST BUY**

The Panasonic PV-M1328/PV-M1328A 13-inch model is one of the smallest TV/VCR combinations without being an LCD (liquid crystal display) model on the one hand or a 27-inch model that is clearly far from portable on the other. This unit uses standard VHS cassettes and will play rental tapes as well as whatever the user chooses to tape off the air or cable. The PV-M1328A is fine for individual and very small group viewing. The cost of this combination is probably less than you would pay for a TV and VCR separately.

Specifications: height, 14⅞"; **width,** 14⅝"; **depth,** 14⅞"; **weight,** 29 pounds. **Warranty: parts,** one year; **labor,** 90 days; **picture tube,** two years.

Approx. retail price
$600

Approx. low price
$599

SONY GV 300 WATCHMAN

✔**BEST BUY**

The Sony GV 300 Watchman is clearly the most portable TV/VCR combination with the added feature of high-fidelity stereo sound and a 4-inch digital color picture. The price reflects the cost of the very newest technology, but this is still a genuine value. For the traveling TV addict, the GV 300 Watchman is especially attractive.

Specifications: height, 2⅞"; **width,** 5⅛"; **depth,** 8⅞"; **weight,** two pounds. **Warranty: parts,** one year; **labor,** 90 days.

Approx. retail price
$1,400

Approx. low price
$959

Prices are accurate at time of printing; subject to manufacturer's change.

Videocassette Recorders, Laser Videodisc Players, and Videotape Rewinders

Over 60 percent of all households in the United States have at least one videocassette recorder (VCR). Unlike VCRs, laser videodisc players have been slow to catch on because they cannot record, and also because the format has limited playing time. For those who want to record televised programs, copy recorded tapes, and edit tapes made with camcorders, a VCR is the machine of choice. VCRs also remain the prime choice for many because rental tapes are widely available, and laser videodiscs have limited availability. The video and audio quality of laser videodiscs is generally superior to tape quality; as videodiscs become more available and the price of players come down, their popularity will grow. They will never become as popular as VCRs, though, until they can record as well as play. In an attempt to overcome this great disadvantage, companies are now introducing units that play all videodisc and audiodisc formats.

A VCR has a television tuner, a tape playback section, and a recorder section. Because a VCR has its own tuner, you can record a program on one channel and use the tuner in your TV to watch a program on another channel. If you want to record from another tape, you need two VCRs, or a VCR and a VCP (videocassette player), or a VCR and a camcorder.

VCR Formats

There are three basic video formats: 8mm, Beta, and VHS. A fourth format, VHS-C, is a cassette one-fourth the size of a regular VHS cassette that can be played in a VHS VCR with an adapter. Even though these formats are physically incompatible, they are electronically compatible. This means that you can easily transfer a recording made on one format to another by connecting the two different VCRs with the proper cables.

The original VCR formats are continuously being improved. VHS units now have HQ (high-quality) circuitry, and Beta now has SuperBeta circuitry. There is also ED Beta (extended definition Beta), S-VHS (Super VHS), and Hi8 with improved horizontal definition; these formats are encountering consumer resistance because you also need a much higher quality television set to get the improved results with these VCRs. Also looming on the horizon is HDTV (high-definition television), a completely new method of broadcasting that will require new TV sets. When HDTV will become a major factor is currently a matter of conjecture.

Choosing Tapes

If you are going to record on a tape only once or twice, and then not play it back very often, high-standard grade tapes are fine. But if you plan to record and play back the same tape many times, such as when time shifting (recording at one time to watch later), use the highest grade tape available; you can even use S-VHS tape in a standard VHS VCR for this purpose. Use brand-name tapes such as Fuji, Kodak, Konica, Maxell, Scotch, TDK, Sony, etc., rather than cheap tapes from unknown manufacturers. Many of them are so poorly made that they can cause expensive damage to the heads of your VCR.

Choosing a VCR

One reason that shopping for a VCR is so confusing is the array of features and combinations of features. One sales promotion may advertise a VCR's programmability, another will publicize its six heads. Since not every consumer needs or wants every feature, it is important to understand what is available and to know what you want.

Hi-fi sound: There is a difference between stereo sound and high-fidelity sound. Stereo means that the sound is recorded and played back through two channels, while hi-fi refers to high-quality sound, whether stereo or monaural.

Index search: Many VCRs now record an electronic index code at the beginning of each recording. To scan your recordings on a tape, you press "index search"; the VCR then stops at each index mark and plays back a few seconds of the recording. Some VCRs now even allow you to tell it which index mark to go to and start playing that section back.

Number of heads: To record and play back a tape, you need only two video heads. Additional heads are used for special effects such as freeze-frame and on-screen search.

Programmability: If you are buying a VCR primarily to record television broadcasts, programmability is an important consideration. Almost all VCRs can be programmed to record at least one program. The simplest programming uses a built-in clock timer that you set to start and stop within the next 24 hours. More elaborate programming allows you to record several different programs over a period of a month or more; other program operations let you record the same program every day or every week.

Quick access/quick play: Many VCRs now provide quick play from the stop position. There are also more VCRs that provide quick access from fast forward or fast rewind to visual scanning, and quick access from visual scanning to play.

Tape speeds: Most VCRs let you choose between two or three different recording speeds; playback speed is automatically set, and even VCRs that record in only two speeds play back all three speeds. The faster the tape moves, the less recording time available. While faster speeds limit recording time, they produce higher quality recordings.

Best Buys '91

Our Best Buy and Recommended VCRs, laser videodisc players, and videotape rewinders follow. The VCRs and laser videodisc players were evaluated on the basis of their performance when they were connected to a Toshiba C2269 26-inch stereo monitor/receiver. All these units were tested directly through the monitor as well as through the receiver. The units were evaluated on the basis of their recording and playback images and on their sound quality, as well as on their features and overall operational design. Within each format designation, Best Buys are listed first, followed by Recommended products. A Best Buy or Recommended designation applies only to the model listed, not to other models from the same manufacturer.

BETA VIDEOCASSETTE RECORDER

SONY SL-HF360

✔ **BEST BUY**

The Sony SL-HF360 is a stereo hi-fi SuperBeta VCR that offers freeze-frame. There is no TV/CATV selector switch because the SL-HF360 tunes in both broadcast and cable signals automatically. This VCR records and plays back at Beta II and Beta III speeds; it also plays back at the Beta I speed used by Beta camcorders. The SuperBeta circuitry can be switched off for recording tapes to be played back on Beta VCRs that don't have SuperBeta. A three-position color selector and a sharpness dial let you fine-tune the playback picture. The linear time counter shows the tape position in hours, minutes, and seconds. The one-event/seven-day timer takes you step-by-step through program setting. The wireless remote controls tape recording, playback, and channel switching.

Specifications: height, 3¾"; **width,** 17"; **depth,** 14⅝". **Warranty: parts,** one year; **labor,** 90 days.

Approx. retail price	Approx. low price
$500	$376

8MM VIDEOCASSETTE RECORDER

SONY EV-C3 `RECOMMENDED`

The Sony EV-C3 is an 8mm VCR deck with edit and synchro edit capabilities. Because it is a deck, the EV-C3 does not have a television tuner; however, you can record TV programs directly off the air if your television or monitor has *F* cable or RCA pin plug outputs. You can connect the EV-C3 to any VCR or camcorder with an *S* cable jack for synchro editing that allows you to control the start and pause of both units with the controls of one unit. There is also an edit position to be used with any other unit that has an edit switch to produce the best possible rerecording. Recordings on the EV-C3 can be made at either the single-play or long-play tape speeds. The EV-C3 has a linear tape counter that keeps track of lapsed time in hours, minutes, and seconds at either speed, making it easy to keep track of your recordings and to locate exact scenes on your tapes. Playback special effects include still picture, frame-by-frame advance, slow-motion playback at $\frac{1}{10}$ or $\frac{1}{5}$ normal speed, two-times normal speed playback with sound, momentary picture viewing during fast forward and reverse, as well as high-speed picture search in fast forward and reverse. This unit comes complete with high fidelity AFM (audio frequency modulation) sound. All special effects are controlled by the wireless remote commander.

Specifications: height, 3½"; **width,** 7⅛"; **depth,** 10⅛"; **weight,** 5½ pounds. **Warranty: parts,** one year; **labor,** 90 days.

Approx. retail price	Approx. low price
$500	$393

VHS VIDEOCASSETTE RECORDERS

TOSHIBA M-641

The Toshiba M-641 is a four-head hi-fi stereo VHS VCR with a quick-access tape transport system and a 181-channel cable-compatible frequency synthesized (FS) tuner. The quick-access system loads the tape as soon as you insert the cassette into the M-641. With the tape preloaded, it takes about one second to start recording or playback after you press the function button on the VCR or the wireless remote controller (instead of the six to ten seconds it takes most VCRs to start playing or recording). The full operation quick-access system provides instantaneous switching between fast forward or rewind and visual search, and immediate switching from visual search to play; switching directly to play from fast forward or rewind takes about 2½ seconds, which is three or four times faster than other VCRs. When rewinding or fast forwarding the tape, the M-641 has a brake system that slows the high speed down as it nears its stopping point to reduce strain on the tape and the VCR mechanism. The FS tuner automatically pulls in any signal when you press the channel up or down button, so there is no need for you to go through any tuning operations for VHF, UHF, or cable channels. The real-time tape counter keeps track of lapsed time in hours, minutes, and seconds. A useful feature of the M-641 is the tape-remain button on the remote that tells you the amount of time left on a tape at the speed the tape is running or at the speed at which the VCR is set if the tape is in the stop position. The on-screen programming allows you to set up to eight events over a one-year period. There is also a one-touch timer that lets you quickly set up one timer recording within a 24-hour period. The one-touch timer can also be used to program a recording in progress to shut off in up to four hours in 30-minute increments. The M-641 has auto indexing that puts a signal on the tape at the start of every recording; you can also add indexing to tapes manually with the index control on the remote. The VCR also features a normal and accelerated visual search, frame-by-frame picture advance, and slow play at ⅐ or 1/15 of normal speed. The Toshiba M-641 is about the most user-friendly sophisticated VCR available.

Specifications: height, 3¾"; **width,** 14³¹/₃₂"; **depth,** 13²⁵/₃₂"; **weight,** 14³/₁₀ pounds. **Warranty: parts,** one year; **labor,** 90 days.

Approx. retail price	Approx. low price
$549	$374

PANASONIC PV-4070

The Panasonic PV-4070 is a sophisticated four-head hi-fi stereo VHS VCR with a learning infrared remote for controlling other electronic components, and video or audio dubbing onto previously recorded tapes. The PV-4070 is especially designed for those who are interested in editing and rerecording. Along with the audio or video dubbing, there is a flying erase head that provides clean cuts between segments, synchronized editing with any compatible VCR or camcorder with a synchro jack, and a jog/shuttle. The jog is a dial on the remote that gives you very fine control of frame advance or reverse to locate the exact frame where you wish to start editing. The shuttle ring around the jog dial is used to control the forward or reverse speed of the tape from still to slow to normal to fast scan. There are seven learning-function buttons that allow you to control one or more functions of a TV or another VCR, regardless of the make. The eight-event/30-day timer recording can be programmed either on the screen with the remote or with the supplied bar code scanner that is displayed on the screen when programming is transmitted. There is also 4-week delayed recording and one-touch timed recording. The PV-4070 has a rapid-access system that starts to play or record about 1½ seconds after the command button is pressed; the time-lapse is equally short when switching from play to forward or reverse search and back to play. The PV-4070 puts an index signal on the tape at the beginning of a recording for index search operation; you can also manually record or erase an index signal with the remote. There is also time search: You enter the time from the beginning of the tape where you want to start playing back. The VCR goes that recorded distance and begins playback. During play, you can check a channel with the monitor button, which puts the tape in pause while

Prices are accurate at time of printing; subject to manufacturer's change.

displaying the channel. Other special playback effects include variable slow playback, studio ½-speed playback, and two-times normal speed. The Panasonic PV-4070 is an excellent choice for those who want to do more than just record and play back with their VCR.

Specifications: height, 3¾"; **width,** 15¾"; **depth,** 11⅝"; **weight,** 9⁹⁄₁₀ pounds. **Warranty: parts,** one year; **labor,** 90 days.

Approx. retail price	Approx. low price
$729	$673

MITSUBISHI HS-U52 ✓BEST BUY

The Mitsubishi HS-U52 is a four-head hi-fi stereo VHS VCR with rapid-access tape transport that has direct-function switching and automatic digital tracking. When you put a tape in the HS-U52, the rapid-access tape transport starts recording or playback in about 1½ seconds; when you press the "play" button on the VCR or the wireless remote, the digital tracking system goes into operation to adjust the tape moving across the heads to provide the best possible picture. There is a two-speed search mode in fast forward and rewind, and high-speed search, which is 10 times faster in SP and 30 times faster in EP than normal play. Switching from high-speed search to play takes only one second. In fast forward or rewind, you can switch to visual search by pressing and holding the fast forward or rewind button to scan the tape. Along with index search, the HS-U52 has time search. You enter the amount of time from the beginning of the tape where you want to start playing back, and the VCR goes that recorded distance and begins playback. The HS-U52 has a real-time counter in hours, minutes, and seconds, and displays time remaining on the screen in hours and minutes; a bar graph that shows you the approximate location between the beginning and end of the tape appears on the VCR's display panel when you are in either fast forward or rewind. The remote-controlled on-screen programming of the eighth event within the Saturday of the fourth week is unnecessarily complicated, but you are taken through each option step by step. The one-touch recording (OTR) and 24-hour standby recording buttons, located on the VCR, set the start and record times in 15-minute increments; by pressing the repeat button after starting OTR, the tape will be automatically rewound to the beginning of the recording before the VCR shuts off. Special playback effects include still, single-frame play in forward and reverse, slow-motion play in forward and reverse, reverse play at standard speed, and double-speed playback. The Mitsubishi HS-U52 is an excellent, multitalented VCR designed for the videophile. **Specifications: height**, 3⅝"; **width**, 16¾"; **depth**, 13½"; **weight**, 13 pounds. **Warranty: parts**, one year; **labor**, six months.

Approx. retail price	Approx. low price
$650	$491

RCA VR675HF

✔ **BEST BUY**

The RCA VR675HF is a four-head hi-fi stereo VHS VCR with quick play and dual remote control with auto edit. A unique and interesting feature of the VR675HF is its monitor function: When you press the monitor button on the wireless remote during tape playback, put the the tape in pause mode, and the channel that the VCR is tuned to appears on your screen. To return to tape play, you press the monitor and play buttons again. When you load a cassette in the VCR, it is loaded into a ready position so that when you press the play or record buttons, the VR675HF starts in a little over one second. The dual remote has VCR1 and VCR2 buttons that allow you to control most RCA VCRs with one control; when copying a tape using the one controller, the AutoEdit button simultaneously controls the starting and stopping of both VCRs. There is also a synchro edit jack for synchro editing with another VCR or camcorder that also has a synchro edit jack. The VR675HF has a linear time counter in hours and minutes that makes it easy to keep track of your recordings. Along with its auto indexing and index search, the VR675HF also has time search, which makes it easy to go directly to a particular spot within a recording by entering the hours and minutes of recorded time, and then pressing rewind or fast forward. There is an eight-event/one-year on-screen programming, 24-hour delayed-start express recording (XPR), and programmed stop for a recording in progress. The VR675HF also features auto play with repeat, still image, single-frame advance, slow motion, double-speed playback, and auto tracking. The RCA VR675HF is a fine, multifeatured VCR.

Specifications: height, 3½"; **width,** 14⅝"; **depth,** 12⅝"; **weight,** 11 pounds. **Warranty: parts,** one year; **labor,** 90 days.

Approx. retail price	**Approx. low price**
$579	$363

TOSHIBA M-441 ✓ BEST BUY

The Toshiba M-441 is a monaural VHS VCR with a quick-access system and front-panel input jacks. The front-panel RCA-type input jacks for video and audio provide handy access for people wishing to dub from their portable camcorder. The quick-access system starts to play or record about 1½ seconds after you press the play or record buttons; the quick-access also gives you rapid shifting from play to picture search to fast forward or rewind, or back again. Picture search is at five-times normal speed in forward and reverse; pressing and holding the fast forward or rewind buttons moves the tape into accelerated search, which increases the search speed to seven times in SP and 21 times in EP. The M-441 has a linear counter that gives you the recording and playback time in hours, minutes, and seconds. The 181-channel frequency synthesized tuner needs no tuning because it automatically tunes itself whenever you press the channel up or down buttons. Programming the on-screen eight-event/30-day timer is as simple as the step-by-step display can make it. Whenever the end of the tape is reached in playback or record, the M-441 automatically rewinds the tape. When you press the record button, an index signal is recorded on the tape; you can also manually insert index signals on a tape with the wireless remote. These signals are used in index search, which plays back about five seconds at the beginning of each signal. The remote has controls for single-frame advance, slow playback, and slow playback tracking. In playback, you can adjust the tracking manually or activate the automatic digital tracking.

Specifications: height, 3⅜"; **width,** 14³¹⁄₃₂"; **depth,** 12¹⁹⁄₃₂"; **weight,** 12⅖ pounds. **Warranty: parts,** one year; **labor,** 90 days.

Approx. retail price	**Approx. low price**
$390	$282

Prices are accurate at time of printing; subject to manufacturer's change.

PANASONIC PV-4024

The Panasonic PV-4024 is a four-head HQ VHS VCR with a flying erase head and synchro edit. The PV-4024 has a real-time counter displaying hours, minutes, and seconds and a time-search feature that lets you enter the time in minutes and/or seconds, from which the VCR fast forwards or rewinds to that time and starts playback. A monitor button puts the tape in pause and displays the channel set on the VCR; press the monitor button again and tape playback resumes. The quick-start feature starts playback or record about one second after the play or one-touch record buttons are pressed. The PV-4024 has many playback special effects such as frame-by-frame advance, variable slow motion, double-speed playback, and rewind with power off after play. Tape playback tracking and still image jitters are electronically controlled from the wireless remote. Auto programming of the 155-channel quartz tuner locks in all broadcast or cable channels in your area. There is an eight-event/30-day on-screen programming, instant start one-touch recording (OTR), and delayed OTR up to 11:30 of the following night. If you plan to edit tapes, the flying erase head keeps cuts virtually unnoticeable. The PV-4024 has provisions for synchro editing with a similarly equipped VCR or camcorder, and also has provisions for video or audio dubbing. The Panasonic PV-4024 is a fine, reasonably priced monaural VCR with many features.

Specifications: height, 3¾"; **width,** 15¾"; **depth,** 11⅝"; **weight,** 9⅖ pounds. **Warranty: parts,** one year; **labor,** 90 days.

Approx. retail price $400	**Approx. low price** $361

SAMSUNG VR3700

RECOMMENDED

The Samsung VR3700 is a reasonably priced HQ VHS VCR with a linear time counter, index search, and quick-start play (QSP). The time counter in the LED display on the VCR registers only hours and minutes; however, the on-screen display shows hours, minutes, and seconds. When you put a cassette in the VR3700, it immediately loads the tape so that when you press the play button, you are watching a picture in less than two seconds. Shifting from normal or fast search to play also takes less than two seconds, while going to play from fast forward or rewind takes only three seconds. The VR3700 puts an index signal on the tape at the beginning of every recording, and also allows you to manually enter or erase index marks. An auto program feature cycles through the 181-channel tuner and locks in every channel in your area. A monitor switch lets you quickly check a channel during tape play by putting the tape in pause and switching to the TV tuner. The wireless remote is used for on-screen programming of the eight-event/ one-year program timer, while the simple one-event timer is on the VCR. An unusual feature usually only found on expensive machines is electronic tracking controlled from the remote. The Samsung VR3700 is an inexpensive monaural VCR that is packed with features.

Specifications: height, 3⅜"; **depth**, 12¼"; **width**, 15"; **weight**, 11 pounds. **Warranty: parts**, one year; **labor**, 90 days.

Approx. retail price	**Approx. low price**
$340	$218

SHARP VC-H860U   `RECOMMENDED`

The Sharp VC-H860U is a four-head hi-fi stereo VHS VCR with a tamperproof function, channel flashback to recall the last station watched, and a four-favorite-channel system for easy selection of your preferred channels. The unique tamperproof function, located on the wireless remote, locks in whatever operation you have put the VC-H860U in, and no matter what controls are pressed, the VCR will continue the operation you have entered before locking it in. The tamperproof function is particularly useful if you have children around the house and you want to program the timer to record while you are out. There are two timer setting methods: the programmable eight-event/one-year timer and the simple recording timer. The simple timer is unique because it can be set to start and stop at any minute in any given 24-hour period, while other VCR simple timer operations can only be set at the hour and half hour, and record in 30-minute increments. Like more and more top-of-the-line VCRs, the VC-H860U lets you select the speed for each program set, so that you can set different recording speeds for different programs. In both the program timer and simple timer modes, the VC-H860U returns the tape to the start of the recording and ejects the cassette when the recording is complete. The full-loading mechanism moves from stop to play or record in two seconds, and from fast forward or rewind in four seconds. The VC-H860U has auto indexing when a recording is started, index search, and time search.

Specifications: height, 3½"; **width,** 16$\frac{15}{16}$"; **depth,** 13$\frac{45}{64}$"; **weight,** 14$\frac{1}{20}$ pounds. **Warranty: parts,** one year; **labor,** 90 days.

Approx. retail price	Approx. low price
$700	$338

RCA VR341 RECOMMENDED

The RCA VR341 is a monaural two-head VHS VCR with multi-language on-screen programming. To select the on-screen language of the VR341, you press the program button, select VCR setup, and then select either English, French, or Spanish. The VCR setup will also automatically tune in the broadcast or cable channels in your area by cycling through the 181-channel tuner. Programming the eight-event/one-year timer is done with the wireless remote control, as are all other on-screen operations. The remote can also control basic functions of compatible television sets. An XPR (express recording) button on the VCR allows you to immediately start a timed recording without programming the timer. The VR341 has auto play and auto rewind with automatic shutoff: When you insert a cassette with the record-protect tab removed, the tape automatically starts to play; at the end of the tape, it is automatically rewound and the VCR shuts off. The RCA VR341 is especially handy for those families with members whose primary language is French or Spanish.

Specifications: height, 3½"; **width,** 14$\frac{5}{8}$"; **depth,** 12$\frac{5}{8}$"; **weight,** 11$\frac{7}{10}$ pounds. **Warranty: parts,** one year; **labor,** 90 days.

Approx. retail price	Approx. low price
$349	$252

Prices are accurate at time of printing; subject to manufacturer's change.

LASER VIDEODISC PLAYERS

A laser videodisc is an optical medium for playing video and digital audio recordings in which pits cut into a disc are read by a laser beam. Because there is no physical contact, the acrylic-coated discs should last for a very long time. Laser videodiscs also produce excellent image quality with ordinary hookups to your television set, and are capable of producing superb images with nearly twice the horizontal resolution of standard videotapes when hooked up to newer TVs that have S-VHS connections. The newer laser videodisc players play back all available formats of audiodiscs and videodiscs.

One of the peculiarities of laser discs is the different types of counters used for CAV- and CLV-recorded discs (see below). A frame counter is used to keep track of the recording on standard CAV discs, while long-play CLV discs use elapsed-time counters. The counters are recorded on the discs, and the players automatically display the counter recorded on the disc being played.

Laser Videodisc Terminology

LD: Laser videodisc

LDP: Laser disc player

CD: Compact (audio) disc

CDV: Compact disc with video

CAV: Constant angular velocity: LDs spin at a constant speed of 1,800 rpm with a playing time of 30 minutes per side; all CAV discs can be played back with special effects.

CLV: Constant linear velocity: LDs spin at speeds varying from 1,800 rpm for the inner tracks to 600 rpm for the outer tracks with a playing time of 60 minutes per side. Special effects with CLVs are only possible with players that have digital frame memory.

Random access: All laser disc players have random access, which lets you quickly find a particular spot on a disc.

Chapter numbers: These numbers recorded on discs are used to indicate sections or chapters, and are used to find scenes with a chapter-search function. For example, a symphony with four movements will have four chapters, and the movie *Bat-*

man will have chapters such as: Chapter 1—Main title/credits; Chapter 2—Robbery in Gotham City, "I'm Batman"; Chapter 3—Press conference, "Meet Jack Napier"; and so on.

PIONEER CLD-1080

The Pioneer CLD-1080 is a CD/CDV/LD player with a zero-cross distortion-free (ZDF) digital-analog (D/A) converter with double-step noise shaper. The results of this new ZDF D/A converter system is a reasonably priced multidisc player with clean, rich sound. The CLD-1080 has two sets of RCA pin plug audio and video outputs and an *F* cable output so that you can permanently connect the player to a variety of components such as a TV, VCR, and audio system. The CLD-1080 can be connected to any TV with the *F* cable, or to any monitor/TV with RCA pin plug connectors. A last-memory function for laser discs allows you to turn the player off part way through a disc, and turn it on later to start where you left off. A motor opens and closes the disc table for easy loading. Once a disc is loaded, the CLD-1080 automatically detects the type of disc to be played. For recording on an audiotape, the CLD-1080 has auto-program editing where you enter the amount of time on a tape, and the player programs the tracks that will fit into that time span. Synchro editing is also possible with Pioneer units that have synchro jacks. The CLD-1080 has multispeed playback, single-frame advance with CAV discs, and six repeat modes from chapter repeat to full-program repeat. There are a number of video displays that range from simple time or frame and chapter display for videodiscs, to audio output level meters with elapsed time and total chapter display. The Pioneer CLD-1080 is a fine, basic multidisc player.

Specifications: height, 4¹³/₁₆"; **width,** 16⁹/₁₆"; **depth,** 16⅜"; **weight,** 16½ pounds. **Warranty: parts and labor,** one year.

Approx. retail price	Approx. low price
$600	$463

SONY MDP-333 [RECOMMENDED]

The Sony MDP-333 is a laser multidisc player with a dual-scan mode shuttle control that allows you to command its clear scan. The dual-scan mode shuttle control, a dial found on both the player and the wireless Unicommander remote control, gives you either 10-times or 30-times clearer scanning of CAV discs as well as clear scanning of CLV discs. All other special playback effects such as image still, frame-by-frame advance, and multispeed playback variable from $\frac{1}{90}$ normal speed to 10-times normal speed only work with CAV laser discs. The Unicommander is so called because it can also be used to control the major functions of remote-capable Sony TVs. The motorized disc drawer can be opened and closed with a button on the remote or player. The MDP-333 has intro scan for the first few seconds of each chapter, frame or time search, auto program play, custom indexing, and next or beginning of chapter search. This model's unique custom index provides easy access to CD passages or laser disc scenes. There are video on-screen displays of chapters, time or frame lapse, and special function operations. The MDP-333 features an S-VHS output and an optical-digital audio output for connection to audio equipment with an optical-digital audio input; there are also standard pin plug or *F* cable connections for standard hook-ups. The Sony MDP-333 is a fine multidisc player with special connections for advanced audio and video equipment.

Specifications: height, 4⅜"; **width,** 17"; **depth,** 15¾"; **weight,** 16¾ pounds. **Warranty: parts and labor,** one year.

Approx. retail price	**Approx. low price**
$650	$549

VIDEOTAPE REWINDERS

Rewinding and fast forwarding videotapes, especially when it is done frequently, puts undue wear on the mechanism of your VCR. Those who often rent or borrow tapes are prime examples of people who should use a rewinder to rewind these tapes, rather than using their VCRs as a rewinder. Many new VCRs operate with the tape partially or fully loaded, and some experts suggest that fast forwarding and rewinding not only puts undue stress on the mechanism of the VCRs, but also adds wear to the tapes. The following VHS rewinders will help to add life to your VCR.

Prices are accurate at time of printing; subject to manufacturer's change.

AMBICO VIDEO TAPE WINDER/CLEANER V-0755

✔ BEST BUY

The Ambico Video Tape Winder/Cleaner V-0755 winds tapes in both fast forward and rewind, which is especially useful to people who do a lot of playing on different sections of their tapes. The V-0755 also has a wet cleaning system that uses four pads to clean both sides of the tape. Tapes that are used often, such as those used for time shifting, should be cleaned after about every half-dozen uses to remove any loose oxides or other particles picked up during playing and recording. To insert a tape, you lift up the hinged dust cover, put the cassette in place, slide the cassette locking hooks in place, and press either fast forward or rewind. A braking system slows the tape down as it nears the end of the tape, and, when winding is complete, a tone sounds. When a tape is being cleaned, the cleaning pads disengage themselves when the winding is complete.
Warranty: parts and labor, six months.

Approx. retail price	Approx. low price
$70	$60

VIVITAR VRW-1

RECOMMENDED

The Vivitar VRW-1 is a basic unit that only rewinds a tape. You pop open the cassette compartment, insert the tape, and close the cover to start the rewinding. A T-120 tape is fully rewound in about 2½ minutes. When rewinding is complete, the cassette compartment pops open, and the VRW-1 turns off.
Warranty: parts and labor, one year.

Approx. retail price	Approx. low price
$30	not available

Prices are accurate at time of printing; subject to manufacturer's change.

Camcorders

The camcorder, which combines a video camera and a videocassette recorder in one unit, allows you to capture live action on tape and immediately play it back on your television. The hit TV show *America's Funniest Home Videos* attests to the incredible popularity of camcorders and their near-professional quality. Rapid advances in technology have greatly improved picture quality and variety of features since the introduction of the first camcorders less than a decade ago. One major advance is that several models now include stereo hi-fi sound. Prices have not fallen as rapidly as those of other electronics, but they have shown significant erosion over the past year, especially on full-size VHS models. While picture quality between models varies only modestly, the feel and operational ease differ dramatically.

When traveling overseas with your camcorder, be aware that outside of Japan, Korea, and Taiwan, you cannot watch your tapes on local TV sets. Most of the world uses a different video standard than we do. Airport security devices, unless grossly defective, will NOT damage your camcorder or your tapes. When flying with your camcorder, always be sure that its battery is charged. Airport security will often ask you to turn it on to prove that what you are carrying is actually a camcorder.

Camcorder Formats

VHS camcorders have a longer recording capacity (up to eight hours at the slow EP speed with T-160 tapes) than recorders using other formats. However, $\frac{1}{2}$-inch-wide VHS tapes require a relatively large camcorder. An upgraded VHS format, S-VHS (Super VHS), uses a specially formulated, much more expensive tape that records up to 400 lines of resolution, and far outperforms conventional VHS at the EP speed. S-VHS camcorders are now available. North America is one of the few places in the world where full-size VHS still dominates sales with a 50 percent market share.

Beta camcorders intended for home videos are no longer being manufactured.

VHS-C is a variation of the VHS format that uses cassettes about the same size as audiocassettes, but which are twice as thick. VHS-C threads the tape through a shorter path than full-size VHS, but both formats record identical signals. This allows VHS-C cassettes to record and play on any VHS VCR with the use of an adapter. Some new VCRs play these small tapes without an adapter. Tapes record for 30 minutes at SP and 90 minutes at EP. During the past year, several exceptionally compact models have been introduced. S-VHS-C camcorders are also available. VHS-C has been losing its market share to the 8mm format.

8mm cassettes are thinner than other videocassettes because the tape is only about $\frac{1}{3}$-inch wide. By using metal tape technology to increase recording density, 8mm tapes reproduce an image equal to or better than most $\frac{1}{2}$-inch VHS tapes. Camcorders that use this format, like those that use VHS-C, are becoming increasingly more compact and lightweight. An 8mm camcorder records for two hours at the fast (SP) speed. The slow (EP) speed is not available for recording on most camcorders, but permits four hours of recording on home VCRs.

Hi Band 8mm (Hi8) offers the same resolution as S-VHS (about 400 lines), but Hi8 records with slightly less color noise, so the picture quality is subtly better than S-VHS. Standard 8mm tapes will record and play on Hi8 machines, but tapes recorded on Hi8 will not play back on conventional 8mm machines. Hi8 camcorders require special tape, and two new metal tape formulations have been developed: a premium metal evaporated tape (Hi8-ME), and an improved metal particle tape (Hi8-MP). Both are more expensive than the standard tape.

The standard 8mm mono soundtrack is high fidelity, unlike VHS. Until recently, the only stereo hi-fi soundtrack for 8mm was a complex digital system available only on one or two of the most expensive models. Now many 8mm camcorders also use the simpler AFM (audio frequency modulation) stereo hi-fi soundtrack, similar to Beta Hi-Fi.

Unlike VHS, the 8mm format was designed for camcorder use since its inception. Perhaps this explains its recent surge in popularity. Both of these reasons account for our expanded listings of 8mm camcorders.

The VHS and 8mm formats are electronically compatible. This allows you, for example, to connect your 8mm camcorder to your VHS VCR and copy your 8mm videos onto VHS tape, or directly to your TV for viewing. You do not have to buy a camcorder that uses the same format as your VCR.

Features and Terminology

Before shopping for a camcorder, you should be familiar with the following terms:

Aperture designation tells you the maximum opening of the iris, or the greatest amount of light that can be admitted. The designation is given as an f-stop rating, such as f/1.6. The iris automatically adjusts in all camcorders. Some offer a desirable manual adjustment as well.

Autofocus describes a feature that focuses the lens as the distance between the camcorder and the subject changes. Some camcorders also have manual focus. Each company uses a proprietary autofocus system, with varying degrees of speed and accuracy. While most companies have switched to some form of a computerized through-the-lens (TTL) system, the simpler infrared system often works better. Be sure to try out the autofocus when evaluating a camcorder for purchase.

CCD (charge-coupled device) is a solid-state imaging device that replaces the pickup tube. CCDs eliminate most image lag, which looks like a streaking highlight on a moving subject. CCDs function well in a broad range of lighting conditions and are rarely damaged by excessive light. All CCDs used in camcorders are based on MOS (metal-oxide semiconductor) devices. The CCD is the system by which electrons are collected and moved through the imaging device. The MOS is the type of light-sensitive transistor making up the CCD. References to CCD or MOS in camcorder specifications are arbitrary and bear little relationship to the quality of the product.

Character generators allow you to add the time, date, titles, or other written information to the images you are recording.

Continuous white balance is used to keep the color of video images true to life. An inaccurate white balance can result in a picture that is too red or too blue.

Fade-in/fade-out is a feature of some camcorders that automatically takes the image to or from a blank screen.

Flying erase head is a special video head that is used for editing videotapes. Because it is mounted on a spinning drum along with the other heads, the flying erase head allows you to make smooth transitions between scenes without noise bursts.

High-speed shutter allows less light into the camcorder than a normal shutter. This improves the camcorder's ability to freeze action. The fastest high-speed shutters operate at speeds up to $\frac{1}{40000}$ of a second.

Lux is a method of measuring the amount of light that is falling on a photo subject. Many camcorders have a low light level rating of around ten lux; this is the amount of light on a subject about 12 feet from a single 60-watt light bulb. While sensitive camcorders deliver a picture signal with two lux, you are more likely to get a good image with 80 lux. The best color and depth of focus require several hundred lux.

Microphones are built into all camcorders, and most can also be connected to external mikes as well.

Minimum illumination tells you the minimum amount of light, stated in lux, that you need to record a clear picture. Many camcorders deliver a picture signal with about four lux and can be used with ordinary indoor lighting.

Pixels, which is short for picture elements, convert electric signals into points of light. In general, a high pixel count produces a more detailed video image, but because the size and type of imaging devices vary, comparing pixel counts between two different devices doesn't always determine which one yields the more detailed image.

Resolution is the ability to produce fine detail in a video picture. It is usually measured in horizontal lines. A good video monitor reproduces more than 500 lines, TV broadcasts are about 340 lines, conventional VHS reproduces 240 lines, and 8mm yields slightly more.

Superimposer is a digital memory function that can store images or titles. At the push of a button, you can superimpose the stored image over the picture that is currently being recorded.

Best Buys '91

Our Best Buy and Recommended camcorders follow; they were all evaluated on their performance from tapes recorded under a variety of conditions and played back directly on a Sony 32-inch XBR color television/monitor. The camcorders are listed within each category according to their quality, features, and value. The unit we consider the best of the Best Buys is first, followed by our second choice, and so on. Keep in mind that a Best Buy or Recommended rating applies only to the model listed, not to other models by the same manufacturer or in the same product line.

8MM CAMCORDERS

SONY CCD-TR4

The Sony CCD-TR4 is an 8mm camcorder that is about the same size and weight as a 35mm still camera. The new model CCD-TR4, available in a black or white body, has even more features and is slightly smaller and lighter than last year's revolutionary CCD-TR5. It is more of a Best Buy because Sony has substantially lowered the price from the previous model. A new ⅓-inch high-sensitivity imager with 270,000 pixels and a five-lux minimum illumination rating ensures good quality pictures under a wide range of lighting conditions. To freeze fast-moving objects, the four-position high-speed shutter's fastest speed is $1/4000$ of a second. The CCD-TR4 includes a six-power zoom lens with autofocus, continuous auto white balance, and automatic exposure with backlight compensation. The only weakness of the CCD-TR4 is its slow autofocus. A specially designed noise-canceling microphone mounted nearly flush on top of the body and just behind the lens complements the high-fidelity mono soundtrack. An edit switch invokes circuitry that compensates for copying losses. An LCD (liquid crystal display) screen on top of the camcorder displays vital information, including a real-time counter that shows elapsed recording time. A built-in clock/calendar powered by a separate battery provides a time-and-date display on the screen. The electronic viewfinder duplicates much of this information, and the date and time can be recorded onto the tape at the push of a button. The camcorder's superimposer has a one-page memory for graphics and titles. A new quick-recording mechanism significantly reduces the interval between the time the "record" button is pressed and the start of recording. The CCD-TR4 owes its compact size and a four-layer circuit board to an innovative tape transport only half the thickness of the one used in most other 8mm camcorders. **Specifications: height,** $4\frac{1}{8}$"; **width,** $4\frac{3}{8}$"; **length,** $6\frac{5}{8}$"; **weight,** $1\frac{3}{5}$ pounds without battery and tape. **Warranty: parts,** one year; **labor,** 90 days.

Approx. retail price	Approx. low price
$1,100	$916

RCA PRO880HB ✓ BEST BUY

The RCA Pro880HB is a Hi8 camcorder with approximately 400 lines of horizontal resolution and high-fidelity stereo sound in a relatively small, handsome package. RCA refuses to follow the pack by using a sometimes problematic through-the-lens autofocus system. The Pro880HB retains a fast, highly accurate infrared autofocus, which also has a telemacro position, not often found on infrared autofocus. The eight-power zoom lens is coupled with a $\frac{1}{2}$-inch CCD imager with 380,000 pixels, which requires only two-lux minimum illumination. It has a two-page superimposer for graphics and titles, plus a character generator for creating titles. Six shutter speeds are available, the highest being $\frac{1}{10000}$ of a second. An unusual feature is a negative/positive switch for transferring film negatives onto tape. The unit's LCD screen is large and easy to read, displaying date/time, elapsed tape time, and important settings and warnings, which are also visible in the electronic viewfinder. RCA provides a wireless remote control for convenience when using the Pro880HB as a home VCR. **Specifications: height**, $4\frac{3}{8}$"; **width**, $3\frac{7}{8}$"; **length**, $11\frac{1}{2}$"; **weight**, $2\frac{9}{10}$ pounds without battery and tape. **Warranty: parts**, one year; **labor**, 90 day

Approx. retail price	Approx. low price
$1,688	$1,142

OLYMPUS VX-81 RECOMMENDED

The Olympus VX-81 is a highly unusual 8mm camcorder. The compact, lightweight unit is shaped like a pair of binoculars. This shape and the conveniently arranged controls make for a very stable shooting grip. The VX-81 uses a $\frac{7}{10}$-inch, 270,000-pixel CCD requiring four-lux minimum illumination. The six-power zoom will automatically focus as close as $\frac{3}{5}$-inch. The fastest setting of the five-position high-speed shutter is $\frac{1}{4000}$ of a second. The automatic white balance samples 64 separate zones in the picture for precise color values. An LCD (liquid crystal display) panel on top of the camcorder shows date/time (maintained by a separate battery), a real-time tape counter, and important operating information, which is also displayed in the electronic viewfinder. The VX-81 is the first camcorder to incorporate a "fuzzy logic" computer chip that analyzes auto focus in order to fine-tune for the best picture. The unit comes supplied with wireless remote control. The camcorder's superimposer has a one-page memory for graphics and titles.
Specifications: height, $3\frac{1}{10}$"; **width**, $6\frac{2}{5}$"; **length**, $7\frac{1}{5}$"; **weight**, $1\frac{1}{5}$ pounds without battery and tape. **Warranty: parts**, one year; **labor**, 90 days.

Approx. retail price	Approx. low price
$2,000	not available

Prices are accurate at time of printing; subject to manufacturer's change.

SONY CCD-TR7 RECOMMENDED

The Sony CCD-TR7 shows a strong family resemblance to the CCD-TR4, and it includes all the features listed for that model. By adding fractions of an inch and a few ounces, Sony loaded this 8mm model with additional features, such as stereo hi-fi sound. The CCD-TR7's eight-power zoom lens is coupled with a ½-inch, 410,000-pixel CCD imager for excellent picture quality. It requires four-lux minimum illumination. The one-page superimposer allows scrolling the image from the bottom to the top of the screen. With the fader you cannot only fade out, but fade to black. The optional SPK-TR water-resistant housing ($250) and the MPK-TR waterproof housing ($1,000) increase the versatility of the CCD-TR7.

Specifications: height, 4¼"; **width,** 4⅜"; **length,** 7¼"; **weight,** 1⅘ pounds without battery and tape. **Warranty: parts,** one year; **labor,** 90 days.

Approx. retail price	Approx. low price
$1,400	$1,266

FULL-SIZE VHS CAMCORDERS

PANASONIC PV-602

The Panasonic PV-602 is the camcorder designed for every person. It is not only truly affordable, it incorporates all necessary features for convenience and good recording, except for a flying erase head. (That feature is available for $100 more on the virtually identical PV-604.) However, the PV-602 compensates for this lack with "book mark search," which marks where recording stopped, and cues up the tape so as to cover up glitches left by the "stop/start" process. Panasonic calls this 3-inch-wide camcorder the "Switch Hitter" because it is designed for easy use by either right- or left-handed people. Panasonic achieves this by building the hand grip into the center of the body underneath the lens barrel, and placing major controls on the grip. The viewfinder can be flipped to either side. The PV-602 needs a minimum illumination of only two lux to record a picture. The three-position high-speed shutter's fast speed is $\frac{1}{1000}$ of a second. A self-timer lets the user set the camcorder for delayed recording, so he or she can be in the video. It will also do time-lapse recording of one second each minute. The infrared autofocus adjusts quickly and accurately.

Specifications: height, $8\frac{1}{4}$"; **width**, 3"; **length**, $15\frac{1}{2}$"; **weight**, $4\frac{2}{5}$ pounds without battery and tape. **Warranty: parts**, one year; **labor**, 90 days.

Approx. retail price	Approx. low price
$799	not available

RCA CC510

✔ **BEST BUY**

The RCA CC510 camcorder includes desirable features in addition to good recording quality. A ten-power zoom lens is coupled with a ½-inch CCD imager with 250,000 pixels. A ten-watt color enhancement light complements the CC510's two-lux minimum light sensitivity. The highest speed of the six-mode shutter is $\frac{1}{10000}$ of a second. A built-in speaker located near your ear when holding the camcorder in recording position lets you hear what you're recording, and it allows you to hear as well as see your efforts on playback. The CC510 includes a flying erase head for seamless edits, in addition to RCA's Synchro-Edit feature that controls compatible VCRs while dubbing. The video/audio dub feature permits adding new video or audio segments to existing tapes. The CC510 has a two-page superimposer with character generator.

Specifications: height, $8\frac{1}{10}$"; **width**, $5\frac{9}{10}$"; **length**, $14\frac{3}{5}$"; **weight**, $5\frac{3}{4}$ pounds without battery and tape. **Warranty: parts**, one year; **labor**, 90 days.

Approx. retail price	Approx. low price
$1,199	$1,099

PANASONIC PV-S540

RECOMMENDED

The Panasonic PV-S540 records with the superior resolution of S-VHS (approximately 400 lines of resolution). A ten-watt color enhancement light complements its five-lux minimum light sensitivity. The eight-power zoom lens couples with the

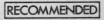

Prices are accurate at time of printing; subject to manufacturer's change.

½-inch CCD with 330,000 pixels. The PV-S540 includes a flying erase head for seamless edits, as well as audio/video dubbing, which permits adding new video or audio to existing tapes. The four-speed shutter's fastest speed is $\frac{1}{1000}$ of a second. A self-timer initiates delayed recording so that the user can be in his or her own videos. Time-lapse recording runs the tape for a brief period of time every hour. The infrared autofocus is fast and accurate. The clock/calendar with its own backup battery is displayed in the electronic viewfinder along with other operating information including tape time remaining. A built-in speaker, located near your ear when recording, lets you hear as well as see your recordings. The VHS Index Search System aids in locating specific points on the tape. This full-size camcorder is made to be rested on the shoulder while shooting.

Specifications, height, 8⅜"; **width,** 4¾"; **length,** 15½"; **weight,** 5⅘ pounds without battery and tape. **Warranty: parts,** one year; **labor,** 90 days.

Approx. retail price	Approx. low price
$1,650	$1,436

VHS-C CAMCORDERS

JVC GR-AX7U

The JVC GR-AX7U is the smallest VHS-C camcorder, highly competitive in size and weight with the smallest 8mm models. Its six-power zoom lens is coupled with a new ⅓-inch CCD with 270,000 pixels. It requires a minimum of three-lux illumination. The highest speed of its six shutter settings is $\frac{1}{4000}$ of a second. It has automatic backlight compensation. The superimposer has a one-page memory. An edit mode enhances videos for copying. The GR-AX7U lacks an LCD (liquid crystal display), but includes date/time, tape time remaining, and other settings and warnings in the electronic viewfinder. This well-shaped tiny camcorder easily fits the hand. Even though it is small, battery life is almost an hour of continuous shooting. It includes an "encore" function for instant replays and a fader. An optional remote control is available.

Specifications: height, 4⅝"; **width,** 6⁷⁄₁₆"; **length,** 4⅝"; **weight,** 1³⁄₁₀ pounds. **Warranty: parts,** one year; **labor,** 90 days.

Approx. retail price	Approx. low price
$1,200	$966

PANASONIC PV-40 "PALMCORDER"

The Panasonic PV-40 "Palmcorder" is the top-of-the-line in the company's aptly named series of "Palmcorders." Although not quite as small as the JVC GR-AXU, its under-two-pound weight makes it easy to tote along. The PV-40's eight-power zoom lens is coupled with a ⅓-inch CCD imager with 250,000 pixels, which requires a minimum illumination of five lux. The seven-position variable-speed shutter's highest speed is ¼₀₀₀ of a second. A flying erase head permits seamless edits. The clock/calendar, with its own backup battery, displays time and date both on the LCD (liquid crystal display) screen and in the electronic viewfinder. A real-time tape counter visible both on the LCD and viewfinder shows tape time remaining. A superimposer stores one page of graphics or titles. The circuitry that provides a digital freeze-frame on playback also supplies a digital strobe function when recording. With digital strobe you can record a progression of momentary still-frame images. What makes the PV-40 unique is a proprietary Panasonic feature called Digital Electronic Image Stabilization (E.I.S.). This minimizes the jitter of unwanted camcorder movement, such as shaky hands. It permits walking and riding while shooting without the irritating unsteadiness in the picture that usually accompanies shooting while in motion. A bit of resolution is lost with Digital E.I.S., but most people will find it a desirable trade-off.

Specifications: height, 5⅛"; **width,** 3¾"; **length,** 5¾"; **weight,** 1⁷⁄₁₀ pounds without battery and tape. **Warranty: parts,** one year; **labor,** 90 days.

Approx. retail price	Approx. low price
$1,299	$1,031

Prices are accurate at time of printing; subject to manufacturer's change.

Stereo Components

Stereo components are now just part of home entertainment complexes that usually center on a television screen. The line between audio and video that existed in the past has almost disappeared because of the increasing popularity of videocassette recorders that record soundtracks in true stereo high fidelity and the rapid expansion of stereo TV broadcasts.

While some manufacturers offer special audio systems to complement their video products, most standard audio components mate easily with TVs and VCRs equipped with stereo output jacks. Just be careful not to place the speakers too close to the TV screen. Unless they were specially designed for this kind of placement, the speaker magnets can distort the color of the picture.

Buying stereo components instead of a system allows you to upgrade your system at any time without having to discard the entire system. If you cannot afford all the components you want, you can begin with just a receiver and two speakers that will provide high-fidelity FM stereo radio. Later you can add a turntable, CD player, or cassette deck.

Over the past 20 years, technology has continuously raised the performance level of audio components while lowering the prices. This steady decline in prices reached its end with the weakening of the U.S. dollar in world markets and the soaring cost of computer memory chips, which are used in many audio components. Both the dollar and the price of memory chips seem to have stabilized, so component prices in 1991 will continue to offer good values.

Best Buys '91

Our Best Buy and Recommended stereo components follow. They are presented in the following categories: loudspeakers, headphones, receivers, compact disc players, turntables, phono cartridges, cassette decks, and DAT recorders. (Stereo systems and portable audio products are discussed in other chapters.) Within each category, components are listed by quality; the item we consider the best of the Best Buys is first, followed by our second choice, and so on. Remember that a Best Buy or Recommended designation applies only to the model listed; it does not necessarily apply to other models made by the same manufacturer or to an entire product line.

LOUDSPEAKERS

Choose loudspeakers carefully before you select other components for your sound system. Speakers often determine the personality of the system, and they always determine your choice of receiver because some speakers require more power than others. Discerning the sonic difference between two electronic components often requires intense concentration, but the differences between similarly priced speakers come through loud and clear. Insist on the privilege of returning speakers that do not meet your expectations. Speakers interact dramatically with room acoustics. What sounds splendid in the store may sound tinny or muddy in your home. The size of the speaker enclosure and the number of individual speakers (woofers, tweeters, and midrange) do not always correlate with sound quality. The following are some of the terms you should know when shopping for speakers.

Power requirements: Different speakers apply different laws of physics to produce sound. High-efficiency *ported*, or *ducted*, systems, which are most common among larger speakers, take advantage of the air within the speaker enclosure, allowing it to move in and out with the speaker. They use the receiver's power efficiently and require modest power to produce ample sound levels. Low-efficiency *acoustic-suspension*, or *air-suspension*, speakers, which are most common among bookshelf-size speakers, seal the enclosure tightly and force the speaker to fight the air within. Large floor-standing speakers can produce throbbing levels with 25 watts of power, while compact bookshelf models require twice that much power.

Too much power can damage speakers, but speaker ratings and amplifier ratings do not always match. Speakers rated at 100 watts maximum may be powered safely by 300-watt amplifiers, but if you force all 300 watts into the speaker the sound would become so loud that it would cause you pain as well as damaging the speakers.

Speaker impedance: Speakers are listed as having either a four-ohm or eight-ohm impedance. This is a technical description of the amount of resistance the speaker offers to the flow of electrical signals. Under normal circumstances, impedance makes little difference to sound quality, but many receivers need a minimum of four ohms to work properly. Two pairs of four-ohm speakers connected to play at the same time equal two ohms as far as the receiver is concerned. A good receiver may work with two ohms, but other receivers will automatically shut off or blow a fuse. A two-ohm load can actually destroy a poorly designed receiver. If you intend to use two pairs of speakers, choose loudspeakers rated at eight ohms.

Woofers, tweeters, and other speaker elements: The woofer is the largest speaker component. It reproduces bass notes and often the lower midrange sounds. The tweeter is the smallest speaker component. It reproduces treble notes and often the upper midrange. Some speakers include a midrange speaker component that reproduces the range of sound between the woofer and tweeter, the range of the human voice. Where a speaker component starts and finishes varies from one speaker to another.

The crossover network is a series of resistors, capacitors, and coils that divide the incoming sound from the receiver, ensuring that the bass goes to the woofer and the treble to the tweeter. These individual speaker components are *drivers*. The size of the driver and the material from which it is manufactured offer no intrinsic advantages. An 8-inch woofer sometimes reproduces more bass than a 12-inch woofer, and paper surpasses some plastics in the quality of the speaker cone.

NHT ONE

The NHT (which stands for "Now Hear This") One is an unconventionally attractive small bookshelf speaker made in the U.S.A. An angled front baffle is responsible for the distinctive appearance of this nonrectangular speaker. The 6½-inch woofer and 1-inch dome tweeter produce a smooth, natural sound with good bass for such a small box. (A matching subwoofer is available for super low bass.) The NHT One comes finished in real oak veneer, although other optional finishes are available. The stereo image is lifelike. The speakers come magnetically shielded, making them an ideal choice for a high-quality video system. NHT is now owned by the electronics conglomerate International Jensen.
Specifications: height, 12"; **width**, 7"; **depth**, 10"; **weight**, 11 pounds each. **Warranty: parts and labor**, five years.

Approx. retail price
$340/pair

Approx. low price
$226/pair

B&W DM-310 ✔BEST BUY

The B&W DM-310 represents the bargain in a new line of B&W speakers, which use components similar to much more expensive models without the elaborate and costly matrix enclosure. The ported enclosure holds an 8-inch polypropylene woofer and a 1-inch metal dome tweeter. The enclosure comes finished in simulated walnut, black ash veneer, or brushed anthracite, with a charcoal-gray cloth grille. B&W pays attention to small details, such as the precise flare of the woofer cone, and molding nonconcentric grooves around the tweeter for the clearest possible sound. The DM-310 reproduces rich, full

---

Prices are accurate at time of printing; subject to manufacturer's change.

sound with good clarity. The frequency response ranges from below 60 hertz in the bass to over 20,000 hertz in the treble. Distortion is low, and the DM-310 handles power well. **Specifications: height**, 19"; **width**, 10"; **depth**, 8½"; **weight**, 15⅘ pounds. **Warranty: parts and labor**, five years.

Approx. retail price	Approx. low price
$500/pair	not available

CELESTION 5

The Celestion 5 is a good small speaker system that is made in England. There's nothing fancy about these speakers. Their plain wood cabinets are finished in simulated oak or black ash veneer with a black cloth grille. Inside the sealed acoustic-suspension enclosure is a 6-inch felted-fiber cone woofer in a polycarbonate basket and a 1-inch titanium dome tweeter. The Celestion 5 is the response to the complaint of a lack of bass in the company's excellent, smaller Celestion 3. To realize full bass from the Celestion 5, it should be used on a bookshelf or a rigid stand near the wall. These speakers are pleasingly low in distortion and withstand large amounts of power, while they need relatively little power (as little as 10 watts) for good sound. The frequency response ranges from below 60 hertz in the bass to 20,000 hertz in the treble. Versatile recessed rear binding posts secure bare wire, banana plugs, or lugged wire. **Specifications: height**, 14"; **width**, 8"; **depth**, 10"; **weight**, 10⅘ pounds each. **Warranty: parts and labor**, five years.

Approx. retail price	Approx. low price
$400/pair	$400/pair

MISSION/CYRUS 782

The Mission/Cyrus 782 speakers reproduce a remarkable stereo image with clarity of sound. This English-made speaker sounds virtually transparent. It contains a pair of 6½-inch polypropylene woofers in die-cast magnesium baskets, and a ¾-inch fabric dome tweeter in a sealed, infinite baffle internal acoustical design. The standard wood veneer enclosure comes finished in black with a black knit grille, but other finishes are available. The cabinet is not elegant, as Mission has chosen to make its investment entirely in the sound, rather than in the appearance. The bass response goes below 50 hertz, with a smooth treble response past 20,000 hertz. Although classified as a bookshelf design, the Mission/Cyrus 782 produces its best sound on floor stands away from the wall.

Specifications: height, 20"; **width**, 10"; **depth**, 13"; **weight**, 30⅘ pounds. **Warranty: parts**, five years; **labor**, one year.

Approx. retail price	Approx. low price
$899/pair	not available

MB QUART 280 RECOMMENDED

The MB Quart 280 bookshelf speakers are designed with great attention to both sonic and visual detail. When we first recommended them two years ago, they cost considerably less than they do now and we considered them a Best Buy. With the rising value of the Deutsche mark, these West German-made speakers look and sound as good as ever, but offer less value. The speaker consists of a 1-inch titanium dome tweeter and an 8-inch woofer. They are housed in a dense enclosure finished with thick wood veneers and solid wood corners and edges, since solid wood resists damage better than veneer. The sound is totally smooth from deep bass to very high treble. The stereo image is so real that it seems to float in the air around the speakers. Standard finishes include walnut, oak, white matte lacquer, or black matte lacquer. Three additional finishes are available at extra cost.

Specifications: height, 17¼"; **width**, 10½"; **depth**, 11¼"; **weight**, 22 pounds. **Warranty: parts and labor**, five years.

Approx. retail price	Approx. low price
$600/pair	$555/pair

POLK 5 JR+ SERIES 2 RECOMMENDED

The Polk 5jr+ Series 2 are three-way speakers that offer good value. Each speaker uses a 6½-inch woofer, 6½-inch midrange, and 1-inch dome tweeter. A passive radiator, which is a dummy bass driver, works with the woofer to improve bass response (it goes until just below 20,000 hertz and begins to fall off sharply). The high sensitivity of the Polk 5jr+ requires only 20 watts of amplifier power. The cabinet is available in three vinyl finishes: black ash, walnut, and oak.

Specifications: height, 19½"; **width**, 9"; **depth**, 10"; **weight**, 20½ pounds. **Warranty: parts and labor**, five years.

Approx. retail price	**Approx. low price**
$350/pair	$288/pair

KEF REFERENCE 104/2 　　　RECOMMENDED

The KEF Reference 104/2 speakers have a unique woofer arrangement that couples two woofers together to obtain a deep, utterly solid bass. To extend the bass response further, the speakers offer an optional electronic enhancement called KUBE (KEF Universal Bass Equalizer) that connects to the tape monitor loop of your receiver. The Reference 104/2 has two 8-inch woofers, two 4½-inch midranges, and a 1-inch dome tweeter in a wooden enclosure that is made of black ash, rosewood, or walnut. A proprietary circuit matches this speaker to any amplifier that produces at least 50 watts per channel. The resulting sound is smooth and has a wide range. Only the high price keeps the KEF Reference 104/2 from being a Best Buy. Consider this a first choice if you are shopping for a luxury speaker.

Specifications: height, 35½"; **width**, 11"; **depth**, 16⅜"; **weight**, 70½ pounds. **Warranty: parts and labor**, five years.

Approx. retail price	**Approx. low price**
$2,200/pair	$1,950/pair

HEADPHONES

Like speakers, headphones are best judged according to how they sound. But unlike speakers, headphones are unaffected by room acoustics, and their sound quality needs to please no one but their owner. The general criteria for good headphone performance include a full bass response with accurate tonal definition and balance from the midrange frequencies up to the highest frequencies.

A headset must also be comfortable. Weight and fit should be considered carefully. The three basic designs for headphones are **circumaural phones**, which cover your entire outer ear and block out all external sound; **supra-aural phones**, which do not completely block external sound; and **open-air phones**, which rest lightly against the outer ear and usually have a foam pad that separates the actual phone from your head, so that outside sounds can be heard while wearing them.

As a general rule, circumaural phones provide the best bass while open-air phones usually provide the least bass. Another style of phone inserts directly into the ear. These tend to be difficult to keep in the ear and uncomfortable. They also tend to have less fidelity than other types of headphones.

SIGNET EP700

 BEST BUY

The Signet EP700 headphones not only offer superb sound but they are extremely comfortable. These eight-ounce dynamic phones are a cross between circumaural and supra-aural. Their soft velourlike ear pads surround the ear, but the back of the headphone cup remains open. This allows the phones to block some but not all external noise. They can deliver excellent bass and still have the airiness of open-air phones. A rigid plastic headband supports the ear cups, while a soft, flexible plastic band rests on your head. The headband is easily adjusted in click-stops, and the ear cups swivel in both the horizontal and vertical planes. The EP700 is supplied with a 10-foot flat cord and a standard ¼-inch stereo phone plug. (An adapter is needed to use the EP700 with a personal portable.)
Warranty: parts and labor, one year.

Approx. retail price	Approx. low price
$150	$150

KOSS TNT/88

 BEST BUY

The Koss TNT/88 circumaural headphones have titanium nitride-coated diaphragms that are stronger and more rigid than titanium but extremely lightweight. These diaphragms pro-

Prices are accurate at time of printing; subject to manufacturer's change.
CONSUMER GUIDE®   121

duce greater clarity throughout the midrange and treble. The phones are rated for a high-frequency response of up to 30,000 hertz. The TNT/88 phones weigh five ounces. Soft foam-filled leatherette ear cushions fit over the ear and seal out external sounds, as well as aiding good bass response. The TNT/88 uses a double headband with a rigid outer band supporting the ear cups and a soft inner band resting on the head. The ear cups swivel in multiple planes for maximum comfort. The TNT/88 comes with a 10-foot flat cord, which employs DuPont Kevlar fibers that make the cord nearly indestructible. The cord has a gold-plated ⅛-inch mini stereo phone plug and is supplied with a gold-plated ¼-inch adapter.
Warranty: parts and labor, lifetime.

Approx. retail price	**Approx. low price**
$90	$83

KOSS PORTA PRO

✔ **BEST BUY**

The Koss Porta Pro headphones are comfortable, and they sound good. Adjustable foam pads take the pressure off the ear in this open-air design. The phones press gently against the temporal bone between your ear and forehead. Without the cord, the phones weigh only 2 ⁹⁄₁₀ ounces, making it easy to forget they are on your head. These headphones do not have a crisp, extended treble response, but the 60-ohm impedance and moderately high sensitivity make them suitable for use with all electronic equipment. The 6-foot dual-control cord has a ⅛-inch mini phone plug, but the headphones come with a ¼-inch adapter. These collapsible phones fold into a ball that stuffs into a supplied pouch.
Warranty: parts and labor, lifetime.

Approx. retail price	**Approx. low price**
$50	$37

SONY MDR-CD555

RECOMMENDED

The Sony MDR-CD555 headphones combine the best attributes of supra-aural and open-air designs. The phones are lightweight and comfortable, and they reproduce sound with unerring accuracy over the entire audible range. Their moderately high impedance (45 ohms) works well with all electronic equipment, and their high sensitivity permits very loud volumes. The 10-foot cord is made of flexible flat wire. It has a stereo UniMatch plug, which fits all equipment. These phones are somewhat fragile.

Warranty: parts and labor, one year.

Approx. retail price	Approx. low price
$130	$84

RECEIVERS

A receiver combines a radio tuner with a preamplifier and a power amplifier into one well-matched system that receives and amplifies audio signals. Separate tuners and amplifiers appeal primarily to listeners with special interests and considerable amounts of money to spend on stereo equipment.

The preamplifier section serves as a kind of switchboard for the entire system. It contains the program, or function, switch; volume and tone controls; and input and output terminals for program sources, such as turntables, cassette decks, and compact disc players. The preamplifier also boosts the level of electrical signals to a level suitable for the power amplifier section of the receiver.

The power amplifier boosts the signal it gets from the preamplifier to levels that are strong enough to cause the loudspeakers to deliver undistorted sound.

Here are some of the terms that you should know before you purchase a receiver:

dB Quieting tells you the amount of signal that is needed at the antenna terminals to provide noise-free, acceptable reception. The lower the number, stated in microvolts or dBf, the better.

Frequency response should be uniform, or "flat," over the entire range of human hearing from 20 to 20,000 hertz.

Power output is stated in watts. Be sure that the wattage applies to each channel and not to the sum of both stereo channels. Most amplifiers deliver higher power when hooked up to four-ohm speakers than they will when they are driving eight-ohm speakers. When you compare power outputs, make sure that they are referenced to the same speaker impedances.

Selectivity is the ability of a tuner to pick up and isolate stations that are close in frequency to each other. It is quoted in dB (decibels); the higher the number, the better. Look for at least 60 dB.

Sensitivity is usually stated in microvolts (millionths of a volt) or in dBf (femtowatts). Excellent sensitivity figures of 2.0 microvolts or 10 to 12 dBf are typical. Sensitivity concerns you if you are attempting to receive weak radio stations or live in an area with poor reception.

Signal-to-Noise ratio (S/N) is a measure of how much background noise, or hiss, is present along with even strong signals. S/N is stated in dB; the higher the number, the better, but anything above 75 dB is adequate for normal listening.

Stereo separation is the amount of separation between left and right stereo channels when receiving stereo FM broadcasts. While manufacturers often list separation figures as high as 50 dB, anything above 30 dB is adequate. (The best phonograph cartridges rarely exceed 30 dB in separation.)

Tape monitor (Loop) is a set of output and input jacks that allows you to interpose an external audio component in the signal path of an amplifier to monitor recordings as you make them or to process the signal through a device, such as a graphic equalizer.

SONY STR-AV220/ STR-AV320

The Sony STR-AV220 and STR-AV320 receivers are the same, except that the STR-AV320 comes with a wireless remote control and 10 watts of additional power. The STR-AV220 produces 40 watts per channel, and its quartz-frequency synthesized tuner has direct-access tuning. A numbered keypad lets you tap in the exact station frequency. For example, if you want to tune in a station at 98.7, you just press 9-8-7. You can also scan up and down. Once tuned, you can assign the station one of 30 presets and recall it at the push of a single button. The STR-AV220 also includes a video input. A "matrix surround" button widens the breadth of the stereo image, providing the illusion of surround-sound while using only stereo speakers. Although the STR-AV220 lacks fancy features, it performs both well and reliably, making it an excellent stereo receiver for most homes.

Warranty: parts and labor, two years.

Approx. retail price	Approx. low price
$210 (STR-AV220)	not available
$240 (STR-AV320)	not available

ONKYO TX-844 ✓BEST BUY

The Onkyo TX-844 receiver has a larger-than-necessary power supply coupled with high-current output transistors. On musical peaks it can deliver more than its rated 60 watts per channel. The TX-844 has as much power as its predecessor and more features at a lower price, making it an even better Best Buy. The quartz-frequency synthesized AM/FM stereo tuner has 40 station presets, with battery-free backup to prevent memory loss. The presets, when used with the tuning memory scan, can be divided into six categories, such as rock, jazz, classical, etc. The TX-844 also has direct-access tuning with a numbered keypad that lets you key in the desired station frequency by number. Automatic Precision Reception (APR) monitors the FM reception and switches between stereo/mono, local/distance, and hi-blend on/off as needed for the best sound. This receiver also includes a CD direct mode, which bypasses the preamp, and a video input. An unusual extra is a sleep timer that shuts off the receiver automatically after a predetermined amount of time. The tone controls are more precise than on many receivers, and they are designed for the way your perception of high and low frequencies varies at different volumes. The bass boost is limited to deep bass, so it does not muddy the midrange. The TX-844 can create a simulated stereo sound from a mono source. It comes supplied with wireless remote control and can be used with Onkyo's optional multiroom remote.

Warranty: parts and labor, two years.

Approx. retail price	Approx. low price
$350	$295

Prices are accurate at time of printing; subject to manufacturer's change.

TECHNICS SA-GX500

The Technics SA-GX500 receiver initially appears intimidating with its dozens of controls, but it is actually easy to operate. Technics returns to old-fashioned knobs to adjust volume, balance, tone, and the quartz-frequency synthesized tuning. The different-sized knobs show you at a glance which control you are turning. There are 24 AM/FM station presets. A versatile, precise tone-control system, called parametric equalization, provides greater control over tonal adjustments. A switch permits totally bypassing the tone-control system for the most natural sound. Technics includes a Dolby surround-sound decoder for use with video systems, which sometimes can also enhance music recordings. There are two video inputs. The SA-GX500 delivers 80 watts per channel for the front channels, and an additional 15 watts per channel for the rear channels. A large fluorescent display fills a third of the front panel. It shows the relative frequency levels of what you're listening to, as well as the levels and actions of the tone controls. It shows all settings, radio frequency, and more. The supplied 48-key remote control can operate other Technics and Panasonic components.

Warranty: parts and labor, one year.

Approx. retail price	Approx. low price
$380	$330

LUXMAN R-115

RECOMMENDED

The Luxman R-115 receiver performs exceptionally well, but its steadily escalating price prevents it from being a Best Buy. This is an expensive receiver that performs so well that its price is justified. While it is rated at 270 watts per channel, it can actually produce twice that much power during loud musical passages. The R-115 is very stable and can drive the most unstable speakers. The digitally synthesized tuner delivers superb, low-noise FM stereo reception and reasonably good AM as well. The receiver features 20 presets. One excellent feature of this receiver is CD straight circuitry, which routes the input from a compact disc player directly to the power-

Prices are accurate at time of printing; subject to manufacturer's change.

amplifier section for the utmost sonic accuracy.
Warranty: parts and labor, five years.

Approx. retail price	Approx. low price
$850	$719

JVC RX-503BK

The JVC RX-503BK 80-watt-per-channel receiver employs unique convenience circuitry. CSRP (COMPU LINK Source-Related Presetting) memorizes your favorite settings (such as volume, tonal equalization, balance, etc.) for each source and even for individual radio stations. Switch to that source or station and all adjustments are made automatically. A computerized seven-band graphic equalizer (a versatile set of tone controls) works in conjunction with ten memory banks. You can create your own equalizations and name them, along with the five preprogrammed equalization settings that come from the factory. The amber and red fluorescent display spells out your equalization names (as well as indicating all other settings and functions). There are 40 AM/FM station presets, with the ability to display 20 sets of call letters. A simple surround-sound synthesizer circuit has outputs for use with an additional amplifier and speakers for a surround-soundlike enhancement. Operating this receiver can be slightly confusing, since all controls are similar-looking keys (buttons). The supplied remote control operates other JVC audio/video components.
Warranty: parts and labor, two years.

Approx. retail price	Approx. low price
$360	$272

PIONEER VSX-3600

The Pioneer VSX-3600 audio/video receiver offers considerable flexibility and value. In addition to 100 watts per channel, it also delivers 15 watts per channel for two rear channels. The rear channels are fed from the unit's Dolby surround-sound decoder with adjustable digital delay to compensate for your room size and the program source. There's also a stereo simulation mode for mono program sources. In addition to three audio inputs, the VSX-3600 includes two video inputs that will switch the audio and video from a VCR or laser videodisc player. The unit contains presets for 30 AM/FM stations, along with a custom memory tuning that categorizes your favorite stations in groups. A sleep timer turns the receiver off after 30 or 60 minutes. An auto-dimmer circuit dims the display. A seven-band graphic equalizer with indicator LEDs permits fine-tuned adjustments. The VSX-3600 will interface with Pioneer's multiroom control system adapter. Model VSX-3700S is the same receiver supplied with a programmable universal smart remote control, rather than the standard A/V remote.

Warranty: parts and labor, one year.

Approx. retail price	Approx. low price
$440	$330

COMPACT DISC PLAYERS

Compact discs (CDs) have revolutionized home sound reproduction. Until a few years ago, all home audio equipment stored and reproduced sound in analog form. The minute wiggles in the grooves of a vinyl record replicate actual sound vibrations; they are analogous to the original sound they represent. For instance, louder sounds increase the depth of the groove.

CDs store sound as a string of numbers. A digital recorder samples the sound thousands of times each second and assigns each sample a numerical value, based on a binary code of zero and one. These numbers represent electrical voltage pulses (one) or the absence of pulses (zero) that can be read and converted into sound by computer chips in CD players. The CD stores this digital information as a series of microscopic depressions, or pits, arranged in a continuous spiral pattern below its clear plastic surface. The player reads the reflection of a laser beam that tracks these pits, so nothing but a beam of light actually touches the CD while it plays.

CDs surpass the sound quality of LPs and analog tapes in many ways. Besides having virtually inaudible distortion and flat (uniform) frequency response, CDs do not produce the annoying noise and hiss of analog recordings. When you hear hiss on a CD, you are actually hearing the hiss from the original analog master tape. (Some CDs originate from analog recordings.) In addition, CDs add no wow and flutter, the annoying speed variations that cause a wavering of pitch.

CD players usually ignore small scratches and dust specks on the disc, although larger flaws can cause problems. Since CDs have no grooves to be worn away, with proper care they should last indefinitely. Always store your discs in their plastic boxes in a cool place. If you leave a CD in your car on a hot summer day, it can warp. The label side of a CD is more fragile than the silver data side, and writing on the label can damage the aluminum film.

Beware of CD gimmicks. Use no labels, adhesive rings, chemicals, or markers on the disc itself. The past year has seen a rise in such "magic" accessories that at best fail to improve performance and at worst harm the disc.

Programmability

The chief difference between CD players is in programming capabilities. "Programming" is a machine's ability to store instructions in its electronic memory and execute them in a given order.

CDs are divided into tracks. A disc that offers a dozen songs will have 12 tracks, numbered 1 through 12. For classical music, such as a symphony, track numbers are used to separate the piece's movements. Some CDs have other divisions. For example, a symphonic movement may have more than one melodic theme; such themes can be assigned index numbers in a given track.

A programmable CD player can, at the very least, play specific tracks in ascending sequence, such as tracks 1, 4, 7, 9, and 12, in that order. More sophisticated units can play tracks in a random but specified order, such as tracks 5, 2, 4, 3, and 9, in that order. A few CD players also let you program index numbers. Some machines can store six instructions in their memory; others accept 30 or more.

Many CD players also offer "repeat play." If you press a button they will play a disc or certain programmed tracks until the instruction is canceled. Many machines randomly shuffle the order in which tracks are played. A newly available programming feature permanently memorizes your favorite tracks on a disc. Some players with this feature store several hundred selections.

Features and Terminology

AAD to DDD: Virtually all discs now display a code indicating the origin of the program material. The letter A stands for an analog source, and the letter D stands for digital. The first letter indicates the nature of the original tape. The second letter reveals how the original recording was processed and mixed. The final letter shows that the material on the CD is digital.

Digital-to-analog (D/A) converters are microchips that translate digital numbers back to an analog form. The CD standard uses 16 bits, meaning that all discs contain blocks of 16-bit information. However, manufacturers encountered great difficulty in producing large quantities of perfect 16-bit D/A chips. Thus, many use 18- and 20-bit chips to retrieve information from the disc. They cannot retrieve additional sound, but often provide a greater margin of error for improved accuracy in the decoding process. The improvement is not always audible. A bad 20-bit converter is not always better than a good 16-bit converter.

Recently engineers developed a method of converting digital information to analog in a rapid stream of single bits. This 1-bit system is often known by its trade name of Bitstream. Each company proclaims a proprietary version of this technology, such as MASH, PEM, or PWM, along with a number-crunching technique called noise shaping that shifts what would have been audible noise outside the range of human hearing. One-bit D/A conversion improves sound at a lower cost than other methods, generally improving the sound of low-cost CD players. However, even among 1-bit conversion systems there are differences in quality, so this alone does not guarantee the best sound quality.

Error correction and tracking: Some manufacturers claim that a three-beam laser system is superior to a single-beam system. Both systems use only one laser, which is either split with lenses and prisms into three beams or used as a single beam. While either system can be effective, there are differences in tracking accuracy and stability between various CD players that are not due to how many beams are used.

If a CD player cannot read one or more numbers on a disc, an error may result, producing a crashing sound. If several errors occur in a short time, the sound becomes very distorted. Fortunately, CD players use error-correction systems, so you will not hear anything wrong. Dropouts (missing or obscured numbers) may be caused by a scratch or dirty area on the disc's surface. In testing CD players, we use a disc with calibrated dropouts that simulate scratches, dust, and fingerprints.

You can judge a CD player's tracking stability, as well as its resistance to external vibration and shock, by tapping lightly on the top and sides of the player's cabinet with your finger. CD players with superior tracking stability will play through such testing without missing a beat. Inferior machines may mistrack when tapped; you will hear a moment of interrupted sound or the machine will skip and move to another part of the disc.

Is Your Stereo Digital Ready?

You can connect a CD to most stereo systems, but you may not get the sound quality you expect. While you probably will not want to play your CDs any louder than you play LPs or tapes, the occasional peaks that occur in music will be 10 to 15 dB louder than if you were playing an LP or tape. So your amplifier must deliver 10 to 15 dB more power when playing CDs. A 10 dB increase represents a ten-to-one increase in power rating. This means your 30-watt receiver must deliver 300 watts per channel. Since most receivers do not usually operate at their maximum limit, you may not need to purchase a new amplifier for your CD player.

Another way to increase acoustic power is to switch to more efficient speakers. Efficiency is the amount of acoustic power you can get from a speaker that is fed a given amount of electrical audio power. If you own acoustic (air) suspension speakers or if your speaker enclosures are small, sealed boxes, you probably have low-efficiency units. Speakers with openings on their front surfaces are usually more efficient; they tend to be large, floor-standing models.

Sensitivity ratings can give you an idea of a speaker's efficiency. Low-efficiency speakers have sensitivity ratings of 80 to 85 dB per watt; medium-efficiency models have ratings between 86 and 89 dB; and high-efficiency units offer ratings higher than 90 dB, some as high as 98 dB or more.

A CD player must be connected to a receiver's high-level inputs, which are usually labeled "Aux" or "Tuner." If these inputs are not available, "Tape" or "Tape Play" may be suitable. Before connecting a CD player, check out the maximum input level permitted at the input jack. If the rating is less than two volts, choose a CD player that has an output level control.

TECHNICS SL-PS70

The Technics SL-PS70 CD player represents the company's top-of-the-line at a budget price. By using multiple 1-bit MASH D/A converters, Technics delivers superb sound with excellent linearity at a moderate cost. The system uses an eight-times oversampling filter, plus the MASH noise shaper operating at 32-times oversampling for remarkably clean sound. The analog circuitry is also quite good. Mechanically, the player includes special antivibration and antiresonance construction that reduces tracking errors. The linear transport motor that moves the laser benefits from Technic's expertise in direct-drive linear motors. The SL-PS70 has 20-track programming with direct-track access from a numbered keypad on the front panel or supplied remote control. The fluorescent display above the center-located disc-loading drawer shows track and index numbers. The deck automatically programs tracks to fit specific-length audiocassettes and finds the highest level on the disc.

Warranty: parts and labor, one year.

Approx. retail price	**Approx. low price**
$450	$364

Prices are accurate at time of printing; subject to manufacturer's change.

DENON DCD-660

The Denon DCD-660 improves upon last year's model at the same price. It uses dual 18-bit D/A converters, with 20-bit, eight-times oversampling digital filters. Although it does not use 1-bit technology, it does use noise shaping, which results in an impressively low noise level for such an inexpensive player. An exceptional new feature is a digital pitch control, unique on digital devices, but common on analog turntables. This feature allows you to vary the pitch of a CD if you wish to tune it to the instrument you play, practice dance steps at a different rhythm, or just speed up a song to fit it onto a tape. This digital circuitry also permits programmable digital fades, allowing you to select the length of the fade from the numeric keypad. Digital fades are lower in noise than analog fades. The laser pickup is mounted in a new floating suspension for even greater shock and vibration isolation. The DCD-660 arranges tracks for the best fit onto an audiocassette, as well as peak level search. The player has 20-track programming, with direct-track access from a numbered keypad or the supplied remote control. The six-digit fluorescent display includes a music calendar for easy programming and shows track numbers (and total disc tracks) as well as toggling between playing time, total playing time, and total remaining time. Defective/dirty discs cause the DCD-660 few problems, and it survives most shocks and vibration.

Warranty: parts and labor, one year.

Approx. retail price
$300

Approx. low price
$286

SONY CDP-X55ES

The Sony CDP-X55ES performs nearly identically to the top-of-the-line CDP-X77ES, but for $1,000 less. By eliminating the use of obscure materials, a professional output, and hand-selected parts, the CDP-X55ES has virtually the same specifications (and critical internal components) as the more expensive model, with equally fast and dependable mechanical performance. In fact, the CDP-X55ES even includes a few programming features Sony left off its top model. The CDP-55ES uses Sony's proprietary 1-bit D/A system with multiple D/A converters, eight-times oversampling, and 45-bit noise-shaping circuitry. This quality runs through the entire player all the way to the gold-plated output jacks. It offers 24-track programming, with direct-track access from a numbered keypad and supplied remote control. A "custom file" feature memorizes your favorite tracks on up to 185 discs, and includes a memo feature that displays the title of, or note about, the disc playing on the fluorescent display. That display also shows track and timing information, plus a music calendar for ease of programming. The shuffle play feature plays tracks in random order. Sony's most advanced electronic and mechanical technology results in impeccable sound and plenty of operating convenience.

Warranty: parts and labor, three years.

Approx. retail price	**Approx. low price**
$900	$814

MAGNAVOX CDB624   RECOMMENDED

The Magnavox CDB624 CD player represents leading-edge technology at a popular price. The mechanical system may be lightweight, but the electronics are first rate. The CDB624 uses dual 1-bit Bitstream D/A converters. It's also one of the lowest-priced players to include a digital output, which will come in handy if you want to make direct digital dubs to DAT. It includes Favorite Track Selection (FTS), which memorizes your favorite tracks on over 200 CDs. The 31-button remote control provides direct-track access. You can program up to 20 tracks.

Warranty: one year.

Approx. retail price	**Approx. low price**
$300	not available

COMPACT DISC CHANGERS

SONY CDP-C705

The CDP-C705 five-disc CD changer contains virtually all of the circuitry and more features than Sony's more expensive

---

Prices are accurate at time of printing; subject to manufacturer's change.

"ES" version. The CDP-C705 uses dual 18-bit D/A converters with eight-times oversampling digital filters and Sony's proprietary noise-shaping technique. This results in sound equivalent to many of the 1-bit systems. The changer has a carousel that works like a lazy Susan. This system is more convenient and less expensive than a magazine system, and it can hold CDs without adapters. The CDP-C705 offers 32-track multidisc programming (although the fluorescent display shows only 20 tracks at a time), with direct-track access to any disc from the supplied remote control. A music calendar display simplifies programming. Sony's Custom File stores your favorite tracks on up to 185 discs, including a title or memo for the fluorescent display. The CDP-C705 plays damaged and dirty discs very well.

Warranty: parts and labor, one year.

Approx. retail price	**Approx. low price**
$380	$329

TECHNICS SL-PC25/SL-PC15 ✓BEST BUY

The Technics SL-PC25 and SL-PC15 are the same, except the SL-PC15 comes without remote control. The Technics SL-PC25 is the successor to one of the most popular CD changers on the market, offering improved circuitry at a lower price. That price decrease was made possible by the installation of an entirely automated robotic assembly line. The SL-PC25 is a carousel CD changer, which lets you lift the lid and change four of its five discs while the fifth one is playing. This feature also allows you to see what discs are loaded without interrupting the music. The SL-PC25 uses a very fast linear motor to move the laser. It employs four of the very latest 1-bit D/A converters with four-times oversampling digital filters and MASH noise shaping. The SL-PC25 includes 32-track programming and shuffle play among the discs. It can also randomly play your 32 programmed selections. Direct-disc and track access is available from both the front panel and supplied remote control. The player automatically calculates CD track lengths and arrangement for optimal recording onto audiocassettes. The two-color, easy-to-read fluorescent display shows all necessary information. Considering the player's lightweight construction, it withstands considerable abuse before mistracking.

Warranty: parts and labor, one year.

Approx. retail price	Approx. low price
$260 (SL-PC25)	not available
$230 (SL-PC15)	not available

SONY CDP-C75ES RECOMMENDED

The Sony CDP-C75ES is a top-quality five-disc magazine-loading player. The magazine design permits loading of single discs without difficulty. The CDP-C75ES uses a one-bit converter with eight-time oversampling digital filters and Sony's proprietary noise shaping. The Custom File can be programmed to recognize individual magazines as well as discs (a total of 185 discs). The player offers 32-track programming, as well as shuffle play. There are optical digital outputs for connection with other digital components. Considering that it juggles five discs, the CDP-C75ES operates quickly. It is rarely affected by shock and vibration, and plays damaged and dirty discs very well.

Warranty: parts and labor, three years.

Approx. retail price	Approx. low price
$400	$400

TURNTABLE

Compact discs and cassette tapes with improved sound are rapidly replacing conventional records. But many music lovers have large collections of conventional LP records and want to play them on a good turntable.

The function of a turntable is simple. All it has to do is rotate at a constant speed while introducing no audible noise or vibration via the tonearm and mounted cartridge that trace the minute undulations found in a record groove. Turntables are either direct driven or belt driven. In a belt-driven turntable, a rubber or neoprene belt couples the motor shaft to the platter. In a direct-driven turntable, the shaft of a slow-speed motor revolving at the required revolutions per minute (rpm) actually forms the center spindle of the turntable platter. The method of drive is less important than the performance specifications that result from a particular design.

TECHNICS SL-QD33

✓**BEST BUY**

The Technics SL-QD33 is a fully automatic turntable that features quartz direct drive to prevent even minor speed changes. Its low wow and flutter is $^{24}/_{1000}$ percent. A straight low-mass tonearm accepts easily installed P-mount cartridges. The base of the turntable is supported by large insulated feet with damping qualities to absorb external vibrations.
Warranty: parts and labor, one year.

Approx. retail price	**Approx. low price**
$200	$160

PHONO CARTRIDGES

A phonograph cartridge is a transducer; it translates one kind of signal into another, converting the movement of the stylus into electrical signals. There are three basic phono cartridge designs:

P-mount cartridges plug into sockets in the front of tonearms that are designed to accept them.

Moving-magnet cartridges use magnetic induction, and all preamplifiers, integrated amplifiers, and receivers have inputs that can deal with signals from them.

Moving-coil cartridges are more expensive than moving-magnet cartridges, and some listeners insist they offer superior sound quality. Most moving-coil cartridges must be sent to an authorized service center when the stylus, or needle, needs to be replaced. Some preamplifiers, integrated amplifiers, and receivers need a special pre-preamplifier, or a step-up transformer, to use signals from this type of cartridge.

Prices are accurate at time of printing; subject to manufacturer's change.

SHURE VST V

The Shure VST V is the last phono cartridge that you will ever need to buy. Twenty-five years of engineering are evident in the performance of this budget-priced cartridge. It is basically the scaled-down version of the famed Shure V15 Type V-MR. It simply costs $200 less. The VST V comes without the fancy box, the printed individual response curve, and all the frills. You still get the incomparable Micro-Ridge (MR) stylus shape and beryllium cantilever. The VST V will track the most difficult records with a clean, clear, neutral sound. The user-replacement stylus makes future stylus replacement easy. Shure remains committed to replace any stylus for the life of the company. The easy-to-install VST V will provide indefinite hours of listening pleasure.

Warranty: one year.

Approx. retail price	**Approx. low price**
$100	$85

SHURE V15 TYPE V-MR

The Shure V15 Type V-MR is a moving-magnet cartridge that has exceptional tracking ability. The MR suffix stands for "Micro-Ridge," which means that the stylus tip is shaped to hug the walls of any record groove. This cartridge weighs less than 6 $\frac{3}{5}$ grams and uses a stylus tip that measures $\frac{15}{100}$ mils in its narrowest dimension and 3 mils along its longer axis.

Warranty: parts and labor, one year.

Approx. retail price	**Approx. low price**
$297	$155

AUDIO-TECHNICA AT 120E/T

RECOMMENDED

The Audio-Technica AT 120E/T is a moving-magnet cartridge that employs a titanium-bonded stylus. It has an overall frequency response capacity from 15 to 25,000 hertz. Special dual-magnet construction provides excellent response and good separation (29 dB at midfrequencies). The tracking force range is from 1 to 1 $\frac{4}{5}$ grams.

Prices are accurate at time of printing; subject to manufacturer's change.

Warranty: parts and labor, one year.

Approx. retail price
$95

Approx. low price
not available

CASSETTE DECKS

An audiocassette recorder is nearly as common in most households as a television or telephone. However, before you shop for a single- or dual-transport cassette deck for your stereo system, read through this brief explanation of the major specifications that you may want to evaluate when choosing a deck.

Frequency response, distortion, and signal-to-noise ratio are closely related. *Frequency response* sometimes is improved at the expense of distortion and signal-to-noise ratio. But achieving the true hi-fi range of 20 to 20,000 hertz may not mean that the overall sound quality is better, since most humans (especially as they get older) cannot hear much above 15,000 hertz and few instruments other than a grand pipe organ produce tones that go much below 30 hertz. When you compare the frequency response of two machines, be sure that the response of each is accompanied by a tolerance, usually stated as plus or minus a certain number of decibels (dB); otherwise the frequency response statement is meaningless.

Distortion is quoted by tape manufacturers for a 0 dB recording level, the maximum level at which you will want to record. This specification depends on the type of tape, but it should be no higher than one percent.

Signal-to-noise ratios (S/N) for cassette decks should be a prime consideration. Once you have selected a tape deck, you should use one of the types of tape recommended by the manufacturer of that recorder. Avoid bargain brands of tape for all but voice-taping applications.

Wow and flutter is a measurement of tape-speed fluctuation. It is usually listed as a percentage, followed by the acronym WRMS. For example, a wow and flutter specification might

Prices are accurate at time of printing; subject to manufacturer's change.

read "$\frac{1}{10}$ percent WRMS." Look for the lowest percentage available within your budget limitations.

Bias, equalization, and level setting adjustments are not available on all cassette decks, but some tape decks offer fine-tuning controls that let you adjust for slight differences in the bias of recording tapes. Other decks control adjustments with microprocessor chips. These circuits test the tape and adjust for the optimum bias, equalization, and sensitivity to provide the best performance from a tape.

Three-head cassette decks have one head for erase, another for recording, and a third for playback. This arrangement provides the same sort of rapid off-the-tape monitoring capability found on professional open-reel machines.

Types of Tape

Several different types of recording tape are used by cassette recorders. The different types of tape require different levels of recording bias voltage, which is a high frequency signal that must accompany all audio signals being recorded on tape to achieve low levels of distortion and high levels of output.

Normal tape (Type I) is coated with ferric oxide and requires a moderate amount of recording bias voltage. **Chrome tape** (Type II) refers to either a formulation of chromium dioxide particles or ferric oxide tape that has been treated with cobalt particles. This kind of tape requires a higher level of bias. **Metal tape** (Type IV) requires the highest bias level of any of these three kinds of tape. It offers better high-frequency recording capability, particularly at high volume levels, and better overall frequency response. A little-known benefit is that it is less subject to gradual erasure from magnetized tape heads and stray magnetic fields. Recently the cost of metal tape has declined, making it a good choice for most music recordings. Many companies now offer metal tapes (Type IV) at chrome (Type II) prices.

Tape Brands

The brand of tape you choose determines the quality of recording as much as the machine you buy. For ultimate performance, pick one representative of each tape type (normal, chrome, metal) and have a service technician adjust the deck for that tape. Then stick with it. The instruction manuals of some decks already specify the tapes for which the machine comes adjusted. We recommend three tape brands for the most reliable service and highest fidelity: Maxell, TDK, and Sony. These brands employ superior shells and internal mechanisms for superior mechanical stability.

Noise-Reduction Systems

Even with the very best cassette tape and the very best cassette recorder, you will probably notice some tape hiss, or noise, when playing back your recordings. Hiss is especially noticeable during playback of softer musical passages. Several electronic techniques are available to reduce the audible effects of tape noise.

Dolby B reduces high-frequency noise by a factor of 10 dB; this is equivalent to the noise having been reduced to half its perceived intensity. Another system, **dbx noise reduction**, not only reduces noise by as much as 35 dB but also permits you to record the full dynamic range (loudest louds and softest softs) of a music program without having to compress that range. Unfortunately, dbx is incompatible with other systems. **Dolby C** offers twice as much noise reduction as Dolby B. While Dolby C-encoded tapes can be played back successfully on decks that have Dolby B, the tapes are incompatible with decks that have no Dolby decoding.

Dolby HX-Pro is a headroom-expansion (HX) system that, unlike noise-reduction systems, works only while recording. Dolby HX-Pro adjusts the recording current, or bias, to allow higher levels of high frequencies (treble) on the tape. With more signal on the tape, the signal-to-noise ratio is improved. A deck with HX-Pro will make superior tapes.

Dolby S is a consumer version of the professional Dolby SR system. It provides the greatest degree of noise reduction on the market with the least adverse effect on the sound quality of music. Dolby claims that Dolby S-encoded tapes can be decoded by Dolby C-equipped machines without a highly noticeable effect on sound quality. Several companies have announced plans for Dolby S-equipped decks, but problems in fabricating a single Dolby S computer chip have slowed actual deck introductions. Expect Dolby S-equipped decks to sell in the same price range as DAT machines, with sound close to DAT quality.

Single-Transport Cassette Decks

SONY TC-K620

The Sony TC-K620 cassette deck combines the most important features for good sound with the fewest frills. Three motors provide durability and smooth tape handling. Three tape heads specialize in erase, record, or play, and permit tape/source monitor. Dolby B and C noise reduction, coupled with Dolby HX-Pro, assure low-noise recordings with wide dynamic range. Large, logically arranged, clearly labeled controls make the TC-K620 easy to operate. The unit includes a real-time tape counter as part of its fluorescent display. The deck automatically senses the type of tape (normal/chrome/metal) loaded. A manual bias adjustment can fine-tune for different brands of tape. The automatic music sensor (AMS) system skips forward or back to locate individual songs on the tape.

Warranty: parts and labor, one year.

Approx. retail price	Approx. low price
$350	$300

TECHNICS RS-BR465

The Technics RS-BR465 uses two motors for good tape control in this quick-auto-reverse cassette deck. Dolby B and C noise reduction coupled with Dolby HX-Pro provide low noise with wide dynamic range. The deck automatically senses tape type, while a manual fine-tuning control adjusts bias for different brands of normal and chrome tapes. The tape counter that is a part of the multicolor fluorescent display shows arbitrary numbers rather than real time. The auto-reverse operates very rapidly. When the RS-BR465 is used in conjunction with a

---

Prices are accurate at time of printing; subject to manufacturer's change.

Technics CD player, the Synchro-Edit function makes CD-to-tape copies easy. The deck can be operated with remote controls supplied with other Technics components.

Warranty: parts and labor, one year.

Approx. retail price	Approx. low price
$230	$184

PIONEER CT-M6R

✔**BEST BUY**

The Pioneer CT-M6R is a unique cassette deck that makes quality recordings, but also is an auto-reverse cassette changer. It can record or play any of the six cassettes you load—that means up to nine hours of uninterrupted recording or playback. Yet the deck makes few compromises in recording quality. It incorporates Dolby B and C noise reduction coupled with Dolby HX-Pro for low noise and wide dynamic range. The deck has many automatic features including cassette-scan, which plays the first ten seconds of each cassette to remind you of its contents, and music skip search for up to 15 selections in either direction. The fluorescent display includes a real-time tape counter. The deck automatically senses tape type. When used with a Pioneer CD changer, the CT-M6R can automatically copy multiple discs making optimum use of the tape and never missing a song.

Warranty: parts and labor, one year.

Approx. retail price	Approx. low price
$450	$315

ONKYO TA-2200

RECOMMENDED

The Onkyo TA-2200 is an affordable cassette deck with a two-motor tape transport for smooth tape motion and good longevity. The motors (one for the capstan that drives the tape and one for the tape spindles) are controlled by a computer chip. The deck automatically adjusts for tape type. The fluorescent display includes a real-time tape counter. The deck has Dolby B and C noise reduction, as well as Dolby HX-Pro. The TA-2200 includes an autoscan feature that automatically skips ahead to find the next selection(s) and a repeat mode that can replay individual selections or blocks of sections.

Prices are accurate at time of printing; subject to manufacturer's change.

Warranty: parts and labor, one year.

Approx. retail price	**Approx. low price**
$330	not available

NAKAMICHI CR-4A RECOMMENDED

The Nakamichi CR-4A performs like a Best Buy, but its high price and professional design suggest that it is more for a person looking strictly for uncompromised recording quality without other features. This three-head, three-motor deck includes Dolby B and C noise reduction. To compensate for the lack of Dolby HX-Pro, the deck uses proprietary tape heads that increase headroom without the HX-Pro circuitry. These heads permit a high-frequency response of 21,000 hertz, which is rarely reached on most tape decks. Nakamichi provides test tones and adjustment controls to precisely match bias and Dolby level to the tape being used. An asymmetrical transport design eliminates resonances to ensure ultrasmooth tape motion. The Nakamichi tape transport employs a motor-driven cam just to engage the various functions, such as fast rewind and play. The functions are so gentle that you may have to look to reassure yourself that the tape is actually moving. The machine displays recording level with highly accurate, easy-to-read LED indicators. The only oversight is a lack of a real-time tape counter.

Warranty: parts and labor, one year.

Approx. retail price	**Approx. low price**
$995	$895

Dual-Transport Cassette Decks

AIWA AD-WX515

The Aiwa AD-WX515 cassette deck offers essential recording features at very good value. It's a simple, budget deck that still includes Dolby B and C noise reduction. It offers high-speed dubbing, continuous playback, and automatic tape-type selection. An antimodulation tape stabilizer, normally found in more expensive decks, improves tape-drive stability to reduce

a particularly annoying form of distortion.
Warranty: not available.

Approx. retail price	**Approx. low price**
$200	$147

SONY TC-WR90ES

The Sony TC-WR90ES delivers maximum versatility from a dual-transport auto-reverse cassette deck without compromising recording quality. The TC-WR90ES plays and records on both transports, permitting you to make two copies at once from another source or sequential recordings that start recording on transport B when transport A is finished. This is ideal for concerts and opera. Relay play does the same thing in playback, starting transport B when transport A has finished. The deck features high-frequency Super Bias with laser amorphous tape heads, as well as Dolby B and Dolby C noise reduction and Dolby HX-Pro. A real-time tape counter on the fluorescent display tells you the tape position in minutes and seconds. As with most dual-transport machines, you can copy tapes at double speed. The TC-WR90ES also includes automatic sensing for the type of tape loaded and an automatic music sensor that can skip forward to the next selection or back to the beginning of the current selection.
Warranty: parts and labor, one year.

Approx. retail price	**Approx. low price**
$400	not available

JVC TD-W803BK   RECOMMENDED

The JVC TD-W803BK dual-transport auto-reverse cassette deck plays and records on both transports for up to three hours of uninterrupted recording. The deck will also continuously play two tapes for "endless" music. It incorporates Dolby B and C noise reduction along with Dolby HX-Pro for low-noise recordings with wide dynamic range. The intelligently laid out controls assisted by computer logic make operation easy. The deck automatically senses tape type. It has high-speed dubbing. The music-scan feature works on both transports and can scan from tape to tape. The only drawback

Prices are accurate at time of printing; subject to manufacturer's change.

to this machine is JVC's use of mechanical tape counters rather than an electronic display.

Warranty: parts and labor, one year.

Approx. retail price	Approx. low price
$370	$319

ONKYO TA-RW490 RECOMMENDED

The Onkyo TA-RW490 may seem to be high priced, but it is actually two complete cassette decks with all the features of separate decks. The TA-RW490 uses dual transports, each of which has two motors and is computer controlled. Both transports can record and play back. The quick auto-reverse is triggered by a fast-acting infrared sensor rather than the tension of the tape reaching the end of its leader. This means you'll miss barely a second of recording when the tape reverses. The TA-RW490 includes Dolby B and C noise reduction, as well as Dolby HX-Pro. Like most dual-transport decks, both transports offer sequential play. In addition, both transports can record sequentially, providing three hours of virtually uninterrupted recording. You can also make two recordings of the same source simultaneously. Direct music search on both transports skips forward or backward to find selections for dubbing. There is even an individual real-time tape counter for each transport. This deck lacks little in features or performance. The TA-RW490 has dropped a notch in our listings only because of its relatively high price in relation to the competition.

Warranty: parts and labor, one year.

Approx. retail price	Approx. low price
$630	$432

DAT

Digital Audio Tape (DAT) made its long-delayed appearance in June 1990 when Sony began shipping the first DAT decks to dealers. DAT is to the analog cassette as CD is to the analog LP record. It records digitally using a system similar, but not iden-

---

Prices are accurate at time of printing; subject to manufacturer's change.

tical, to CD. DAT records using 16 data bits, but with a sampling rate of 48,000 hertz, rather than the CD rate of 44,100 hertz. Otherwise, the quality specifications that apply to CD apply to DAT.

The reason the record industry fought DAT's arrival was that the system is capable of recording with fidelity virtually identical to the source material. Whereas regular tapes lose a bit of fidelity with each copy, you can digitally copy from one DAT to another DAT to another, etc., with the final copy still sounding like the original. This assumes that you make all the copies digitally. DAT decks can also make unrestricted copies with their analog inputs and outputs, but the results are not as perfect as when using the digital inputs and outputs, because the signal must first go through a digital-to-analog converter (D/A) and then back again through an analog-to-digital (A/D) converter.

The record industry and DAT manufacturers reached a compromise during the summer of 1989. Dutch electronics giant Philips, which invented the analog compact cassette, developed a microchip that would limit digital copying without affecting sound quality. This chip, called Serial Copy Management System (SCMS), allows you to make a digital DAT copy from a digital source. For example, you can copy a CD onto DAT using the digital output from the CD player and the digital input on the DAT, but you can't make digital copies of that copy. You can copy that same CD as many times as you like onto DAT. You can also copy DAT to DAT digitally one time. Analog sources such as LPs or radios can be recorded on DAT, and then be digitally copied from DAT to DAT once, but no more.

DAT not only far surpasses the fidelity of conventional cassettes, it also offers superior tape handling. Any selection on a tape can be located within a minute by the touch of a button. DAT cassettes are about half the size of analog cassettes, and come in lengths of up to two hours.

As we go to press, recording artists and composers are vowing to block the sale of DAT machines in the United States until the imposition of a royalty tax on DAT machines and tapes.

SONY DTC-700

The Sony DTC-700 Digital Audio Tape deck offers all the performance advantages of DAT at a lower price than a premium analog cassette deck. The DTC-700 includes all the convenience features you've come to expect from CDs, although most functions operate more slowly, since the deck must shuttle the tape back and forth to locate selections. When recording, the deck automatically marks the beginning of each recording; you can also push a button to mark each selection individually. It comes equipped with the SCMS chip, permitting direct digital copying from CD. Sony has been selling digital recorders longer than any other company, and the design and fidelity of the DTC-700 prove it. Model DTC-75ES is essentially similar with a few minor refinements, such as a copper-clad chassis.

Warranty: parts and labor, one year.

Approx. retail price	Approx. low price
$900	$800

TECHNICS SV-DA10

The Technics SV-DA10 includes all standard DAT performance and convenience features, such as easily marking selections for rapid locating. Tape motion is exceptionally smooth. Technics uses its proprietary 1-bit MASH circuitry not only for the D/A converters, but also for the A/D converters. This means that recordings from analog sources, such as live music, might actually sound better than some professional DAT recorders that still use less sophisticated A/D converters.

Warranty: one year.

Approx. retail price	Approx. low price
$900	$800

Stereo Systems

Stereo systems, which are often called rack systems, are audio component systems that are designed to work well together. When you shop for a stereo system, consider which components it includes, its audio power, and its sound quality. Additional features you may wish to consider are remote-control selection of program source and automatic shutoff of one component, such as the tuner, when another program source, such as the tape player, is selected. The speakers are usually the weakest component of rack systems. Most electronics manufacturers do not make good loudspeakers. If possible, you should select different speakers than the ones supplied with the system. A recent trend has been toward compact, or "mini," systems. These fit big sound into stylish downsized components.

For additional information about stereo components, please refer to the preceding chapter.

Best Buys '91

Our Best Buy and Recommended stereo systems follow. They are divided into full-size stereo systems and compact stereo systems. Within each category, systems are listed by quality; the item we consider the best of the Best Buys is first, followed by our second choice, and so on. Remember that a Best Buy or Recommended designation applies only to the model listed; it does not necessarily apply to other models made by the same manufacturer or to an entire product line.

Prices are accurate at time of printing; subject to manufacturer's change.

FULL-SIZE STEREO SYSTEMS

ONKYO FUSION A/V 900C

The Onkyo Fusion A/V 900C combines separate high-quality components into a reasonably priced rack system housed in attractive simulated oak cabinetry. The 100 watt-per-channel integrated amplifier includes a pair of video inputs as well as the standard array of audio inputs, including CD direct. The very good AM/FM stereo tuner features 20 station presets with a battery-free memory backup. The dual-transport cassette deck with Dolby B and C noise reduction permits high-speed dubbing and continuous play. The CD player uses dual 18-bit D/A converters with eight-times oversampling digital filters. It has 20-track programming with a music calendar display. The system comes with a semiautomatic, belt-driven turntable. It has a vibration-absorbing mat, which is important in a rack system where the turntable is often close to the speakers. The tower three-way bass reflex speakers feature a 12-inch polypropylene woofer, a 5-inch midrange, and a 1-inch tweeter. The identical system is available with a five-disc carousel CD changer for $100 more as the A/V 910C, which is also considered a Best Buy.

Warranty: parts and labor, one to two years, depending on component.

Approx. retail price	Approx. low price
$1,560	$900

TECHNICS SC-S210

The Technics SC-S210 stereo system offers high power and high technology at an affordable price. The SC-S210 combines a 110-watt-per-channel integrated amplifier with very low distortion, a five-disc carousel CD changer, a quartz-synthesized AM/FM stereo tuner, a dual-transport auto-reverse cassette deck, and a servo-controlled belt-driven semiautomatic turntable. The amplifier, electronically matched to the tower speakers, includes a special bass boost circuit called Super Bass. The CD changer uses Technics' 1-bit D/A converters with MASH noise-shaping circuitry. The CD player synchronizes with the cassette deck for dubbing discs to tape. The cassette deck has Dolby B noise reduction and high-speed dubbing. The quartz-synthesized tuner has 24 station presets with direct station access. A large, easy-to-read fluorescent display shows station frequency, preset number, and band. The three-way speakers include a 10-inch woofer. The supplied full-function remote control provides direct track access for the CD player, and also controls Panasonic TVs and VCRs. A graphic equalizer is an option.

Warranty: parts and labor, one year; **speakers, parts and labor**, three years.

Approx. retail price	Approx. low price
$1,100	$983

SONY R-2000CD

The Sony R-2000CD manages to offer high power and good performance in a bargain-priced system. While the amplifier, tuner, and cassette deck look like separate units, they are powered by a single power supply. The 100-watt-per-channel amplifier includes a five-band graphic equalizer with an LED display. The tuner uses an LCD (liquid crystal display) and has 25 station presets, with other conveniences such as scan and auto-tuning. The dual transport cassette deck includes Dolby B noise reduction and features high-speed dubbing. The CD player incorporates dual D/A converters with four-times over-sampling digital filters. Rounding out this complete system is a belt-driven semiautomatic turntable. The three-way tower speakers, finished in simulated oak veneer (as is the equipment rack), feature 10-inch woofers. An added bonus is the supplied remote control.

Warranty: parts and labor, one year.

Approx. retail price	Approx. low price
$750	$583

PIONEER SYSCOM X6600BK ✔BEST BUY

The Pioneer Syscom X6600BK not only combines every component and feature you could desire, but adds an additional twist: It can serve as the center of a multiroom sound system and will function with Pioneer's multiroom remote control. The X6600BK redefines convenience, with both CD and cassette changers. At the center is a 130-watt-per-channel integrated amplifier incorporating a five-band graphic equalizer with a colorful fluorescent spectrum analyzer display showing you the relative levels of each adjustable frequency. The amplifier includes switching and input/output for a Dolby surround-sound processor. The quartz-phase-locked-loop AM/FM stereo tuner has 36 station presets. The six-disc magazine-style CD changer uses dual 18-bit D/A converters with 20-bit eight-times oversampling digital filter. It has 32-track programming and a memory hold for instant recall of programmed plays, last-played discs, etc. The CD changer works in conjunction with the six-cassette changer. Synchronization circuitry allows accurate, uninterrupted copying of up to six discs. The cassette changer offers many of the same features as a CD player, such as cassette scan and cassette random play. It has Dolby B and C noise reduction, an automatic tape selector, and an electronic tape counter. The tower speakers are fairly narrow and include dual 8-inch woofers, 2½-inch tweeters, and ¾-inch supertweeters with a built-in protection circuit. The speakers and equipment cabinet come finished in either black or simulated oak. Pioneer supplies a full-function remote control. A fully automatic direct-driven turntable and Dolby surround-sound processor are optional. A similar, but not identical, system (X5600SBK) at the same price trades the cassette changer for a dual-transport cassette deck and a turntable, as well as a few watts of power for a surround-sound equipped amplifier.

Warranty: parts and labor, one year.

Approx. retail price	**Approx. low price**
$1,550	**$1,400**

SONY R-7000CD5

RECOMMENDED

The Sony R-7000CD5 offers high performance in an expensive rack system. It's designed for the listener who desires flexibility and first-rate sound, but who lacks interest in purchasing and connecting separate components. The system can serve as the center of a whole-house system. The four-channel integrated amplifier produces 150 watts per channel for the front channels and 30 watts per channel for the rear channels. It includes a digital Dolby surround-sound processor with adjustable rear-channel delay. It has four audio and four video inputs, plus two video outputs. The sensitive, selective tuner has 30 station presets, with auto-tuning and station scan. The dual-transport auto-reverse cassette deck has both Dolby B and C noise reduction. Its full-logic controls make it simple to operate. It offers high-speed dubbing. The CD player is a five-disc carousel changer with dual D/A converters and four-times oversampling digital filters. You can program up to 32 tracks. Completing the system is a servo-controlled, belt-driven, semiautomatic turntable. Four speakers accompany the R-7000CD5. The two main three-way tower speakers each have a 12-inch woofer, with a 12-inch passive radiator for added bass. The much smaller rear-channel speakers are for the Dolby surround-sound effect. The entire system is finished in simulated oak veneer. The same system, with the addition of an equalizer, but finished in real oak veneer, costs an additional $600 (not a very good value unless furniture is very important to you). A sophisticated programmable remote control is supplied with the system. The remote can be programmed to control almost any audio or video equipment at which you point it.

Warranty: parts and labor, one year.

Approx. retail price	Approx. low price
$1,800	$1,400

COMPACT STEREO SYSTEMS

YAMAHA YST-C11

The Yamaha YST-C11 is a compact system with contemporary styling that uses advanced technology to deliver big sound from its small speakers. The system combines an amplifier featuring Yamaha's active servo technology, AM/FM stereo tuner, dual-transport auto-reverse cassette deck, four-band

Prices are accurate at time of printing; subject to manufacturer's change.

graphic equalizer, and a CD player in a petite package. Each component matches or exceeds the performance of many components found in full-size systems. The active servo technology custom-matches the speakers to the amp, and by using special feedback circuitry, produces low, accurate bass from these miniature speakers. The redesigned speakers supplied with the YST-C11 offer better bass performance than those supplied with the previous YST-C10 model. The system includes a phase-locked-loop synthesized AM/FM stereo tuner with direct station access and ten station presets. Direct track access is also available on the CD player. The dual-transport cassette deck with Dolby B noise reduction records on only one transport, but features auto-reverse on both transports. The CD player has 20-track programming capability.

Warranty: parts and labor, two years.

Approx. retail price	Approx. low price
$1,000	$1,000

JVC MX-1

The JVC MX-1 is one of the most flexible mini systems on the market. The six modules that make up the MX-1 can be stacked in several combinations, such as a minitower if shelf space is limited, or a sleek horizontal system only a few inches high. JVC borrows a page from expensive audiophile systems by providing a separate amplifier for the bass subwoofer in addition to the stereo amplifiers. The miniature amplifier even uses a new cooling technology allowing it to produce 30 watts per channel, plus 40 watts to the subwoofer, without ugly cooling fins. The other components include a CD player, a dual-transport auto-reverse cassette deck with Dolby B, a quartz-synthesized AM/FM stereo tuner with 40-station presets, and a seven-band graphic equalizer with computer memories. Direct CD track access and station preset access is provided by the supplied full-function remote control. The MX-1 offers a variety of CD-to-tape dubbing options, including auto-fade at the end of a tape and high-speed dubbing from tape to tape.

Warranty: parts and labor, one year.

Approx. retail price	Approx. low price
$1,000	$800

Prices are accurate at time of printing; subject to manufacturer's change.

Personal Stereos

Sony celebrated the tenth anniversary of its Walkman in 1989. Yet it's hard to believe that the headphone stereo, also known as a personal portable, hasn't always been around. The same period saw the rise of the larger all-in-one portable stereo system commonly called a "boom box." The personal stereo can be as small as a set of headphones with integral radio, while the boom box can be as large as a suitcase. Personal stereos can combine radios, tape players (and recorders), or CD players. The even more versatile boom box can contain any combination of radio, tape player, and/or CD player, and even tape-dubbing dual-cassette transports.

Various portable models offer a variety of the following features: Dolby B and Dolby C noise reduction, auto-reverse, automatic music search (AMS), a graphic equalizer for fine-tuning frequency response, bass boosters, water resistance, and recording capability. Portables may also supply integral rechargeable batteries, solar power, TV sound (on units with radio tuners), and digitally synthesized tuning. Many of these features are marketing ploys rather than performance enhancements. However, you may find auto-reverse and digitally synthesized tuning with preset station buttons a great convenience. Dolby noise reduction provides an appreciable improvement in the sound of tapes.

Choosing a Portable

Most major brand-name portable stereos perform impressively under ideal conditions, but the true test of a portable is how it performs when it is in motion. Listen for tape skewing (a varying amount of treble) and wow and flutter (warbling or off-speed sound) while you shake and vibrate the unit to simulate jogging or cycling.

The critical test of FM reception occurs in cities where the unit may overload from nearby transmitters. This is often compounded by multipath distortion caused by signals bouncing between tall buildings. A stereo/mono switch or a local/distant switch helps in these situations. Some FM-only models use automatic stereo/mono blending to help smooth out the rapid and distorting change between stereo and monaural sound that can occur when you are downtown. Another test of reception occurs inside steel and concrete buildings that shield the stereo's antenna from radio signals. The length of the headphone cord determines the quality of FM reception in units where the cord acts as the FM antenna. A few inches more or less than the ideal 31 inches makes a difference.

Upgrading Your Portable System

Even though the electronics used in portable stereos are constantly being improved, many units come with inferior headphones. The only remedy is to purchase better phones. You may also want to consider small, powered speakers that allow you to turn your portable into a system that can fill a room with sound.

Best Buys '91

Our Best Buy and Recommended portable stereos follow. They are divided into portable CD players, personal radio-cassette player/recorders, personal radio-cassette players, personal cassette players, personal radios, personal headset radios, and boom boxes. In each category, the units are arranged in order of preference. The best of the Best Buys is listed first, followed by our second choice, and so on. Remember that a Best Buy or Recommended designation applies only to the model listed; it does not necessarily apply to other

Prices are accurate at time of printing; subject to manufacturer's change.

models made by the same manufacturer or to an entire product line.

PORTABLE CD PLAYERS

SONY D-35

The Sony D-35 is one of the most expensive portable CD players on the market, yet it qualifies as a Best Buy. The reason is that even though it is one of the smallest, lightest portable CD players, it's also the only one that can fully double as a home player. Exactly one inch thick, this tiny player's lid contains nearly every control found on a full-size CD player, including a numbered keypad for direct track access. An LCD (liquid crystal display) screen, much larger than found on other portable CD players, presents the same information commonly found on the fluorescent displays of home players. The D-35 calculates the best track arrangements for optimal dubbing onto cassettes. The D/A converter uses an eight-times over-sampling digital filter. The sound quality is quite good. Its built-in rechargeable battery powers the D-35 for two hours. Two alkaline AA cells inserted in the outboard detachable battery compartment power the unit for about 3½ hours. The rechargeable and outboard batteries can be used in conjunction for about 5½ hours. A separate lithium button cell maintains the D-35's memory and clock functions. The clock, besides displaying time of day on the LCD, can be programmed to stop and start the D-35 and even fade in and out at desired times. You can program up to 22 tracks. Sony's MegaBass circuit boosts bass, a useful feature for headphones. A remote control module is in the middle of the headphone cord. Remote control only operates when using the supplied in-the-ear headphones.

Specifications: height, 1″; **width,** 5″; **depth,** 5⁷⁄₁₆″; **weight,** 13⁷⁄₁₆ ounces without batteries. **Warranty: parts,** one year; **labor,** 90 days.

Approx. retail price	**Approx. low price**
$400	$338

Prices are accurate at time of printing; subject to manufacturer's change.

PANASONIC SL-NP1

The Panasonic SL-NP1 portable CD player is all performance and no frills. It's one of the smallest and lightest players, yet it has a surprisingly low price. Panasonic uses the same basic chassis for both the budget SL-NP1 and the deluxe SL-NP12 (which is identical to the Technics SL-XP2). The NP1 and NP12 even look alike, with the more expensive model a barely noticeable two decibels better in noise level. The SL-NP1 sounds quite good and travels extremely well. The unit uses a four-times oversampling digital filter. You can program up to 18 tracks. A small LCD (liquid crystal display) screen on the front edge shows timings and track numbers, and it aids in programming. Panasonic supplies the unit without rechargeable batteries or headphones. It is furnished with an AC adapter, a cable for connecting its line output to your stereo, and a carrying belt. Since most people already own a set of lightweight headphones that will work with the SL-NP1, not supplying them makes sense. The unit operates for about four hours on a pair of alkaline AA batteries. You can use generic rechargeable batteries (with an external charger) for 2½ hours of playing time.

Specifications: height, 1⅜"; **width**, 5"; **depth**, 5¹¹⁄₁₆"; **weight**, 11⁹⁄₁₆ ounces without batteries. **Warranty: parts and labor**, one year.

Approx. retail price	Approx. low price
$190	$173

PERSONAL RADIO-CASSETTE

PLAYER/RECORDERS

SONY WM-AF67

The Sony WM-AF67 is the personal radio-cassette player/recorder that has every feature you could want, including auto-reverse. Rather than a built-in microphone, the recorder comes with an external single-point stereo microphone, which gives you much more flexibility in recording. It even has a pocket/tie clip. The AM/FM stereo radio includes three feather-touch presets for your favorite FM stations. You can switch the FM to mono to quiet noisy reception. For tape playback, there is Dolby B noise reduction and equalization for chrome/metal tape. The tape player has a deluxe version of MegaBass that offers three levels of bass boost to compensate for the lack of bass in the lightweight, in-the-ear headphones. **Specifications: height**, 4⅝"; **width**, 3½"; **depth**, 1½"; **weight**, 9 ounces. **Warranty: parts**, one year; **labor**, 90 days.

Approx. retail price	**Approx. low price**
$175	$105

AIWA HS-J505 RECOMMENDED

The Aiwa HS-J505 radio auto-reverse cassette player/recorder offers more features and better sound than the previous year's model at the same substantial price. If this unit was just a little less expensive we'd rate it a Best Buy. While most headphone stereos include bass enhancement circuits, as does Aiwa with its Dynamic Super Loudness (DSL), the HS-J505 is one of the rare models to include a midrange and treble enhancement circuit. BBE, used in recording studios and similar to the APHEX sound-enhancement system, makes the midrange and treble sparkle. The improved, supplied headphones sound very good and are reasonably comfortable. You can play tapes back with Dolby B noise reduction. An LCD (liquid crystal display) screen shows time or radio station frequency. There are five AM and five FM station presets. The HS-J505 will also sample all local radio stations and program the five strongest AM and FM, in addition to your presets. This is a nice feature when traveling. The digital tuner adjusts to broadcast standards around the world, and offers wideband AM for higher AM fidelity. The clock stores five different time zones, and it doubles as an alarm clock. The quick-charge battery plays for two hours on a 15-minute charge.

Specifications: height, 4³⁄₁₆"; **width**, 3"; **depth**, 1¹⁄₁₆"; **weight**, 7⅜ pounds. **Warranty: parts**, one year; **labor**, 90 days.

Approx. retail price	**Approx. low price**
$270	$192

Prices are accurate at time of printing; subject to manufacturer's change.

PERSONAL RADIO-CASSETTE PLAYERS

SONY WM-F2015

✓ **BEST BUY**

The Sony WM-F2015 is a basic Walkman that plays tapes and receives good radio reception. It lacks the bells and whistles of higher priced units, but measures and weighs only fractions more than models twice its price. Sony still includes necessary features like automatic shutoff, equalization for all tape types, and a local/distant sensitivity switch for the FM stereo tuner. You may find that the FM will overload near transmitter sites in the center of large cities. The on-the-ear headphones with their foam pads are even somewhat more comfortable that Sony's more expensive in-the-ear variety. The unit operates on two AA batteries for about four hours.

Specifications: height, 5⅜"; **width,** 3¾"; **depth,** 1½"; **weight,** 8 ounces without batteries. **Warranty: parts,** one year, **labor,** 90 days.

Approx. retail price	Approx. low price
$37	$31

SONY WM-F2085

✓ **BEST BUY**

The Sony WM-F2085 radio-cassette player comes packed with features. The auto-reverse tape player features automatic shutoff. It offers Dolby B noise reduction and correct equalization for any type of tape. The AM/FM stereo digitally synthesized tuner displays the station frequency on an LCD (liquid crystal display) screen. The unit includes ten station presets. It will automatically scan up and down the radio dial. A built-in clock displays the time on the LCD screen when the radio is not in use, and it doubles as an alarm clock. Two AA batteries power the unit for over four hours. A rechargeable battery and AC adapter are options.

Specifications: height, 4¾"; **width,** 3⁷⁄₁₆"; **depth,** 1½"; **weight,** 8⅗ ounces without batteries. **Warranty: parts,** one year; **labor,** 90 days.

Approx. retail price	Approx. low price
$95	$83

Prices are accurate at time of printing; subject to manufacturer's change.

AIWA HS-T70 RECOMMENDED

The Aiwa HS-T70 radio-cassette player includes many of the features of Aiwa's HS-J505 without the recording circuitry and the quick-charge battery. Aiwa builds in DSL (Dynamic Super Loudness) for ample bass and BBE, used in recording studios and similar to the APHEX sound-enhancement system, for better midrange and treble. Dolby B noise reduction helps assure low-noise tape playback. The digitally synthesized tuner offers five AM and five FM presets, plus automatic presets that lock onto the strongest stations in any given location. The tuner functions anywhere in the world, and permits wideband AM for higher AM fidelity. The built-in clock remembers five time zones, and it doubles as an alarm clock. Aiwa supplies reasonably comfortable, high-fidelity headphones.

Specifications: height, $4^{11}/_{16}$"; **width,** $3^7/_{16}$"; **depth,** $1^7/_{16}$"; **weight,** 8½ ounces without batteries. **Warranty: parts,** one year; **labor,** 90 days.

Approx. retail price	**Approx. low price**
$170	$100

PERSONAL CASSETTE PLAYERS

SONY WM-2051

The Sony WM-2051 fills the bill for someone on a budget looking for a tape-only personal cassette player. It's as rugged as the more expensive models, and while it lacks fancy features, it does have auto-reverse. This unit costs about one fourth the price of the original Sony Walkman and sounds better while weighing about half as much. The WM-2051 has equalization for all tape types. The on-the-ear headphones with their foam pads are somewhat more comfortable than Sony's in-the-ear variety.

Specifications: height, $4^7/_{16}$"; **width,** $2^{11}/_{16}$"; **depth,** $1^9/_{32}$"; **weight,** $4^4/_5$ ounces without batteries. **Warranty: parts,** one year; **labor,** 90 days.

Approx. retail price	**Approx. low price**
$40	$40

Prices are accurate at time of printing; subject to manufacturer's change.

SHARP JC-K99

RECOMMENDED

The Sharp JC-K99 may be the world's lightest personal cassette player, weighing only 3½ ounces with batteries. The black carbon-fiber body is not only light, but strong. That makes the JC-K99 not only easy to carry, but durable as well. Few compromises are made in the quality of tape playback. It includes Dolby B noise reduction and proper equalization for all tape types. The auto-reverse player includes the standard antirolling mechanism to keep the tone steady while the player is in motion. A multifunction wired remote control makes operation easy. The ear-bud style headphones (two ear pieces without a headband) employ a twin-circuit design that sounds fairly good if you can fit them in your ears properly. The JC-K99 operates for 2½ hours on a one-hour charge with the supplied rechargeable battery. By using the optional screw-on "sidecar," you can substitute a single AA battery for three hours of play, or use both together for four to five hours. Sharp also supplies a leatherette carrying case.

Specifications: height, $2^{27}/_{32}$"; **width**, $4^7/_{32}$"; **depth**, $\frac{3}{4}$"; **weight**, 3½ ounces with battery. **Warranty: parts and labor**, one year.

Approx. retail price	**Approx. low price**
$270	not available

PERSONAL RADIOS

TOSHIBA RP-2059

✓BEST BUY

The Toshiba RP-2059 is a deluxe personal radio. Its frequency synthesized tuning is displayed on a large, clear LCD (liquid crystal display) screen. It has ten station presets, five for AM and five for FM. The preset buttons are well spaced and arranged in an arc across the front of the unit. The LCD also functions as a clock. The clock has an alarm function so that the RP-2059 can be used as a personal portable clock radio. There is a power backup for the clock, alarm, and station presets. You can switch the unit to mono to reduce noise in poor reception areas. DBSS (Dynamic Bass Sound System) boosts the bass. The unit comes with on-the-ear headphones and a belt clip.

Prices are accurate at time of printing; subject to manufacturer's change.

Specifications: height, 4⅜"; **width,** 2⁷⁄₁₆"; **depth,** ²⁹⁄₃₂"; **weight,** 3⅕ ounces. **Warranty: parts,** one year; **labor,** 90 days.

Approx. retail price	Approx. low price
$65	$46

SONY SRF-4

✓BEST BUY

The Sony SRF-4 is a basic, nearly indestructible FM stereo radio with a rugged, water-resistant design. Its on/off buttons, volume knob, and tuning knob are easily distinguishable both by touch and by shape. A small light-emitting diode on the front acts as a stereo indicator light and shows the condition of the batteries. Its bright yellow case is resistant to moisture. The radio circuit is based upon a single computer chip for simplicity, dependability, and good reception. The radio comes with water-resistant in-the-ear headphones, designed for superior frequency response and sound reproduction. Two AAA alkaline batteries power the unit for 30 hours.

Specifications: height, 4¼"; **width,** 2¼"; **depth,** ²⁷⁄₃₂"; **weight,** 3⁹⁄₁₀ ounces. **Warranty: parts,** one year; **labor,** 90 days.

Approx. retail price	Approx. low price
$45	$34

PERSONAL HEADSET RADIOS

TOSHIBA RP-2031

✓BEST BUY

The Toshiba RP-2031 is a simple, nondigital lightweight AM/FM stereo headset radio. It offers very good reception in most locations, although it can be overloaded near radio transmitters, such as in the centers of large cities. The retractable rod antenna works much better than in models that come with antennas built into the headband. Adjusting the length of the antenna can somewhat compensate for signal strength. Two AAA batteries power the unit for about 20 hours.

Specifications: weight, 4⅖ ounces without batteries. **Warranty: parts,** one year; **labor,** 90 days.

Approx. retail price	Approx. low price
$50	$30

Prices are accurate at time of printing; subject to manufacturer's change.

SONY SRF-M50

The Sony SRF-M50 FM stereo headset radio is part of Sony's "Sports" line of bright yellow, water-resistant personal portables. The ergonomically shaped earpieces are connected with dual adjustable headbands for a very good fit and to stay on your head while you're in motion. The digitally synthesized tuner and retractable rod antenna provide excellent reception. The unit has five station-preset buttons along the left earpiece, with a small LCD (liquid crystal display) screen for manual tuning. The SRF-M50 provides a good fit with good sound. It operates for about 30 hours on two AA batteries. This unit's self-contained cordless design makes it suitable for a wide range of activities and sports.

Specifications: weight, 6½ ounces without batteries. **Warranty: parts**, one year; **labor**, 90 days.

Approx. retail price	**Approx. low price**
$55	$49

BOOM BOXES

SANYO MCD-Z30

The Sanyo MCD-Z30 CD boom box has an amazing number of sound sources and features packed into a fairly modest package. Think what a CD player, cassette recorder, and AM/FM radio would cost individually. This model comes equipped with a CD skip feature. When you record onto a tape from a CD and the tape runs out, all you have to do is turn the tape over. The CD will automatically back up to the start of the track of whatever selection is playing so you won't miss any music and won't have to hunt for the break. The automatic level control helps casual recorders from oversaturating tapes being made from CDs. The remote makes this an extremely useful machine.

Specifications: height, 9⅝"; **width**, 26¹³⁄₁₆"; **depth**, 10¹⁵⁄₁₆"; **weight**, 13⅞ pounds. **Warranty, parts**, one year; **labor**, 90 days.

Approx. retail price	**Approx. low price**
$280	$250

Prices are accurate at time of printing; subject to manufacturer's change.

CASIO CD-950

The Casio CD-950 CD boom box is a solid performer with detachable speakers for true stereo. The clear labeling and sensible layout make this unit easy to use even though it is packed with such features as a graphic equalizer and high-speed dubbing. This CD boom box is a practical solution for dormitory, apartment, picnics, and quiet work sites.

Specifications: height, 9⅛"; **width,** 25⅛"; **depth,** 9⅛"; **weight,** 15¼ pounds. **Warranty: parts and labor,** 90 days.

Approx. retail price	Approx. low price
$340	$290

PANASONIC RX-DT5

RECOMMENDED

The Panasonic RX-DT5 CD boom box has a sleek design with a serious purpose. It has several features that make this machine great for recording from CDs and tapes. The RX-DT5 will turn itself off when the recording tape runs out. It will automatically fit the CD to a given tape length and fit the most music onto that tape without a break. The automatic level control helps casual recorders make good tapes. The remote is a very useful and desirable feature.

Specifications: height, 7¹³⁄₁₆"; **width,** 26"; **depth,** 9⅞"; **weight,** 14⁹⁄₁₆ pounds. **Warranty: parts and labor,** one year.

Approx. retail price	Approx. low price
$380	$324

SAMSUNG RCD-1200

RECOMMENDED

The Samsung RCD-1200 CD boom box offers maximum utility and portability at a very modest price. The stereo headphone jack permits you to get the full glory of CD sound. (None of these boxes can do CDs justice with the tiny speakers provided.) The 2½-watt-per-channel amplifier can't cope with the dynamic range of CDs or cassettes either. But if you don't push it, this unit provides a very pleasant sound.

Specifications: height, 8½"; **width,** 23⅞"; **depth,** 7¾"; **weight,** 9½ pounds. **Warranty: parts and labor,** one year.

Approx. retail price	Approx. low price
$280	$175

Prices are accurate at time of printing; subject to manufacturer's change.

SONY CFD-770

 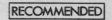

The Sony CFD-770 CD boom box is as much a home (or dorm) music and recording system as it is a portable. Indeed, at more than 24 pounds without batteries, it is hardly a machine that most of us would tote down the street. It offers solid sound and very convenient recording facilities. The synchro dubbing makes it easy to fit CDs and tapes of various lengths onto cassettes of alternate lengths. The feather-touch controls are a welcome contrast to the standard switches on most boom boxes. The detachable speakers allow for true stereo separation.

Specifications: height, $9^{27}/_{32}$"; **width,** 27"; **depth,** $9^{7}/_{32}$"; **weight,** 24 pounds (without batteries). **Warranty: parts,** one year; **labor,** 90 days.

> **Approx. retail price**
> $550
>
> **Approx. low price**
> $419

EMERSON AC2350

The Emerson AC2350 is a very straightforward and portable boom box. The double cassette wells make this a useful recorder and playback machine. The slim shape matches the slim price. A CD player would be nice, but each additional feature impacts on the price and portability of these units.

Specifications: height, $5^{1}/_{4}$"; **width,** 19"; **depth,** $3^{1}/_{4}$"; **weight,** 6 pounds. **Warranty: parts and labor,** 90 days.

> **Approx. retail price**
> $100
>
> **Approx. low price**
> $53

Clock Radios

Whether they prefer music, the weather forecast, or the friendly banter of a disc jockey, most consumers want a clock radio they can count on to wake them every morning. But different models of clock radios can do a lot more. Some lull you to sleep with prerecorded personal improvement tapes played back on a built-in cassette player. Others have a built-in telephone. There are even models that have a television set and are designed to be mounted under the cabinet in the kitchen.

When you shop for a clock radio, look for one with easy-to-read instructions, both radio and alarm wake-up functions, dual alarms, and easy operation in the dark. The unit should also be sturdy enough so that you don't push it off your nightstand when you fumble for the controls. A dimmer for the time display is also a helpful feature.

Clock radio terminology should be familiar to you if you have ever bought stereo or video equipment. Most clock radios deliver distortion-free sound, so your goal in purchasing a clock radio is finding one that has the features that match your needs.

Clock Radio Features

The **doze** or **snooze** bar allows you to catch a few minutes of extra sleep after the alarm goes off by waking you up a second time.

The **sleep** feature lets you fall asleep to music, which plays for a predetermined period of time and then shuts itself off automatically.

Best Buys '91

Our Best Buy choices follow. The unit we consider the best of the Best Buys is listed first, followed by our second choice, and so on. Remember that a Best Buy designation applies only to the model listed; it does not necessarily apply to other models made by the same manufacturer or to an entire product line.

PANASONIC RC-X250

The Panasonic RC-X250 is an AM/FM stereo electronic digital clock radio that looks like a small, black boom box. Its two circular 3-inch dynamic speakers are located on each side of the unit. This model produces unusually good sound quality in FM stereo. It has a cassette tape player/recorder that can be used to fall asleep to or wake up to tapes. It can also be used as a personal message center; an LED message indicator lets you know a message is waiting. The RC-X250 has "doze/snooze" and "sleep" functions, a green LED display, a headphone jack, a booster switch, dual alarms, and a battery backup system to ensure the alarm goes off on time in case of a power failure.
Specifications: height, 4¼"; **width**, 13⅛"; **depth**, 5¹¹⁄₁₆".
Warranty: parts and labor, one year.

Approx. retail price	Approx. low price
$85	$84

PROTON 320

The Proton 320 is a high-fidelity AM/FM clock radio that offers excellent sound for its moderate price. Other brands with comparable sound cost much more. This model comes in black or white. It has 3 watts of power, a dual alarm, and a 5-inch diameter cone speaker. It uses a 9-volt battery to back up the electronic clock during power outages. The "doze/snooze" bar lets you catch a few winks after the alarm goes off and then wakes you a second time.
Specifications: height, 5³⁄₁₀"; **width**, 10⅗"; **depth**, 3⅕".
Warranty: parts and labor, one year.

Approx. retail price	Approx. low price
$110	$110

Prices are accurate at time of printing; subject to manufacturer's change.

PANASONIC RC-6190

The Panasonic RC-6190 is an AM/FM electronic digital clock radio. It has two alarms and two FM presets, so each sleeper can awaken at a different time to a different station. This model also has "doze/snooze" and "sleep" functions, a 9-volt battery backup, an earphone jack, and a 3-inch dynamic speaker. **Specifications: height**, 2⅝"; **width**, 9⅝"; **depth**, 5½". **Warranty: parts and labor**, one year.

Approx. retail price	Approx. low price
$40	$35

SONY ICF-CS950

The Sony ICF-CS950 is an AM/FM stereo electronic digital clock radio. Its two 4-inch speakers produce unusually good sound quality for a model in this price range. It has a dual alarm, "sleep" and "doze/snooze" functions, a 9-volt battery backup (not supplied), and a contemporary black design. Most controls are located on top of the unit. **Specifications: height**, 4⅝"; **width**, 13"; **depth**, 3⅞". **Warranty: parts and labor**, one year.

Approx. retail price	Approx. low price
$60	$53

SONY ICF-CS970

The Sony ICF-CS970 is an AM/FM stereo electronic digital clock radio with unusually good sound for a model in this price range. Its speaker system consists of two 4-inch speakers and a woofer. A surround function further enhances the sound. A stereo input jack enables playback of a personal CD player or cassette player through the unit's sound system. Model ICF-CS970 has a dual alarm, "sleep" and "doze/snooze" functions, a blue fluorescent display, and a 9-volt battery backup. **Specifications: height**, 5½"; **width**, 14⁹⁄₁₆"; **depth**, 4¾". **Warranty: parts and labor**, one year.

Approx. retail price	Approx. low price
$100	$70

Prices are accurate at time of printing; subject to manufacturer's change.

Cameras

Some sixty billion pictures are taken every year around the world. Sixty billion pictures a year is not such a large figure when you consider the fact that you no longer have to be an expert to operate many cameras that produce high-quality images. Many of these cameras automatically focus the lens, meter the available light, set the correct aperture and shutter speed, and even activate the built-in or attached flash for you if the light level is too low for a good exposure. Some of the more sophisticated models will allow you to either use them as fully automatic cameras or make your own picture-taking decisions. There are also fully manual cameras for those who always want to be in control of their photographs. You should be careful in choosing a camera that will give you the type of pictures you want.

Types of Cameras

With a **single-lens reflex (SLR) camera**, you view the subject of your picture through the lens so that you see exactly what the camera sees.

With a **viewfinder camera**, you see the image you are going to photograph through a window, or viewfinder, in the camera's body.

With a **range finder camera**, you view your subject through a viewfinder, and the range finder projects a second image of the subject in the viewfinder. The lens is in focus when the two images coincide.

A **zone-focus camera** is a viewfinder camera that uses symbols or a distance scale to focus the lens. You estimate the distance and set the lens according to your estimate. Some autofocus cameras use zone-focus symbols in the viewfinder to indicate where the camera is focused.

A **fixed-focus camera** (usually called a point-and-shoot camera) is a viewfinder camera that has a lens fixed at a certain point, so that everything from a specified minimum distance to infinity is in focus.

An **autofocus camera** is any kind of camera that uses one of several different methods to focus the lens automatically when you touch the shutter-release button.

Features and Technology

Aperture, or **f-stop**, is listed as a ratio of the diameter of the lens opening to the focal length of the lens. All lenses are identified by their focal length and their largest aperture. A standard, or normal, lens for a 35mm camera is usually listed as a 50mm f/2 lens. (A normal lens produces a picture that approximates the perspective and degree of magnification that is seen by the human eye, excluding peripheral vision.) The f-stop is a function of the lens aperture setting. The standard series is f/1.4, f/2, f/2.8, f/4, f/5.6, f/8, f/11, f/16, f/22, and f/32. The smaller the number, the larger the aperture and the more light that will strike the film. Most lenses do not cover the full range of settings, but some may extend higher or lower.

A **dedicated hot shoe** is a clip found on most 35mm SLR cameras that interfaces accessories—such as electronic flashes—with the camera's electronics. Some dedicated systems provide through-the-lens-of-the-film (TTL-OTF) flash control.

DX coding imparts information about the film directly to the camera. Cassettes for 35mm film have metal strips that make contact with the pins in a camera—telling the camera the film speed, exposure latitude, and the number of exposures on the roll. Most SLR's offer both DX coding and manual film-speed settings. Compact 35mm cameras offer only DX coding.

EV compensation corrects the automatic exposure of subjects that are either very light or very dark. One EV (exposure value) is equivalent to one full f-stop.

A **focal-plane shutter** uses curtains or blades that travel either vertically or horizontally across the film plane to make an exposure. Almost all 35mm SLR cameras use this shutter because it allows the camera to use interchangeable lenses.

ISO (International Standards Organization) is a numerical system that indicates the relative speed of film. The higher the ISO number, the faster the film records an image. To take photographs in low light, use a high-speed film.

A **leaf shutter** uses a series of blades arranged in a circle that open and close to make an exposure. Compact 35mm cameras with fixed lenses use leaf shutters.

A **self-timer** is a switch found on most 35mm cameras that delays the operation of the shutter for about ten seconds, allowing the photographer to get into the picture.

Viewfinder information is a visual display in the camera's viewfinder of the exposure information you need to take good pictures. Autofocus SLR cameras also have signals that indicate when an image is in focus, and some signal out-of-focus conditions. Most cameras also provide flash signals that tell you when the flash is needed for good exposures.

Exposure Systems

Most 35mm SLR cameras have built-in TTL exposure meters that allow for accurate exposures no matter which lens you have on the camera. These meters use silicon photodiodes, which react instantly to light and are not blinded by very bright light. Most SLR cameras provide both automatic- and manual-exposure operation.

Most 35mm autofocus and compact cameras also have built-in meters that parallel the lens to meter the image area. These parallel meters are so sophisticated that they provide accurate exposures even for zoom lenses.

There are three basic kinds of automatic-exposure (AE) systems in cameras:

Aperture-priority AE lets you set the lens opening (f-stop), and the camera's metering system selects the shutter speed.

Shutter-priority AE lets you select the shutter speed, and the camera selects the lens opening automatically.

Programmed AE automatically selects both the aperture and shutter speed that will give you the appropriate exposure for the film in use. A microcomputer connected to the metering cell determines the correct settings. Programmed AE is used in most 35mm autofocus cameras, 35mm compact cameras, and instant-print cameras.

Best Buys '91

Our Best Buy and Recommended cameras follow. They are presented in eight categories: 35mm manual-focus SLR cameras, 35mm autofocus SLR cameras, 35mm autofocus cameras, 35mm compact cameras, underwater camera, snapshot 110 cartridge camera, instant-print cameras, and 35mm disposable cameras. Within each category, products are listed according to overall quality. The best of the Best Buys is first, followed by our second choice, and so on. Recommended cameras follow our Best Buy selections. Remember that a Best Buy rating applies only to the model listed and not necessarily to other models in the same product line or by the same manufacturer.

35MM MANUAL-FOCUS SLR CAMERAS

The 35mm SLR (single-lens reflex) camera is probably the most widely used professional camera. Newspaper, combat, and sports photographers use 35mm SLRs, as do fashion and nature photographers, scientists, and doctors. The research and development that has perfected professional SLR systems is passed on to amateur photographers in the form of advanced, but less expensive, 35mm SLRs. Our manual-focus SLR selections provide TTL exposure metering with manual-exposure adjustment so that you have full control over your images.

NIKON FM2

✓ **BEST BUY**

The Nikon FM2 is a professional-quality mechanical camera. It has a top shutter speed of $\frac{1}{4000}$ second and an electronic flash synchronization up to $\frac{1}{250}$ second. The high-speed flash synch provides more versatility for flash-fill in sunlight, and it also stops action better than slower shutter-speed syn-

Prices are accurate at time of printing; subject to manufacturer's change.

chronizations. The FM2 uses battery power only for its through-the-lens (TTL), center-weighted metering system, which uses two silicon photodiodes (SPD) for accurate full-aperture metering. Three LEDs (a plus sign, a minus sign, and a zero) in the viewfinder are used for metering; the correct exposure is indicated when only the zero is lighted. The aperture and shutter-speed settings appear in the viewfinder that, coupled with the TTL metering, give the photographer great control over his or her pictures. The FM2 features an easy-to-use multiple exposure lever, depth-of-field preview, interchangeable viewing screens, and a simple hookup for a motor drive. The body is chrome; black adds $20 to the cost.

Warranty: parts and labor, one year.

Approx. retail price	Approx. low price
$525	$368

RICOH KR-5 SUPER II ✔BEST BUY

The Ricoh KR-5 Super II is a compact 35mm single-lens reflex camera that uses all popular K-mount lenses from wide angle to telephoto. The KR-5 Super II has mechanical shutter speeds from one second to $\frac{1}{2000}$ second, plus a special *B* shutter speed for long exposures, and a flash synchronization of $\frac{1}{125}$ second. The shutter speeds and apertures are coupled to a built-in, through-the-lens, center-weighted meter. There are three LEDs in the viewfinder: a green circle for correct exposure, a red plus that indicates overexposure, and a red minus that indicates underexposure. To take an exposure reading, you move the film-advance lever to its 30-degree standoff position, then depress the shutter-release button partway to activate the meter. Film speeds are manually set from ISO 25 to ISO 1600 on a collar around the rewind knob. The only other control is a self-timer. A well-designed finger grip gives you a firm hold of the camera. The KR-5 Super II is a basic, reliable SLR that gives you full control over your pictures at a reasonable price.

Warranty: parts and labor, two years.

Approx. retail price	Approx. low price
$310 (with 50mm f/2 Rikenon lens)	$125

35MM AUTOFOCUS SLR CAMERAS

Autofocus (AF) SLR cameras have CCD (charged-coupled device) sensors that use subject contrast to achieve the correct focus. Some CCDs are so sensitive that they can focus on low-contrast subjects in light so low that you can hardly see the AF frame in the viewfinder. Many AF SLRs now have built-in near-infrared AF illuminators to automatically project a focusing pattern so that the camera can focus on subjects with no contrast, and even on subjects in total darkness. Highly efficient microprocessors and micromotors have made autofocusing very fast and accurate, even with long telephoto lenses.

Microcomputers in camera bodies interface with microcomputers in lenses and electronic flashes to perform many sophisticated functions automatically. All of this technology provides you with a photographic tool that helps create excellent pictures if you read the instruction booklet and learn to use the camera's many sophisticated automatic features.

MINOLTA MAXXUM 8000i

The Minolta Maxxum 8000i is a sophisticated AF SLR with intelligent autofocus and metering. The 8000i has multiple AF sensors to give you an autofocus area that is up to 12 times wider than that of other AF SLRs, allowing you to focus on off-center subjects. The multiple AF sensors provide focusing on vertically, horizontally, and diagonally oriented subjects. A built-in AF illuminator, with a range of 30 feet, automatically switches into predictive focus control when it detects a moving subject, and continues to focus up to the instant of exposure. The 8000i has three metering devices: spot for pinpoint metering; standard center-weighted average; and an AF Integrated Multi-Pattern with six metering segments, which uses autofocus information to determine the best exposure for each subject. There is also automatic contrast compensation that corrects for backlit and spotlit situations. The 8000i uses the Maxxum Creative Expansion Card System with 13 software cards for special effects and automatic operation of complicated photographic procedures—such as exposure

Prices are accurate at time of printing; subject to manufacturer's change.

bracketing and highlight/shadow metering. The top shutter speed is $\frac{1}{8\,000}$ second; the top flash synch speed is $\frac{1}{200}$ second. The long eye-relief viewfinder is one of the best we have ever seen for providing a complete view of the image frame and the information panel below it for eyeglass wearers. In spite of its many operations, the 8000i is user friendly: All major controls are set up so that they can be used with the camera at eye level and all necessary information appears in the uncluttered viewfinder. Simply put, the sophisticated Maxxum 8000i is easy to use.

Warranty: parts and labor, two years.

Approx. retail price	Approx. low price
$812	$583

CANON EOS 10S

The Canon EOS 10S is the first AF SLR to use the innovative flexible autofocus system. Three sensors, capable of working individually or together, are spread across half the frame, and the location of each one is marked in the viewfinder. The flexible AF system automatically evaluates your subject for accurate focusing even when it is off center, and the flexible focus marks are lightly illuminated in red. This flexible system is particularly good at predicting the actual focus point of moving subjects at the instant of exposure. It will also focus on any subject—no matter what its orientation. In the 10S's depth-of-field mode, the flexible focus marks are placed over the near-and-far focus points, and the microcomputer sets the right aperture for a sharp picture of the scene. For special focus situations, you can select to use only one focus mark. There is a built-in focusing aid light that automatically projects a pattern in low light for any of the three AF sensors to focus on. The novel eight-zone Evaluative Metering is coupled to the flexible AF system so that the meter always knows the location of your main subject when evaluating the brightness levels around it for the best exposure. There is also partial metering—which meters only the central 8½ percent of the scene—for tricky lighting situations. The 10S is also the first advanced camera to have a built-in pop-up flash for fast-flash illumination when there is not enough time to attach a separate flash.

Prices are accurate at time of printing; subject to manufacturer's change.

Other convenient features built in to the 10S are: automatic program shifting for different focal lengths; camera-shake compensation, which automatically shifts to a higher shutter speed to avoid blurred pictures; autoexposure bracketing to vary the exposure rendition of a subject; multiple-exposure control; interval timer for time-lapse photography; film advance of five frames per second; four programmed image-control settings; and custom-function control for setting up the camera the way you want it to operate. In spite of having too many operations, the EOS 10S is one of the very best AF SLRs available because of its flexible autofocus, eight-zone meter, built-in flash, and very fast motor drive.

Warranty: parts and labor, one year.

Approx. retail price	Approx. low price
$730	$478

CHINON GENESIS III

The Chinon Genesis III is an ergonomically designed AF SLR with a fixed 38mm-to-110mm power zoom lens. When you slip your hand through the hand strap, the camera nestles in your palm, your fingers rest in the finger grip on the top of the camera, and your forefinger is on the shutter-release button. This ergonomic design allows you to take sharp pictures even with one hand. The Genesis III features both a through-the-lens contrast autofocus system and a three-beam infrared autofocus system for accurate focusing in all situations—from distant subjects to subjects in total darkness. Zooming can be controlled by the photographer via the telephoto and wide buttons on top of the camera. For snapshooting, you let the automatic composition system zoom the lens for you in any one of three modes: landscape/group mode for scenic and large group shots, sport/portrait mode for action and people shots, and standard program mode for general shooting. The sport/portrait mode also has automatic close-up operation when your subject is from 33½ to 39⅖ inches from the camera. The focal plane shutter has speeds from 1 to ¹⁄₁₀₀₀ second, plus long-time exposures for nighttime scenic shots. The pop-up flash, which stands 2½ inches above the film plane to reduce red-eye, normally sets the shutter speed to ¹⁄₁₀₀ second, but it can be overridden to produce balanced ambient and flash pictures by holding the flash button down while you press the shutter-release button. DX coding handles film speeds from ISO 25 to ISO 3200. The silicon photodiode produces very accurate exposures for all types of film. Film speeds can be fine-tuned with the ±2 EV control, which is also used to compensate for unusual lighting situations without using a flash. The Chinon Genesis III is an excellent camera for those who want an autofocus SLR, but do not want to bother with changing lenses.

Warranty: parts and labor, two years.

Approx. retail price	**Approx. low price**
$699	$353

MINOLTA MAXXUM 5000i `RECOMMENDED`

The Minolta Maxxum 5000i is a simple AF SLR that can use the Minolta Creative Expansion Card System. The 5000i has built-in programmed AE and metered manual-exposure modes, but you can expand these to include aperture-priority AE and shutter-priority AE with the A/S Mode Card. Other special application cards that can be used with the 5000i are: sports action, portrait, automatic depth control, and closeup cards. Each of these cards automatically sets up the camera to produce the best possible picture for the given application. For example, the portrait card automatically uses a sufficiently wide aperture for your main subject. A second meter cell, located in the mirror box, controls the exposure of the built-in flash or attached Maxxum flash. A thumb-operated AE Lock Button allows you to lock in an exposure setting before recomposing and making the exposure. The phase-detection autofocus system focuses in low-light levels, and a built-in AF illuminator automatically projects a focus pattern up to 16 feet when the light level or subject contrast is too low for the AF sensors to focus on. The 5000i uses DX-coded film with film speeds from ISO 25 to ISO 5000, and non-DX-coded films of ISO 100. Shutter speeds are $\frac{1}{2000}$ second to 4 seconds.

Warranty: parts and labor, two years.

Approx. retail price	**Approx. low price**
$470	$310

Prices are accurate at time of printing; subject to manufacturer's change.

35MM AUTOFOCUS CAMERAS

The 35mm leaf shutter autofocus (AF) camera is popular because it is an easy way to shoot high-quality 35mm film. An AF camera does more than focus the lens automatically. It loads the film, advances it after each exposure, and rewinds the film after the last exposure. An AF camera may also have a sophisticated meter that activates a built-in flash in difficult lighting situations—such as backlight—to produce a well-lit subject that is balanced with the background exposure. Some models, called dual-lens cameras, have both a normal and a moderate telephoto lens. Others have a zoom lens with a variety of focal lengths. Some cameras now have a special flash operation to reduce or eliminate red-eye, a problem caused by the flash being too close to the film plane. For your picture-taking enjoyment, be sure to acquaint yourself with a camera's features.

KONICA A4

The Konica A4 is a compact, shirt-pocket-size 35mm autofocus camera that has superior optics and an accurate exposure system that produces excellent images. When you press the power switch, the lens cover slides open, the lens extends from the camera body, and the shutter-release lock is canceled. The 35mm f/3.5 lens focuses from two feet to infinity in its standard mode and from $13\frac{4}{5}$ to $23\frac{3}{5}$ inches in its macro mode. There are 11 autofocus steps in the macro mode, and another 12 steps for the normal range, which produce accurate focusing in both ranges. The A4 normally operates in an automatic-flash mode, but it can also be operated in a flash-on mode for backlit subjects or in a flash-off mode for available-light pictures. DX coding is indexed for films from ISO 50 to ISO 3200. The built-in winder loads the film to the first frame automatically, advances the film after each exposure, and rewinds the film after the last exposure. The A4 is small in size, but it delivers big performance.

Warranty: parts and labor, one year.

Approx. retail price	Approx. low price
$310	**$196**

Prices are accurate at time of printing; subject to manufacturer's change.

RICOH SHOTMASTER ZOOM

The Ricoh Shotmaster Zoom creates sharp, finely detailed images over its entire 38mm-to-76mm zoom range and over its entire focus range of 2⅕ feet to infinity. The exposure system adds accurate metering to each picture to combine with the optics in order to produce superb images. You can operate the zoom lens with two buttons on top of the camera or set it for three-position zooming in which a touch of a button zooms the lens to 38mm, 54mm, or 76mm for quick subject framing. The Shotmaster Zoom has modes to handle a wide range of picture-taking situations: night/panorama, which is used for shooting through windows; available-light night shots; flash-plus-available-light exposures; TV, which is used for photographing television and computer screens; continuous, which is used for sequence pictures at 1½ frames; interval, which exposes one frame every 60 seconds; and multiple exposure, which allows you to make two or more exposures on one frame. The continuous mode can be combined with the self-timer to make two successive exposures. The built-in winder provides automatic film loading, automatic advance after each exposure, and automatic rewind after the last exposure.

Warranty: parts and labor, one year.

Approx. retail price	Approx. low price
$390	$199

OLYMPUS INFINITY ZOOM 200

The Olympus Infinity Zoom 200 introduced the innovative S-mode flash operation that eliminates the red-eye effect in most subjects. Red-eye occurs when you take pictures of people in low-light levels with a flash that is too close to the film plane. When light levels are low, the iris opens up, and the retina reflects back the red spectrum of the flash. In the S-mode, the Infinity Zoom emits about 15 low-level preflashes that effectively close the iris down before the shutter opens and the full-power flash exposure is made; with the iris closed down, not enough red light is reflected back to be recorded on your film. The flash has variable power, putting out less light for close subjects than for distant subjects, so that subjects even as close as two feet away are properly exposed. There is also a multiflash mode that makes four flash exposures in ⅙ second on one frame. The Infinity Zoom 200 makes both spot and average readings to measure contrast, and it will automatically fire the flash in situations such as backlighting. You can shift to spot metering, which also switches autofocus operation from multifocus to spot focus. The optical real-image viewfinder shows only the image that is being seen by the 38mm-to-80mm zoom lens. The Infinity Zoom 200 also features auto-zoom framing for portraits and a remote control that allows you to trip the shutter from up to 16 feet away. All these features are neatly packaged in the compact Olympus Infinity Zoom 200.

Warranty: parts and labor, one year.

Approx. retail price	Approx. low price
$440	$267

KONICA Z-UP28W

The Konica Z-UP28W is a wide-angle-to-normal AF compact with a sharp, snappy 28mm-to-56mm zoom lens. Complementing the superb lens is an accurate exposure system for both ambient light and the built-in electronic flash that produces perfect exposures even at its closest focusing distance of 1⅗ feet in its macro mode. The normal focusing range is 2½ feet to infinity, and the macro mode focuses from 1⅗ to 2½ feet. The green focus lamp in the viewfinder blinks when you are in the macro mode. The Z-UP28W also has a snapshot mode where the lens is fixed at 28mm and the range of sharp focus is 3³⁄₁₀ to 16 feet. In the snap mode, you can select to use autoflash, flash-on, flash-off, and two-frame self-timer operation. In standard autofocus operation, the self-timer operation is one frame, and there is also the addition of an infinity mode for sharp images of distant subjects. The real-image viewfinder shows you only the composition that is being recorded on the film, just like the viewfinder of an SLR. All types of DX-coded film from ISO 25 to ISO 3200 can be used. Because it produces such fine images, the Konica Z-UP28W is much more than just a reasonably priced wide-angle auto-focus camera.

Warranty: parts and labor, one year.

Approx. retail price	Approx. low price
$370	$205

OLYMPUS INFINITY SUPER ZOOM 330

The Olympus Infinity Super Zoom 330 is an improved version of the Super Zoom 300, a Best Buy two years ago. The excellent real-image viewfinder (like an SLR, it shows you the view that will be recorded on the film) has been improved by extending it to the back of the camera and adding an adjustable diopter to fine-tune the eyepiece to your vision. Another improvement is the addition of the red-eye-eliminating Auto-S operation to its other flash modes. The Auto-S mode emits a rapid series of low-level preflashes to close down the iris before the shutter opens and a full-flash burst is fired. Olympus has also redesigned the hand strap so that it now has a detachable shoulder strap for easier camera portability. The hand strap is so versatile that you can take pictures with one hand, if necessary. The Super Zoom 330 retains all the fine features of its predecessor, including a 38mm-to-105mm zoom lens with macro focusing at 105mm, which shifts the viewfinder image to provide correct macro-image framing. All DX-coded film types from ISO 25 to ISO 3200 can be used, and film speeds can be fine-tuned with the exposure compensation control, which also provides compensation for unusual lighting situations. Two autozoom modes can be used for head-and-shoulders portraits or full-length portraits.

Warranty: parts and labor, one year.

Approx. retail price	Approx. low price
$610	$331

RICOH SHOTMASTER AF SUPER

RECOMMENDED

The Ricoh Shotmaster AF Super is a pocket-size camera with multimode operation. The 35mm f3.5 lens has a focus range of

Prices are accurate at time of printing; subject to manufacturer's change.

2⅗ feet to infinity, and the LED AF monitor lamp in the view-finder blinks if your subject is closer than that. The built-in flash automatically pops up in low-light levels; it also pops up when the meter detects a backlight scene to provide fill-in lighting. There are six other modes besides the auto-flash mode: The panorama mode sets the lens to infinity for sharp landscape pictures, even when taken through windows; the night mode sets the lens to infinity and uses shutter speeds down to ¼ second for evening panoramas; the TV mode sets the camera so that it synchronizes with the scanning lines of television screens and computer monitors; the continuous mode allows you to take sequences of moving subjects, and when combined with the self-timer, to get two sequential frames; the interval mode makes an exposure every 60 seconds until the end of the roll is reached or you turn off the mode; the last mode is for multiple exposures, and it allows you to put two or more exposures on one frame. The camera uses DX-coded film from ISO 100 to ISO 1600. The Shotmaster AF Super is a fine pocket-size AF camera for the snapshooter who wants quality images.

Warranty: parts and labor, one year.

Approx. retail price $230

Approx. low price $85

PENTAX IQZOOM 700 RECOMMENDED

The Pentax IQZoom 700 is a compact 35mm autofocus cam-era. The 35mm-to-70mm lens has two zooming speeds. When you move the spring-loaded zoom lever lightly, the lens zooms slowly, and when you press the lever hard, the lens zooms quickly. The normal focusing range is 3⁹⁄₁₀ feet to infinity, and a button on top of the camera switches the lens into its macro mode with a range of 2 to 3⅕ feet. The flash and the viewfinder zoom along with the lens; when you press the macro button, the lens zooms to macro, the recticle in the viewfinder shifts over to correct for parallax, and the flash adjusts to cover the close-up area. When the green focus lamp in the viewfinder flickers in either the normal or close-up mode, your subject is out of the focusing range of the AF system. The camera's modes of operation are automatic flash, flash-on for flash-fill

Prices are accurate at time of printing; subject to manufacturer's change.

and slow-speed synchro-shooting, flash-off, exposure compensation for light and backlit subjects, bulb for long night shots, bulb with flash, continuous film advance, multiple exposure, self-timer, and two-frame self-timer. To easily return to the standard shooting mode of automatic flash and single-frame shooting, you simply press the mode/drive-clear button. The IQZoom 700 is a multitalented AF compact that produces sharp, well-exposed pictures.

Warranty: parts and labor, one year.

Approx. retail price	Approx. low price
$315	$189

CHINON AUTO GL-AF RECOMMENDED

The Chinon Auto GL-AF is a basic 35mm autofocus compact with full automatic-exposure operation. A built-in flash is tied in to the exposure system so that it will always fire when the light level is too low for correct exposure. The flash has a range of $4^{13}/_{50}$ to $13^{1}/_{10}$ feet with ISO 100 and ISO 200 film, and $5^{1}/_{5}$ to $15^{7}/_{10}$ feet with ISO 400 film. The 35mm f/3.9 lens has a focus range of $4^{3}/_{10}$ feet to infinity. The shutter speed is $1/_{125}$ second to prevent blurred pictures due to camera-shake. A sliding lens cover shuts off the power from the lithium battery when it is closed. The power winder provides continuous frame advance when you hold the shutter-release button down, and it also supplies power rewind, which is activated by a rewind switch. A self-timer completes the features of this decision-free autofocus camera.

Warranty: parts and labor, two years.

Approx. retail price	Approx. low price
$205	$110

35MM COMPACT CAMERAS

The 35mm compact is a relatively inexpensive camera with a fixed lens. Many 35mm compact cameras are simple point-and-shoot cameras with simple exposure systems designed for color negatives. Some compacts are more versatile and take high-quality photographs. Although these cameras

Prices are accurate at time of printing; subject to manufacturer's change.

demand more input from the photographer than the point-and-shoot autofocus compacts, they often produce excellent results.

MINOX 35 GT-E

The Minox 35 GT-E is a sophisticated, high-quality compact that weighs only seven ounces with its lithium batteries and fits into a shirt pocket. It has a folding flatbed that protects the 35mm f/2.8 multicoated Minoxar lens when you are not taking pictures. Zone focusing is from 28 inches to infinity, with a footage scale on the focusing ring. The 35 GT-E is an aperture-priority AE camera with f-stops from f/2.8 to f/16, and the meter selects shutter speeds from 8 seconds to $\frac{1}{500}$ seconds. The shutter-speed scale in the viewfinder has a shaded area below $\frac{1}{30}$ second to remind you to use a tripod or flash. An optional 35 FC-E flash has two automatic-exposure ranges as well as manual. Film speeds from ISO 25 to ISO 1600 are manually set with a dial on the camera base. On top of the camera is a +2 EV switch used to compensate for backlighting, a self-timer switch, and a battery-check switch. The 35 GT-E is another tiny camera with big performance.

Warranty: parts and labor, one year.

Approx. retail price	Approx. low price
$385	$286

KONICA KANPAI

The Konica Kanpai is named after the Japanese word for "cheers," which is just what you say to the camera once it is set up at a party or family gathering—it is the world's first sound-activated compact camera. The sound trigger has three sound level positions: low for a moderate sound level of $\frac{1}{5}$ second or longer, medium for a $\frac{3}{10}$-second duration, and high for a $\frac{1}{2}$-second duration. A built-in timer controls the rate of frames exposed, extending the completion of a 24-exposure roll of film to between 20 and 40 minutes. The Kanpai comes with a special mini tripod that will aim the camera at one area or will let the camera operate in free-swing framing to cover an area of 100 degrees. In free-swing framing, the Kanpai takes a picture, swings about 40 degrees, takes another picture, then swings back another 40 degrees through a 100 degree arc until the last frame; sound still activates each exposure as set by the sound level and governed by the timer. To make subject-framing easier when placing the camera near a wall for sound-activated operation, a second viewfinder is located on top of the camera. The Kanpai is a fully automatic point-and-shoot camera with automatic flash, flash on for fill-flash, flash-off for low-light pictures, and self-timer operation. The Kanpai is a fun camera designed to capture the excitement of fun times. **Warranty: parts and labor**, one year.

Approx. retail price	**Approx. low price**
$216	$168

RICOH L-20 RECOMMENDED

The Ricoh L-20 is a simple, inexpensive point-and-shoot camera that goes one step further than most cameras in this price range: When taking pictures of distant subjects such as land-scapes, you slide and hold the infinity switch in the infinity position while you take the picture. The infinity switch, which is located below the 35mm lens, is spring-loaded so that the lens returns to its snapshot position when you release it. The camera's flash and automatic winder are powered by either two AA alkalines or one 3-volt lithium battery, which gives you fast recycling times. A red LED lights up in the viewfinder telling you when to turn on the flash for correctly exposed pictures. A switch on the front panel is used to set the camera for the film speed in use—color-negative films of ISO 100, 200, 400, and 800/1000. The Ricoh L-20 is a better-than-average point-and-shoot snapshot camera.
Warranty: parts and labor, one year.

Approx. retail price	**Approx. low price**
$90	$56

UNDERWATER CAMERA

An underwater camera is waterproof. Do not confuse it with a weatherproof camera, which can be used in the rain and snow. A waterproof camera has O-rings that compress under water pressure to seal the camera. The depth to which an underwater camera can be used is listed in the instruction booklet that comes with the camera.

MINOLTA WEATHERMATIC DUAL 35

 ✔BEST BUY

The Minolta Weathermatic Dual 35 is an autofocus dual-lens camera that is waterproof to a depth of 16 feet. Lens selection of 35mm or 50mm is done by a push button on top of the camera; as the lens changes, the viewfinder changes to give you the proper framing for the lens in use. An underwater close-up button shifts the focus from $1\frac{7}{10}$ to $4\frac{3}{10}$ at 35mm and 2 to $3\frac{3}{10}$ feet at 50mm. The built-in flash automatically fires in low-light levels. The Weathermatic Dual 35 uses DX-coded film from ISO 100 to ISO 1000, and it is designed to be used with color-negative film. Film loading, film advance, and film rewind are automatically handled by the camera's built-in autowinder. Because it is waterproof, the Weathermatic Dual 35 is also an excellent all-weather camera that is fully protected from dust, sand, snow, and water. When the camera gets dirt or sand in it, you simply rinse it and dry it before changing film.
Warranty: parts and labor, one year.

Approx. retail price	Approx. low price
$303	$211

SNAPSHOT 110 CARTRIDGE CAMERA

The 110 cartridge camera used to be the most popular snapshot camera, but most people now prefer 35mm compact cameras. The only advantage to a cartridge camera is that you never have to touch the film.

KODAK EKTRALITE 10

RECOMMENDED

The Kodak Ektralite 10 is a basic 110 cartridge camera for taking snapshots with color-print film. The 25mm f/8 lens has a fixed focus from five feet to infinity. The built-in flash, activated

---

Prices are accurate at time of printing; subject to manufacturer's change.

by a switch on top of the camera, has a range of 5 to 14 feet with ISO 100/200 film, and 5 to 20 feet with ISO 400 film. The flash is powered by two AA batteries. The film is advanced by a two-stroke thumb lever, and the shutter release is locked until the film advance is completed to prevent double exposure.
Warranty: parts and labor, one year.

Approx. retail price	Approx. low price
$34	$30

INSTANT-PRINT CAMERAS

Instant-print cameras produce a finished black-and-white or color print in between 15 seconds and a few minutes.

MINOLTA INSTANT PRO

The Minolta Instant Pro is a versatile instant-print camera with many features that give you both image and creative control. The Instant Pro produces rectangular pictures with an image area that measures 3⅗ by 2⁹⁄₁₀ inches. On the back of the Instant Pro is the LCD (liquid crystal display) information panel, system-control buttons, and flash-status LEDs. The modes are: automatic flash, with a normal shooting range of 2 to 15 feet, which can be turned off for available light pictures; sonar autofocus system, which can be switched to manual focus for special-focus situations; audio signals for focus, self-timer, and film-pack empty, which can be turned on or off; automatic exposure, which can be adjusted to lighten or darken the picture; time-exposure mode, which provides long exposures beyond the automatic-exposure range of six seconds; backlighting mode to provide exposure adjustment for backlit scenes; sequential mode, which allows you to take a series of pictures at various time intervals from 3 seconds to 19 minutes; and finally, multiple exposure, which allows you to make up to five exposures on one picture. An auto-reset button returns the camera to its basic automatic modes when pressed. The normal shooting range of the Instant Pro is two feet to infinity, but a close-up lens supplied with the camera allows you to take pictures at ten inches; a built-in measure provides exact measurement for close-ups. The Minolta Instant Pro is a sophisticated instant-print camera that gives you great control over your images.

Warranty: parts and labor, five years.

Approx. retail price	Approx. low price
$219	not available

POLAROID PROPACK

The Polaroid ProPack is a folding camera that uses ten kinds of instant pack film: four color films, one color positive transparency film, and five black-and-white films. The ProPack is used in any application where instant prints are needed, such as real-estate displays of houses for sale. Though called a pro camera, it is easy to operate. Focusing from three feet to infinity is done via a distance scale on the focusing lever. There is a film-type selector for ISO 80 or ISO 3000 film used outdoors, and a 3000 ER (extended range) setting for indoor available-light photography. A lighten/darken switch is used to control the brightness of your prints. Development takes from 15 to 60 seconds, and a built-in timer beeps when it is time to peel the print from the negative. An optional off-camera flash provides plenty of light when needed, up to 75 feet with ISO 3000 film.

Warranty: parts and labor, one year.

Approx. retail price	Approx. low price
$157	$93

POLAROID IMPULSE AF

RECOMMENDED

The Polaroid Impulse AF is an instant-print camera that uses a sonar auto-focus system for accurate focusing from two feet to infinity. The AF system tells the digital dual-photodiode exposure system the focusing distance so that it can provide the correct amount of fill-flash or full-flash for each subject. When you touch the top of the flash, it pops up, the lens cover opens, and all circuits are activated. The flash has a range of 2 to 14 feet. A soft-touch electronic shutter release provides shake-free pictures. The viewfinder shows 100 percent of the picture area, and it has a soft, flexible eyepiece. A 12-second

Prices are accurate at time of printing; subject to manufacturer's change.

self-timer lets the photographer get into the picture. The Impulse AF uses Polaroid 600 Plus film that has an image area of 3⅛ by 3¹/₁₆ inches.

Warranty: parts and labor, one year.

Approx. retail price	Approx. low price
$110	$76

35MM DISPOSABLE CAMERAS

There is a growing group of point-and-shoot cameras known as disposables. These cameras, which range is price from $8 to $14, are handed in to a photo lab when the preloaded film is exposed, and your processed prints and film are returned to you. Although inexpensive, they produce quality images that can be enlarged to 8 by 10 inches. The disposables started out as a solution for those people who had forgotten their cameras at amusement parks, circuses, and so forth, and wanted to take pictures. Now there are specialty disposables that allow the ordinary photographer to take panoramic pictures and underwater shots for very little investment. On an environmental note, both Kodak and Fuji have set up recycling programs for their disposable cameras, so that you know that your processor is not throwing them away.

FUJICOLOR QUICKSNAP AND QUICKSNAP FLASH

 ✓BEST BUY

The Fujicolor Quicksnap, with its f/11 lens, takes well-exposed pictures only in bright sunlight and slightly overcast days. The Quicksnap Flash has a built-in flash and battery and a range of ten feet to provide its own light when there is not enough ambient light. Both cameras are loaded with 24-exposure rolls of Fujicolor film and have thumbwheels to advance the film after each exposure. The focus for both is fixed to produce sharp pictures from three feet to infinity.

Approx. retail price	Approx. low price
$8 (Quicksnap)	$8
$14 (Quicksnap Flash)	$12

KODAK STRETCH 35

The Kodak Stretch 35 produces twelve 3½-by-10-inch panoramic prints via a 25mm f/12 lens that has a 75 degree angle of view, which is about twice the angle of coverage that is covered by a standard 50mm lens. Because the lens is wide angle, it is protected from stray light by a built-in lens shade. The focus is fixed to produce sharp pictures from three feet to infinity. The Stretch 35 is designed to produce good exposures in bright sunlight to partially cloudy days. When you bring in the Stretch 35, make sure you tell your processor that you want stretch prints.

Approx. retail price	Approx. low price
$13	not available

KODAK WEEKEND 35

The Kodak Weekend 35 has a transparent housing that is waterproof up to a depth of eight feet for taking pictures underwater. The waterproof housing also makes the Weekend 35 a good camera to use when taking pictures at the beach or when boating. The focus-free Weekend 35 has a fixed focus from four feet to infinity. Because it will be used underwater, the Weekend 35 has a viewfinder that it easy to use with goggles, a large film-advance knob that is easy to use with gloves on, and a wrist strap for safety. The Weekend 35 produces 24 prints.

Approx. retail price	Approx. low price
$14	not available

Telephones and Answering Machines

In the past few years, telephone technology has become highly advanced. For the consumer, this means greater options and more versatility; it can also mean greater confusion when it comes to picking a phone with just the options you need! Getting what you need or want from a phone, no more and certainly no less, is the key to making an intelligent telephone purchase. A buyer needs to know what each feature does and whether or not it's necessary for his or her purposes. It doesn't pay to purchase a phone that's full of complex features when all that's needed is a basic model. There are top-quality telephones available in all categories ranging from the basic lines to the high-tech cellular models.

A telephone depends on the kind of service the local telephone company supplies. This can be either UDK (universal dialing keyset), more commonly called pulse (or rotary) dialing, or it can be DTMF (dial tone multiple frequency), known as tone dialing. If your area is wired for tone, you can use either a pulse or tone phone. About half the United States is wired for the tone system; the rest still uses the pulse system.

Many phones are tone/pulse switchable, so they can use either system. These phones can also be used for long-distance services in pulse-dialing areas: First dial the number of the system, then switch to tone dialing. Tone dialing allows you to access beeperless-remote answering machines, computer information, and telephone banking services.

Telephone Features

Automatic last-number redial automatically redials the last number dialed if you've reached a busy signal. It will redial the number a set number of times (10 to 15) at regular intervals (usually once every minute or 45 seconds) until the party is reached. If the number being called is busy, the telephone automatically hangs up. If the number is free, the caller will hear it ringing and take the call. This feature is usually found on telephones that have speakerphones so you do not have to lift the receiver to make a call.

Hearing-aid-compatible telephones provide distortion-free conversations for people who wear hearing aids.

Hold temporarily cuts off the line so that neither party can speak to or hear the other.

Last-number redial temporarily stores the last number dialed in the phone's memory so you can redial that number by pressing one or two buttons.

Memory stores phone numbers so they can be called by pushing one or two buttons. Almost all new phones have some memory. Basic models can store about ten numbers, while feature phones can retain 30, 40, or even 100 numbers in memory.

Mute is similar to hold. By pressing the mute button, you can have a conversation with someone in the room without the person on the other end of the line hearing you.

Speakerphone means that, like the handset, the base of the telephone has a microphone and a speaker. You don't have to lift the handset to send and receive calls; you just speak in the direction of the phone. Almost all speakerphones are simplex, rather than duplex, which means that both parties cannot speak at the same time.

Best Buys '91

Our Best Buy and Recommended telephones and answering machines follow. They are categorized as follows: basic telephones, feature telephones, cordless telephones, cellular mobile telephones, portable telephones, and answering machines. The best of the Best Buys is listed first, followed by our second choice, and so on. Recommended products follow our Best Buys and may be substituted if their features meet your needs. Remember that a Best Buy or Recommended designation applies only to the model listed; it does not apply to other models by the same manufacturer.

Basic Telephones

AT&T TRIMLINE 210

The AT&T Trimline 210 is a top-quality table or wall phone. It is fully modular, comes in six colors, and features a lighted keypad, receiver and ringer-volume controls, mute, last-number redial, and switchable tone/pulse dialing.
Warranty: two years.

Approx. retail price	Approx. low price
$50	$32

COBRA MODEL ST 512

The Cobra Model ST 512 is a trim desk or wall phone. It is fully modular, sturdy, and less expensive than similar models. The unit is equipped with last-number redial, switchable tone/pulse dialing, ringer on/off switch, and a ten-number memory dialer. It comes in almond, black, dusty rose, red, and silver.
Warranty: one year.

Approx. retail price	Approx. low price
$35	$22

CODE-A-PHONE STYLELINE I   RECOMMENDED

The Code-A-Phone Styleline I is a desk or wall phone that's fully modular. It features a compact design with bigger buttons

---

Prices are accurate at time of printing; subject to manufacturer's change.

and easy-to-read numbers and letters. The dial pad is backlit to make dialing easier. It has a ringer-volume control, last-number redial, and is available in white, cream, and gray.
Warranty: one year.

Approx. retail price	Approx. low price
$30	not available

GENERAL ELECTRIC 2-9210 `RECOMMENDED`

The General Electric 2-9210 is a desktop model that features a good-looking design that sets it off a bit from other basic phones. It's equipped with last-number redial, mute, a hold button, hearing-aid compatibility, ringer-volume control, and a 12-number memory. Three of the 12 memory numbers are accessed by one touch. The fully modular phone comes with an extra-long ten-foot cord.
Warranty: one year.

Approx. retail price	Approx. low price
$25	$25

Feature Telephones

AT&T MEMORY TELEPHONE 610 ✓BEST BUY

The AT&T Memory Telephone 610 is a good choice if you want a bit more capability than a basic model provides. Besides ringer-volume control, last-number redial, and switchable tone/pulse dialing, this desk or wall-mount model offers a 16-number one-touch dialing memory feature, hold with remote release, flash for custom calling, and pause.
Warranty: two years.

Approx. retail price	Approx. low price
$60	$47

SONY IT-D150 ✓BEST BUY

The Sony IT-D150 is a single-line phone with 32-number memory, scratch pad memory that lets you jot down a number

---

Prices are accurate at time of printing; subject to manufacturer's change.

directly into the phone's temporary memory, and an LCD (liquid crystal display) that shows you what number you've dialed and the date and time of the call. An automatic busy redial makes ten attempts to get your call through after you've hung up. It's complete with programmable pause and flash functions.

Warranty: one year.

Approx. retail price	**Approx. low price**
$110	not available

GENERAL ELECTRIC 2-9435 [RECOMMENDED]

The General Electric 2-9435 is a two-line phone with dual ringers and conference call. An LED indicator tells you if the automatic redial, mute, or speakerphone functions are in use. In addition, it has a 32-number memory, last-number redial, pause, and flash.

Warranty: one year.

Approx. retail price	**Approx. low price**
$100	$72

AT&T TWO-LINE SPEAKERPHONE 622 [RECOMMENDED]

The AT&T Two-Line Speakerphone 622 features a 16-number one-touch dialing memory and hold. It also has LED indicators for the speakerphone and to show what line is in use. Other features include an incoming call identification, last-number redial, mute, flash, and pause.

Warranty: two years.

Approx. retail price	**Approx. low price**
$120	$99

SONY IT-A850 [RECOMMENDED]

The Sony IT-A850 is the phone to look at if you've decided that you need just about every feature you can get. It's a sophisticated speakerphone with an integrated TAD (telephone answering device). This phone also offers last-number redial, hold, mute, and a 20-number memory. It's fully modular and has

Prices are accurate at time of printing; subject to manufacturer's change.

switchable tone/pulse dialing. The built-in answering device features beeperless remote, remote turn-on, automatic disconnect, and dual microcassettes. It allows you to select VOX (to allow incoming messages to be any length) or determine the incoming message length manually. An LED counter numbers and times the calls. Messages are retrieved by dialing a three-digit security code or with an automatic message transfer that forwards important messages to a preprogrammed number. Calling party control eliminates blank tape when no messages are left.

Warranty: one year.

Approx. retail price	**Approx. low price**
$220	$169

Cordless Telephones

Mobility is the number-one feature of cordless telephones. Whether you are working in the garage or barbecuing with the neighbors, you can always be ready to place or receive a call.

Cordless telephones use a special radio, not a cord, for transmissions between the base and handset. The transmissions carry the voice signals and operate the telephone's functions. Cordless phones have many features, such as memory, hold, mute, and last-number redial. However, the most important feature to look for is clear transmission between the base and the handset. Security features and channel selections are used to deal with the problems of interference and static. The FCC (Federal Communications Commission) allocated ten different channels in the frequency range used by cordless phones. Some phones are equipped to use only one channel, and others can be switched among two, three, or all ten channels, allowing you to search for the clearest transmission.

Although manufacturers cite a maximum distance between the base and the handset, which is usually between 700 and 1,500 feet, clear reception is based upon several factors. Electrical storms, dense trees and foliage, and other cordless phones in use in your immediate vicinity can have an impact on the operation of your unit.

Prices are accurate at time of printing; subject to manufacturer's change.

Two other features found on cordless phones are **intercom** and **paging**. Intercom allows you to speak between the base and the handset. Paging lets you send a tone signal between the base and the handset. If two-way paging is offered, the signal can be sent either way. With one-way paging, the signal can be sent only from the base to the handset. The paging feature can be used to locate your handset.

SOUTHWESTERN BELL FREEDOM PHONE FF 1725

The Southwestern Bell Freedom Phone FF 1725 functions as two phones. The base unit is a full-function speakerphone, and you can make or receive calls from either the base or the handset. In addition, it features a nine-number memory, intercom, last-number redial, and switchable tone/pulse dialing. The durable handset has a 1,000-foot range and features an extending antenna, snap-out battery pack, and ten channels with programmable security codes. The circuitry on this model is designed to improve clarity and reduce interference. **Warranty:** one year.

Approx. retail price	**Approx. low price**
$185	$179

CODE-A-PHONE 7010

The Code-A-Phone Model 7010 has fewer features than other cordless models and for that reason is very affordably priced. It's an attractive, ultracompact phone that offers one-way paging, large easy-to-read buttons, user replaceable battery and antenna, ringer-volume control, pause, flash, and last-number redial. **Warranty:** one year.

Approx. retail price	**Approx. low price**
$75	$60

SONY SPP-120

RECOMMENDED

The Sony SPP-120 is a compact cordless that's fully featured with ten-number speed dialing (two-step memory) and three

Prices are accurate at time of printing; subject to manufacturer's change.

one-touch memory numbers, ten channels with programmable security, and a dual battery system to ensure that either the base or handset is working at all times. This cordless has a channel button that allows you to change the channel during a call in case of interference.

Warranty: one year.

Approx. retail price	Approx. low price
$230	$182

COBRA INTENNA AN-8525   `RECOMMENDED`

The Cobra Intenna AN-8525 is a cordless phone with an integrated telephone answering system. The handset features Cobra's built-in antenna, noise-reduction circuitry, digital security coding, and a nine-number memory. The beeperless-remote answering device uses a digital voice chip for outgoing messages and records incoming messages on a micro-cassette. With the handset, you can screen messages that are being left on the tape, interrupt, and take the call if you like.

Warranty: one year.

Approx. retail price	Approx. low price
$230	$94

SONY SPP-320   `RECOMMENDED`

The Sony SPP-320 is a combination cordless phone and full-function base telephone. From the base you can place and receive calls using a receiver or the speakerphone. The cordless handset is designed to deliver seven-day standby time. It features a dual battery system, noise-reduction circuitry, ten-number memory, channel button, and two-way intercom.

Warranty: one year.

Approx. retail price	Approx. low price
$340	$266

Cellular Mobile and Portable Phones

The mobile telephone is an essential business tool for anyone who needs to be in continuous contact with clients. Cellu-

---

Prices are accurate at time of printing; subject to manufacturer's change.

lar telephone service is now widely available, and prices are coming down. If you live near a major city, you probably have a choice between two carriers. The FCC regulates cellular services and allocates cellular licenses to two carriers in each area.

The cellular system divides each area into a number of cells with one central mobile telephone switching office (MTSO) that ties the cells to a conventional phone system. When you dial a number from your cellular phone, this signal is transmitted to an MTSO that transmits it to the telephone system. As you drive around, you move from one cell to another. Each cell site has a radio receiver/transmitter that hands you off to an adjacent cell. If you move from one cellular service area to another, you are automatically switched to the service in the new area.

For cellular phone service you pay both fixed and ongoing access and usage fees that are similar to the monthly fees you are charged for your home telephone. The fixed costs are the cost of the cellular phone itself and the initial installation and service activation fee.

In addition to standard cellular phones installed in your automobile or boat, transportable and portable cellular phones are also available. These three kinds of cellular phones differ not only in size, but also in price and the amount of power. Standard and transportable models transmit at three watts, while portables operate at ⅗ watt.

Cellular telephones offer most of the features of standard phones including memory dialing, last-number redial, and speakerphone. Many offer on-hook dialing, which lets you dial a number without picking up the handset. One difference between cellular and standard phones is that the cellular service charges you for both the calls you send and the calls you receive.

DIAMONDTEL 95M

The DiamondTel 95M is a deluxe, compact cellular telephone with a duplex speakerphone. It has a 100-number memory with a directory scan, last-number redial, and a silent scratch pad that lets you enter a number into a temporary memory instead of jotting it down. It's a car phone that can be converted into a transportable with an optional kit. A turn-off override feature lets you continue talking once the car ignition is off. There's a call timer and counter as well as an electronic lock that prevents unauthorized calls. It has the full 832-channel capacity.

Warranty: parts and labor, three years.

Approx. retail price	Approx. low price
$1,050	$620

RADIO SHACK CT 102 ✔**BEST BUY**

The Radio Shack CT 102 is a low-priced mobile phone that offers all the basic features. It has a permanent car mount that offers hands-free operation. A 30-number memory and last-number redial and recall features are also included. There's a call-in-absence indicator as well as a call-lock feature that prevents unauthorized calls. It also has a backlit LCD.

Warranty: one year.

Approx. retail price	Approx. low price
$299 (with activation)	$299

Cellular Portable Phones

OKI PHONES 750

The OKI PHONES 750 is a portable weighing just $17\frac{3}{16}$ ounces. A permanent car mount is an optional accessory. This phone has a 200-number memory, last-number redial, and re-call. Once recharged, it offers over two hours of talk-time. Re-charging takes 90 minutes, and the batteries are replaceable. It comes with a call-in-absence indicator and a call-lock feature that prevents unauthorized calls. All of its features are easily accessible through user-friendly menus.

Warranty: three years.

Approx. retail price	Approx. low price
$1,299	$746

MOTOROLA MICROTAC DIGITAL PERSONAL COMMUNICATOR TELEPHONE (950 DPC)

RECOMMENDED

The Motorola Microtac Digital Personal Communicator Telephone (950 DPC) is a portable cellular that weighs $6\frac{7}{10}$ ounces. With its special slim-line battery, the unit is at its most compact, but there's an interchangeable regular battery as well. It features on-hook dialing, automatic last-number redial, a 120-number memory, and two lines. With this model, there is no permanent car mount. It has a call-in-absence indicator and a car-lock feature that prevents unauthorized calls. Once recharged, it offers about an hour of talk-time. Recharging takes 10 hours.

Warranty: three years.

Approx. retail price	Approx. low price
$2,495	not available

Answering Machines

Answering machines offer the convenience of never having to miss a phone call. They are easy to install; simply plug one into a modular phone jack and an electrical outlet. Two-line answering machines are especially convenient for someone who has a small business at home and needs both the home and business numbers answered.

Most answering machines include two tapes, one for your outgoing messages (OGM) and one to record the incoming messages (ICM). These tapes can be either standard C-cassettes or microcassettes. The only difference is in size; microcassettes allow manufacturers to make smaller machines.

Less expensive, smaller single-tape machines put both the outgoing and the incoming messages on one tape. These units are designed for someone who does not get many messages. The machine sits in position at the beginning of the outgoing message and waits for a call. When the phone rings, it plays the outgoing message and then moves over any already-received calls while sounding a beep tone. It is then ready to record another incoming call. If there are many messages, the beep tone can last as long as a couple of seconds and be annoying to callers. Some single-tape machines use digital recording voice chips for the outgoing message. Since the tape is only for incoming messages, there is plenty of capacity and no problem with the beep tone. Some manufacturers offer machines that record incoming and outgoing messages on chips, but the number of incoming messages is limited to three 15-second messages.

Features and Terminology

Autodisconnect allows you to pick up any telephone in your home while the answering machine is taking a message and stop the answering machine automatically.

Beeperless remote lets you call in to get your messages from any touch-tone phone. You access your machine with a security code.

Call screening allows you to listen to a call as it comes in.

Memo lets you put a message on the machine while you are at home for someone who is coming home later. When that person comes in and listens to the phone messages, your memo will be heard.

Remote turn-on allows you to turn on your machine, usually by calling it and letting it ring about ten times.

Toll saver lets you call long distance for your messages and not pay for the call if there are no messages. The answering machine will ring more often before answering the first message (usually four times) and then only once before answering subsequent calls. When you call your phone number, if the telephone rings more than once, you know there are no messages and you can hang up.

VOX allows the incoming message to be any length, up to the maximum capacity of the tape. The machine continues recording as long as the person keeps speaking. It will not chop off the end of the message or leave a dead space or dial tone at the end of the message. The machine usually waits a few seconds after the caller stops speaking before hanging up. This is a very practical feature for anyone who wants to make sure that all of his or her messages are received in full.

COBRA TIMEKEEPER AN-8537

The Cobra Timekeeper AN-8537 is a microcassette system answerer that features VOX and a time and date voice "stamp." It has a beeperless remote with autodisconnect, a digital call counter, and a switchable musical or standard beep tone that follows the outgoing message.

Warranty: one year.

Approx. retail price	Approx. low price
$110	$80

AT&T ANSWERING SYSTEM 1304

RECOMMENDED

The AT&T Answering System 1304 is a basic answering machine that's perfect for someone who doesn't get a lot of calls. It is a beeperless-remote system with autodisconnect, toll saver, an LED message-received indicator, and personal memo feature.

Warranty: one year.

Approx. retail price	Approx. low price
$80	$72

CODE-A-PHONE MODEL 1920

RECOMMENDED

The Code-A-Phone Model 1920 is a relatively inexpensive answering machine that features a digital message counter and personal memo. It has a beeperless remote with a toll-saver function. Ring delay lets you determine how many times the phone will ring before the answering machine takes the call. It comes in black and can be mounted on the wall.

Warranty: one year.

Approx. retail price	Approx. low price
$70	not available

Prices are accurate at time of printing; subject to manufacturer's change.

Computers

There are hundreds of computers from which to choose. To help you find the right one, our reviews are divided into five categories: under $1,000; $1,000 to $2,000; $2,000 to $3,000; over $3,000; and portable computers. We usually describe computers without any extras, but some "extras" are required. For example, some systems are sold without video monitors, but you must have one to use the computer. An incomplete system may cost less initially, but better-equipped systems may offer superior value if they have the "extras" you need.

The Ratings

Ratings at the end of each review use a scale of one (worst) to ten (best) to rate the computer's overall value, performance, ease of use, documentation, software (how much is offered for that computer), and expandability (the availability of and capacity for add-ons). Portable computers are rated for portability, not expandability.

The Overall Value rating measures how well the computer's price compares to its performance, ease of use, and features. An overpriced system will not have a high rating. The Performance rating tells how well the computer functions. The Ease of Use rating measures how easy the computer is to learn to use; most systems are easy to use after you have become familiar with them. The Documentation rating tells how well the manuals explain the computer's functions and if the manuals are well organized.

Understanding Computer Terminology

You do not need a technical understanding of computers to select and use one. But you do need to know some terms.

A computer's "brain," the **central processing unit (CPU)** or **microprocessor**, resides on one **chip**, which is a tiny silicon wafer with thousands of electronic parts. The CPU and the **operating system software** regulate the data transfer between the computer's parts as well as between the computer and a peripheral such as a printer. The CPU does math and tests hypotheses that are "true" or "false," which it indicates by allowing or preventing electricity to flow through a circuit.

The CPU usually receives data from a disk drive (see below), a keyboard (as on a typewriter), a **modem** (a device used to send data over telephone lines to another computer), or a **mouse**, which is a small device that you roll on a desktop or a special pad to move the **cursor** (the on-screen pointer that shows where a character will be inserted, deleted, or moved). The mouse's button(s) lets you access on-screen functions. Another input device is a **joystick**, which is a small box with a vertical lever that you tilt to move an on-screen figure.

The CPU uses **random-access memory (RAM)** to manipulate data and programs. **Read-only memory (ROM)** may store the operating system, utility programs, and/or applications, such as word processing, that will be sent to the RAM. The contents of RAM are usually lost when the electricity is shut off; ROM retains its memory. RAM changes constantly; ROM does not. Peripherals also use RAM and ROM. For example, printers use RAM **buffers** to store data received from the computer until it can be printed.

RAM and ROM are measured in **bytes**, which are made up of **bits**. A bit (*Binary dig/T*) is the smallest unit of data. Its value is either one or zero (yes or no). A group of bits, usually eight, make up one byte that represents a letter, number, or symbol. A byte is treated as a unit of data. Roughly 1,000 bytes are equal to one **kilobyte (K or Kb or K byte)**. A **megabyte (M or Mb or M byte)** is about one million bytes.

The more RAM in a computer, the better. This allows for larger, more powerful programs that run faster. Some programs hide in RAM until you need them. These **RAM-resident programs** steal RAM from the main program in use, reducing the amount of data you can create. The operating system also uses RAM, unless it exists in ROM.

Programs and data are saved on magnetic **disks** and **tapes**. **Floppy disks** (or **diskettes**) are circular and flexible, although they have square, stiff housings. **Hard disks** are rigid and hold more data than floppy disks. Hard disks also speed up the loading of software into RAM and make programs run faster.

Single-sided floppies use one side of the disk; double-sided floppies use both sides. Quad-density (or high-density) disks hold more data than double- and single-density disks. You must know how many sides and the density your computer needs when you buy blank disks. Avoid no-name bargain-priced disks.

A **disk drive** transfers data and programs between RAM and a disk. A **disk operating system (DOS)** is an operating system that stores data on disks. The most common one is Microsoft's MS-DOS and its IBM version, PC-DOS; both systems are used by IBM-compatible computers (or clones). A **proprietary operating system** is used by only one manufacturer, so programs written for other computers cannot normally be used. If you work closely with other computer users, you should use the same operating system.

The CPU sends the data it has processed to an output device, such as a video monitor, printer, modem, or disk drive. The CPU, RAM, ROM, other chips, and connecting circuits are on the main circuit board, called the **motherboard**. This board often has slots for **expansion cards** (small circuit boards) that add functions, speed, or memory to the computer.

A computer's **ports** (connectors for peripherals) and operating system limit the devices and programs a computer can use. Software is often sold for only one operating system. In addition, a computer with an RS-232C port can only use devices that have RS-232C **interfaces** (software and hardware that permit the transfer of data). The words "port" and "interface" are used interchangeably. There are many varieties of the two most common interfaces, RS-232C serial and Centronics parallel.

Prices

Manufacturers constantly change their prices or add "free" items to their systems. Prices also vary in different parts of the country. Plus, the fluctuations in the value of the U.S. dollar may affect costs. Therefore, the retail and low prices in this buying guide may not be the same as those offered by a local store or a nationwide mail-order outlet. Compare prices from several computer dealers, and check advertisements.

Where to Buy

Computers are sold primarily by department stores, computer stores, and mail-order firms. Department store prices can be low, but their clerks often cannot give you technical help. Such stores do not offer a wide selection, and they usually send items to the manufacturer for repair, which may take a long time unless the manufacturer has a local repair center.

A computer store usually offers a wider selection, hands-on evaluations, knowledgeable salespeople, training, technical help, and factory-trained repair service, which eliminates shipping time. Discounts vary greatly between stores, but you can often obtain a sizable discount when you buy a complete system.

Mail-order firms advertise in computer magazines. They offer a wide selection and low prices. A few companies promote new items before they are released or fail to ship items for which your credit card has been billed, so check out the firm by contacting a satisfied client and the Better Business Bureau. Use the firm's toll-free number to confirm the product's description, price, and compatibility. Accept brand names only. Place your credit-card order cautiously. Make your first order a small one. When a shipment arrives, report any damage to the box *before the driver leaves* on all copies of the receipt or on the proper form. If a box is severely damaged, don't accept it, and immediately call the mail-order firm to ask for a new shipment.

Best Buys '91

Our Best Buy and Recommended computers follow. Within each category, the Best Buys are listed first, followed by our

Recommended choices in order of decreasing overall value. If all the ratings for two items are identical, the reviews appear in alphabetical order. A Best Buy or Recommended designation applies only to the model listed; it does not necessarily apply to other models made by the same manufacturer.

COMPUTERS UNDER $1,000

COMPUADD 216

The CompuAdd 216 delivers hefty performance and good flexibility in a low-profile, very reasonably priced package. This dual-speed (8 or 16 MHz) IBM-compatible system uses an Intel 80286 microprocessor. The $895 base model 216 includes a 101-key keyboard, 512Kb of memory, and your choice of a 5.25-inch 1.2Mb floppy disk drive or a 3.5-inch 1.44Mb microfloppy drive.

Featuring very good expandability, the 216 can support two additional disk drives, and it has three 16-bit (AT-compatible) expansion slots that accept full-size cards and two 8-bit (XT-compatible) slots that handle half-size cards. Because the main circuit board contains the one parallel and two serial interfaces and the floppy and hard disk drive controller circuitry, four expansion slots will be free, even after a display card is added to the system.

Adding another 512Kb of RAM to the system's standard 512Kb costs $95. The main circuit board can hold up to four single inline memory modules (SIMMs). That translates to a maximum capacity of from one to four megabytes, depending on the type of SIMMs used. If more memory is desired, a memory board can be used in a free expansion slot.

Although the CompuAdd keyboard lacks crisp tactile response, its overall feel is markedly better than we have come to expect from inexpensive personal computers.

In our performance tests, the 216 yielded impressive results for a low-cost AT-compatible. It was over twice as fast as a standard 8-MHz IBM AT. Our 216's computational speed was complemented by a 40-megabyte Western Digital hard drive that exhibited good overall performance.

Prices are accurate at time of printing; subject to manufacturer's change.

Several 216 packages add a hard drive, a house-brand display card, and a monitor. The pricing of systems with Hercules-compatible monochrome displays depends on the hard drive: $1,459 with a 40-megabyte drive, $1,729 with an 80-megabyte drive, and $1,929 with a 110-megabyte drive. Opting for color VGA graphics adds $330 to the package. CompuAdd-brand monitors and display cards are of good quality. The firm also discounts brand-name peripherals.

No software is included with the base model 216, but MS-DOS 4.01 is available for $89. CompuAdd systems purchased with hard drives include PC-Fullbak+ backup software.

We judged the overall construction of the CompuAdd 216 to be excellent. The instruction booklets are complete, easy to follow, and clearly illustrated.

CompuAdd systems may be purchased at CompuAdd retail outlets in most metropolitan areas, or by telephone from the company's mail-order facility. Free assistance is available to CompuAdd customers through local stores and a toll-free technical support line.

There are many AT-compatible systems being sold in catalog showrooms and appliance stores that may cost a few hundred dollars less than a fully configured CompuAdd system. However, the 216 offers significantly higher performance, the ability to configure the system to meet your specific needs, and better after-sale support. Hardware sold by CompuAdd carries a 30-day money-back guarantee.

Specifications: RAM, 512Kb; **operating system**, MS-DOS, MS OS/2; **included hardware**, system unit with CPU, keyboard, 1.44Mb microfloppy or 1.2Mb floppy disk drive, Centronics parallel port, two RS-232C serial ports, game port interface, clock/calendar; **included software**, none. **Warranty**, one year.
Ratings: overall value, 9; **ease of use**, 8; **software**, 10; **performance**, 9; **documentation**, 10; **expandability**, 9.

Approx. retail price	Approx. low price
$895 (Part No. 64776)	$895

COMMODORE AMIGA 500   RECOMMENDED

The Commodore Amiga 500 (A500) is a fairly powerful system with both unique graphics and sound at an attractive price. Its

7.16-MHz Motorola 68000 microprocessor can work faster thanks to chips that control graphics, animation, and sound. Commodore's A501 card expands the 512Kb of RAM to a full megabyte and adds a clock/calendar. Using this $159 card and external modules, you can increase the RAM to 9Mb.

The multitasking operating system can run many programs simultaneously. For example, you can edit a word processing file while sorting a database. Kickstart, part of the operating system, is in ROM, so you don't have to load it from a disk. The easy-to-use Workbench user interface employs windows (on-screen areas) and icons (tiny pictures depicting programs or files). The two-button mouse lets you move the cursor (on-screen pointer) to select an icon.

Commodore's 1084S monitor ($399) is an analog and digital RGB color monitor that has a built-in stereo speaker. Besides being attached to a computer, it can be used with a TV tuner or a videocassette recorder. The A500 can display 16-color graphics at a resolution of 640-by-400 pixels (dots). In the 320-by-400 or the 320-by-200 mode, the A500 displays 32 colors chosen from 4,096 hues.

The 94-key keyboard feels solid and offers function keys, cursor-control keys, and a numeric keypad. A 3.5-inch 880Kb microfloppy disk drive is built into the side of the system; a front-mounted drive would be easier to use. Commodore's A590 Hard Drive Plus ($800) is a 20Mb external hard disk that has a board to which you can add 2Mb of RAM.

The stereo ports, sound coprocessor, and four-voice, two-channel sound are ideal for music applications. The crude speech synthesizer is of little use, however.

Commodore sells a 1200-bps (bits per second, or baud) modem and an external 360Kb 5.25-inch floppy drive. Other firms offer MIDI (musical instrument digital interface) devices, color video digitizers, and a unit that mixes computer images with those from sources such as camcorders.

Amiga entertainment, graphics, music, and video programs are excellent. Solid word processors, database programs, and spreadsheets are also available. However, the selection of business software is very limited compared with that for IBM computers. Commodore now bundles the A500 with a television adapter and free software: the Textcraft Plus word processor, the popular Tetris game, and the entertaining and educational Where in the World is Carmen Sandiego?

The 200-page indexed manual is clearly written and heavily illustrated, making the A500 easy to set up. The on-disk tutorial is very helpful.

In addition to the $799 consumer package described in this review, Commodore announced a $799 professional version of the Amiga 500, which includes a full megabyte of RAM, the AmigaDOS operating system, and AmigaVision. The television adapter and other software provided with the consumer version do not come with the professional package. AmigaVision is software that simplifies the combination of graphics, text, video, and audio in order to create multimedia presentations. AmigaVision requires one megabyte of RAM and is also sold separately for $149.

Commodore recently announced CommodoreExpress, a new 24-hour toll-free "helpline" and door-to-door customer service program. The helpline offers assistance in setting up and operating A500 computers. CommodoreExpress also includes free pickup and return delivery by Federal Express for warranty repairs. Repairs will be completed within 24 hours after the computer is received. This program is offered to owners of new A500 computers purchased in the U.S. after January 1, 1990. Owners of older A500 systems can also use the helpline at no charge and use the pickup, return delivery, and repair service for an applicable fee.

Specifications: RAM, 512Kb; **operating system**, proprietary; **included hardware**, system unit with CPU and integral keyboard, 880Kb microfloppy disk drive, video display circuitry, mouse, external power supply, Centronics parallel port, RS-232C serial port, external disk drive port, mouse/joystick/light pen ports, stereo sound ports, system expansion bus port, monochrome composite video port, analog RGB color video port; **included software**, AmigaDOS operating system; AmigaBASIC; Amiga Tutorial. **Warranty**, one year. **Ratings: overall value**, 9; **ease of use**, 10; **software**, 9; **performance**, 8; **documentation**, 10; **expandability**, 8.

Approx. retail price	Approx. low price
$799	not available

COMPUTERS FROM $1,000 TO $2,000

ALR POWERFLEX MODEL 40 ✓BEST BUY

The ALR PowerFlex Model 40 offers solid performance and value; it is also easily upgraded. Its standard processor is a 12.5-MHz Intel 80286. However, a slot on the main circuit board allows you to upgrade the PowerFlex to a 80386 or 80486 computer. The upgrade modules simply plug in, and the PowerFlex reconfigures itself automatically.

The $1,149 base system comes with one 3.5-inch 1.44Mb microfloppy disk drive, while adding a 40Mb hard drive raises the price to $1,495. The compact system unit (15 inches wide by 17 inches deep) manages to pack a lot of power and expandability into that space. The microfloppy disk drive and hard drive are mounted vertically, leaving enough space for two more data storage devices. If you install a 16-bit (AT-compatible) video card, one 8-bit (XT-compatible) and three 16-bit expansion slots remain open.

The main circuit board contains the disk drive controller circuitry, serial and parallel ports, and a math coprocessor socket. The board had no last-minute wiring changes and few electronic components, which means that long-term reliability should be better than average. You can expand the one megabyte of memory to 5Mb by simply adding memory modules to the main circuit board. Using a memory expansion card, the RAM can be increased to 16Mb.

The 101-key keyboard is comfortable, but its feedback lacks a solid sense of touch. We prefer keys that have more "click." The front-mounted power switch is convenient.

The CPU performance of our stock PowerFlex was good, measuring about 1.8 times as fast as an 8-MHz IBM AT. Adding ALR's 16-MHz 80386SX processor card ($395) increased performance by another ten percent. That's not much, but it does allow you to use software that requires an 80386 processor. ALR also offers a 20-MHz 80386SX processor card for $595, which we did not test. We also did not have access to ALR's $1,995 i486 processor card, which contains a 25-MHz 80486 processor. ALR claims that it gives the PowerFlex 9.7 times the power of the original IBM AT.

Prices are accurate at time of printing; subject to manufacturer's change.

The 40Mb Western Digital hard disk was praiseworthy, too. Its very good performance can be augmented by special disk caching software that ALR supplies. (Disk caching allows the use of RAM to store data often accessed from a disk.)

Our ALR Model 1413 VGA monitor ($499) had good color and reasonable sharpness, but our test unit had a tendency to "ghost" when displaying black text on a white background. The supplied Paradise VGA card, which costs an extra $329, was also a modest performer. We recommend opting for a better monitor and display card if your budget permits.

Although not for novices, the quick-reference guide is straightforward, easy to follow, and clearly illustrated. A more detailed reference guide costs extra.

You may have to go out of your way to find an ALR dealer, but the extra effort is well worth it. The performance, low cost, and expandability of the PowerFlex Model 40 make it a highly desirable system.

Specifications: RAM, one megabyte (1,024Kb); **operating system**, MS-DOS; MS OS/2; **included hardware**, system unit with CPU, keyboard, 1.44Mb microfloppy disk drive, Centronics parallel port, RS-232C serial port, clock/calendar; **included software**, setup and utility software. **Warranty**, one year. **Ratings: overall value**, 10; **ease of use**, 9; **software**, 10; **performance**, 9; **documentation**, 8; **expandability**, 10.

Approx. retail price	Approx. low price
$1,149	not available

HYUNDAI SUPER-386S | RECOMMENDED |

The Hyundai Super-386S is a compact 80386SX-based computer with a price to match. When Intel first announced the 386SX in the spring of 1988, it expected most manufacturers to jump on the SX bandwagon. After all, the 386SX cost less than an Intel 80386 chip, and offered equivalent speed. However, the 386SX can address only 16Mb of memory and its 16-bit data bus (the electrical pathway for data flow) had the potential to send only half the amount of data as an 80386 could. "Power users" looked down on the 386SX. About a year later, Intel repriced the 386SX to be competitive with the high-speed 80286 chips being manufactured by its competitors. Within a few months, the 386SX became a very popular medium-priced computer.

A 16-MHz 386SX system does not have any more processing power than a 16-MHz 80286 system. Paying slightly more for a computer equipped with a 386SX processor is akin to buying an insurance policy to be sure that your computer can use any software designed for 386 processors. Although relatively few programs of that type are on the market today, their number and capabilities are sure to increase.

The Super-386S comes with one 5.25-inch 1.2Mb floppy disk drive, one serial port, one parallel port, a math coprocessor socket, and one megabyte of memory. The main circuit board has room for up to eight megabytes of RAM, and a special expansion slot accepts a proprietary card that can hold another eight megabytes. We were surprised at the large numbers of chips and switches on the main circuit board, however. Most newer systems use fewer, though more dense, chips. They also use software rather than manual switches to change system options. Even so, the board was of high quality, with no last-minute wiring changes.

With a 16-bit Hyundai VGA graphics card ($345) installed, one 8-bit (XT-compatible) and three 16-bit (AT-compatible) expansion slots remained free. Our evaluation unit was also equipped with a 40Mb hard disk drive, which adds $750 to the system price and left room for one more data storage device. Hyundai's 14-inch VGA monitor ($645) displayed pleasingly sharp, rich colors.

System performance is where we expect it to be. In the "fast" mode, the dual-speed 8-MHz/16-MHz 386SX processor yields twice the power of an 8-MHz IBM AT, and the 40Mb Conner-made hard drive is quiet and speedy. The power switch and reset button are front-mounted, and the 101-key keyboard has a light touch with positive click action.

MS-DOS 3.3 and GW-BASIC is included with the Super-386S. The manuals for this software are very good. An otherwise fine user guide for the computer is marred only by the omission of illustrations that would help first-time users.

Given the discounts associated with Hyundai computers, it's likely that a well-equipped Super-386S could be acquired for about the same price as 80286 machines with more famous

Prices are accurate at time of printing; subject to manufacturer's change.

nameplates. When competitively priced, the Hyundai's "SX appeal" and longer-than-usual warranty may make this machine one of the best bargains in its class.

Specifications: RAM, one megabyte (1,024Kb); **operating system**, MS-DOS, MS OS/2; **included hardware**, system unit with CPU, keyboard, 1.2Mb floppy disk drive, Centronics parallel port, RS-232C serial port; **included software**, MS-DOS 3.3, GW-BASIC, system diagnostics. **Warranty**, 18 months. **Ratings: overall value**, 10; **ease of use**, 8; **software**, 10; **performance**, 8; **documentation**, 9; **expandability**, 8.

Approx. retail price	Approx. low price
$1,445	$1,026

COMPUTERS FROM $2,000 TO $3,000

COMPUADD 320 ✓BEST BUY

The CompuAdd 320 offers impressive power and expandability at a price that is much lower than other 20-MHz 80386-based systems. Free one-year on-site service in 250 cities; toll-free support; and a 30-day money-back guarantee place it on our list of most-affordable 80386 systems.

With a 40Mb hard drive and your choice of either a 5.25-inch 1.2Mb floppy drive or a 3.5-inch 1.44Mb microfloppy drive installed, the system unit can hold three more data storage devices. The one megabyte of RAM resides on a card attached to a special slot on the main circuit board. This card holds up to 16Mb. After installing the standard Hercules-compatible graphics display card and floppy disk controller card, one 8-bit (XT-compatible) and four 16-bit (AT-compatible) expansion slots remain free. The unit also has a math coprocessor socket.

The feel of the 101-key keyboard is not very crisp, but it is better than average. CompuAdd's 16-bit VGA display card (made by Paradise) and 14-inch VGA color monitor cost $330 more and are of good quality. Brand-name display adapters and monitors may be substituted at extra cost. The one parallel and two serial ports were not labeled on the case or clearly identified in the "quick user's guide."

Prices are accurate at time of printing; subject to manufacturer's change.

We judged the CompuAdd 320's computational performance to be slightly better than other low-cost 20-MHz 80386 machines we have tested. It was about 2.7 times faster than a standard 8-MHz IBM AT. That's a little over 70 percent of the power afforded by an IBM PS/2 Model 70, which costs over $5,000 more than the 320. The 40Mb Western Digital hard drive was a better performer, though a little noisier, than average. We also tried an Imprimis-built 80Mb drive ($270 extra), which yielded one of the best performance scores we have ever logged. For more data storage, fast 110Mb ($470 extra) and 320Mb (an additional $1,440) units may also be substituted.

The system construction is good, although the chassis is made of slightly lighter-gauge metal than more costly systems. The main circuit board had six last-minute wiring changes. The hard drive in our unit failed after two weeks and had to be replaced under warranty. We had no further problems during the remaining three months of our evaluation period.

Complete CompuAdd 320 systems come with setup and utility software, MS-DOS 4.01, and a version of the Microsoft Windows graphical user interface. The well-illustrated documentation is adequate for experienced users, but a bit tough for novices. Help is available from dealers and a toll-free technical support line. During the warranty period, CompuAdd provides free on-site service in 250 metropolitan areas. CompuAdd computers may also be brought to local outlets, or shipped to a Texas repair facility. Systems may be purchased at CompuAdd retail outlets in most metropolitan areas, or by phone from the firm's mail-order facility. Hardware sold by CompuAdd carries a "30-day no-questions-asked" money-back guarantee.

A fully configured CompuAdd 320 costs hundreds of dollars less than units with more familiar names. The CompuAdd 320 offers excellent expandability and solid performance, and it is backed by CompuAdd's strong support policies and highly competitive pricing.

Specifications: RAM, one megabyte (1,024Kb); **operating system**, MS-DOS; MS OS/2; **included hardware**, system unit with CPU, keyboard, 1.2Mb floppy or 1.44Mb microfloppy disk drive, 40Mb hard disk drive, monochrome monitor, video display card, Centronics parallel port, two RS-232C serial ports, clock/calendar; **included software**, MS-DOS 4.01, CompuAdd licensed version of Microsoft Windows, setup and utility software. **Warranty**, one year. **Ratings: overall value**, 10; **ease of use**, 8; **software**, 10; **performance**, 9; **documentation**, 9; **expandability**, 10.

Approx. retail price	Approx. low price
$2,259 (Part No. 64965)	$2,259

AST BRAVO/386SX   RECOMMENDED

The AST Bravo/386SX adds the performance of Intel's 80386SX microprocessor to the popular Bravo lineup, which is less costly (and less expandable) than AST Research's well-respected Premium line. Very good construction, easy-to-follow instructions, and compatibility with 80386-specific software make this model a capable computer with a reasonable price.

The $2,095 list price may seem too high compared to some lower-cost 386SX-based systems. However, the standard VGA Plus display card is normally a $329 option, making the Bravo/386SX one of the lowest-priced brand-name systems of its type. The Bravo comes with a choice of a 5.25-inch 1.2Mb floppy or 3.5-inch 1.44Mb microfloppy disk drive.

The system unit has one XT-compatible (8-bit) and three AT-compatible (16-bit) expansion slots, and a math coprocessor socket. One of the 16-bit slots holds AST's VGA Plus display card. Expansion cards must be mounted in the slots horizontally rather than vertically. The left edges of mounted cards are supported by a screw-on bracket that was awkward to remove and reattach as we added cards. With a 40Mb hard drive installed ($750), there is room for one more data storage device. We rate expandability to be good enough for the average home user or small business.

You can expand the 2Mb of RAM to 4Mb without using an expansion card. The keyboard connector, reset button, and on/off switch are on the back panel, as are the parallel and serial ports. The 101-key keyboard has a slightly vague feel; it may take a while to get used to it. We prefer a greater sense of touch in the keyboard response.

The internal fit and finish are impressive, despite the dense plastic chassis. Heavy-gauge metal is used for the system unit's cover. The main circuit board has few components, which should extend the long-term reliability. The overall quality of construction is very good.

Our Bravo turned in an overall CPU performance of about 2.1 times that of an 8-MHz IBM AT. If desired, the Bravo can be slowed down to the speed of an IBM XT or AT system. The 40Mb hard drive was quiet and fast, and exhibited a higher-than-average data transfer rate. The AST Premium VGA monitor ($695) produced sharp, colorful images with almost no distortion, and AST's VGA Plus adapter was one of the quickest and most capable VGA cards we ever tested.

The user manual combines a straightforward style with helpful illustrations. A "quick start" instruction pamphlet is also included. Advanced users will find the manual a bit short on technical content, however. The included utility programs and diagnostics are handy and well documented. MS-DOS 3.3 and GW-BASIC cost an additional $95. Version 1.1 of the OS/2 operating system retails for $340.

AST's product quality, longevity, user-friendly documentation, and capable technical support make the Bravo/386SX a good buy. Bravo computers are often discounted. If you are looking for a solid value in a brand-name 386SX-based computer, strongly consider the AST Bravo/386SX.

Specifications: RAM, two megabytes (2,048Kb); **operating system**, MS-DOS, MS OS/2; **included hardware**, system unit with CPU, keyboard, 1.2Mb floppy or 1.44Mb microfloppy disk drive, video display card, Centronics parallel port, RS-232C serial port; **included software**, diagnostics, setup, utilities. **Warranty**, one year. **Ratings: overall value**, 10; **ease of use**, 8; **software**, 10; **performance**, 9; **documentation**, 9; **expandability**, 8.

Approx. retail price	Approx. low price
$2,095	$1,515

HYUNDAI SUPER-386C | RECOMMENDED

The Hyundai Super-386c is a strong contender among 80386 computers when combined with its highly competitive prices,

Prices are accurate at time of printing; subject to manufacturer's change.

good reliability, and a longer-than-average warranty.

The full-size system unit has two 8-bit (XT-compatible) expansion slots and four 16-bit (AT-compatible) slots. The slots, disk drive controller circuitry, parallel port, and serial port are built into one of two circuit boards in the system unit. A math coprocessor socket is also included. The CPU, memory, and logic chips reside on a separate board that plugs into a special slot next to the expansion slots. The 386c comes with one 5.25-inch 1.2Mb floppy disk drive. After adding a Hyundai hard drive, there is still room for two more data storage devices.

The 20-MHz Intel 80386 processor can be run at 8 MHz if desired. This system comes with one megabyte of RAM. The system board can be expanded to 8Mb of RAM, and an optional "daughterboard" allows adding another 8Mb without using an expansion slot. The overall expandability is excellent.

The keyboard has a nice "clicky" feel that is a bit light, but otherwise satisfactory. The on/off switch and reset button are conveniently mounted in front.

The Super-386c provides 2.5 times the speed of an 8-MHz IBM AT. However, the performance of the 40Mb hard drive supplied with our test unit (for an extra $600) was rather puzzling. The drive looked identical to the 40Mb Conner-built hard drive that came with our less powerful Hyundai Super-386S. However, the drive in the 386S outperformed the 386c's hard drive, yielding almost twice the data transfer rate of its apparent twin. We found that the Super-386c's drive was a Conner CP 342, which has been superseded by an improved model. The 386S, being of more recent manufacture, came with the newer CP 344. We recommend that 386c purchasers insist on the newer Conner drive if their system has a 40Mb hard disk supplied by Hyundai.

We tested Hyundai's HMM-1900 ($1,099), a large-screen monochrome monitor and display card combination. We enjoyed using the 19-inch (diagonal) screen with text-based programs, but it flickered noticeably when running Microsoft Windows 386 (a graphical user interface). On the other hand, Hyundai's 14-inch VGA display ($645) produced vibrant, sharp, and colorful images when coupled with a different Hyundai display card (actually the 16-bit VGA Wonder made by ATI Technologies), which retails for $345.

Prices are accurate at time of printing; subject to manufacturer's change.

We found no fault with the MS-DOS and GW-BASIC manuals. The user guide for the system was marred only by many misspellings and the omission of several illustrations.

A discounted Super-386c is likely to be priced on a par with brand-name 80286 and 80386SX computers that offer far less expandability and performance. Note that the Super-386c has an 18-month warranty, which is 50 percent longer than most other units. That, plus its low price, make this highly competent, but ordinary, computer a good bet.

Specifications: RAM, one megabyte (1,024Kb); **operating system**, MS-DOS; MS OS/2; **included hardware**, system unit with CPU, keyboard, 1.2Mb floppy disk drive, Centronics parallel port, RS-232C serial port, clock/calendar; **included software**, MS-DOS 3.3, GW-BASIC, diagnostics, setup utilities. **Warranty**, 18 months. **Ratings: overall value**, 10; **ease of use**, 8; **software**, 10; **performance**, 8; **documentation**, 8; **expandability**, 10.

Approx. retail price	Approx. low price
$2,195	not available

APPLE MACINTOSH SE | RECOMMENDED |

The Apple Macintosh SE (which differs from the Mac SE/30) resembles its predecessor, the Mac Plus. The SE retains the old Mac's size and shape, but has a platinum color. Gone are the louvers that let heat escape through the top of the Mac Plus. An internal fan eliminates the heat buildup that caused power supply problems in the original Mac Plus and earlier Macs. The SE also adds an internal expansion slot.

Performance has been improved, not by boosting the speed of the SE's 7.83-MHz Motorola 68000 processor, but by rewriting the operating system. The Mac SE performs almost 20 percent better than a similarly equipped Mac Plus.

To access the SE's one expansion slot (which is *not* compatible with the NuBus slots in the Mac II series), the case must be opened; this is a job for technicians. Orange Micro sells a $499 board that adds an Intel 8086 microprocessor to the Mac SE, allowing it to run IBM-type software and use IBM-compatible floppy drives.

The $2,569 base Mac SE has two 3.5-inch microfloppy disk drives that hold 1.4Mb each, and can read and write data stored in IBM format. In the $2,969 SE, one floppy drive is replaced with a 20Mb internal hard drive, while the $3,369 system has 2Mb of RAM and a 40Mb internal hard drive.

The nine-inch black-and-white screen has a resolution of only 512-by-342 pixels (dots), but it seems sharper due to the small screen size. On the back are serial ports for a modem and a printer. There are also ports for an external microfloppy drive ($429) and up to seven SCSI (Small Computer System Interface, pronounced "scuzzy") devices, like external hard drives. Two Apple Desktop Bus ports accept the mouse and extra-cost keyboard. Apple's 81-key keyboard ($129) feels good, but some users may find the keys to be too close together. A 105-key keyboard that follows IBM's enhanced layout costs $229.

The colorful manuals are easy to understand, and the Desktop Tour programs introduce new users to the unique aspects of Mac operation in an easily mastered format.

The operating system can run in two modes: Finder is for normal operations; MultiFinder is for multitasking, which allows you to use more than one program at the same time. For instance, you can sort a database file in the background (off-screen) while using a word processing program. Employing the Orange Micro board mentioned above, MultiFinder lets you use IBM-compatible and Mac programs simultaneously, and share information between them.

The supplied HyperCard software can be used to write interactive programs that mix text, graphics, animation, music, voice, and video. A Mac SE with only one megabyte of RAM cannot run HyperCard and MultiFinder simultaneously. The SE's one megabyte of RAM may be expanded to 4Mb.

Most Mac software runs on the SE. Icons (tiny on-screen images depicting files and commands) are still the basis of the Mac's user-friendly interface. Using the mouse, you move the cursor (on-screen pointer) to an icon and press a button on the mouse to access the desired function.

The four-voice sound generator supports excellent music composition and MIDI (musical instrument digital interface) programs. A $99 interface lets you connect MIDI devices (such as keyboards and electronic drum boxes) to a Mac, transforming it into a multitrack recorder and controller for music composition. Special software is required.

Prices are accurate at time of printing; subject to manufacturer's change.

If you need greater power, consider the Macintosh SE/30, which uses a 68030 chip and offers about 3.5 times the speed of a Mac SE and an additional expansion slot for an extra $1,300. Although not as powerful as the more costly Mac SE/30, the SE is still useful and a very good value.

Specifications: RAM, one megabyte (1,024Kb); **operating system**, proprietary; **included hardware**, system unit with CPU and integral monochrome monitor, 1.4Mb microfloppy disk drive, video display circuitry, mouse, two serial ports, external microfloppy disk drive port, SCSI port, two Desktop Bus ports, sound port, clock/calendar; **included software**, Finder and MultiFinder operating systems, Apple File Exchange, Guided Tour, HyperCard, System Tools, utilities. **Warranty**, one year.
Ratings: overall value, 9; **ease of use**, 10; **software**, 10; **performance**, 8; **documentation**, 9; **expandability**, 8.

Approx. retail price	Approx. low price
$2,569 (Model M0029LL/A)	$2,379

COMPUTERS OVER $3,000

COMMODORE AMIGA 3000/16 AND 3000/25

✓ BEST BUY

The Commodore Amiga 3000/16 and 3000/25 computers are very powerful systems that set new standards of price and power. They retain all the video and audio features that have come to be hallmarks of the Amiga line, and they can stand toe-to-toe with expensive IBM-compatible and Apple Macintosh "power" machines. When used for desktop video applications, the Amiga 3000 can run rings around the competition.

The system is about 15 inches square and five inches high. Our unit, which utilized a 25-MHz Motorola 68030 processor, yielded over five times the power of an Amiga 2000. (Commodore also offers a 16-MHz version of the Amiga 3000.) The 16-MHz Amiga 3000 has a Motorola 68881 math coprocessor, and the 25-MHz Amiga 3000 comes with the faster 68882. The two megabytes of RAM on the main circuit board can be expanded to 18Mb.

Standard drives include an 880Kb 3.5-inch microfloppy disk drive and a 50Mb hard disk, leaving room for one more data storage device. That's not a serious handicap, since the Amiga 3000 has connections for external floppy drives and SCSI (Small Computer System Interface, pronounced "scuzzy") compatible peripherals. Substituting a 100Mb drive for the 50Mb unit in the 25-MHz Amiga 3000 costs an extra $500. The parallel and serial ports allow you to attach printers, scanners, modems, and other devices.

The system unit has two free Amiga-only expansion slots, and two combination Amiga/IBM AT slots. Either IBM slot can accept a Bridgeboard that adds IBM XT ($699) or AT ($1,599) compatibility to the Amiga 3000. A special slot supports video devices such as internal genlock boards (that can merge computer and video images) or signal encoders. A "fast slot" on the main circuit board provides for future expansion options, such as an accelerator card containing a 68040 CPU chip, thus increasing the computer's speed.

The overall quality of construction is very good. The chassis is well laid out, but adding memory requires some disassembly, which should be left to a technician. The main circuit board is neatly laid out, with only one last-minute change. The 94-key keyboard is Commodore's best yet, with snappy response and a solid feel.

Special circuitry built into the main circuit board greatly improves the clarity of the video output. The 3000 is at its best with a high-quality multiscanning monitor. Our system came with Commodore's Model 1950 monitor ($799). It yielded distortion-free, sharp images with vivid color.

The 3000's extra processing speed and quick Quantum-built hard drive significantly enhanced the ease of use of AmigaDOS 1.3, which we tested because AmigaDOS 2.0 was not quite finalized. The system's overall feel and speed equaled that of Apple's Macintosh IIc series computers. We were also impressed by an early release of AmigaDOS 2.0, which adds a more polished look and new functions to the Amiga's friendly, mouse-driven user interface. The provided AmigaVision software makes it relatively easy to combine graphics, text, video, and audio in order to create multimedia presentations.

Prices are accurate at time of printing; subject to manufacturer's change.

The indexed manuals are excellent, detailing every aspect of system operation. A "quick start" pamphlet makes getting up and running an easy five-minute process, and the system's hard disk comes already loaded with the provided software. A hardware reference manual provides plenty of information.

Shoppers can save $700 by opting for the 16-MHz Amiga 3000. For $3,299, the 3000/16 teams all the features of its more expensive cousin with a bit less than two thirds of the power of the 3000/25, which costs $3,999. Commodore also announced expansion cards ($230 to $350) and software ($150 to $200) that allow the 3000 to participate in Arcnet and Ethernet local-area networks (LANs).

The Amiga 3000 should be rapidly accepted by desktop video professionals who need a powerful graphics processor and general purpose computer. Both Amiga 3000s offer outstanding graphics processing and number-crunching power at a terrific price. Anyone considering the purchase of a high-end Macintosh or IBM-compatible computer should try an Amiga 3000 for a few hours before making a final decision.

Specifications: RAM, two megabytes (2,048Kb); **operating system**, proprietary; **included hardware**, system unit with CPU, keyboard, 880Kb microfloppy disk drive, 50Mb hard disk drive, video display circuitry, mouse, Centronics parallel port, RS-232C serial port, internal and external SCSI ports, two RGB color video ports, two mouse/joystick ports, internal and external disk drive ports, stereo audio output ports, clock/calendar; **included software**, AmigaDOS 2.0 operating system, Amiga BASIC, AmigaVision, Amiga Workbench; system utilities. **Warranty**, one year. **Ratings: overall value**, 10; **ease of use**, 10; **software**, 9; **performance**, 10; **documentation**, 10; **expandability**, 9.

Approx. retail price	Approx. low price
$3,299 (3000/16)	$2,948
Approx. retail price	Approx. low price
$3,999 (3000/25)	not available

APPLE MACINTOSH IICX | RECOMMENDED |

The Apple Macintosh IIcx offers an easy-to-use mouse-driven interface, a potent Motorola 68030 CPU running at 15.667

MHz, and good expandability. Most programs run 3.5 to 4.5 times faster on the IIcx than on the Mac SE. Like the Mac IIx, the IIcx runs about 25 percent faster than the original Mac II. Programs (like Microsoft Excel) that heavily use the Mac IIcx's 68882 math coprocessor can run nearly twice as fast. Barely 12 inches wide, the system is six inches slimmer than the Mac II and IIx, the result of reducing the number of expansion slots from six to three. With a video card installed, two NuBus (not IBM standard) slots remain open. Many cards are available, like Orange Micro's $1,399 board with an Intel 80286 processor that lets any Mac II run IBM-compatible software.

The IIcx has a 1.4Mb 3.5-inch microfloppy drive that can also read and write data in IBM format. The system cannot hold another floppy drive, but you can attach an external unit. Macs use SCSI (Small Computer System Interface, pronounced "scuzzy") hard drives. The 40Mb hard drive in our IIcx ($5,369 for the entire system) was much faster than the SCSI drives in the Mac SE we tested. A IIcx with an 80Mb hard drive and 4Mb of RAM lists for $6,569.

Apple sells three black-on-white monitors for the Mac II series: A 12-inch model ($399) and two large-screen units that can display one ($1,099) or two ($2,149) full pages of data at the same time. These monitors are sharp and easy on the eyes; the one-page model has the sharpest display we've seen. The larger units are ideal for desktop publishing and computer-aided design (CAD). Exhibiting excellent color and sharpness, the 13-inch AppleColor RGB monitor ($999) can display in color or black and white.

Although adding a video card leaves only two expansion slots free, we rate expandability as very good, since many peripherals can simply plug into the SCSI port on the IIcx. The 12-inch monochrome and AppleColor monitors use the same $499 video card, which supports 16 colors or shades of gray. Both the one-page and two-page monochrome monitors require $599 video cards that produce four shades of gray as supplied, or 16 shades of gray for another $149.

For those who do not need color or gray scales, a 1-bit video card retails for $199. All Apple monitors can use Apple's 8-bit video card ($649), which supports 16 shades of gray on Apple's one-page and two-page displays. It supports 256 grays on Apple's 12-inch monochrome display, and 256 simultaneous colors or shades of gray on an AppleColor RGB monitor. If the 8-bit card is upgraded to 24 bits ($250), then photographic quality images with up to 16 million simultaneous on-screen colors can be produced.

The $129 keyboard is adequate, but its 81 keys seem too close together for some users. A 105-key keyboard with an enhanced IBM layout costs $229. The easy-to-follow manuals lack details, but the quick-reference guide is handy.

The operating system runs in one of two modes: Finder is for normal operations; MultiFinder is for multitasking, which means you can use more than one program at a time. For instance, you could sort a database file in the background (off-screen) while using a word processing program. Employing the Orange Micro card mentioned above, MultiFinder lets you use IBM-compatible and Mac software simultaneously and share information between them.

The provided HyperCard software can be used to write interactive programs that mix text, graphics, animation, music, voice, and video. You don't have to be a programming whiz to use it. HyperCard programs, called "stacks," cost little or nothing. HyperCard and MultiFinder take up lots of RAM. The main circuit board can hold 8Mb of RAM. We feel that one megabyte is not enough; 2Mb are barely acceptable.

The newer Mac IIci, which costs $1,600 more than a IIcx, has built-in video display circuitry. However, many IIci owners purchase a video card anyway because using the built-in circuitry can make the IIci run slower than a IIcx. Using a separate video card makes the IIci run 40 percent faster than a IIcx. Adding special memory can boost the IIci to 1.8 times the speed of a Mac IIcx.

Apple's newest Mac, the IIfx, yields three times the power of a Mac IIx or IIcx. For $8,969 you can buy a IIfx with 4Mb of memory, one microfloppy drive, and five empty NuBus slots. Both the 80Mb ($900 extra) and 160Mb (an additional $2,000) internal hard drives are fast and quiet. Apple's new $1,999 color graphics display card speeds up the screen display from 5 to 30 times.

Priced to compete with most high-powered brand-name, 80386-based IBM clones, the Mac IIcx offers superior power

Prices are accurate at time of printing; subject to manufacturer's change.

and a friendly user interface that is not a costly add-on.
Specifications: RAM, one megabyte (1,024Kb); **operating system**, proprietary; **included hardware**, system unit with CPU, 1.4Mb microfloppy disk drive, mouse, math coprocessor, two RS-232/RS-422 serial ports, external microfloppy disk drive port, SCSI port, two Desktop Bus ports, stereo audio output port, clock/calendar; **included software**, Finder and MultiFinder operating systems, Apple File Exchange, Guided Tour, HyperCard, System Tools, System Utilities. **Warranty**, one year. **Ratings: overall value**, 9; **ease of use**, 10; **software**, 10; **performance**, 10; **documentation**, 9; **expandability**, 9.

Approx. retail price	Approx. low price
$4,669 (Model M5660)	$3,760

AST PREMIUM 386/25 RECOMMENDED

The AST Premium 386/25 is extremely fast, adaptable, and reasonably priced. The flexibility of the Premium 386/25 is due to AST's CUPID-32 architecture. CUPID stands for Completely Universal Processor I/O Design. The main circuit board contains only components related to input/output (I/O) operations, including one parallel and two serial ports, disk drive controllers, and expansion slots. The processor, memory, and math coprocessor sockets are on a board that plugs into the main circuit board. If you need more power than the 25-MHz Intel 80386 CPU chip provides, you can remove the processor card and swap it for another based on a 33-MHz 80386 ($2,395) or a 25-MHz i486 chip ($3,995).

There's a price to be paid for this versatility. For example, a base model of the AST Premium 486/25 retails for $6,995. The sum of the list prices of a base Premium 386/25 and the i486 upgrade is $8,490, not counting the extra 2Mb of RAM in the Premium 486/25. The cost difference is significant, but paying it is probably preferable to disposing of one system and replacing it with a new one.

The expandability and construction of the AST Premium 386/25 are excellent. The system is very sturdy and well built. There are few components on the processor and main circuit board, which should enhance long-term reliability. One 5.25-inch 1.2Mb floppy drive is standard, leaving room for four data storage devices. Two of the system's five 16-bit (AT-compatible) expansion slots have connections for proprietary AST memory expansion cards. One 8-bit (XT-compatible) slot is also provided.

The processor card, which has the standard two megabytes of RAM, can hold up to 4Mb. Separate sockets are standard, so that Intel 33-MHz 80387 and Weitek 33-MHz 3167 math coprocessors can be added. A memory card with one megabyte installed and a capacity of 16Mb retails for $650. The maximum system memory is 36Mb.

AST's 101-key keyboard has a slightly vague feel. It took us a while to get used to it. We prefer keys with more of a "click" and a somewhat firmer touch.

The Premium 386/25 has almost 3.5 times the number-crunching ability of an 8-MHz IBM AT. Our system included a 110Mb hard drive ($1,450), an AST VGA Plus display card ($329), and an AST Premium VGA color monitor ($695). The speed of both the hard disk and graphics adapter nicely complemented the CPU performance. In addition, the AST color monitor delivered a sharp and undistorted image.

The first-rate manuals are suitable for both novices and expert users. The menu-driven setup program sailed us smoothly through installation of both MS-DOS and AST's useful utility software. GW-BASIC is also included.

The Premium 386/25 may not be the fastest 80386 machine, but its unique architecture and quality construction make it much less susceptible to obsolescence than its competitors. Don't let its relatively high list price cause you to scratch it off your list without shopping around; AST's list prices are often heavily discounted.

Specifications: RAM, two megabytes (2,048Kb); **operating system**, MS-DOS, MS OS/2; **included hardware**, system unit with CPU, keyboard, 1.2Mb floppy disk drive, Centronics parallel port, two RS-232C serial ports; **included software**, MS-DOS 3.3, GW-BASIC, diagnostics, setup, utilities. **Warranty**, one year. **Ratings: overall value**, 9; **ease of use**, 8; **software**, 10; **performance**, 9; **documentation**, 10; **expandability**, 10.

Approx. retail price	Approx. low price
$4,495 (Model 5)	$2,998

Prices are accurate at time of printing; subject to manufacturer's change.

PORTABLE COMPUTERS

TOSHIBA T1000SE

The Toshiba T1000SE is one of the best blends of performance, flexibility, and portability we've ever seen. This well-thought-out, slickly engineered package offers a very reasonable list price and a host of useful options.

At 5.9 pounds, the T1000SE is the lightest notebook computer with a 3.5-inch 1.44Mb microfloppy disk drive we've tested. Measuring 12.4-by-10.16 inches and only 1.78 inches thick, the T1000SE easily slips into a standard briefcase or its $99 fitted carrying case.

The large, backlit liquid crystal display (LCD) is very good, featuring adjustable brightness and contrast. The shape of its blue-on-white characters seemed odd at first, but after a short time, their unique shape improved the readability of on-screen information. The display is CGA (Color Graphics Adapter) compatible and its higher resolution 640-by-400-pixel (dot) mode is supported by some popular software. The keyboard is very comfortable to use.

The T1000SE has one megabyte of RAM. A slot under a hatch on the right side accepts one ($699) or two megabytes ($1,199) of additional memory that is easy to install. Memory above 640Kb can be used as a fast, nonvolatile RAM disk (memory that mimics a very fast disk drive). This can make the T1000SE seem quicker than it actually is (2.2 times faster than the original IBM XT).

The back panel on the T1000SE houses the serial port, a connector for "to be announced" options, and a parallel port that can also connect to an external 5.25-inch 360Kb floppy drive ($499). There is room for a 2400-bps (bits per second, or baud) internal modem ($349), but there's no video output for an external monitor. To extend the battery life, the modem can be turned off and the backlit display can be set to shut off at a time interval selected by the user. A convenient "auto-resume" feature lets you shut off the T1000SE in the midst of a program and automatically return to where you left off when the computer is turned back on. Colored LEDs (light-emitting diodes) alert you to the status of seven different system functions.

Our T1000SE's rechargeable battery lasted almost three hours before a loud beep and flashing LED indicated the need to replace or recharge the battery. The easily removed NiCad battery is light enough to make carrying a spare ($79) quite feasible. Recharging using the supplied AC power supply/recharger took around four hours. A quick charger unit that can recharge three batteries at once lists for $349, and a power adapter that connects to an automobile's cigarette lighter costs $129.

The first-rate manuals are well organized, complete, and illustrated in color. The only faults were a few erroneous page numbers in the index of the reference manual. A box labeled "First Time" contains everything a novice needs to quickly get the T1000SE up and running. The inclusion of on-disk versions of the MS-DOS and system reference manuals makes carrying the paper manuals on the road unnecessary. Besides MS-DOS in ROM, Toshiba supplies an easy-to-use setup program, diagnostics, and Multisoft's PC-Kwik Power Pak, which is a collection of useful system utilities.

Toshiba promises a two-business-day turnaround on repairs while the T1000SE is under warranty. A toll-free number for technical support is also provided. For modem users, Toshiba offers a computerized bulletin board and a support area on the popular CompuServe information service.

The newer 6.2-pound T1000XE substitutes a 20Mb hard drive for the T1000SE's floppy drive. To compensate for the absence of an internal floppy drive, this $2,699 system includes LapLink software, which allows you to connect the T1000XE to a desktop computer and transfer files. An external 1.44Mb microfloppy drive costs $249.

When a hard drive is not needed, the T1000SE is our preferred notebook computer. Its portability, many features, keen engineering, and exceptional construction make it a pleasure to use and an excellent value.

Specifications: RAM, one megabyte (1,024Kb); **operating system**, MS-DOS; **included hardware**, system unit with CPU and keyboard, 1.44Mb microfloppy disk drive, liquid crystal display, video display circuitry, Centronics parallel port, RS-232C serial port, clock/calendar; **included software**, MS-DOS 3.3 (ROM and diskette), PC-Kwik Power Pak, setup program, system utilities, on-disk reference manuals. **Warranty**, one year. **Ratings: overall value**, 10; **ease of use**, 10; **software**, 10; **performance**, 8; **documentation**, 10; **portability**, 10.

Approx. retail price
$1,699

Approx. low price
not available

TANDY 1100 FD   [RECOMMENDED]

The Tandy 1100 FD is Radio Shack's MS-DOS notebook computer that offers light weight, usability, and reasonable cost. Weighing 6.4 pounds with a battery, the 1100 FD is sleekly styled and travels very well. It slips into a briefcase with room to spare, measuring about 2.5 inches thick, 10 inches deep, and a foot wide. Despite its small size, the keyboard is among the most comfortable we have used on a laptop computer. Most of the 84 keys are large and well spaced, with positive click action and a very solid overall feel. The layout of cursor keys is logical and easy to use.

Though the 1100 FD's large CGA (Color Graphics Adapter) compatible liquid crystal display (LCD) is not backlit, it is very readable under all but the dimmest light. Its dark blue characters stand out sharply against the reflective yellow-green background. The battery in our unit lasted for well over four hours before requiring a ten-hour recharge. The low cost ($30) and light weight of a spare battery make the 1100 FD ideal for extended use away from an electrical outlet. The 1100 FD includes an AC power supply/recharger.

The 8-MHz NEC V-20 processor is not speedy by today's standards, but it manages to provide twice the processing of the original IBM XT. A full 640Kb of RAM is standard, but it cannot be expanded. The 1100 FD has only one 720Kb 3.5-inch microfloppy drive. We would have preferred a 1.44Mb unit. However, the drive is very quiet. The disadvantage of its smaller storage capacity is lessened by having MS-DOS in ROM. Also in ROM is Tandy's DeskMate graphical user interface. Some DeskMate programs come on a floppy disk and others are in ROM. They include simple word processing, spreadsheet, database, and telecommunications programs.

For this portable, Tandy offers a $200 internal modem that runs at 2400 bps (bits per second, or baud). A fold-down panel

Prices are accurate at time of printing; subject to manufacturer's change.

on the back of the computer covers the ports. There is no video output for an external monitor.

The well-written manuals have plenty of illustrations. Unfortunately, the user manual has no index. A "getting started" guide eases novices into laptop computing. Service and accessories are sold by most Radio Shack stores and a few other dealers authorized to sell Tandy systems by mail.

The 1100 FD provides a solid foundation for computing on the run that's light on weight and your budget. It's not as expandable as some notebook systems, but its advantages far outweigh its limitations. The excellent keyboard, legible screen, long battery life, easy-to-use DeskMate interface and applications, MS-DOS in ROM, and compact size make the 1100 FD one of today's best values in low-cost laptops.

Specifications: RAM, 640Kb; **operating system**, MS-DOS; **included hardware**, system unit with CPU and keyboard, 720Kb microfloppy disk drive, liquid crystal display, video display circuitry, Centronics parallel port, RS-232C serial port; **included software**, MS-DOS 3.3 (in ROM); GW-BASIC; DeskMate Interface, Text word processing, and Spell Checker (in ROM); DeskMate productivity software. **Warranty**, 90 days. **Ratings: overall value**, 9; **ease of use**, 9; **software**, 10; **performance**, 8; **documentation**, 8; **portability**, 9.

Approx. retail price	Approx. low price
$799	not available

Home Office Products

More and more working Americans choose to work at home, where some of the products formerly found in the office have found a home as well. But manufacturers saw opportunities to use technology to bring just about all the features of office machines into the home at reasonable prices.

Best Buys '91

Our Best Buy and Recommended home office products follow. They are categorized into word processors, electronic typewriters, desktop copiers, and fax machines. (Computers, telephones, and answering machines are reviewed in the two preceding chapters.) Within each category, products are listed by quality; the best of the Best Buys is first, followed by our second choice, and so on. Recommended products follow the Best Buys. A Best Buy or Recommended designation applies only to the model listed; it does not necessarily apply to other models made by the same manufacturer.

Word Processors

A word processor is a computer that is designed primarily for producing letter-quality reports, manuscripts, correspondence, and other documents. The differences between a computer and a word processor have decreased in the past few years. Some word processors can also be used to create spreadsheets and perform some of the other functions of a computer.

Most home office word processors are portable and produce letter-quality correspondences. They vary considerably in size, weight, number of features, and cost. Your choice of a word processor depends on your anticipated needs and your budget. Before you buy a word processor, you should consider whether a laptop or desktop computer or an electronic typewriter might better suit your needs. If you decide to purchase a word processor, buy the most advanced model available.

PANASONIC KX-W1510

 ✔ BEST BUY

The Panasonic KX-W1510 is a fully-featured word processor that has a 9-inch CRT (cathode-ray tube) and a daisy-wheel printer in a cabinet with a separate keyboard. It prints at a rate of 12 characters per second. The CRT displays 80 characters on 25 lines and can be adjusted for either white characters on a black screen or black characters on a white screen. The unit's built-in text memory can store 58,000 characters, including 2,000 characters of user-programmed phrases. Its 3½-inch floppy disk drive provides unlimited external storage. Its cut-sheet feeder lets you stack-feed up to 50 sheets. The KX-W1510 offers an autocolumn function that lets you set up figures in tabular form and perform basic arithmetic. An address list lets you store a file of up to 999 names, addresses, and phone numbers on a floppy disk. This model has a 63,000-word built-in spelling checker, which can be programmed for 120 additional words. The thesaurus has 45,000 root words and 500,000 synonyms. This model also has mail-merge and mailing-list functions, so you can create personalized letters. The printer's carriage accommodates paper up to 12 inches wide with a maximum typed line of 10 inches wide. Other features include word search, next-word search, word replace, word wrap, bold, underline, centering, justification, lift-off correction, one-line correction memory, and one-touch erase of an entire word. The KX-W1510, which is AC powered, comes with a self-demonstration program and a tutorial diskette. **Specifications: height,** $10^{3}/_{16}$"; **width,** $17^{3}/_{4}$"; **depth,** $13^{1}/_{8}$"; **weight,** $21^{9}/_{16}$ pounds. **Warranty: parts,** one year; **labor,** 90 days.

Approx. retail price	Approx. low price
$830	$649

BROTHER WP-95

The Brother WP-95 is a fully featured word processor with a 9-inch CRT and daisy-wheel printer in a cabinet with a detachable keyboard. This model also has built-in spreadsheet software and preformatted templates for financial calculations, business letters, and resumes. Its printing speed is 15 characters per second. The CRT displays 15 lines of 91 green characters against a black background. The unit's 3½-inch floppy disk drive provides unlimited external storage. A tractor-feeder uses continuous-form paper, and an optional cut-sheet feeder lets you stack-feed up to 50 sheets. Built-in grammatical aids include a 70,000-word spell checker, 204 user-programmable words, and a 45,000-word thesaurus. The carriage accommodates paper up to 12 inches wide with a maximum 9-inch-wide typed line. Other features include address merge, search and replace, block move/copy/delete, justification, lift-off correction with single keystrokes to erase a word or a whole line, centering, bold, superscripts and subscripts, and several spreadsheet features. The WP-95 is AC powered. It comes with a built-in demo and tutorial.

Specifications: height, $7^{7}/_{10}$"; **width,** $15^{9}/_{10}$"; **depth,** 17"; **weight,** $27^{1}/_{5}$ pounds. **Warranty: parts,** one year; **labor,** 90 days.

Approx. retail price	Approx. low price
$999	not available

SMITH CORONA PWP 7000LT

The Smith Corona PWP 7000LT is the first of a new generation of truly portable word processors that, with an optional, rechargeable battery pack, can be used anywhere to create documents. It must be hooked up to a separate printer to generate typed pages. When first introduced last year, the PWP 7000LT came with a daisy-wheel printer; this year, the printer is optional at an approximate retail price of $300. In addition to its word processing functions, an optional, downloadable spreadsheet software package, CoronaCalc, lets you perform financial analysis. This model has a backlit LCD (liquid crystal display) screen showing 80 characters on 16 lines. It has 50,000 characters of editable memory and unlimited external storage on 100,000-character disks used in the unit's built-in disk drive. Built-in grammatical aids include a 90,000-word dictionary, thesaurus, and punctuation checker. Other features include address merge, block move/copy/delete, search and replace, underlining, bold, and word erase. Its built-in, standard RS-232C port lets you connect to the optional printer, to compatible serial interface printers, or with an optional Hayes-compatible 1200-baud compatible modem, to personal computers or on-line services. It is AC powered. Other optional accessories include a carrying case, a rechargeable battery pack that lasts between six and eight hours of operation, and a 100-sheet feeder for the matching printer.

Specifications: height, 3½"; **width**, 13⁹⁄₁₀"; **depth**, 10"; **weight**, 6½ pounds. **Warranty: parts**, one year; **labor**, 90 days.

Approx. retail price	**Approx. low price**
$600	$554

Electronic Typewriters

Prices of fully featured electronic typewriters plummeted in the last decade as electronic technology made manual and electric typewriters obsolete.

When you shop for an electric typewriter, think about the ways in which you plan to use it. A basic model may suit your needs, or you may need a typewriter that has many of the features of a word processor. If you plan to use the typewriter to address letters produced by a computer, make sure the typewriter and your computer printer have the same pitch (characters per inch), size of print characters, and font (type style).

Prices are accurate at time of printing; subject to manufacturer's change.

BROTHER AX-350

The Brother AX-350 is a portable daisy-wheel electronic typewriter with a built-in spelling checker of 56,000 words. Lift-off correction enables you to erase a letter, a word, or an entire line. This model can be set for pica (ten-pitch, or ten characters per inch) or elite (12-pitch). It has a clear plastic shield over the carriage to reduce noise. Other features of this AC-powered typewriter include bold printing; automatic centering and underlining; superscript and subscript; and built-in demo, handle, and lid cover.

Specifications: height, $5\frac{1}{10}''$; **width,** $16\frac{1}{5}''$; **depth,** $14\frac{2}{5}''$; **weight,** $9\frac{9}{10}$ pounds. **Warranty: parts,** five years; **labor,** 90 days.

Approx. retail price	Approx. low price
$300	$146

SMITH CORONA XL 1700

The Smith Corona XL 1700 is a value-priced, portable daisy-wheel electronic typewriter with lift-off correction, which can be used to erase a letter, a word, or a line with a single keystroke. This model can be set for pica or elite. It features bold printing, automatic centering, superscript and subscript, and a built-in demo. Model XL 1700 is AC powered. Daisy wheels in many styles and other supplies for this machine are widely available.

Specifications: height, $4\frac{9}{10}''$; **width,** $16\frac{3}{10}''$; **depth,** $14\frac{2}{3}''$; **weight,** 12 pounds. **Warranty: parts,** one year; **labor,** 90 days.

Approx. retail price	Approx. low price
$230	$142

SMITH CORONA XD 5700

The Smith Corona XD 5700 is a portable electronic typewriter that has a 24-character LCD (liquid crystal display) screen and a 7,000-character internal memory. You can see your work before it is printed on the page. Lift-off correction enables you to erase a letter, a word, or an entire line. The 50,000-word spelling checker beeps when it detects a word it cannot recognize and then displays alternative, correctly spelled words.

Other features include stop codes, bold printing, automatic center/return/underline, two pitches, and end-of-page warning. Model XD 5700 is AC powered. Many styles of daisy wheels and other supplies for this machine are widely available.

Specifications: height, 5"; **width,** 16⁹/₁₀"; **depth,** 16½"; **weight,** 13⁷/₁₀ pounds. **Warranty: parts,** one year; **labor,** 90 days.

Approx. retail price	Approx. low price
$300	$217

PANASONIC KX-R530

 ✔ **BEST BUY**

The Panasonic KX-R530 is a portable electronic typewriter with a 15-character LCD (liquid crystal display) screen that lets you see your work before it is printed on the page. You can store 7,000 characters, or three pages of double-spaced text, in the internal memory. The spelling checker has a built-in dictionary of 86,000 words. You can connect this typewriter to certain personal computers using an optional KX-R60 parallel interface adapter. Other features include lift-off correction with the ability to erase a letter, a word, or a whole line with one keystroke. There is also search and replace, block move/copy/delete, justification, bold printing, automatic center, and underline. Print speed is 12 characters per second. Model KX-R530 is AC powered.

Specifications: height, 4⅜"; **width,** 16¹³/₁₆"; **depth,** 14⅜"; **weight,** 11 pounds. **Warranty: parts,** one year; **labor,** 90 days.

Approx. retail price	Approx. low price
$240	$221

Desktop Copiers

Three factors have made photocopiers popular for use in the home. Most importantly, they are built and designed to be simply serviced by the user, unlike office copiers, which typically require periodic servicing by a technician. When the toner runs out, you simply replace the old cartridge with a new one. Second, they are small enough to fit on a desktop. And third, they are more convenient and cost-effective than run-

Prices are accurate at time of printing; subject to manufacturer's change.

ning out to a print shop or coin-operated copier every time you need copies.

Before you buy a copier, test a floor model in the store to make sure it produces clear copies.

CANON PC-3II

The Canon PC-3II produces excellent-quality copies. It is a single-sheet manual-feeding machine capable of making copies from business-card size to 8½ by 12 inches using plain paper. Its easily replaceable cartridge is available in black, brown, blue, green, or red and sells for under $100. The cartridge contains enough toner for about 1,500 copies. **Specifications: height**, not available; **width**, not available; **depth**, not available; **weight**, 25½ pounds. **Warranty: parts and labor**, 90 days.

Approx. retail price	Approx. low price
$795	$501

PANASONIC FP-820

The Panasonic FP-820 is a desktop photocopier that has a 100-sheet stack feeder and can be set to produce up to 99 copies. The paper supply tray holds 100 sheets. Model FP-820 will reproduce originals from 4 by 6 inches up to legal size. This machine can be adjusted to make copies 67 percent, 79 percent, or 122 percent of the size of the original. Its easily replaceable toner cartridge comes in black, brown, blue, green, or red. Model FP-820 produces eight copies per minute. **Specifications: height**, 11"; **width**, 18⅖"; **depth**, 18³⁄₁₀"; **weight**, 55 pounds. **Warranty:** 120-day end-user warranty.

Approx. retail price	Approx. low price
$1,495	$915

Desktop Fax Machines

Fax is the commonly used term for facsimile machine and electronic facsimile transmission of documents. Faxing has

---

Prices are accurate at time of printing; subject to manufacturer's change.

become known as a type of electronic mail, as everything from orders for goods and deli food to love letters and song requests are faxed. Fax machines are selling at the rate of 100,000 a month because desktop faxes have become even less expensive. Desktop faxes use heat-sensitive paper to record transmissions and to make copies of personal documents. Fax machines transmit over ordinary telephone lines, and most include a telephone. Fax transmissions and receptions can be done manually or automatically, and most machines can be programmed for delayed transmission to take advantage of low night phone rates. Most machines have various reproduction modes for transmitting different types of documents.

PANASONIC KX-F220

The Panasonic KX-F220 is a desktop communications center that is a facsimile, a telephone, and a telephone answering machine. The KX-F220 has built-in automatic switching so that it can receive both voice and fax transmissions while you are out: When another fax machine calls, the KX-220 senses the signal and switches into its fax mode; when a desktop fax calls you, your outgoing message (OGM) tells the caller to press the asterisk button if they want to send a fax, or to wait for the tone to leave a voice message. An automatic cutter cuts each page that is transmitted or copied, and deposits each sheet in a tray. An automatic document program holds up to 15 pages, and a delayed transmission program allows you to send documents automatically at a time when the phone rates are low. Transmission controls include resolution, contrast, 16-shade gray scale for photographs, and a verification stamp mark that can be put on each page to confirm correct document transmission. Setting up and using the KX-F220 is easy, since both the machine and the instruction booklet are user-friendly. For example, the KX-F220 records your OGM on the standard microchip and also records it on the tape that records your incoming messages; when there is a power outage, you lose the OGM on the chip, but when power is restored, the KX-F220 automatically rerecords your message on the chip from the tape. You can also access the answering machine from any phone, and remote access is restricted to you because you program your own access code. There are 30 one-touch and 100 speed-dialing numbers that can be entered into the machine. The Panasonic KX-F220 is a sophisticated, yet user-friendly, communication center.

Specifications: height, 5⁵/₁₆"; **width,** 18⁷/₈"; **depth,** 14⁹/₁₆"; **weight,** 20½ pounds. **Warranty: parts and labor,** 90 days.

Approx. retail price	**Approx. low price**
$1,796	$1,380

RICOH RF920 ✓ BEST BUY

The Ricoh RF920 is a sophisticated desktop fax with high-quality, 64-tone gray-scale photo reproduction, and an automatic paper cutter. Since the quality of photographic reproduction depends solely on the sending machine, the 64-tone gray-scale capabilities of the RF920 make it the perfect fax machine for those who want to transmit finely detailed items such as photographs, line drawings, blueprints, and the like. Besides halftones, there are additional contrast and fine-detail settings for transmission and copying. The RF920 has both manual and automatic reception and transmission. A 10-page document feeder transmits up to ten pages automatically, and delayed transmission allows you to send documents during night rates; if the number is busy, it will be automatically redialed five minutes later, or you can program the RF920 to dial an alternate number. There is a voice request alerting the other party to pick up the phone when the fax transmission has ended. You can record an announcement up to 16 seconds long to identify yourself before the fax modem tone is sounded. The RF920 has 25 one-touch and 90 two-touch dialing for frequently called telephone and fax numbers. On-hook dialing and a built-in monitor speaker allow you to transmit manually without using the hand set. The heavy-duty Ricoh RF920 is an easy-to-use fax with one-touch operation.

Specifications: height, 4⅕"; **width,** 12⅗"; **depth,** 12⅘"; **weight,** 15⅖ pounds. **Warranty: parts and labor,** 90 days.

Approx. retail price	**Approx. low price**
$2,295	$1,263

Prices are accurate at time of printing; subject to manufacturer's change.

Personal Care Appliances

It's easy to look your best at all times with the wealth of personal care appliances available today in a wide range of prices. Manufacturers, mindful of the hectic schedules of today's increasing number of two-income families, are continually adding new features to personal care products to increase their versatility and usefulness. And they are making these products better looking, easier to use, and more colorful.

We're traveling more these days. Whether you're dashing from office to health club to home, or from continent to continent clear across the globe, the newest personal care appliances have been designed to follow you with ease. From blow dryers and other hair stylers to electric razors and travel irons, these products offer such helpful features as compact design, fast heat-up times, cordless operation, and dual voltage.

Safety is an important consideration in personal care appliances because many of them are used in damp or wet bathrooms. Since 1987, hair dryers have included a mechanism that prevents electric shock if the dryer falls into water while it is turned off. Even so, the dryer should be disconnected once you are through using it. Most electric appliances today include a reminder that electrical parts are electrically live even when the switch is off, and warn users to unplug the unit immediately after use to eliminate any risk of electric shock. When you shop for a hair dryer or other personal care appliance, make sure that it has a UL seal. This is your guarantee that it meets the most stringent, current safety specifications set by Underwriters Laboratories.

Prices for personal care products are reasonable, and you may be tempted to buy on the basis of price alone. But a low price does not necessarily mean that a product is a good value. Reject products that have weak plastic housings, rough edges where flashing was not trimmed thoroughly after it was molded, or sections that don't fit together properly. Check the balance and the way the product feels in your hand, and make sure that a particular model is designed to handle the job you want it to do. In addition, be certain that the retailer has a reasonable return policy if the product does not perform as you expected.

Best Buys '91

Our Best Buy and Recommended personal care appliances follow, divided into the following categories: full-size hair dryers, compact hair dryers, heated rollers, flexible hair shapers, curling irons, curling brushes, makeup mirrors, men's and women's electric shavers, full-size and travel irons, and garment steamers. In each category, products are listed by quality. The best of the Best Buys is first, followed by our second choice, and so on. A Best Buy or Recommended designation applies only to the model listed, not to other models by the same manufacturer or to an entire product line.

HAIR DRYERS

Hair dryers are available in 1,200-watt, 1,250-watt, and 1,500-watt models. The higher the wattage, the greater the heat output and the faster your hair dries. A 1,200-watt hair dryer is adequate for many people, but if your hair is long or thick or the styling is complicated, a higher wattage will be more effective. Many 1,500-watt models have a dual element that allows them to operate at lower heat settings so you don't have to subject your hair to continual high heat as it dries.

Hair dryers with variable-speed fans and variable-temperature settings let you select the combination best suited to your needs. These dryers are ideal if more than one person uses the same dryer. Nozzle adapters further increase a dryer's flexibility. A concentrator for spot drying and a diffuser that spreads the airflow over a wider area are both useful. Tangle-free cords add to the ease of drying hair. Before buying a hair dryer, hold it in your hands to check its weight and balance, then hold it above your shoulders for a few minutes to see if it is comfortable to use.

Be aware that some manufacturers offer full-powered, mid-size models that have the same features as a full-size model in a slightly smaller size at a lower price.

Full-Size Hair Dryers

WINDMERE SIGNATURE PRO 1500 SLP-15 ✓BEST BUY

The Windmere Signature Pro 1500 SLP-15 is a value-packed hair dryer that offers 1,500 watts of power, with two speeds and two temperature settings to increase versatility. Dual voltage makes the unit ideal for the traveler who prefers a full-size hand-held dryer. Additional features include a styling nozzle and lighted energy indicators.
Warranty: one year.

Approx. retail price	**Approx. low price**
$15	$15

VIDAL SASSOON PROFESSIONAL 1500-WATT STYLING DRYER VS-207

The Vidal Sassoon Professional 1500-Watt Styling Dryer VS-207 is a full-powered unit with four heat settings and two independent speed controls for flexibility in hair styling. The 1,500-watt dryer comes with a professional concentrator attachment. A coil cord eliminates the danger of a long cord acci-

---

Prices are accurate at time of printing; subject to manufacturer's change.

dentally falling in the sink and is a plus when it comes to storage. A hanging ring is convenient for those who prefer to hang their hair dryers on the bathroom wall or any other convenient location.

Warranty: one year.

Approx. retail price	Approx. low price
not available	$19

CLAIROL SALON POWER 1500 PRO DRYER FP-1 ✔ BEST BUY

The Clairol Salon Power 1500 Pro Dryer FP-1 offers 1,500 watts of drying power and high-air velocity as used in salons for ultra-fast drying. The thermostatically controlled heating element has high, medium, and low heat settings that can be run at either high or low speeds. The shatter-resistant body has a swivel hang-up loop for easy storage. The unit comes with a concentrator styling attachment for spot drying, perfect for those who style as they dry.

Warranty: one year.

Approx. retail price	Approx. low price
$27	$17

Compact Hair Dryers

Although compact hair dryers are much smaller than full-size models, they are not necessarily less powerful. There are a number of 1,500-watt units available. What they do lack is versatility because most of them do not have styling attachments. Their compact size and light weight make them more portable, a definite advantage for the on-the-go person concerned with always looking his or her best. Easily packed into a gym bag or suitcase, some even have folding handles to fit in a purse. Look for some of the same features, such as variable fan speeds and heat output, that are found in full-size dryers. If you tend to do a lot of traveling, choose a compact model with multivoltage capacity.

CLAIROL PAZAZZ 1500 SD-2CS

 ✔**BEST BUY**

The Clairol Pazazz 1500 SD-2CS is a powerful little unit. The high velocity 1,500-watt travel dryer has two speed/heat settings and dual voltage for use here and abroad. The lightweight unit is well balanced and easy to hold while in use. It has a thermostatically controlled heating element and a "Flex Guard" to help protect the cord from breakage. Snappy turquoise indicators set off against a black case make it easy to find the setting you want even in the dim light of some foreign hotel bathrooms.

Warranty: one year.

Approx. retail price	Approx. low price
$13	$10

WINDMERE TRAVEL FOLDER W-12F

 ✔**BEST BUY**

The Windmere Travel Folder W-12F is a dual-voltage compact hair dryer that will meet the needs of most international travelers. Its folding handle is a real space saver in crowded suitcases. The dryer has a 1,250-watt heating element with two heat settings and two fan speeds.

Warranty: one year.

Approx. retail price	Approx. low price
$11	not available

VIDAL SASSOON MINI FOLDING DRYER VS-223

 ✔**BEST BUY**

The Vidal Sassoon Mini Folding Dryer VS-223 is perfect for travel. With its folding handle and coil cord, this compact dual-voltage unit takes up just a few inches of space in a suitcase. The lightweight dryer has a strong 1,500-watt heating element with two speed and heat settings.

Warranty: one year.

Approx. retail price	Approx. low price
not available	$16

Prices are accurate at time of printing; subject to manufacturer's change.

HEATED ROLLERS

Today's heated roller sets are versatile units designed to give fullness, volume, or tight curls, depending on your mood or current hair style. Home-use sets contain 20 or more rollers in several sizes, while travel sets generally have eight to 10 rollers. Some rollers are flocked, or covered in a velvetlike fabric; others have hard rubber shafts with spines or brushes. Both kinds of rollers are designed to hold hair in place, while cushioning and protecting it against potentially damaging heat. When choosing heated rollers, consider which cover material you prefer and the speed at which the rollers heat up. The durability and design of the case is also a factor, especially if you plan to travel with a home-use set.

CLAIROL TIME SAVER PTC-20N

The Clairol Time Saver PTC-20N features 20 ribbed rollers in small, medium, and large sizes that heat up in 90 seconds. The unit has an electronic heating system with an indicator dot on each roller to show when it is ready to use. Even though the rollers remain hot for approximately 20 minutes, the edges of the curling rods stay cool to the touch for easy handling. When the lid of the sturdy, oval case is closed, the unit automatically turns off. There's convenient clip and cord storage in the base of the unit.

Warranty: one year.

Approx. retail price	Approx. low price
$35	$24

CONAIR VOLUMAKER HAIRSETTER HS30

The Conair Volumaker Hairsetter HS30 contains 20 fast-heating, soft-cushioned rollers in three sizes for styling versatility. The unit has a "ready" light to indicate when the curling rods have reached the right temperature. The lightweight, easy-to-use rollers secure with unique pullout fasteners, so there's no

---

Prices are accurate at time of printing; subject to manufacturer's change.

need to keep track of separate pins or clips.
Warranty: one year.

Approx. retail price	Approx. low price
$44	not available

WINDMERE SIGNATURE QUICK HEAT SLQ-8 [RECOMMENDED]

The Windmere Signature Quick Heat SLQ-8 is a travel unit that contains eight rollers and ten clips with protective tips. The unit is dual voltage for worldwide travel. With its 90-second heat-up feature and compact size, it's perfect for quick, after-work touch-ups.
Warranty: one year.

Approx. retail price	Approx. low price
$17	not available

FLEXIBLE HAIR SHAPERS

Flexible hair shapers are similar in principle to heated rollers but are more versatile. They are rubber sticks that heat up and bend easily, holding hair in place while the heat sets the curl. The amount of hair you wrap around each heated shaper, the way you twist hair and shaper, and the length of time hair stays wrapped work together to determine whether you get tight curls or loose, bouncy waves.

CONAIR HOT STICKS HS19D

The Conair Hot Sticks HS19D features 20 soft rubber sticks with heating elements inside each of the eight small pink and 12 larger lavender shapers. While the center of each shaper is hot, the ends remain comfortably cool so you can roll hair around it with ease. Once hair is rolled, you bend both ends of the stick together and secure it by inserting one end of the stick through a loop at the other end. No clips or pins are necessary to hold the shapers in place. The sticks are packed in a hard plastic case with a see-through lid. A "ready" dot indi-

---

Prices are accurate at time of printing; subject to manufacturer's change.

cates when the shapers have reached optimum temperature. Dual-heat settings increase versatility. High heat locks in tight, long-lasting curls, while a lower heat setting is used for looser curls and waves. The cord wraps neatly around the base of the unit. An instruction sheet includes styling tips and directions on how to achieve various looks.

Warranty: one year.

Approx. retail price	Approx. low price
$33	$26

CLAIROL LOCK 'N ROLL BT-1 ✓ BEST BUY

The Clairol Lock 'n Roll BT-1 flexible heated stylers feature a unique, round folding flap design that holds hair gently without clips or pins. The unit comes with 24 stylers—20 large green and four small orange—to create soft, natural-looking curls and waves and to add fullness and body to hair. The lightweight stylers have a specially formulated surface that grips the ends for hard-to-hold fly-away hair. They are packaged in a compact heating base that is ready to use in 10 minutes. A step-by-step styling booklet is included that shows you how to create various looks.

Warranty: one year.

Approx. retail price	Approx. low price
$40	$35

CURLING IRONS

Curling irons give body and curl to straight hair and enhance the shape of wavy hair. These appliances are offered with or without electrical cords. Cordless curling irons are powered by a butane cell that is either built into the unit or snapped into place like a battery. The advantage of a cordless unit is convenience. You can use it for touch-ups after work, while traveling, or at home.

The shafts of some curling irons are bare metal; others are flocked or covered with soft rubber. Some curling irons have narrow styling barrels for short, curly, or permed hair. Curling irons with electronic controls take the guesswork out of styling by signaling when it is time to remove the wand from your hair. A few curling irons have an automatic shutoff feature that turns them off after about 60 minutes if you forget to do so.

CLAIROL TIMEWAVE
C-600-CS

The Clairol TimeWave C-600-CS is a versatile unit that heats up quickly and features curling settings for tight, medium, and loose curls at the twist of a dial. An electronic heating system maintains a constant temperature while the unit is in use. A built-in electronic timer beeps softly when a curl is set according to the curling designation chosen. The unit has a mist option; vents are located all around the aluminum barrel for even distribution of steam to hair. The unit also has a heel rest, cool tip, "ready" dot, and tangle-free swivel cord.
Warranty: one year.

Approx. retail price	**Approx. low price**
$17	$13

WINDMERE AUTO-OFF
IRON ASO-I

✔**BEST BUY**

The Windmere Auto-Off Iron ASO-I features an automatic safety shut-off that cuts power to the unit after 60 minutes. The unit, which has a ¾-inch diameter chrome barrel, also has a "ready" dot to indicate when the curling iron is ready for use, a lighted energy indicator, and tangle-free swivel cord.
Warranty: one year.

Approx. retail price	**Approx. low price**
$10	not available

CURLING BRUSHES

Curling brushes are essentially curling irons with bristles. In fact, some curling irons come with brush attachments. When

---

Prices are accurate at time of printing; subject to manufacturer's change.

you choose a curling brush, make sure that the bristles are gentle but secure and that the brush is comfortable to hold. Other important features include a curl-release mechanism, which allows the unit to rotate freely and prevents hair from tangling; a cool tip, which prevents the top of the brush from getting hot; and a swivel cord, which lets the cord turn without twisting.

CLAIROL BODY BUILDER PLUS CB-8

The Clairol Body Builder Plus CB-8 is a versatile steam styling brush that offers a range of options for multiple hair styles. Rows of bristles arranged in loops along the barrel heat up and send heat through all layers of hair to produce a hairstyle with added body and fullness. The "Therma-Loop" bristle design prevents hair from getting tangled in the brush. The unit also comes with small, interchangeable bristles to create curls and waves. A rotating barrel helps prevent tangled curls. Gentle steam action enhances body and fullness and helps set curls and waves. The unit, which has a "ready" dot and tangle-free swivel cord, is dual voltage for use when traveling abroad.
Warranty: one year.

Approx. retail price	Approx. low price
$13	not available

VIDAL SASSOON PROFESSIONAL MINI BRUSH IRON VS-112

The Vidal Sassoon Professional Mini Brush Iron VS-112 has a ½-inch diameter barrel with heat-resistant bristles. The unit heats up quickly and is ready for use in 3-4 minutes, providing steady uniform heat during use. A contoured handle adds to the ease of use. This brush also has an "on/off" switch, a "ready" light, cool tip, and tangleproof swivel cord.
Warranty: one year.

Approx. retail price	Approx. low price
not available	$9

Prices are accurate at time of printing; subject to manufacturer's change.

MAKEUP MIRRORS

Makeup mirrors are designed to help you look your best in any light. You should select a mirror that offers multiple light settings including those that duplicate daylight, fluorescent, and incandescent lighting. The light output should be consistent and evenly spaced around the mirror to eliminate shadows. Look for a sturdy, adjustable frame that lets you set the mirror at an angle that's most comfortable for you when applying makeup. Regular and magnifying mirrors are two other features that help makeup application.

CLAIROL TRUE-TO-LIGHT LIGHTED MAKEUP MIRROR LM-7

 ✔ BEST BUY

The Clairol True-to-Light Lighted Makeup Mirror LM-7 provides four lighting filters to simulate daylight, fluorescent lighting, evening, and incandescent lighting. Strips of light on both sides of the mirror illuminate the glass entirely so that there are no shadows to mar makeup application. The 7½-inch by 5½-inch mirror swivels to allow you to choose regular or magnifying glass. A sturdy wire stand on the back of the unit easily adjusts to the desired angle. An outlet on the mirror frame can be used with other beauty appliances.

Warranty: one year.

Approx. retail price	Approx. low price
$52	$27

CONAIR TRUE REFLECTIONS III TM7

 ✔ BEST BUY

The Conair True Reflections III TM7 has four light settings so you can adjust your makeup for day, evening, home, and office. In addition to a center mirror that swivels from regular to magnified, it has two adjustable wing mirrors to give you a full view for easier makeup application.

Warranty: one year.

Approx. retail price	Approx. low price
$41	$29

Prices are accurate at time of printing; subject to manufacturer's change.

ELECTRIC SHAVERS

There are two basic designs for electric shavers: those with rotary heads that have two or three spring-mounted guards and turn in a circular pattern, and those with foil heads that have a thin, flexible screen over the cutting edges. Shavers come in both corded and cordless rechargeable models as well as cord/cordless versions that do not need recharging.

Top-of-the-line shavers have precision-hardened blades, rugged motors, and a selection of closeness settings. These shavers also include a mechanism to stretch the skin before the whiskers are cut, an ultra-thin screen covering the blades, and rechargeable power. The newest electric shavers are fully immersible for use with foam or in the shower and are cleaned simply by rinsing in water. Also new are charger stands that never need recharging. Most shavers include a coiled cord, a pop-up trimmer, and miniature cleaning brush. Many have dual-voltage capability for international use.

Standard women's shavers are designed specifically for women and are not simply smaller versions of men's shavers. Most are easy to handle and pack well for travel. Bikini shavers are designed to shave the bikini line, facial hair, and other sensitive areas. Epilation shavers pull unwanted hair out at the root line by gripping it in a revolving spiral spring. This new method of hair removal prevents hair from growing back for weeks longer than conventional shaving.

Men's Shavers

PANASONIC SMOOTH OPERATOR ES867BK

 ✔ BEST BUY

The Panasonic Smooth Operator ES867BK is a rechargeable wet/dry shaver that is totally immersible and shaves either wet with lather or dry. The unit, which can be used in the shower, has super-thin titanium-coated foil and precision-serrated inner blades for close shaving. It also features an ergonomically designed T-shaped body for fast shaving, a charger stand

---

with automatic voltage conversion, and improved battery capacity for approximately fifteen shaves on a full 8-hour charge. A built-in low battery indicator light glows when the battery needs recharging. A pop-up trimmer shapes sideburns and moustaches. The unit rinses in tap water. The shaver comes with a hard case and mirror.

Warranty: one year.

Approx. retail price	Approx. low price
$105	$91

REMINGTON MICRO SCREEN ULTIMATE RECHARGEABLE ULT-3

The Remington Micro Screen Ultimate Rechargeable ULT-3 is a cord/cordless shaver with an extra powerful motor, two ultra-thin electroformed screens, and two wide diamond-honed cutters with 120 cutting edges. A beard-lifter feature adjusts to stretch skin and lift whiskers for closer shaving. The shaver comes with a "Perma-Charge" charger stand with indicator light. The stand never needs charging, and shavers stay fully charged when stored in it. The shaver has worldwide voltage to be used with the cord. The unit has a trimmer and comes with a travel kit.

Warranty: one year.

Approx. retail price	Approx. low price
$70	$42

BRAUN SYSTEM 1-2-3 MODEL 3510

The Braun System 1-2-3 Model 3510 is a cord/cordless rechargeable shaver with platinum-plated foil and ice-hardened steel blades for close cutting. The shaver has three positions: the first setting for routine shaving uses the foil-screen blade; the second for awkward areas uses the trimmer and blade; and the third for moustaches and sideburns uses the fully extended trimmer. The 3510 has automatic dual-voltage adjustment capability and a built-in recharger with a three-way indicator

light showing the level of recharging. The shaver can be quick-charged in five minutes for touch-up shaving. An optional special recharging cord for car and boat sockets is included. A cleaning brush is conveniently fitted in the storage case. The unit comes with a 30-day, money-back guarantee.
Warranty: two years.

Approx. retail price	**Approx. low price**
$60	$56

FRANZUS TRAVEL-LITE MINI CORDLESS SHAVER RFS-35

 ✓BEST BUY

The Franzus Travel-Lite Mini Cordless Shaver RFS-35 is an economically priced, battery-operated shaver designed for travel or for late-afternoon office touch-ups. The lightweight, 4½-ounce shaver features an angled, twin-head screen for close shaves. The unit operates on two AA batteries and comes with a protective cover and mirror.
Warranty: one year.

Approx. retail price	**Approx. low price**
$28	$19

Women's Shavers

LADY REMINGTON WER-6100

 ✓BEST BUY

The Lady Remington WER-6100 is a rechargeable shaver with diamond-honed blades for normal shaving, and a "Gentle Touch" cutter for removing long or curly hair. The shaver's contoured shape promotes ease of use. An optional bikini attachment adapts the unit for shaving the bikini area. The shaver features an electronic solid-state built-in charger. The unit comes with a travel case that has extra space for cosmetics. The shaver has a 30-day money-back guarantee.
Warranty: one year.

Approx. retail price	**Approx. low price**
$35	$30

Prices are accurate at time of printing; subject to manufacturer's change.

PANASONIC SMOOTH OPERATOR ES176HK

The Panasonic Smooth Operator ES176HK is a ladies' rechargeable wet/dry shaver that is totally immersible for shaving with foam or in the shower or tub. It can also be used as a dry shaver. The ultra-thin shaving foil and precision trimmer are aligned on the same flat surface so both cutting systems work simultaneously. In this way, long hairs are cut by the trimmer, while the foil system smoothly finishes off the shaving. An angled head ensures that the foil/trimmer rests against the skin. A pop-up trimmer for shaving the bikini line is activated with a button. The ES176HK has a charging stand that includes automatic voltage conversion for worldwide use. The unit comes with an AC recharger/storage stand and hard case. **Warranty:** one year.

Approx. retail price	**Approx. low price**
$86	not available

LADY REMINGTON SMOOTH & SILKY HR-1

The Lady Remington Smooth & Silky HR-1 removes hair with a rotating coil that pulls out the hair by the roots so that it takes approximately three weeks for the hair to grow back. Hair as short as $\frac{1}{16}$-inch can be removed. Use on hair longer than $\frac{1}{2}$ inch is not recommended. The lightweight, compact epilation device has a curved handle to fit comfortably in the hand. The unit comes with an extra roller and a travel pouch. **Warranty:** one year.

Approx. retail price	**Approx. low price**
$25	not available

FULL-SIZE IRONS

New irons do a lot more than remove wrinkles from clothes. The most advanced have automatic shutoff if they are left idle for a specific length of time as well as electronic controls to

Prices are accurate at time of printing; subject to manufacturer's change.

maintain consistent heat ranges, burst of steam, self-cleaning vents, "on" lights, warning tones, and up to three levels of steam for different types of fabrics. Some irons are cordless and others have cords that can be attached to either side of the iron for right- or left-handed use.

Automatic shutoff gives you the comfort of knowing your iron will never be left on all day. An added safety feature in some irons is a switch-off mechanism that shuts a unit off in 30 seconds if left unmoved on the soleplate.

Cord/cordless irons allow for more freedom of movement than conventional irons. They are best suited for small jobs since they work at optimum temperatures for a relatively short period of time—about ten minutes.

When you purchase a new iron, look for multiple levels of steam and temperature settings to accommodate a wide range of fabrics, spray and burst of steam functions, shut-off mechanism, self-cleaning vents, and "on" indicator light. Other important features include a body that remains cool to the touch and adaptable cord for right- or left-handed uses.

PROCTOR SILEX
ADJUSTABLE STEAM IRON
12747

The Proctor Silex Adjustable Steam Iron 12747 is a fully loaded steam iron that features three levels of steam, a powerful blast of steam function to smooth out stubborn wrinkles, electronic shut-off that turns the iron off automatically if left unmoved for 30 seconds on the soleplate or 30 minutes on the heel rest, a constant "on" green light, and a red light to signal that the shut-off mechanism is activated. The 12747 has a nonstick coated soleplate with 53 self-cleaning vents and a cool-to-the-touch body for extra safety. The unit also includes a misting function to dampen wrinkled fabrics, a six-ounce, see-through, spillproof water reservoir, a fabric guide for setting correct temperatures, button grooves, and a reversible cord. **Warranty:** one year.

Approx. retail price
$56

Approx. low price
not available

BLACK & DECKER
ADVANCED SYSTEM F640S

The Black & Decker Advanced System F640S is a top-of-the-line unit offering three levels of steam to penetrate most fabrics, a surge of steam for heavy-duty wrinkles, a self-cleaning system to discharge mineral deposits, "wait" and "ready" lights, and a tone alert to signal when the iron is ready for use. The F640S has an electronic automatic shutoff that turns off an idle unit after 30 seconds on its soleplate or 12 minutes on its heel rest. A tone warns the user that the unit is about to shut down. The iron features a pivoting electric cord for greater maneuverability, a full-length button groove, and a nonstick coated soleplate. The F640S has a 30-day, money-back guarantee. **Warranty:** two years.

Approx. retail price	**Approx. low price**
$71	$51

ROWENTA AQUAGLIDE
IRON DA-33

The Rowenta Aquaglide Iron DA-33 features a gleaming non-stick stainless steel soleplate bonded to conductive aluminum to provide high, even heating without hot spots. The iron heats quickly and delivers steady, powerful steam with a choice of light steam for delicate fabrics and normal output for heavier fabrics. In addition, there is the option of extra steam for problem wrinkles. The soleplate features steam channels with fewer holes for greater steam pressure and wide, even dispersion. A transparent, removable water tank makes refilling simple and ironing easy because the tank slips off for pressing such hard-to-reach areas as the inside of cuffs and pockets. The large heel base provides extra stability in an upright position and also functions as a storage unit for the electric cord. The center-mounted cord swivels to accommodate left- or right-handed users. **Warranty:** three years.

Approx. retail price	**Approx. low price**
$65	$62

Prices are accurate at time of printing; subject to manufacturer's change.

TRAVEL IRONS

Travel irons are useful appliances, but they do have their limitations. They lack many of the features of full-size irons—heating power, proper weight, and versatility. But a travel iron does deliver for the traveler, ironing wrinkles out of suits, dresses, shirts, and other items.

Considering their compact size, travel irons do function remarkably well, providing steam, finger-activated sprays, and thermostatically controlled heat settings. And for the international traveler, almost all travel irons have dual voltage.

REMINGTON STEAM/ SPRAY/DRY TRAVEL IRON TI-15

The Remington Steam/Spray/Dry Travel Iron TI-15 has a powerful steam system and finger-activated spray for ironing tough wrinkles. The TI-15 has thermostatically controlled heat settings and a safety "on" light. The unit features a nonstick soleplate for smoother ironing and a fabric guide. Its handle folds over and locks for compact storage. The dual-voltage unit comes with a travel pouch and international adapter plug. **Warranty:** one year.

Approx. retail price	Approx. low price
$23	not available

FRANZUS WRINKLES AWAY TRAVEL IRON LT-10

The Franzus Wrinkles Away Travel Iron LT-10 is a steam and dry iron with excellent maneuverability. Its removable handle is designed for packing convenience. The LT-10 features a detachable clear-plastic water reservoir, a steam/dry button in the handle, a nonstick soleplate for smooth ironing, multiple steam vents, thermostatically controlled heat settings, and color-coded dial for fabric and temperature settings. The dual-

---

Prices are accurate at time of printing; subject to manufacturer's change.

voltage unit comes with a travel pouch and international adapter plug.

Warranty: one year.

Approx. retail price
$34

Approx. low price
$19

GARMENT STEAMERS

Increasingly versatile, garment steamers are for more than just removing wrinkles from clothes. These hand-held units are excellent devices for smoothing wrinkles out of draperies and sheers at home. Today's units deliver abundant amounts of steam and contain bristle brushes, lint removers, and crease attachments—a new innovation that turn the steamers into pressing machines for pants with results approximating those of an iron.

REMINGTON GARMENT
STEAM BRUSH SB-1

The Remington Garment Steam Brush SB-1 offers powerful steaming action quickly. The compact hand-held unit features a built-in lint remover and a soft bristle brush that stretches fabric as steam penetrates fibers and smoothes wrinkles.

Warranty: one year.

Approx. retail price
$25

Approx. low price
not available

ROWENTA STEAM BRUSH
DA-55

The Rowenta Steam Brush DA-55 produces steam in 90 seconds. A built-in brush opens the fabric weave to allow steam to penetrate. The brush detaches for delicate fabrics. The unit features an optional crease attachment (available for $10).

Warranty: three years.

Approx. retail price
$40

Approx. low price
$32

Prices are accurate at time of printing; subject to manufacturer's change.

Home Fitness Equipment

In past decades, home gyms were reserved for so-called muscle-bulging fitness fanatics. But today, a toned body is an expected part of a healthy, desirable lifestyle. Workouts have become part of a daily routine for most, and, as a result, the number of professional gyms has been multiplying. However, most of these health clubs are overcrowded, expensive, and limited in terms of hours of operation and space.

Until recently, a home gym was not an acceptable alternative since most home equipment was terribly inadequate in durability and design. But high-quality fitness equipment is now being manufactured for home use. The most exciting products combine basic performance needs with new technologies. When you purchase home exercise equipment, invest in products that will fulfill your expanding needs, but don't buy high-tech options you will never use. Also stay away from low-end bargains. If the price is too low to believe, it probably is too good to be true.

Always remember that even the best equipment is potentially harmful if you do not work gradually into a regimen which is suited for you. Never start an exercise program without first consulting your physician. He/she will help you to set up realistic goals/limitations and select the appropriate equipment to serve your needs.

Finally, equipment placement is crucial to the success of any home gym. As we all know, if it isn't easily accessible, use may taper off as the novelty of any new purchase does. The basement may be the perfect place because of available square footage. But exercising with no natural light among storage boxes may be unpleasant enough to drive you away from your new home-gym investment. A spare bedroom, den, or enclosed back patio and a smaller equipment set-up might be the better solution.

Best Buys '91

Our Best Buy and Recommended home fitness equipment products follow. We reviewed products in the following categories: exercise cycles, rowing machines, treadmills, home gyms, stair climbers, and ski machines. Within each category, the products are listed by quality. The Best Buy is listed first, followed by our Recommended choices. Remember that a Best Buy or Recommended designation applies only to the model listed; it does not necessarily apply to other models by the same manufacturer.

EXERCISE CYCLES

The stationary exercise cycle is a standard feature in most home gyms. A wide variety of stationary bikes is available. When you are deciding which cycle to buy, take time to use the ones you are considering. Check out their sturdiness of construction and stability. Make sure the seat is adequately padded and its contour feels comfortable during a long ride. Also look for weighted foot pedals (to prevent pedal spinning) with adjustable toe straps. Stationary exercise cycles are good for exercising buttocks and thighs.

TUNTURI TEE 2 ERGOMETER

The Tunturi TEE 2 Ergometer is an excellent cycle featuring digital display (showing speed, distance, and time consecutively at a touch of a button), a robotically balanced fly-wheel for a smoother ride, and seamless steel construction for sturdiness and longevity. Features include adjustable handle-bars, weighted foot pedals with adjustable toe straps, and a calibrated resistance system for a smooth, quiet ride.

Specifications: height, 43"; **width**, 23"; **length**, 37"; **weight**, 90 pounds. **Warranty: parts and labor**, two years.

Approx. retail price	Approx. low price
$399	$356

PRECOR MODEL 825E ✔**BEST BUY**

The Precor Model 825e boasts contemporary design and en-gineering in a compact and attractive cycle. An invisible fly-wheel (horizontally mounted in the base under the cycle) pro-vides direct drive for a smooth, vibration-free ride. A compu-terized control panel (showing speed, time, and distance—displayed consecutively at a push of a button) makes it an excellent choice for the avid indoor cyclist.

Specifications: height, 46"; **width**, 21"; **length**, 37"; **weight**, 65 pounds. **Warranty: parts**, one year; **labor**, 90 days.

Approx. retail price	Approx. low price
$700	$665

PRECOR M8.7SP RECOMMENDED

The Precor M8.7sp stationary cycle is exceptionally well con-structed of high-gauge aluminum. With a 7:1 gear ratio and a 25-pound flywheel, this cycle offers a smooth, quiet ride. Its seat is wide enough to keep you comfortable while the cycle guides you through preprogrammed trips on 30 different courses, including a desert trail and the hills of San Francisco. The simulated bike routes are displayed on a three-dimen-sional split screen. The other part of the screen shows concur-rent readings on data such as speed, distance, calories burned, etc.

Specifications: height, 48"; **width**, 16"; **length**, 37"; **weight**, 70 pounds. **Warranty: parts**, one year; **labor**, 90 days.

Approx. retail price	Approx. low price
$2,400	$2,263

Prices are accurate at time of printing; subject to manufacturer's change.

ROWING MACHINES

When you test a rowing machine, look at the way in which the machine is constructed. In most cases, it should use hydraulic cylinders and sealed ball bearings. The surface should be smooth all over—even at the joints. Make sure the movement of the machine is steady. Rowing machines are good exercise for buttocks, thighs, backs, biceps, triceps, and abdominals, and promote cardiovascular fitness. They can, however, aggravate back problems, and learning proper rowing form is a must.

PRECOR M6.4

The Precor M6.4 integrates innovative design and computer technology in a versatile and compact rowing machine. Its internal track (for smooth operation) and digital display (which consecutively shows elapsed time, stroke rate, and total number of strokes at a push of a button) make this unit a cut above the rest for so little money. It also features unique rear elevation, which allows you to shape and tone hips more effectively. Standard wing-nut tension adjustment is offered. The unit slides under a bed or other low-profile furniture for storage.
Specifications: height, 8½"; **width,** 32"; **length,** 54½"; **weight,** 42 pounds. **Warranty: parts,** one year; **labor,** 90 days.

Approx. retail price	**Approx. low price**
$400	$395

TUNTURI AIR ROWER R701

The Tunturi Air Rower R701 truly simulates real rowing because of a revolutionary design using an actual fan for resistance. A fully electronic display (showing time, distance, speed, calories burned, strokes per minute, and total strokes) and automatic scan feature allow you to cycle through readings automatically. You set tension/difficulty by how hard and fast you stroke. The seat rail folds up to form a right angle that allows the rower to be stored in a closet.

Prices are accurate at time of printing; subject to manufacturer's change.

Specifications: height, 25½"; **width,** 19½"; **length,** 93"; **weight,** 72 pounds. **Warranty: parts and labor,** two years.

Approx. retail price	Approx. low price
$699	$666

LIFE FITNESS LIFEROWER
MODEL 8500   `RECOMMENDED`

The Life Fitness Liferower Model 8500 really feels lifelike. A color graphics screen offers three training levels with 15 intensity settings. Workouts can be programmed in advance for up to 60 minutes. Computerized concurrent display shows readings on time, strokes per minute, and calories burned per hour.

Specifications: height, 36"; **width,** 22¼"; **length,** 108"; **weight,** 190 pounds. **Warranty:** one year.

Approx. retail price	Approx. low price
$2,795	$2,748

TREADMILLS

Treadmills are reliable, safe, and versatile. When you shop for a treadmill, make sure its design will help you in keeping to your exercise program. A resilient running bed that minimizes stress to your feet and legs is important, especially if you plan to run on your treadmill. For the best quality, look for a DC motor. It will provide a broader range of speeds and be more durable under stress and long-term usage than an AC motor. As with other exercise equipment, look for an easy-to-read instrument panel, safety features, quality construction, and a lengthy warranty. Treadmills provide excellent cardiovascular exercise.

AEROBICS PACEMASTER
MODEL 870XAE

The Aerobics Pacemaster 870XAE offers the best combination of features, quality construction, and price. Its powerful DC motor, digital read-out (showing time, speed, distance, and calories burned at the touch of a button), wide mph range, and optional motorized or hand-crank elevation are featured. This treadmill automatically shuts off in the event of a fall. A built-in safety device prevents sudden stops or changes in speed in case of a power failure.

Specifications: height, 51"; **width**, 22"; **length**, 64"; **weight**, 139 pounds. **Warranty:** one year; **motor**, two years; **frame**, five years.

Approx. retail price
$1,800

Approx. low price
$1,731

PRECOR MODEL M9.3

The Precor Model M9.3 has good stability and impact absorption. It features electronic incline with digital read-out showing the slope. There is a scan button that allows for constructive display of distance, time, speed, calories burned, and percentage of incline. It has a safety shut-off switch that stops the belt from turning in the event of a fall.

Specifications: height, 49"; **width**, 38½"; **length**, 58½"; **weight**, 300 pounds. **Warranty: parts**, one year; **labor**, 90 days.

Approx. retail price
$3,000

Approx. low price
$3,000

TROTTER MODEL 540   RECOMMENDED

The Trotter Model 540 treadmill is versatile with push-button speed adjust, electronic incline (up to 15 percent), and digital read-out (showing consecutive display of speed, calories burned, distance, and time) as just a few of its many useful features. Built-in work-out programs for nine levels of difficulty include warm-up, cardiovascular conditioning, weight loss, hill climber, cool down, etc.

Specifications: height, 53"; **width**, 28"; **length**, 61"; **weight**, 260 pounds. **Warranty: parts and labor**, one year or 15,000 miles; **belt**, 90 days.

Approx. retail price
$4,195

Approx. low price
$4,063

Prices are accurate at time of printing; subject to manufacturer's change.

HOME GYM

Because home gyms weigh hundreds of pounds, stability and reliability are the most important factors you should consider. Since weight lifting presents so many possible safety hazards, we do not recommend the use of free weights at home. Even though the use of free weights allows a latitude of movement that many people consider to be conducive to balanced muscle growth, their use is best suited to a gym where other people can spot you while you train. The home gyms we have selected are safe when used properly, and they permit you to work on massing and shaping many different parts of your body. When shopping, look for a gym that allows ease of movement from one exercise station to another with minimal movement of pins to access weight. With a home gym, you can design a workout to suit every member of the household and exercise any bunch of muscle groups. Home gyms tend to take up a lot of space, and beginners need to learn proper ways to use the equipment.

PACIFIC FITNESS MALIBU

The Pacific Fitness Malibu is a value-packed unit of superior construction with a patented four-position incline bench and easy-to-access weight at every station. The unit comes with 195 pounds of weight, but provides a maximum resistance workout of about 300 pounds due to a creative pulley configuration. Among the numerous work stations are: incline bench press, shoulder press, leg kick-back, leg curl, leg extension, front lateral pull-down, etc. The Malibu is capable of approximately 30 exercises. There are additional optional stations including the vertical knee raise/tricep dip and multi-hip. As options, 50 pounds of additional weights and chrome packages are available.

Specifications: height, 82"; **width**, 50"; **length**, 48"; **weight**, 350 pounds. **Warranty:** ten years.

Approx. retail price	Approx. low price
$1,695	not available

Prices are accurate at time of printing; subject to manufacturer's change.

STAIR CLIMBERS

As with all home exercise equipment, be sure to test out each stair climber for an adequate period of time in the store. This is the only true way to test the unit for its appropriateness to your workout needs. You'll be faced with a wide variety of climber styles: some simply simulate a staircase, while others have the feeling of mountain climbing. Stair climbers are an excellent method of lower-body and aerobic exercise and are simple to use.

HEART RATE INC. CL-108H VERSA CLIMBER

✓**BEST BUY**

The Heart Rate Inc. CL-108H Versa Climber has a vertical design requires only 3 feet by 4 feet of floor area, making it a perfect choice for those with limited space. A sophisticated computer allows three levels of difficulty and vital data read-out (calories burned, speed, and preprogrammed workouts). A variable stroke-length (height of the step), from one to twenty inches, allows this climber to be adaptable to all levels of fitness.

Specifications: height, 94"; **width**, 48"; **length**, 36"; **weight**, 65 pounds. **Warranty: parts and labor**, one year.

Approx. retail price	Approx. low price
$1,295	$1,295

PRECOR M7.4 LOW IMPACT CLIMBER

✓**BEST BUY**

The Precor M7.4 Low Impact Climber is a quality machine that's sturdy and features electronic read-out capabilities including time, steps per minute, and total steps. It offers a wide range of difficulty settings and step heights. This is a well-built steel-framed climber at a good price.

Specifications: height, 51"; **width**, 27¼"; **length**, 37½"; **weight**, 77½ pounds. **Warranty: parts**, one year; **labor**, 90 days.

Approx. retail price	Approx. low price
$900	$880

Prices are accurate at time of printing; subject to manufacturer's change.

LIFE FITNESS MODEL 1000
LIFESTEP AEROBICTRAINER RECOMMENDED

The Life Fitness Model 1000 Lifestep Aerobictrainer is a top-ranking fully computerized model with multiple features and program selections including digital step height, calories burned, floors per minute, etc. In this case, price reflects quality. It's an excellent buy for the avid athlete.

Specifications: height, 63½"; **width**, 36"; **length**, 49"; **weight**, 230 lbs. **Warranty: electronic/mechanical**, two years; **housing, drip pan, and grips**, six months.

Approx. retail price	Approx. low price
$3,295	not available

SKI MACHINES

Ski machines are a hot category in fitness equipment because of cardiovascular benefits and the fun of simulating cross-country skiing indoors. Testing equipment before you buy is crucial, since smoothness of operation can only be gauged this way. Ski machines can give you a full-body aerobic workout, and the equipment is usually quite compact.

NORDICTRACK ACHIEVER   ✓BEST BUY

The NordicTrack Achiever skier combines both quality and ample features, including variable upper and lower body resistance settings that let you set the machine to a workout to suit your body and your needs. A front-elevation adjustment is available for a more intense workout. Electronic readout displays consecutive information on speed, time, distance, and a performance index. Real wood tracking makes it attractive and in keeping with a traditional home.

Specifications: height, 60"; **width**, 23"; **length**, 48"; **weight**, 55 pounds. **Warranty: parts and labor**, two years (30-day at-home trial); **electronics**, one year.

Approx. retail price	Approx. low price
$769	$699

Prices are accurate at time of printing; subject to manufacturer's change.

FITNESS MASTER SIERRA EM

The Fitness Master Sierra EM has light weight and fold-to-store capabilities that make this model a true value. Although it conveniently packs away, it's not flimsy. It's sturdy and provides a real workout. The electronic display furnishes consecutive information on calories burned, distance, time elapsed, workout intensity, etc. A memory stores records from one workout to the next for up to four family members. The console has a special slot for a personal stereo or TV.

Specifications: height, 54"; **width,** 19¼"; **length,** 56"; **weight,** 62 pounds. **Warranty:** two years.

Approx. retail price
$699

Approx. low price
$582

CSA E333C ALPINE TRACKER

The CSA E333c Alpine Tracker features a unique weighted pulley system that allows for greater upper body workout. It has computerized monitoring (consecutive display for the following: speed, calories burned, distance, and time) and three tension adjustments for tracking. It folds away conveniently under the bed.

Specifications: height, 72"; **width,** 18"; **length,** 54"; **weight,** 55 pounds. **Warranty: parts and labor,** 90 days.

Approx. retail price
$350

Approx. low price
$299

Lawn Care Products

When you are deciding which lawn mower and weed cutter to buy, keep the requirements of your lawn in mind. If your plot is small and flat, you will not need a powerful mower with lots of features. But if you have a lot of grass to cut or if your property is hilly, you may need more than a basic mower.

There was a time when many homes had two lawn mowers—a large mower for cutting most of the grass and another one for trimming. Even so, much was left to be done by hand. But powered weed cutters have changed this, and most homeowners can groom their lawns with an appropriately powerful lawn mower and a weed cutter.

Best Buys '91

Our Best Buy and Recommended lawn mowers and weed cutters are listed below. They are presented in the following categories: gasoline, electric, and riding lawn mowers; and gasoline and electric weed cutters. The item we consider the best of the Best Buys is listed first, followed by our second choice, and so on. Remember that a Best Buy or Recommended rating applies only to the model listed; it does not necessarily apply to other models made by the same manufacturer.

LAWN MOWERS

When considering the purchase of a power mower, match the mower to your lawn. Rotary mowers are the best choice for heavy, coarse grasses. These are the simplest, the most rugged, and the most common mowers. The cutting action is produced by a spinning blade 18 to 24 inches long rotating at approximately 3,000 rpm (revolutions per minute). Reel-type mowers work best for fine-blade grasses such as zoysia. They are a gasoline-powered version of the old push mower and employ a reel of revolving spiral cutting blades that snip the grass cleanly against a stationary blade, scissors fashion.

Gasoline or Electric

For small flat plots, an electric mower may be adequate. Electric motors are rated in amps instead of horsepower. The most popular is the 12-amp range mower, which has approximately 1¾ horsepower output and should be sufficient for most lawns of this type. Electric mowers are quieter than gasoline and don't require as much maintenance since there is no oil to change or fuel to add. To start an electric motor, you simply flip a switch, but the area you can mow is limited by the length of your electric cord.

Gasoline mowers are more portable and more powerful than electric mowers, but require more maintenance and are more likely to have mechanical problems, even though solid-state ignition systems and refined carburetors have eliminated many previous service requirements. Remember that an air-cooled engine must work much harder at higher temperatures than a water-cooled engine like the one in your car; keep the cooling fins clear of clippings and debris, change the oil and filters regularly, and use only fresh gasoline for many years of trouble-free operation.

Rotary Mowers

Rotary mowers are equipped with special lift blades and decks designed so that the blades vacuum the grass off the lawn and into a container, usually a heavy fabric bag. The container can be mounted to the side or the rear of the deck.

Mulching Mowers

Mulchers are designed to lift the grass cuttings up under the deck and cut them into very small pieces, much like a blender chopping lettuce leaves; the clippings are then scattered into the lawn where they decompose into the soil. They work great unless you let the grass get too high; under these conditions they tend to leave clumps of grass on the lawn.

Push (Walk-Behind) Mowers

Push mowers are the most common and economical. They can be bought at most home centers or neighborhood hardware stores and are fine for the typical lawn if it is relatively flat. The engine spins the blade when the mower is pushed.

Self-Propelled Mowers

In self-propelled mowers, the engine drives either the front or rear wheels in addition to the blade. These mowers cost 30 to 50 percent more than the others and use some of the engine power for the wheel-drive mechanism. A 4-horsepower or larger engine is worth the extra cost. If you have a large lawn with a great deal of slope, a good self-propelled mower is a worthwhile investment.

Riding Mowers

A riding mower is strictly for lawns 15,000 square feet or larger. Be certain that the model you select has sufficient power, since the engine must drive a large blade (some three-blade versions cut up to 46-inch swaths), the self-propelling gear train, and your weight. Many new riders do a good job of cutting, but their size and maneuverability limit their usefulness for trimming operations. For this reason, many rider owners also have a smaller push-type mower for the final touches.

Most riding mowers for home use range from 5 to 14 horsepower. When selecting a riding mower, look for one with a wide stance and wide tires; this improves its stability and reduces damage to your lawn caused by impressions of smaller tires. A riding mower must be used with care when cutting on a moderate slope and should never be used on a steep incline.

Finally, get a rider that is maneuverable. A short turning

radius is important, but don't expect a large tractor-type mower to cut right against your favorite tree in one smooth motion. There are differences in models and makes, however, so select your size first and then ask for a hands-on demonstration so you can see if it will meet your requirements.

Safety Features

The Consumer Product Safety Commission set new standards for lawn mowers in 1982. Since the tips of the blade are spinning at over 100 miles per hour and can make projectiles out of the smallest foreign object, all are required to have some sort of blade brake. For this reason, most mowers have a "dead man" control on the handle that must be kept depressed when the mower is in use. Others have a blade/brake clutch, which stops the blade quickly but allows the engine to keep running.

Gasoline-Powered Lawn Mowers

BOLENS 8655/8656 ✔BEST BUY

The Bolens 8655 (electric start)/8656 (recoil start) is the latest version of the Bolens pioneering mulching mower. It has one of the best height-adjustment mechanisms we have found, using a single crank handle to elevate all four wheels at the same time. It is available in electric start and recoil versions; both are self-propelled.
Specifications: weight, 93 pounds. **Warranty:** three years.

Approx. retail price	Approx. low price
$559	not available
(8655)	
not available	$477
(8656)	

HONDA HR215PXA ✔BEST BUY

The Honda HR215PXA is a two-speed self-propelled mower with a 4½-horsepower overhead valve engine, rust-free aluminum deck, and rear bag; a side discharge adapter is available as an option. This is a good quality, durable mower, although some routine repair parts are costly and some routine maintenance (changing the air filter) is difficult.

Specifications: weight, 92 pounds. **Warranty:** two years.

Approx. retail price	Approx. low price
$590	$516

JOHN DEERE 14SB

The John Deere 14SB has a blade/brake clutch and discharges to the side or rear. This model comes equipped with a cast-aluminum deck, a 4½-horsepower overhead valve engine, and electric start. A five-speed geared transaxle regulates over-the-ground speed.

Specifications: weight, 97 pounds. **Warranty:** two years.

Approx. retail price	Approx. low price
$659	$589

SEARS CRAFTSMAN 37228

The Sears Craftsman 37228 is a self-propelled, rear-bagging mower with front-wheel drive and five drive speeds. The 4-horsepower engine starts with a lighter pull than most mowers. This model has four-position height adjustments.

Specifications: weight, 81 pounds. **Warranty:** one year.

Approx. retail price	Approx. low price
$378 (plus shipping)	not available

Electric Mowers

SEARS CRAFTSMAN 37031

The Sears Craftsman 37031 is the lightest full-featured electric mower. Features include a "cord minder" automatic cord reel, dial-type cutting height adjustment, and a two-bushel hardtop catcher. With its 12-amp electric motor and fully baffled deck, this mower cuts an 18-inch path.

Specifications: weight, 56 pounds. **Warranty:** one year.

Approx. retail price	Approx. low price
$250	not available

Prices are accurate at time of printing; subject to manufacturer's change.

LAWN CARE PRODUCTS

HOMELITE HE20

✔**BEST BUY**

The Homelite HE20 electric mower has a 20-inch cutting path, a Briggs & Stratton 1000-watt (9 amp) four-pole permanent magnet motor, and direct drive. The wheels are lever adjusted for cutting height. This model discharges on the side; a rear-bagging attachment is optional.
Specifications: weight, 54 pounds. **Warranty:** two years.

Approx. retail price	**Approx. low price**
$260	$212

BLACK & DECKER 8019

✔**BEST BUY**

The Black & Decker 8019 is a good value in an 18-inch side-bagging model. Its permanent magnet motor with 400-rpm no-load speed results in especially good cutting characteristics for an electric mower. This model has a stamped-steel deck and four cutting-height positions.
Specifications: weight, 37 pounds. **Warranty:** one year.

Approx. retail price	**Approx. low price**
$237	$138

Riding Mowers

SEARS 25632

The Sears 25632 12-horsepower lawn tractor offers dramatic styling and power at a good price. It has a steel high-lift mower deck and five forward speeds. Its unique sector-and-pinion steering allows precise control, allowing a tight 24-inch turning radius.
Warranty: one year.

Approx. retail price	**Approx. low price**
$997	not available

TROY-BILT 3312GR/3312HR

The Troy-Bilt 3312GR (manual) and 3312HR (hydrostatic) yard tractors offer heavy-duty, rugged construction. Features include an electric power takeoff clutch, a fuel gauge, head-

Prices are accurate at time of printing; subject to manufacturer's change.

CONSUMER GUIDE®

277

lights, and disk brakes. This model has a 12-horsepower engine. The mowing deck is sold separately; the price for the 36-inch deck is $556.

Warranty: three years.

Approx. retail price	Approx. low price
$1,949	not available
(5-speed manual)	
$2,349	not available
(hydrostatic)	

HONDA H3013HSA

The Honda H3013HSA has a 13-horsepower Honda engine, electric start, hydrostatic drive, and a twin-blade 38-inch deck. Although a good mower, its price is high.

Warranty: two years.

Approx. retail price	Approx. low price
not available	$2,500

HOMELITE RE1030E

The Homelite RE1030E rider mower features a 12-horsepower Briggs & Stratton synchro-balanced engine, electric start, electric blade clutch, and five forward speeds. This model has a high-vacuum deck and rack and pinion steering. It's a good choice for medium-size yards.

Warranty: two years.

Approx. retail price	Approx. low price
$1,700	not available

WEED CUTTERS

String trimmers use a nylon cord attached to a hub at one end of a flexible shaft. The weed cutter is driven by either a gasoline engine or an electric motor. Smaller electric versions are usually hand-held; larger gasoline-powered models have a harness and handlebars to allow the user to control the movement and placement of the hub. As the hub turns, the protruding strings lash weeds and tall grass down, but the "whipping" action reduces the possibility of injury to the operator.

Thoroughly clear an area of debris before using a weed trimmer and wear goggles, leather shoes, and socks when you operate this equipment. The cord, particularly on high-powered units, can turn stones or other debris into dangerous projectiles.

Special Applications

The versatility of a weed cutter can be increased by replacing the string trimmer head with a special saw blade, allowing it to cut heavier brush and even small trees. Extreme caution must be used to avoid getting the saw blade near hands or feet. Be sure to use only a blade specified for that particular trimmer.

Gasoline or Electric

Gasoline-powered versions are more powerful, more portable, and more expensive. They also generally require more maintenance than their electric counterparts. They have two-cycle engines that require oil to be blended with the gasoline. A centrifugal clutch engages the hub when the engine is accelerated, usually by a trigger-type control. For large yards, farms, and for clearing heavy brush, they are the best choice.

For most typical yards, one of the larger electric-powered models or smaller gas-powered models is adequate. You may be disappointed in the performance and durability of the least-expensive electric models promoted in discount stores; it's worthwhile to pay a little more for a heavy-duty version that will not only last longer but will have enough power for all your tasks.

Gasoline Models

JONSERED LR 220B

The Jonsered LR 220B is an excellent Swedish-built weed cutter that features a bicycle-type handle and strap with a waist loop. It has a 2 ½ cubic-inch engine. The balance is excellent,

Prices are accurate at time of printing; subject to manufacturer's change.

an important consideration when choosing a weed cutter.
Warranty: two years.

Approx. retail price	Approx. low price
$300	not available

HOMELITE ST175 | RECOMMENDED

The Homelite ST175 offers a lot of trimmer for the money. The
$1\frac{1}{10}$-horsepower engine has heavy-duty features that perform
flawlessly under tough conditions. This model has a dual-line
head.
Warranty: two years.

Approx. retail price	Approx. low price
$120	$95

Electric Models

Beware! Many bargain electric weed trimmers are poor per-
formers in all but the smallest yards. We chose those that in our
experience handled heavier jobs well, even though they cost a
little more.

TORO 1410 ✓BEST BUY

The Toro 1410 is a super-heavy-duty trimmer (by electric trimmer standards) that can do the work of some smaller gas-powered models thanks to its series-wound $4\frac{1}{2}$-amp motor and
heavy construction. The full hand-grip trigger is easier to
manipulate in tight spots than a conventional control. The
shaft separates for storage or transportation, and the second
handle is adjustable for handling ease. This model cuts a full
14-inch path.
Warranty: one year.

Approx. retail price	Approx. low price
not available	$58

SEARS 79804 ✓BEST BUY

The Sears 79804 is an excellent value. Its $\frac{3}{4}$-horsepower 5-
amp motor has sufficient power for a 17-inch cutting head.

The two-handle design provides maximum control. The auto-feed head stores 35 feet of line, which automatically sets to the correct length whenever the motor is started.
Warranty: one year.

Approx. retail price	**Approx. low price**
$65	not available

TORO CORDLESS 51720   RECOMMENDED

The Toro Cordless 51720 may be worth considering if your yard is not large enough to warrant an gas model but too large to have an electric cord following along. Add the cost of the power pack to the base price, which will operate a variety of other Toro cordless tools. Combination tool/power pack prices are available.
Warranty: one year.

Approx. retail price	**Approx. low price**
not available	$57

Snow Removal Equipment

Approach the purchase of snow removal equipment in the same way you would choose a lawn mower. The most important consideration is matching the type and size of the equipment for the job. Choose a power shovel for small jobs such as clearing a porch, balcony, deck, or steps, and a one- or two-stage walk-behind snow thrower for large jobs such as clearing a long drive or walkway. Power shovels are often electric; walk-behind units are usually driven by gasoline engines.

Power shovels work best on light, fluffy snow, but may clog in heavy or wet snow if you try to work too quickly. If you slow down they will get the job done.

Power snow shovels are one-stage devices. Their plastic or metal scoop-shaped housings contain a rotating drum fitted with a set of paddles. When you push the scoop into the snow, the paddles grab a chunk, whisk it around the scoop, and hurl it up and away through a deflector. Most of these units clear a 12- to 20-inch path. They are relatively lightweight, almost as easy to maneuver as a manual snow shovel, and take up little more storage space.

Walk-behind snow throwers are excellent for walks and driveways, especially when the snow is light and powdery. Single-stage snow throwers are the next step up from power shovels. They have a large metal scoop with a rotating auger formed of two reverse-pitch metal spirals that rotate toward common paddles at the center. The augers break up the snow and force it into the center from both sides where the paddles lift it and hurl it upwards through a discharge chute at the top of the scoop. The chute can be positioned to throw the snow in any direction within approximately a 200-degree radius. These machines clear an 18- to 24-inch path in one or two passes, depending on the depth and wetness of the snow. One-stage snow throwers usually have a 3- to 4-horsepower gasoline engine. Both push-type and self-propelled models are available.

Two-stage snow throwers combine a slow-speed auger with a rotating, power-driven, high-speed impeller. The augers break and feed snow to the impeller, which throws it up and out of a chute at the top or side of the machine. Two-stage models can usually clear a path 24 to 32 inches wide, depending on their design, and have engines ranging from 5 to 10 horsepower. Again, the latest versions have refined control systems and newly designed impellers to increase performance and snow-throwing distance, which can range up to more than 30 feet depending on wetness of the snow and the amount of loft required. Almost all two-stage snow throwers are self-propelled and have transmissions that give you a choice of up to five forward speeds in addition to reverse. If you have a large area that you intend to clear and heavy snowfalls are common, you will need one of the larger heavy-duty two-stage snow throwers. Optional accessories include headlights, protective "cabs," and even handlebar warmers.

Features

When you select snow removal equipment, you may want to keep the following features in mind. An electric starter may be helpful in getting the machine running on cold days, although the specially designed engines used on these units include a primer bulb and a large D-ring starting handle that makes manual starting easier than you might expect. It should have a discharge chute or spout that rotates, and it should rotate more than 180 degrees to allow you to work close to objects such as foundation walls and garage door openings. Slow forward speeds, especially in two-stage units, help prevent jamming in heavy and wet snow. It should have a heavy-duty power train that can withstand the shock of ice and other obstructions. At least one reverse gear is recommended; a high- and lower-speed arrangement is even better. The skids should be easy to adjust and should range from ground level to about 1½ inches for clearing unpaved areas. Larger snow throwers should have a limited-slip differential for better traction. A pivoting feature on the bladelike bottom of the scoop and cleats or lugs on the tires help in maneuvering. Every walk-behind snow thrower should have a scraper behind or under its paddle wheel or auger to pick up any snow that the wheel or auger leaves behind. The handle should be comfortable and convenient, or it should be capable of being adjusted to a convenient location.

In compliance with Consumer Product Safety Commission standards, most snow throwers have "dead-man" controls that stop the machine when you release the clutch handles. Self-propelled units have two; one that stops the auger and one that stops the driving wheels. As with any item of outdoor power equipment, check out the service facilities of the dealer from whom you buy.

Tips for Using a Snow Thrower

Fill the fuel tank with fresh fuel in the fall before the snow season starts, and keep it filled to the top at all times. This helps to prevent water condensation caused by sudden temperature changes. Check the engine and gearbox oil levels regularly, according to manufacturer's instructions, and wax the inside of your snow thrower's discharge chute if it's made of metal. This makes it easier for wet or sticky snow to move up the chute. Change the oil at the end of the season so it is ready to go when the next winter arrives.

If your snow thrower has been stored in a heated area, allow the entire unit to cool to outdoor temperature before operation. If you attempt to clean with a warm machine, snow will melt on it and turn into ice, which can jam the controls.

Slipping tires can be a problem with large snow throwers. To improve traction, you may want to equip your unit with tire chains. They are available from the manufacturer for a cost of about $35.

Before you start cleaning, think about what's under the snow. Gravel, stones, and other debris can be scooped up and thrown by the machine. If you think this may happen, keep the clearing height of the snow thrower slightly above the ground. On small snow throwers you will have to control this yourself; on large models you can adjust the skid shoes.

Start removing snow from the center of the area to be cleaned and work outward. To avoid side spills, slightly overlap each path you make. Because snow throwers can hurl foreign objects and chunks of ice as well as snow, never operate snow-throwing equipment when a bystander is in the area.

Best Buys '91

Our Best Buy and Recommended snow removal equipment listed below were chosen on the basis of efficient performance and value. Within each category, products are listed in order of quality. The item we consider the best of the Best Buys is first, followed by our second choice, and so on. Remember that a Best Buy or Recommended designation applies only to the models listed. It does not necessarily apply to other models made by the same manufacturer or to an entire product line.

POWER SHOVELS

Power shovels are lightweight electric snow throwers that are manually guided and handled in much the same manner as a conventional snow shovel. The action of the paddle or auger displaces the snow, so that no lifting is required. They are ideal for light but important jobs such as clearing steps and porches, and are easily transported.

TORO 38310 POWER CURVE

The Toro 38310 Power Curve is a lightweight but powerful (6⅜-amp) electric shovel that will throw dry snow up to 18 feet. The 12-inch width and light weight make it ideal for clearing steps and porches. The single handle grip is supplemented by a nonslip assist handle on the bar. This model has a removable key to prevent unauthorized use. The combination paddle/

auger rotor is driven directly from the motor through the gear train with a rubber coupling to cushion shock from ice and debris.

Specifications: weight, 12 pounds. **Warranty:** one year.

Approx. retail price	**Approx. low price**
$100	$89

SEARS 88201

The Sears 88201 is a hardworking, lightweight power shovel with a 4½-amp permanent-magnet motor. An adjustable assist handle aids in balance and control. The shovel has trigger on-off control.

Specifications: weight, 13 pounds. **Warranty:** one year.

Approx. retail price	**Approx. low price**
$100	not available

SINGLE-STAGE SNOW THROWERS

Single-stage snow blowers are fine for moderate snow areas. They can clear up to ten inches of dry snow or 3 to 4 inches of wet snow, and are light enough to be transportable. They are propelled by pushing and by the pulling action of the paddles on the snow and the ground.

JOHN DEERE TRS21

The John Deere TRS21 is a heavy-duty 4-horsepower machine that handles light to moderate snow very well. Snow-discharge vanes lock in three positions—left, right, or straight ahead. It will clear a 21-inch path and throw snow up to 18 feet. Forward movement is easier than on most single-stage snow throwers that depend on paddle "grip." Hand-operated clutch starts and stops paddle movement. The handlebars fold for storage or transporting. The engine runs on a mixture of gasoline and oil at a 32:1 ratio.

Specifications: weight, 77 pounds (recoil), 89 pounds (electric). **Warranty:** two years.

Prices are accurate at time of printing; subject to manufacturer's change.

Approx. retail price	Approx. low price
$529	$404
(recoil start)	
$599	$484
(electric start)	

SIMPLICITY 350M

✔ BEST BUY

The Simplicity 350M is a 3-horsepower two-cycle thrower that clears a 20-inch path. Scoop-shaped rubber paddles can be replaced when worn by removing bolts on the rotor. Discharge vanes adjust left, right, or forward. A reinforced "buster bar" helps break through drifted snow. The handles fold for storage or to fit in a car trunk.

Specifications: weight, 56 pounds. **Warranty:** two years residential.

Approx. retail price	Approx. low price
$429	$385
(recoil start)	
$479	$450
(electric start)	

SEARS 8829

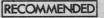
RECOMMENDED

The Sears 8829 has a two-cycle, 3-horsepower engine and clears a 21-inch path. The chute rotates 190 degrees. Its overall quality, features, and price make it a recommended product.

Specifications: weight, 67 pounds. **Warranty:** one year.

Approx. retail price	Approx. low price
$297	not available
(recoil start)	
$300	not available
(electric start)	

TWO-STAGE SNOW THROWERS

All three choices are mid-size units with engines developed and equipped for severe-weather use. Homeowners with needs requiring larger units should select heavy-duty equipment, such as the ones reviewed below.

BOLENS 1032

The Bolens 1032 has a full range of features and excellent overall quality as well as the longest warranty in the business. Options such as the handlebar warmers (powered by an engine-mounted alternator) are nice, but it's the controlled differential that really makes a difference. This is a very well-designed product, and it shows in such standard features as the 220-degree discharge.

Specifications: weight, 315 pounds (shipping weight). **Warranty:** three years; **transmission,** lifetime.

Approx. retail price	Approx. low price
$1,679	$1,363

SIMPLICITY 870S

The Simplicity 870S is a high-quality snow thrower that has new features such as a foot-operated pedal to shift the auger into positions for scraping, throwing, or transporting. It also has a "power boost" system, which is a variable-ratio pulley on the engine output shaft that varies the speed and torque of the second-stage blower according to the load. The result is a claimed 30 percent improvement in snow-throwing distance. The freehand control system allows the operator to maintain operation with one hand while making adjustments with the other; one of the adjustments includes a remote control for the discharge deflector cap. It is an 8-horsepower machine with a 28-inch clearing width and rugged construction.

Specifications: weight, 323 pounds. **Warranty:** two years residential; one year commercial.

Approx. retail price	Approx. low price
$1,489	$1,187

ARIENS ST824

The Ariens ST824 is a full-featured two-stage machine that has excellent quality and design. A large 12-inch diameter im-

---

Prices are accurate at time of printing; subject to manufacturer's change.

peller can throw snow from 3 to 30 feet. Auger shear pins protect the engine and gears from jams. The discharge chute rotates 230 degrees and a deflector shield controls the distance of a throw. A unique friction disk drive allows the operator to choose from five forward gears. This model comes equipped with manual lockout on the differential for easy handling.
Specifications: weight, 280 pounds (shipping weight). **Warranty: labor**, two years; **parts**, five years.

Approx. retail price	**Approx. low price**
$1,219	$1,200

SEARS 8859 [RECOMMENDED]

The Sears 8859 is an innovative, full-featured machine that is an excellent value. Its track-drive system results in better traction and control, and the friction disk drive allows six forward and two reverse speeds. This model has an 8-horsepower engine and a 26-inch clearing width. An electric start and a headlight are standard equipment.
Specifications: weight, 217 pounds. **Warranty:** two years.

Approx. retail price	**Approx. low price**
$1,000	not available

Food Preparation Appliances

Most kitchens in the United States have a coffee maker, a toaster or toaster oven, a food processor, a mixer, and several other standard food preparation appliances. New products that are more efficient, more compact, and easier to use are developed every year. Some are conveniences we learn to use every day; others are passing fads or meet the culinary needs of only a few people.

Best Buys '91

Our Best Buy and Recommended food preparation appliances follow. They are divided into the following categories: food processors, electric mixers, blenders, coffee makers, toasters, toaster ovens, and specialty food preparation appliances. With the exception of toaster ovens, these categories are further divided into appropriate subcategories. Products within a category or subcategory are listed according to quality. The best of the Best Buys is first, followed by our second choice, and so on. A Best Buy or Recommended designation applies only to the model listed; it does not necessarily apply to other models made by the same manufacturer or to an entire product line.

FOOD PROCESSORS

The first home food processor was a basic machine that could handle chopping, mixing, and pureeing with a simple "on/off" pulse motion. Considered by many to be nothing more than a sophisticated toy for culinary artists, the food processor has earned its place in the kitchen alongside coffee makers and mixers.

The original idea has been revised upward and downward. Bigger, more powerful machines can now knead dough for two loaves of bread or slice a whole tomato that has been pushed through an expanded feed tube. Smaller models store compactly on the counter and have smaller work bowls that are efficient for processing a single onion, a handful of parsley, or a cup of mayonnaise. Mini mincers dispense with slicing and shredding discs and specialize in chopping such small amounts of food as a clove of garlic or a tablespoon of herbs. Mini mincers also puree a single serving of baby food or grind coffee or spices.

Since food processors range in price from about $30 to about $350 and because each kind of machine has advantages and drawbacks, you should assess your needs and budget before you go shopping. Ask yourself the following questions:

- How much do I cook? Do I bring home take-out food during the workweek and cook only under duress on weekends? Or do I spend time in the kitchen baking, trying new recipes, and chopping ingredients?
- How many people do I usually cook for?
- How hard will I work the machine? Will I use it to knead bread dough or only for slicing and chopping?
- Do I want a food processor that does more than the basics? Should it be able to cut French fries, juice oranges, or whip cream?

Once you answer these questions, you are ready to consider the major kinds of food processors. In general, size is related to price, but not necessarily to quality. The largest machines have strong motors for big jobs and hard work. They usually come with an impressive warranty that helps justify the high cost. Most have options and attachments, such as specialty cutting discs, juice extractors, citrus juicers, or whipping whisks. Less expensive machines are not nearly as powerful as the big machines, but they are capable of kneading dough for a single loaf of bread. Some offer labor-saving accessories such as a second work bowl or a continuous feed chute.

Many compact models adequately meet the needs of small families. These models slice, chop, mince, and shred. Some knead bread dough or continuously spew out processed ingredients into a waiting bowl. Mini mincers handle only very small jobs, and many cooks use them in conjunction with a larger food processor.

Once you have decided which size food processor is best for your kitchen, carefully read all instructions before you begin. You are likely to overprocess food at first, since most jobs take only a few seconds. Because of their power and speed, you must handle a food processor safely. Keep it out of reach of children, be sure it is stable on the counter and the cord is out of the way, and be very careful when you handle the blades and discs.

Large Food Processors

CUISINART CUSTOM 11 FOOD PROCESSOR

The Cuisinart Custom 11 Food Processor is a powerful, European-styled machine with a direct-drive motor capable of handling any processing task. Designed in snowy white with charcoal-gray accents, the Custom 11 is available exclusively through department and specialty stores. Both large and small feed tubes accommodate whole fruits and vegetables of all shapes and sizes. Cuisinarts' easy-to-operate "on" and "pulse/off" switches make speedy work of everyday tasks. You can process up to 11 cups of sliced or shredded ingredients or about two cups of liquid for puree. The machine comes with a stainless-steel chopping blade, a reinforced plastic dough blade, a serrated slicing disc, a medium shredding disc, and a plastic spatula. Optional attachments include eight slicing and shredding discs, a whisk, a citrus juicer, and a power strainer. Also available exclusively for the Custom 11 is a continuous-feed chute attachment that lets you process unlimited quantities of sliced or shredded produce.

Warranty: three years; **principal motor parts**, 30 years.

Approx. retail price	Approx. low price
$250	$215

CUISINART FOOD PREPARATION CENTER

RECOMMENDED

The Cuisinart Food Preparation Center can stand up to the heaviest workload. Designed for extra-large quantities, this machine boasts 50 percent more capacity than a standard-size processor. Its powerful direct-drive motor and large work bowl process up to 14 cups of sliced or shredded vegetables and grind over two pounds of meat. The machine's large and small feed tubes accommodate fruits and vegetables of all shapes and sizes. Cuisinarts' "on" and "off/pulse" switches are easy to use. The Preparation Center comes with a stainless-steel blade for chopping and pureeing, a plastic dough blade for mixing and kneading, a serrated slicing disc, a shredding disc, and a spatula. Optional attachments include nine slicing/shredding discs, a whisk, a citrus juicer, and a power strainer.

Warranty: three years; **principal motor parts**, 30 years.

Approx. retail price	Approx. low price
$350	$261

Smaller Food Processors

CUISINART CLASSIC DLC 10C FOOD PROCESSOR

✓**BEST BUY**

The Cuisinart Classic DLC 10C Food Processor is a standard-size food processor with the same capacity as the original Cuisinart food processor. Charcoal-brown graphics accent an off-white base that houses a powerful, direct-drive motor. A three-position lever affords easy fingertip control. Standard parts include a large amber-tinted work bowl, a cover with both large and small feed tubes to handle a multitude of processing tasks, a stainless-steel chopping/mixing blade, a reinforced plastic dough blade, a serrated slicing disc, a medium shredding disc, and a plastic spatula for scraping the work bowl.

Warranty: three years; **principal motor parts**, 30 years.

Approx. retail price	Approx. low price
$200	$123

BRAUN MULTIPRACTIC DELUXE VARIABLE-SPEED CONTROL FOOD PROCESSOR UK-40

The Braun Multipractic Deluxe Variable-Speed Control Food Processor UK-40 is an all-in-one processing tool. Electronic dial control lets you select the optimum speed for the job. An adjustable disc system features thick or thin slicing as well as coarse and fine shredding, grating, and French fry/julienne cutting. Besides the standard work bowl, the Braun UK-40 also comes with a small bowl insert for whipping egg whites or cream. Other standard equipment includes a heavy plastic dough blade, a whisk attachment, and a wide feed tube that swings out to allow easy loading of whole fruits and vegetables, and a conventional feed tube for use when mixing or blending. The large work bowl can blend dough for two loaves of bread or shred about six cups of cabbage for cole slaw. This unit also features thermostat-overload protection with a signal light.

Warranty: one year.

Approx. retail price	Approx. low price
$160	$150

REGAL ELECTRONIC FOOD PROCESSOR K663BK `RECOMMENDED`

The Regal Electronic Food Processor K663BK is a powerful, direct-drive unit that features electronic speed control for fast, precise processing. The base is designed in black to complement today's modern kitchens. One dial adjusts the speed selection, while a single "on/off/pulse" button controls operation. Standard equipment for the K663BK includes a two-and-one-half-quart see-through work bowl, a stainless-steel chopping/mixing blade, a reversible stainless-steel slicing/shredding disc, a French fry disc, a thin-slice disc, a julienne/coarse shred disc, and a beater attachment. Optional accessories include a clear-plastic disc storage rack, an extra work bowl, and a machine dustcover.

Warranty: one year.

Approx. retail price	**Approx. low price**
$117	$89

REGAL LA MACHINE I
(K813)

RECOMMENDED

The Regal La Machine I (K813) is an uncomplicated, basic-feature machine. The unit comes with a standard work bowl, a chopping blade, a disc with interchangeable shredding and slicing blades, a food pusher, and a plastic spatula. Process one loaf of bread dough, half a pound of pasta, or three cups of relish in a single batch. The machine has "continuous" and "pulse" settings, which are both controlled by a single knob for simplified operation. The compact styling and convenient cord storage take less counter space. All parts, except the motor base, are dishwasher safe. For added convenience, additional work bowls are available.

Warranty: one year.

Approx. retail price	**Approx. low price**
$76	not available

Compact Food Processors

CUISINART LITTLE PRO
PLUS FOOD PROCESSOR

✓ BEST BUY

The Cuisinart Little Pro Plus Food Processor is a compact version of the traditional food processor. It is not only efficient and versatile, but also remarkably quiet. Standard equipment for the Little Pro Plus includes two work bowls (clear for chopping or mixing and white with a chute for continuous slicing or shredding), a stainless-steel chopping/mixing blade, a serrated slicing disc, a medium-fine shredding disc, a spatula, and a juicer attachment with three stackable reamers for juicing lemons, oranges, and grapefruit. The clear work bowl can accommodate up to three cups of shredded ingredients or up to one-half pound of ground meat in a single batch. With its continuous slicing chute, the white work bowl can speed through unlimited quantities of produce. The single "on/off/ pulse" control makes the Little Pro Plus a cinch to operate. **Warranty:** three years; **principal motor parts**, 15 years.

Approx. retail price	Approx. low price
$115	$74

BLACK & DECKER SHORTCUT CFP10

The Black & Decker Shortcut CFP10 is a space-saving unit that performs virtually all processing tasks. The tinted six-cup work bowl locks into position for hassle-free operation. A bowl handle makes removing ingredients fast and easy. A single touch-control button makes the Shortcut easy to operate in "continuous" or "pulse" settings. The unit comes with a unique chopping blade that is straight on one side and curved on the other to ensure uniform processing. The internal bowl ribs force food to make contact with the chopping blade to produce even results. Other standard equipment includes a reversible slicing/shredding disc, a transparent food pusher that doubles as a measuring cup, and "food fingers"—metal, comblike "teeth" to hold food upright for even slicing. All parts, except the motor base, are dishwasher safe for easy cleanup.
Warranty: two years.

Approx. retail price	Approx. low price
$52	$31

Prices are accurate at time of printing; subject to manufacturer's change.

HAMILTON BEACH EMMIE 3 COMPACT FOOD PROCESSOR 382W

The Hamilton Beach Emmie 3 Compact Food Processor 382W is a well-designed, basic-function compact food processor. Available in white or black, the Emmie 3 comes with a steel chopping blade, a reversible slicing/shredding disc, and a continuous-processing chute. Up to three cups of fruit, vegetables, meats, or grains are processed directly in the work bowl. For larger batches of sliced or shredded produce, attach the continuous-feed chute and go to work. For slightly liquid ingredients, Emmie's capacity is reduced to about one cup. An effortless twist of the lid starts the machine. The machine operates in both "continuous" and "pulse" motions for uniform results. Other features include cord storage and suction cups on the base for stability.

Warranty: one year.

Approx. retail price	**Approx. low price**
$50	$38

BRAUN MULTIPRACTIC MC 100

RECOMMENDED

The Braun Multipractic MC 100 is a basic-function compact food processor with added power and capacity. Mix, chop, slice, shred, grate, blend, and knead your favorite ingredients to perfection. The machine's liquid capacity is about three cups; dry capacity is about two cups. The clear lid has a feed tube for slicing and shredding tasks and for adding liquids or other ingredients during mixing and blending. The machine offers both "continuous" and "pulse" speeds. It has nonslip rubber feet and convenient cord storage.

Warranty: one year.

Approx. retail price	**Approx. low price**
$80	not available

Prices are accurate at time of printing; subject to manufacturer's change.

Mini Mincers

BLACK & DECKER SUPER CHOPPER MINCER/ CHOPPER SC25

✔**BEST BUY**

The Black & Decker Super Chopper Mincer/Chopper SC25 is superb for mincing onions, garlic, and fresh herbs; grinding small amounts of nuts or coffee beans; pureeing baby food; and even whipping a dollop of whipped cream. The easy-to-use fingertip control has three settings—"on," "off," and "pulse." In just a few seconds, you'll process up to one and a half cups of dry food or up to one cup of liquid ingredients. Produce such as apples and onions must first be cut into small pieces to ensure uniform processing. With the wire whipping attachment, you can whip cream, mayonnaise, light sauces, or salad dressings. An insert hole in the unit's lid facilitates the addition of liquids during processing. A curly, telephone-type cord reduces counter clutter, and rubber feet provide stability. All parts, except the base, are dishwasher safe, but you may find it easier to simply rinse them after each use. The unit is compact enough to store in a drawer or cabinet.
Warranty: two years.

Approx. retail price	Approx. low price
$30	$26

KRUPS "MINIPRO" MINI FOOD PROCESSOR #708

✔**BEST BUY**

The Krups "Minipro" Mini Food Processor #708 is a compact yet powerful mini processor. This unit offers more power than other units in its class. The clear, 19 ounce work bowl can accommodate up to one ounce of parsley, one-half cup of chopped onion, or about one cup of chopped apples. A touch-and-release button affords easy control and uniform results. The see-through lid is contoured to facilitate the addition of liquids during processing—especially useful when making sauces or mayonnaise. Also included with the unit is a plastic spatula for scraping the work bowl. This machine also features wraparound cord storage. For extra convenience, Krups also

Prices are accurate at time of printing; subject to manufacturer's change.

makes a "Minipro Extra" which features an extra work bowl for an additional $10 to $15.

Warranty: one year.

Approx. retail price	Approx. low price
$40	$38

CUISINART MINI-MATE PLUS CHOPPER/GRINDER

The Cuisinart Mini-Mate Plus Chopper/Grinder mixes and blends salad dressings or seasoned butters, purees baby food, grates cheese or chocolates, and minces garlic or herbs in an instant. The motor is housed in a white plastic cover that sits on top of the clear work bowl. Two blade positions and dual operating speeds make this unit extremely versatile. The tiny blade has a sharp edge for chopping soft foods and a blunt edge for grinding, grating, or pureeing. Up to two ounces of food pieces may be processed in each batch. Large foods must first be cut into half-inch pieces, while herbs, spices, nuts, and coffee beans can be processed whole. Push-button operation allows precise control. A tiny spatula is also included for scraping the work bowl. The bowl and blade are dishwasher safe, although rinsing them under tap water cleans them quickly. Rubber feet add stability.

Warranty: two years.

Approx. retail price	Approx. low price
$40	$34

MOULI "VARCO" ELECTRIC MINCER MODEL 534 ✔BEST BUY

The Mouli "Varco" Electric Mincer Model 534 is preferred by chefs for its fast, precision processing. Composed simply of a motor base, bowl/blade assembly, and cover, the Mouli grinds herbs and spices, minces garlic, and chops nuts in seconds. It also purees vegetables, condiments, and cooked meats for baby food. Operation is a bit more complicated with the Mouli than with other mincers; however, once you've mastered the steps, you'll be turning out perfectly minced garlic and ground spices with ease. Fill the two-thirds-cup work bowl no more

Prices are accurate at time of printing; subject to manufacturer's change.

FOOD PREPARATION APPLIANCES

than halfway with desired ingredients (larger foods, such as onions, must first be cut into small pieces), press the lid and cover together, place the assembly on the motor base, and press down on the cover to start the motor. A touch-and-release pulsing motion affords the best results. Vary the pulses for a fine mince or a coarse puree. A tiny spatula is included for scraping the work bowl. Both the bowl and cover are dishwasher safe, although rinsing under running tap water is just as easy.

Warranty: one year.

Approx. retail price	Approx. low price
$33	not available

SUNBEAM OSKAR JR. CHOPPER/GRINDER 14131 `RECOMMENDED`

The Sunbeam Oskar Jr. Chopper/Grinder 14131 is a small yet powerful mini food processor. Designed in white with a tinted work bowl, the Oskar Jr. has the advantage of a pouring hole in its lid for adding water or other liquids during processing (useful when making mayonnaise). The lid twists easily to engage the motor. A special blade design ensures uniform results. The unit will chop or grind up to one-half cup of cheese, chocolate, meat, or nuts; it can also puree single portions of baby food. As with other mincers, food must be cut into small pieces to ensure even processing. All parts, except motor base, are dishwasher safe.

Warranty: two years.

Approx. retail price	Approx. low price
$28	not available

ELECTRIC MIXERS

Electric mixers have the unique ability of incorporating air into whatever is being mixed. This makes them invaluable for whipping cream, beating cake batter, and creaming frosting. For frequent and heavy mixing jobs, you'll want a sturdy stand mixer. These powerful workhorses can handle even the most rigorous jobs with ease. Light and occasional mixing can be completed quickly and conveniently with hand mixers. For the ultimate in convenience, a cordless mixer adds portability to the already long list of desirable features.

Portable Mixers

KITCHENAID ULTRA POWER HAND MIXER MODEL KHM3WH

 BEST BUY

The KitchenAid Ultra Power Hand Mixer Model KHM3WH is a sturdy hand mixer that can stand up to tough mixing tasks such as heavy cookie dough. Exclusive self-cleaning "Turbo Beaters" have no center posts for dough to "climb" and clog mixing action. Made of sturdy wire, these beaters cut cleanly through ingredients for optimum mixing, beating, and whipping action. The smooth, rounded design and angled handle allow for easy cleanup and a comfortable grip. A thumb-operated control lets you switch from "low" to "medium" to "high" in an instant. An electronic sensor automatically adjusts when more power is needed to maintain steady speed. The unit also features a heel rest for added stability.

Warranty: one year.

Approx. retail price	Approx. low price
$55	$55

CUISINART CORDLESS HAND MIXER CM-3

 BEST BUY

The Cuisinart Cordless Hand Mixer CM-3 beats eggs, mixes batter for cakes, cookies, and brownies, and whips cream in record time. Best of all, it has no bulky cord to get in the way of mixing. The beaters are made of sturdy wire, enabling them to produce significantly greater volume of egg whites and cream. They can also handle tough mixing jobs like brownie batter. Incredibly powerful for a cordless appliance, the Cuisinart Cordless Hand Mixer is also sturdy and well balanced. It has three speeds—"high," "medium," and a "pulse/low" setting. It

Prices are accurate at time of printing; subject to manufacturer's change.

comes with a convenient charging stand that can sit on the counter or mount on the wall. The mixer charges in its stand when not in use. A red light in the handle indicates connection. **Warranty:** three years.

Approx. retail price	Approx. low price
$70	$43

BLACK & DECKER SPATULA-SMART POWER BOOST MIXER M175

The Black & Decker Spatula-Smart Power Boost Mixer M175 is a compact yet powerful hand mixer that can handle a full range of food preparation tasks. Five speed settings—"blend," "stir," "mix," "beat," and "whip"—make speedy work of routine mixing chores. Sturdy and well-balanced, this mixer also tackles stiff doughs with the help of its extra-large beaters. For extra-difficult tasks, the M175 has a super power boost feature that can be activated at any speed setting. Its sleek design and closed handle make it comfortable to hold, even during extended mixing tasks. The thumb-operated control switch is easy to use.
Warranty: two years.

Approx. retail price	Approx. low price
$30	$29

SUNBEAM 8-SPEED ELECTRONIC MIXMASTER HAND MIXER 03921

RECOMMENDED

The Sunbeam 8-Speed Electronic Mixmaster Hand Mixer 03921 is a well-designed, versatile appliance. Electronic controls adapt power and speed to prevent the motor from slowing or stopping during heavy mixing jobs or racing during light mixing jobs. Two sturdy beaters are positioned in line rather than side-by-side, creating a narrow profile that works well in small spaces and also allows for easy storage in a kitchen drawer or cabinet. The mixer also comes with a whisk, a plastic stir paddle for use with nonstick coated pans, and a chrome-

plated blender rod attachment.
Warranty: two years.

Approx. retail price	Approx. low price
$42	not available

Stand Mixers

KITCHENAID K5SS

✔ **BEST BUY**

The KitchenAid K5SS provides a powerful motor, sturdy base, and efficient rotary mixing action that no other mixer can match. Standard equipment includes a five-quart stainless-steel mixing bowl capable of handling enough dough for two loaves of bread in a single batch, a flat beater, a dough hook, and a stainless-steel wire whisk. Ten speed settings adjust from "high" to "low/stir" for a complete range of mixing tasks. Four large rubber feet protect the countertop while ensuring stability. The mixer is available in white, almond, and cobalt blue (the latter sold exclusively through Williams Sonoma mail-order catalog of fine housewares). With a number of optional accessories, the K5SS converts to a food grinder, a pasta maker, a fruit/vegetable strainer, a sausage stuffer, a rotor slicer/shredder, a grain mill, a citrus juicer, and even a can opener. A fabric cover, a food tray, a two-piece pouring shield, and a temperature-retaining water jacket are also sold.
Warranty: one year.

Approx. retail price	Approx. low price
$400	$274

SUNBEAM 9-SPEED EURO STAND MIXER 01971

RECOMMENDED

The Sunbeam 9-Speed Euro Stand Mixer 01971 is a powerful stand mixer that offers deluxe features at a modest cost. The mixer utilizes electronics to sense load demand and automatically adjust power. The dial control lets you shift settings quickly and easily while mixing takes place in the heavy three-and-one-half-quart glass bowl. Automatic bowl rotation affords hands-free mixing. The machine is also equipped with heavy-duty dough hooks. The unit is efficient and unusually quiet.

Warranty: two years.

Approx. retail price	Approx. low price
$80	$80

BLENDERS

Blenders are still a cook's best choice for mixing frothy drinks, crushing ice, or pureeing liquid food items. Of the two types available, carafe units provide added power and their own receptacles for heavy jobs such as crushing ice. Immersion blenders have the convenience of being able to be inserted right into the saucepan or container you happen to be working in.

Traditional Blenders

WARING FUTURA III
BLENDER BL320-1

✔ BEST BUY

The Waring Futura III Blender BL320-1 features ten blending speeds, including four "pulse/blend" speeds for quick and easy blending. The exclusive carafe design provides vortex action for added efficiency. You can chop, stir, mix, grind, or whip ingredients for a range of food preparation tasks. The Futura III BL320-1 comes with two carafes—a real plus when performing different blending jobs at the same time. The 45-ounce shatter-resistant carafe includes a "strain 'n' serve" lid for pouring off liquids while leaving ice or other solids in the carafe. The 40-ounce heat-resistant glass carafe features an easy-pour spout. Both carafes are designed with Waring's "sure-grip" handle, a spill-guard locking mechanism, and a tip-resistant base. A "twist-lock" removable lid insert doubles as a two-ounce measure.

Warranty: one year.

Approx. retail price	Approx. low price
$52	$23

Prices are accurate at time of printing; subject to manufacturer's change.

BLACK & DECKER HANDYBLENDER II (HB15)

RECOMMENDED

The Black & Decker HandyBlender II (HB15) is a space-saving, easy-to-use blender. A single switch offers three settings: "high," "low," and "pulse." You can chop ice, puree baby food, grate cheese, or mix up a frothy drink. The dishwasher-safe, 32-ounce, unbreakable blending jar features cup, ounce, and metric measurement markings. The "no-drip" lip makes pouring off liquids fast and neat. Other features include a two-piece blender lid with removable insert for adding ingredients during blending, a convenient lock/carry feature that secures the blender jar into its base for stable operation and easy carrying, and a curly, telephone-style cord for minimum counter clutter. **Warranty:** two years.

Approx. retail price	Approx. low price
$32	$26

Immersion Blenders

BRAUN MULTIPRACTIC HAND BLENDER PLUS MINCER/CHOPPER MR-50

 BEST BUY

The Braun Multipractic Hand Blender Plus Mincer/Chopper MR-50 is a powerful, single-speed immersion blender that performs the tasks of a traditional blender without the blender carafe. Designed to fit comfortably in your hand, the MR-50 consists of a slender power base attached to a stem fitted with a standard chopping blade. The multi-purpose mincer/chopper attachment enables the MR-50 to perform chopping and mixing tasks in a convenient splatterproof container. The mincer/chopper has a dry or liquid capacity of about seven ounces. The unit also comes with a mixing beaker and a wall bracket for convenient off-the-counter storage. **Warranty:** one year.

Approx. retail price	Approx. low price
$40	$37

Prices are accurate at time of printing; subject to manufacturer's change.

MOULINEX DELUXE TURBO HAND BLENDER MODEL 071

RECOMMENDED

The Moulinex Deluxe Turbo Hand Blender Model 071 consists of a lightweight mixing rod with a thumb-operated pulse-action switch, a light-duty mixing attachment, a mashing attachment, a stainless-steel filter, and a measuring cup. Perfect for sauces, gravies, or frosty drinks, the Moulinex Deluxe Turbo Hand Blender also includes a wall-bracket for storage.

Warranty: one year.

Approx. retail price	Approx. low price
$50	$19

COFFEE MAKERS

Coffee preparation has become an art thanks to readily available gourmet coffee beans, countertop grinders, and Americans' love of the beverage. Coffee maker manufacturers have changed with the times by offering a wide variety of product styles to satisfy today's convenience-seeking coffee connoisseurs.

The speed of automatic-drip units will always keep them in the forefront. They produce excellent coffee and come in a range of sizes, shapes, and colors. You can choose an insulated carafe (rather than the standard glass pot) to keep coffee hot away from the brewing stand, a drip-stop feature that lets you interrupt brewing to pour a cup of coffee, a timer that starts the coffee maker automatically, and a safety feature that shuts the unit off just in case you've forgotten. With shrinking households, mini one-to-four cup models are the rage, but standard ten- to 12-cup units are still the leaders, since they have the versatility to serve a couple or a crowd. (Remember that one cup is equivalent to 5 ounces of coffee.)

Some people will sacrifice the quick-brewing advantages of automatic drip for the flavor of perked coffee. Those who prefer extra-strong coffee sometimes find this method ideal, especially since percolators now have faster brewing cycles.

Prices are accurate at time of printing; subject to manufacturer's change.

For serving large parties, an oversized electric percolator is usually the coffee maker of choice. Generous capacity and self-serving taps make them an essential convenience item when serving a crowd. Our reviews of electric percolators follow those of auto drip units.

Large-Capacity Automatic Drip Coffee Makers

HAMILTON BEACH 792

The Hamilton Beach 792 is an attractive white coffee maker with a compact, clean design that's well-suited to most countertops. Although it has a ten-cup capacity, it's engineered to take up very little space. The carafe handle swings snugly into a niche in the brewing base, giving the coffee maker a neat, "packed-away" look while keeping it accessible on the counter. Features include an illuminated "on" switch and a thumb-operated hinged lid.

Warranty: one year.

Approx. retail price	Approx. low price
$32	$20

MR. COFFEE SR12

The Mr. Coffee SR12 is a good choice for budget-conscious, coffee-loving households because of its rock-bottom price and generous 12-cup capacity. Its "pause 'n' serve" feature interrupts brewing when the carafe is removed from the warming plate to allow you to sneak a cup before the full pot is finished brewing. Additional features include: traditional styling in white with brown accents, a lighted "on" switch, and a brew basket that hangs on the base instead of resting on top of the coffee maker for quick-pouring ease. The SR12 uses standard cupcake-style filters (several complimentary filters are packaged with the coffee maker).

Warranty: one year.

Approx. retail price	Approx. low price
$25	$20

Prices are accurate at time of printing; subject to manufacturer's change.

BLACK & DECKER THERMAL CARAFE DRIP COFFEE MAKER TCM402

The Black & Decker Thermal Carafe Drip Coffee Maker TCM402 is designed with an eight-cup thermal carafe. The coffee brews directly into this carafe, which keeps it hot away from the brewing stand for about four hours. For added convenience, there's an analog clock/timer that can be set the night before, so there's a fresh pot waiting for you in the morning. An automatic shutoff feature protects you against leaving the coffee maker on accidentally. There's also a "pause-to-serve" feature that interrupts coffee brewing mid-pot, so you can grab a cup without waiting for the cycle to complete.

Warranty: two years.

Approx. retail price	Approx. low price
$80	$61

OSTER 3420 THERMO CAFE

The Oster 3420 Thermo Cafe is a compact coffee maker with a ten-cup capacity. It brews directly into a portable thermal carafe that keeps coffee hot and fresh for hours. Carafe lids have beverage indicators labeling contents (coffee, decaf, tea, or other). Removable water containers fill right at the sink.

Warranty: one year.

Approx. retail price	Approx. low price
$66	$53

ROWENTA FK-27

The Rowenta FK-27 is a great-looking, white ten-cup appliance that produces an excellent cup of coffee. There are two brewing settings (two-to-four cup or five-to-ten cup), which regulate water-flow speed through the filter basket for consistent coffee flavor. For convenience, a permanent 23K gold-plated filter eliminates the need for buying paper filters, and an automatic drip stop allows a cup to be served before the brewing cycle is finished. Cord storage is provided to keep the unnecessary cord length out of sight.

Prices are accurate at time of printing; subject to manufacturer's change.

Warranty: three years.

Approx. retail price	Approx. low price
$80	not available

Small-Capacity Automatic Drip Coffee Makers

MR. COFFEE JR4 ✓BEST BUY

The Mr. Coffee JR4 is a low-priced coffee maker that does not sacrifice quality or great coffee. This attractive coffee maker is both portable and storable at only 11 inches tall and $3\frac{9}{10}$ pounds. A no-nonsense mini coffee maker, the JR4 has a one-to-four cup capacity and an illuminated "on" switch. It uses the smaller cupcake-style filters.

Warranty: one year.

Approx. retail price	Approx. low price
$16	$16

HAMILTON BEACH 788 ✓BEST BUY

The Hamilton Beach 788 is too attractive to hide away in a kitchen cabinet. To increase its aesthetic appeal, it's available in both black and white to suit varied room color schemes. The look and size make this unit a perfect office or college dorm addition.

Warranty: one year.

Approx. retail price	Approx. low price
$29	$18

BLACK & DECKER DCM5 CUP-AT-A-TIME ✓BEST BUY

The Black & Decker DCM5 Cup-At-A-Time is the ultimate in a small product that doesn't sacrifice quality. Designed to brew a single cup at a time, this attractive coffee maker offers a generous 12-ounce cup of true brewed coffee. There's a permanent filter (no paper filter fuss) and automatic shutoff (just in

Prices are accurate at time of printing; subject to manufacturer's change.

case you've mistakenly left the appliance on).
Warranty: two years.

Approx. retail price	Approx. low price
$27	not available

Electric Percolators

PRESTO 02811

The Presto 02811 is made of sturdy stainless steel and features a "ready" light (that illuminates when coffee is finished brewing), a removable cord, cool-to-touch plastic handles, and traditional styling. At standard size, this model has a four to twelve cup capacity, and uses 800 watts of power to brew a full pot in just 12 minutes.
Warranty: two years.

Approx. retail price	Approx. low price
$68	$39

FARBERWARE 138B

The Farberware 138B stainless-steel percolator will probably outlast most countertop appliances due to durability and simplicity of design. This coffee maker brews quickly (a cup a minute) using 1000 watts of power (keeping perked coffee extra-hot). A compact family-size coffee maker, the 138B has a two to eight cup capacity and sturdy stay-cool plastic handles. A detachable cord adds to cleaning convenience.
Warranty: one year.

Approx. retail price	Approx. low price
$68	$56

Large-Capacity Electric Percolators

WEST BEND AUTOMATIC PARTY PERK 57630

The West Bend Automatic Party Perk 57630 brews and keeps warm 12 to 30 cups of coffee. Its "country blue" floral design

---

Prices are accurate at time of printing; subject to manufacturer's change.

on an antique white background complements almost any party buffet table. This percolator's convenience features include a removable cord, which fits inside the urn for easy storage; a two-way dripless faucet for convenient self-service; and a safety light that turns on when the brewing cycle is complete. The parts are top-rack dishwasher safe, but the base is nonimmersible.

Warranty: one year.

Approx. retail price	Approx. low price
$58	$37

TOASTERS

Toast remains a staple of the American breakfast. For fast, even toasting, the standard, reliable toaster does the job best. For more versatility, a toaster oven can bake, broil, and top-brown.

Two-Slice Toasters

BLACK & DECKER WIDE-SLOT COOL-TOUCH TWO-SLICE TOASTER T215

 ✓**BEST BUY**

The Black & Decker Wide-Slot Cool-Touch Two-Slice Toaster T215 offers variable toast color selection, a sensor control for consistent toasting even when using different breads, and a cool-touch, easy-care exterior. The T215 has extra-wide toast slots designed to accommodate thicker breads and pastries. You choose from five color settings, ranging from "light" to "dark," then push down on the extra-wide start lever. Breads, muffins, and bagels are perfectly toasted in minutes. Designed in white, the T215 also includes a swing-out crumb tray for convenient cleaning.

Warranty: two years.

Approx. retail price	Approx. low price
$27	$23

Prices are accurate at time of printing; subject to manufacturer's change.

SUNBEAM ELECTRONIC TWO-SLICE TOASTER 20241

The Sunbeam Electronic Two-Slice Toaster 20241 features electronic controls that reset instantly to eliminate waiting between toasting cycles and to assure consistent results with each use. A stay-cool exterior provides safe handling and easy cleanup. You can toast two hearty slices of bread, bagels, muffins, or pastries in the single, extra-wide slot. A self-centering mechanism holds the food in the proper position during toasting. Special control settings for pastry, bread, frozen pastry, and bagels/English muffins take the guesswork out of toasting. The Sunbeam Electronic Two-Slice Toaster 20241 also features a snap-down crumb tray for easy cleaning.

Warranty: two years.

Approx. retail price	Approx. low price
$40	$19

Four-Slice Toasters

BLACK & DECKER WIDE-SLOT COOL-TOUCH FOUR-SLICE TOASTER T440

The Black & Decker Wide-Slot Cool-Touch Four-Slice Toaster T440 features dual controls to allow independent operation of its extra-wide slots. Ideal for toasting thick slices of bread, bagels, muffins, or pastries, the Black & Decker Wide-Slot Cool-Touch Four-Slice Toaster T440 even lets you toast two different shades at the same time. You can select one of five settings on each easy-to-read dial. The toaster also includes a delicate pastry setting for gentle toasting of your favorite torte. A maintenance-free white and black exterior hides fingerprints and stays cool to the touch during operation. A swing-open crumb tray allows easy cleanup.

Warranty: two years.

Approx. retail price	Approx. low price
$61	$50

Prices are accurate at time of printing; subject to manufacturer's change.

FARBERWARE T295
FOUR-SLICE TOASTER

RECOMMENDED

The Farberware T295 Four-Slice Toaster is an updated version of the Farberware Classic Toaster. It features stay-cool end panels and a variable heat selector that adjusts for delicate pastries, muffins, and frozen food items such as waffles. Wider toast wells are designed to accommodate thick bread slices, bagels, and muffins. Independent push-button operation lets you select a "light" setting for delicate pastries in one well and a darker setting for toast or bagels in the other. The dials and front handle stay cool to the touch and a hinged crumb tray simplifies cleanup.

Warranty: one year.

Approx. retail price	**Approx. low price**
$65	$43

TOASTER OVENS

DELONGHI ALFREDO
DELUX BAKE N' BROIL
OVEN XU-20

✔ BEST BUY

The DeLonghi Alfredo Delux Bake n' Broil Oven XU-20 offers a complete range of toaster and oven features. Three dials individually control oven temperature, toast color selection, and desired function: toast, bake, or broil. The roomy interior is designed to accommodate large food items such as a whole chicken, meatloaf, or even your favorite quiche. The unit comes with its own black-steel baking pan and broil tray. The two-position wire rack adjusts to allow room for taller items and a temperature-resistant bulb lets you keep an eye on cooking. The enamel-coated metal surface resists scratches and wipes clean with a damp cloth. Other features include a continuous-cleaning interior, a removable crumb tray, cool-touch handles, a "power" light, cord storage, and nonslip rubber feet.

Warranty: one year.

Approx. retail price	Approx. low price
$129	$93

BLACK & DECKER SPACEMAKER TOAST-R-OVEN BROILER SO2500

✔**BEST BUY**

The Black & Decker Spacemaker Toast-R-Oven Broiler SO2500 is a versatile appliance with outstanding performance features. This unit can sit on your counter or install under your cabinet with its own "heat-guard" mounting hood. It bakes, broils, top-browns, reheats foods, and toasts. The roomy interior can accommodate a nine-inch pie plate, a full-size muffin pan, a 9 by 13 inch baking pan, or up to six slices of bread for toasting. Standard features include an oven/broil pan, a two-position drip tray, and a continuous-cleaning interior. The easy-to-use dial control includes toast settings from "light" to "dark," standard bake temperatures, and a "broil" setting. Select the desired setting, then activate the "on/off" switch. A handy "power" light reminds you it's working, and recommended cooking times and temperatures for popular food items appear on the front panel.

Warranty: two years.

Approx. retail price	Approx. low price
$128	$93

BLACK & DECKER TR0400 TOAST-R-OVEN BROILER

✔**BEST BUY**

The Black & Decker TR0400 Toast-R-Oven Broiler is a compact oven that toasts, bakes, defrosts, broils, and top-browns. Despite its compact size, the TR0400 can accommodate prepared frozen dinners, six burgers, or a six-cup muffin tin with ease. Two independent dials control toast color selection and "bake/broil" temperature settings. A separate "on/off" switch activates the machine. This model comes with a multi-purpose bake/broil pan, a dual-position broiling grid, a convenient signal light, a swing-open crumb tray, and an easy-care white

Prices are accurate at time of printing; subject to manufacturer's change.

exterior. An under-the-cabinet heat-guard mounting hood is available separately.

Warranty: two years.

Approx. retail price	Approx. low price
$56	not available

TOASTMASTER 336
TOASTER-OVEN-BROILER
WITH ELECTRONIC TIMER   RECOMMENDED

The Toastmaster 336 Toaster-Oven-Broiler with Electronic Timer features electronic toasting circuitry to deliver consistent results. Two dial settings offer independent control of toast color and "bake/broil" temperatures. An "on/off" switch controls toasting; the adjustable thermostat control also includes settings from "keep warm" to "broil." The continuous-cleaning interior can accommodate an eight-inch cake or pie pan or up to four slices of bread. The unit comes with a chrome bake/broil tray and a wire rack that slides forward automatically as the door is opened. Other features include double-wall construction for better heat retention and a cooler exterior surface, a "power" signal light, a crumb tray, and automatic shutoff with a bell signal when toasting is complete.

Warranty: one year.

Approx. retail price	Approx. low price
$89	not available

PROCTOR-SILEX 03030
OVENMASTER ELECTRONIC
TOASTER OVEN/BROILER   RECOMMENDED

The Proctor-Silex 03030 Ovenmaster Electronic Toaster Oven/Broiler, with its continuous-cleaning interior, features a built-in electronic toast sensor that automatically adjusts temperature for precise results. Push-button toast control lets you start and stop toasting in an instant. Separate dials let you select toast temperatures from "light" to "dark" for toasting and oven temperatures from "defrost" to "broil." With 40 percent

Prices are accurate at time of printing; subject to manufacturer's change.

more capacity than a standard toaster oven, the Proctor-Silex 03030 can roast a five-pound chicken or bake a full-size loaf of bread. The unit comes with a multi-purpose, two-position broil pan, a reversible oven rack, a continuous-cleaning interior, an easy-care white exterior, a snap-open crumb tray, and a "power" light. A tone signals the end of the toasting cycle. This product is available in black as model 03020.
Warranty: two years.

Approx. retail price	**Approx. low price**
$76	not available

SPECIALTY FOOD PREPARATION APPLIANCES

Waffle Makers

BLACK & DECKER SWEET HEARTS WAFFLEBAKER G12 ✔BEST BUY

The Black & Decker Sweet Hearts Wafflebaker G12 takes the guesswork out of waffle making. Just preheat the unit—a "ready" light indicates when to pour batter—and bake. A bell tone signals when the waffle is done. An automatic thermostat guarantees golden-brown waffles every time. The Sweet Hearts Wafflebaker G12 bakes a seven and one-half-inch, plate-size waffle that divides into four heart-shaped sections. A nonstick cooking surface simplifies cleanup.
Warranty: two years.

Approx. retail price	**Approx. low price**
$45	not available

TOASTMASTER FASTBAKE WAFFLEBAKER MODEL 275 ✔BEST BUY

The Toastmaster FastBake WaffleBaker 275 bakes a golden, delicious, eight-inch square waffle in half the time required by many other family-size waffle bakers. A "ready" light indicates when to pour the batter and when to remove the finished waffle. Double-duty grids reverse to convert the wafflebaker

Prices are accurate at time of printing; subject to manufacturer's change.

into a large, divided griddle. Leave the griddle open for pancakes or grilling; close for use as a sandwich griddle. Durable Mastercoat surfaces inside and out, a pouring spout, and a full-perimeter grease channel simplify cleanup. An adjustable dial features a full-range of temperatures for waffles, grilling, or sandwiches. The unit stands on end for convenient storage. **Warranty:** one year.

Approx. retail price	Approx. low price
$72	$42

Manual Ice-cream Maker

DONVIER PREMIER

The Donvier Premier is a completely self-contained, portable ice-cream factory. It requires no ice, no salt, and no electricity. The "chillfast cylinder," with its patented refrigerant, provides the cooling power necessary to freeze ice cream, frozen yogurt, even difficult-to-freeze alcohol-based sorbets. Place the cylinder in your freezer for a minimum of seven hours, insert the cylinder into its plastic container, pour in your ingredients, and turn the crank twice every three minutes. In about twenty minutes, you'll have a batch of the freshest, creamiest ice cream you've ever tasted. The Donvier Premier is available in white and two sizes (quart and pint). Extra cylinders are sold separately and come in handy when making multiple batches. **Warranty:** one year.

Approx. retail price	Approx. low price
$50/quart	$38
$40/pint	$35

Electric Ice-cream Makers

SIMAC II GELATAIO SCX2 "DUET" IC-40

The Simac II Gelataio SCx2 "Duet" IC-40 combines versatility with ease of use in this two-pint ice-cream maker. It consists of a sealed cooling chamber with two individual freezer compartments, each with its own electrically powered churning motor. When you pre-freeze the cooling chamber, put a different flavor in each side, and place the motor and mixing blade on top, they churn at the same time. The churning paddle aerates the mixture producing fluffier ice cream. A unique "dipole" action automatically reverses the churning direction when resistance is encountered. The machine makes smooth, creamy ice cream, yogurt, sorbet, or mousse in about forty minutes or less. Other features include an insulated container to retain the cold temperature, clear lids with openings for adding chips, nuts, or fruit during operation, and a nonstick coating for easy cleanup in warm, soapy water.

Warranty: one year.

Approx. retail price	**Approx. low price**
$125	$80

WARING ICE CREAM PARLOR II CF810-1 RECOMMENDED

The Waring Ice Cream Parlor II CF810-1 comes with both an electric motor paddle and a hand crank assembly to suit whatever ice-cream making mood you're in. A specially designed chilling bucket acts as the cooling agent, eliminating the need for ice or salt. Place the bucket in your freezer for at least 16 hours (or overnight), attach the paddle of choice, and pour in your mixed ingredients. The hand crank requires only a few turns every five minutes; the electric motor does the cranking for you and automatically shuts itself off when the proper consistency is reached. In an average of 20 minutes, you'll have up to three pints of soft-serve ice cream. For a harder set, simply place the ice cream in your freezer. The unit also features a see-through lid with an opening for adding nuts, M&Ms, and other last-minute ingredients. The bucket is immersible for easy cleaning.

Warranty: one year.

Approx. retail price	**Approx. low price**
$68	$45

RIVAL 8200 DOLLY MADISON ICE CREAM FREEZER

The Rival 8200 Dolly Madison Ice Cream Freezer is a two-quart, countertop ice-cream freezer. This compact model consists of an electric motor base onto which sits a large, plastic bucket. The two-quart ice-cream container and churning paddle fit inside the bucket. You pour ingredients into the container, then fill the space between the container and the bucket wall with layers of ice cubes and table salt. The clear plastic lid locks into position and allows easy viewing of the churning process. Fresh, creamy ice cream is ready to eat in about 25 to 40 minutes. Because no pre-freezing is required, this unit is ready at a moment's notice. All parts, except the motor, are immersible for easy cleaning.

Warranty: one year.

Approx. retail price	**Approx. low price**
$32	not available

Electric Deep Fryers

DELONGHI ROTO-FRYER D-10

The DeLonghi Roto-Fryer D-10 requires half the amount of oil called for by traditional fryers. It features a rotating basket, which circulates its contents in and out of the oil, producing crisp, golden French fries, onion rings, or batter-fried shrimp in just minutes. This unit is smokeless and odorless thanks to a hermetically sealed lid containing two changeable filters that absorb odors and excess steam. Another added feature is a special handle, which lets you raise and lower the basket while the lid is closed to prevent splattering. You can fry up to two pounds of potatoes in a single batch using only one quart of oil. The rotating design lets the oil flow evenly around the food to prevent sticking and ensure even results. The self-monitoring basket also reverses direction if it encounters resistance. Other standard features include a thermostat dial offering temperatures from 300°F for delicate food items, such as mushrooms, to 370°F for fries and chips; a 20-minute bell timer; and a "ready" light, which signals that the correct oil temperature has been reached.

Warranty: one year.

Approx. retail price	Approx. low price
$169	$157

DAZEY CHEF'S POT DCP-6

The Dazey Chef's Pot DCP-6 is a multi-purpose appliance that can perform a number of different cooking and frying tasks. You add oil to the six-quart pot for frying potatoes or chicken, or fill the pot with broth and vegetables for delicious home-made soup. Steamed broccoli, pot roast, and chicken cacciatore are accomplished just as easily. Set the removable thermostat control to the desired temperature, and plug in the cord. In all, the Chef's Pot bakes, roasts, stews, simmers, blanches, boils, steams, deep fries, and even pops popcorn. Standard features include a steam/fry basket with a "drip-grip" handle for easy drainage, an immersible die-cast aluminum pot with nonstick coating inside and out to facilitate cleaning, cool-touch handles and feet, and a glass lid that lets you keep an eye on cooking. The Dazey Chef's Pot DCP-6 is stable on its feet.

Warranty: one year.

Approx. retail price	Approx. low price
$49	$33

Juicers

BOSCH "GROVELAND" JUICER MCP 100170

The Bosch "Groveland" Juicer MCP 100170 is a compact, easy-to-use citrus juicer that will leave your oranges and other citrus clean to the skin. This unit features a powerful motor

---

Prices are accurate at time of printing; subject to manufacturer's change.

base, a clear plastic pitcher container with handle and pouring spout, and a cone/strainer attachment. You press down on the large, grooved cone to start the motor. Up to three cups of orange, grapefruit, lemon, or lime juice can be squeezed quickly and efficiently. The reamer reverses direction when you lift and reinsert the fruit for maximum juice extraction. Both the pitcher and cone/strainer are dishwasher safe. Other features include convenient cord storage and three nonslip rubber feet.

Warranty: one year.

Approx. retail price	Approx. low price
$40	$38

SANYO JUST JUICE PLUS SJ60

 ✓BEST BUY

The Sanyo Just Juice Plus SJ60 is a lightweight, sturdy appliance that can stand up to pressure. It consists of a motor base, a clear plastic container with pouring spouts on either end, a cone, a strainer, and a dustcover. The wide juicing cone is perfect for all types of citrus. Its angled grooves dig in to extract every drop of juice, and a small pusher foot ensures that no juice gets left behind in the strainer. Press down on the cone and the high-speed motor goes right to work extracting up to two-and-a-half cups of juice in a single batch. The Just Juice Plus also features handy cord storage.

Warranty: one year.

Approx. retail price	Approx. low price
$20	not available

BRAUN JUICE EXTRACTOR MP-80

✓BEST BUY

The Braun Juice Extractor MP-80 is a sleek, sophisticated machine that can transform ordinary fruits and vegetables into a delicious, healthful beverage in seconds. An easy-to-use "on/off" dial activates the motor. The top-loading chute has a unique tray attachment, which holds bulk produce for continuous processing. To prepare produce to be juiced, wash and cut larger fruits and vegetables into sections, and peel

Prices are accurate at time of printing; subject to manufacturer's change.

citrus fruit and bananas. Then feed small quantities through the chute and watch juice flow into the supplied beaker or, if you prefer, your own glass for immediate consumption. Pulp is automatically ejected into a swing-out container for easy disposal.

Warranty: one year.

Approx. retail price	Approx. low price
$90	not available

Popcorn Popper

PROCTOR-SILEX HOT-AIR POPCORN PUMPER H7340

The Proctor-Silex Hot-Air Popcorn Pumper H7340 is a compact, efficient appliance that uses hot air, rather than oil, to heat the popcorn kernels. The Popcorn Pumper yields about five quarts of fluffy popcorn in less than three minutes. The half-cup plastic measure can also be filled with butter and placed on top of the unit for melting. Popcorn is fed into the machine and is then ejected out a chute into a waiting bowl. Both the chute and measuring cup detach for easy cleaning and then stack together with the pumper base to save storage space.

Warranty: one year.

Approx. retail price	Approx. low price
$26	$17

Barbecue Grills

With nutrition consciousness on the rise, and the desire to keep cholesterol and calorie counts down, grilled food is enjoying great popularity. Today's barbecue grill goes beyond the hamburger and hot dog to tackle full-course grilled meals featuring seafood and vegetables. But if you're a die-hard fan of purist charcoal-cooked burgers, don't despair. The basic, affordable metal charcoal tray on legs, with all of its classic simplicity, is still a hot item!

Charcoal or Gas?

Fans of barbecued food love the taste of charbroiled meat, poultry, fish, and even vegetables. Only charcoal grills give you this taste, and they also cost less than gas grills. A new advantage—smoker grills, which offer the option of double- and sometimes triple-decker cooking—allow full-course meal preparation using various cooking techniques from steaming to smoking on grills of all sizes.

On the downside, charcoal takes a long time to heat up (although the new quick-heating briquette pitchers help to speed this process), and you have less control over the heat and flame while you are cooking. Other substantial drawbacks: After a meal, you have to clean up the messy ash, and there's also the expense and hassle of keeping briquettes on hand.

Gas grills are usually more expensive than charcoal grills, but they have many more features, heat up quickly, and clean up easily. The lava rock, used instead of charcoal, remains in the grill so that you don't have to add new coals every time you use the grill. Also, gas fuel tanks have to be refilled when the gas has been used up. Gas grills will never give you char-broiled taste, but mesquite and other wood formulated for use with gas grills offer a great-tasting alternative.

Features and Terminology

Btus are a measure of the amount of heat produced by a gas grill. Select the appropriate power level for your cooking needs.

Cooking surface is usually measured in square inches. Some manufacturers add the dimensions of the warming racks to the cooking surface, so when you compare dimensions make sure you are considering only the area over the coals.

Best Buys '91

Our Best Buy barbecue grills follow. They are arranged in these categories: large charcoal, small charcoal, tabletop charcoal, fixed gas, portable gas, and tabletop gas. All these grills have been selected on the basis of their features, performance, and overall value. Within each category, the item we consider the best of the Best Buys is listed first, followed by our second choice, and so on. Remember that the Best Buy designation applies only to the model listed.

Large Charcoal Grills

WEBER ONE-TOUCH KETTLE #71001

The Weber One-Touch Kettle #71001 offers an ample 397 square inches of cooking surface in a no-nonsense grill. (It's large enough to cook a whole turkey and vegetables.) You will not have trouble finding this model in local stores since it has been a top-seller due to its simplicity of design and sturdiness. It gets its name from a patented single-lever feature that sweeps ashes into a lower bowl for ease of disposal. The bowl and lid are constructed of heavy-gauge steel sealed with rust-resistant black porcelain enamel.

Prices are accurate at time of printing; subject to manufacturer's change.

Specifications: weight, 35 pounds. **Warranty:** five years, limited.

Approx. retail price	Approx. low price
$80	$68
(black)	
$90	not available
(other colors)	

COOK 'N' CA'JUN S-80B

✓ BEST BUY

The Cook 'n' Ca'Jun S-80B is a double-decker cylinder-shaped smoker-style grill that's versatile and good-looking. It has two stacked cooking grids making up a total of 376 square inches of cooking surface that can handle a total of 50 pounds of food. An eight-quart water pan allows the grill to function as a smoker. Optional accessories include a vinyl cover, smoking spice, hickory wood sticks, and rib rack.

Specifications: weight, 25 pounds. **Warranty:** one year, over the counter.

Approx. retail price	Approx. low price
not available	$50

Small Charcoal Grills

CENTURY SPORTSMAN 420

✓ BEST BUY

The Century Sportsman 420 is made of durable cast iron. A grill surface made of the same material provides excellent cooking results. (Cast iron's flavor-enhancing advantages increase with use and age.) This model has its own removable legs to free table space for serving food and a cooking surface that measures 173 square inches. This model is not easily portable; it performs best as a permanent backyard or short-distance picnic grill.

Specifications: weight, 39 pounds. **Warranty:** written—none. Defective products will be replaced if they are relatively recently purchased.

Approx. retail price	Approx. low price
$103	$102

Prices are accurate at time of printing; subject to manufacturer's change.

BRINKMANN SMOKE 'N' PIT
805-2106-0

The Brinkmann Smoke 'n' Pit 805-2106-0 grill sports bright-yellow styling and four-way cooking capabilities including barbecuing, roasting, smoking, and steaming. The grill is constructed of enamel over rustproof steel and cooks up to 25 pounds at once. A cleverly designed lid tucks inside the grill lip to prevent spillover accidents. An optional Smoke 'n' Stack (#807-2307-0) fits on top of the Smoke 'n' Pit to double cooking area to a 50-pound capacity.

Specifications: weight, 22 pounds. **Warranty:** one year, over the counter.

Approx. retail price	Approx. low price
not available	$56

Tabletop Charcoal Grill

MECO 9600-6

The Meco 9600-6 is a grill with impressive design. Although it functions like a simple covered charcoal cooker, its red-and-black styling and sleek, cylindrical shape make it a generation ahead of the others. With a hinged lid and 225 square inches of cooking surface, this compact grill will handle more than most tabletop versions. Optional accessories include a warming rack (90 square inches, about $6) and a grill cover (about $9).

Specifications: weight, 22 pounds. **Warranty:** 90 days.

Approx. retail price	Approx. low price
$60	not available

Fixed Gas Grills

NORDICWARE NATURAL
GAS GRILL 74100

The Nordicware Natural Gas Grill 74100 is a full-featured post-style grill. The cooking surface measures 365 square inches with an additional 140 square inches of warming space. The grill is rated at 34,000 Btus. Luxuries include a temperature indicator, dual controls, automatic ignition, and two mahogany side shelves. It is available in black. An optional kit converts the grill for permanent installation in your yard, where it is attached to a gas line to eliminate the need to refill a gas tank as with most portable cart-style grills.

Specifications: weight, 110 pounds. **Warranty:** one year; **casting and burner,** five years.

> **Approx. retail price**
> **not available**
>
> **Approx. low price**
> **$160**

SUNBEAM 9560N

The Sunbeam 9560N offers powerful grilling capabilities with a 40,000 Btu dual burner designed for a natural gas connection. (This means freedom from refilling portable propane tanks.) It has a generous 332 square inches of cooking surface and an additional 231 square inches of warming area. Convenience features include two fold-away redwood side shelves, a push button ignitor, a temperature indicator, and a viewing window. Plentiful optional accessories include rotisseries, grill covers, and cooking tool kits.

Specifications: weight, 76 pounds. **Warranty:** one year; **burner,** five years; **casting,** 10 years.

> **Approx. retail price**
> **$320**
>
> **Approx. low price**
> **$225**

Portable Gas Grill

SUNBEAM 20711

The Sunbeam 20711 is an impressive patio cart grill for the price with three redwood shelves (one on each side and one up front) to provide space for trays of food, utensils, plates, etc. This grill measures up with 225 square inches of main cooking area and 116 square inches of warming space. There's a 24,000 Btu dual burner, pushbutton ignitor, lower storage shelf, and viewing window. A variety of accessories are available includ-

Prices are accurate at time of printing; subject to manufacturer's change.

ing grill covers (starting at about $23) and rotisserie.
Specifications: weight, 75 pounds. **Warranty:** one year (except
lava rock); **glass window**, one year; **burners**, five years; **casting**, 10 years.

Approx. retail price	Approx. low price
$129	not available

Tabletop Gas Grill

WEBER 1530

The Weber 1530 is a compact grill with folding legs for maximum portability and storage capabilities. To further enhance
carry-along-ease while decreasing food scorching flare-ups,
this grill uses heated bars instead of standard lava rock. It features a 160-square-inch cooking surface and heats up with
10,000 Btus. This mini grill even has a push-button ignitor—
quite a luxury for such a small model. The jet-black porcelain-
on-steel unit uses disposable LP cylinders or can be adapted
(by purchasing an optional hose attachment) to use refillable
tanks.
Specifications: weight, 12 pounds. **Warranty:** limited, five
years.

Approx. retail price	Approx. low price
$45	$38

Microwave Ovens

An estimated 75 percent of American households have one or more microwave ovens, which are used to augment, rather than replace, other cooking appliances. According to a consumer survey, the specific tasks for which they are most frequently used are reheating leftovers, baking potatoes, heating rolls and bread, and cooking vegetables. However, the biggest reason for using a microwave oven is to prepare frozen convenience foods, which survey respondents are reluctant to admit, according to authorities.

Microwave recipes are formulated for units 600 to 700 watts of cooking power; using a less powerful model will jeopardize your results. We recommend an oven with a capacity of at least 0.70-cubic foot, 600 watts of power, and no fewer than three power levels (low, medium, and high).

Safe Microwave Cooking

Microwaves are electromagnetic waves similar to radio, heat, and light waves. They are created in a magnetron tube inside the oven and are contained inside the oven by its metal walls and door. Metal reflects microwaves (that is why metal containers are not used for microwave cooking), but the waves pass directly through glass, paper, and plastic. Microwaves cause the water molecules in food to vibrate; the friction from the molecules bumping against each other causes heat that cooks the food.

Microwave ovens are covered by a radiation safety standard enforced by the Food and Drug Administration. This standard requires ovens to be equipped with two independent interlock systems to stop the production of microwaves the moment the door latch is released. A monitoring system stops the oven if one of the interlock systems fail. There have been no documented cases of radiation injury from microwave ovens.

Features and Terminology

Cooking power is the level of its power a microwave oven uses to defrost food or to cook different foods properly. Some microwave ovens have as many as ten power levels, but high, medium, and low are sufficient to prepare most foods.

Humidity sensor lets you enter a code for the kind of food you are cooking. Then the oven figures out the cooking time and power level by monitoring changes in the moisture level within the oven.

Memory allows you to program the oven for a sequence of two to four cooking stages. For example, you can set the oven to bring food to a boil, reduce to simmer, and then hold at the proper serving temperature.

Temperature probe works like a continuous-reading meat thermometer, measuring the interior temperature of the food during cooking. Preprogrammed probes automatically vary the power level, and some probes have a "hold" function to keep food at a specified temperature.

Weight cook/defrost is an electronic cooking control. You enter a code for the kind of food you are cooking and enter its weight. Then your microwave oven automatically determines the cooking time and power level.

Best Buys '91

Our Best Buy and Recommended microwave ovens follow. They have been selected on the basis of overall value and efficient performance. The microwave ovens are presented in the following categories: full-size ovens with a capacity of more than 1.0 cubic foot; medium-size ovens with a 0.8- to 1.0-cubic-foot capacity; compact ovens with a 0.5- to 0.8-cubic-foot capacity; subcompact ovens with a 0.4-cubic-foot capacity; over-the-range microwave ovens; and microwave/convection ovens. Within each category, ovens are listed in order of quality. The item we consider to be the best of the Best Buys is listed first, followed by our second choice, and so on. Remember that a Best Buy or Recommended designation applies only to the model listed, and not necessarily to other models made by the same manufacturer. Microwave ovens that are built into gas or electric ranges are reviewed in the next chapter.

Full-Size Microwave Ovens

PANASONIC NN-6500

The Panasonic NN-6500 is a full-size countertop microwave oven with electronic controls, a turntable, and several one-touch automatic functions. This brand new model has automatic start; turbo weight defrost; automatic reheat; timed cooking up to 100 minutes; three-stage memory; memory recipe; and one-touch keypads for popcorn, potatoes, and three types of convenience foods—entrees, dinners, and vegetables. Power levels range from 90 to 800 watts. It comes in a simulated woodgrain cabinet with a black door. A kit for built-in installation is optional.

Specifications: height, 12¹⁄₁₆"; **width,** 21⅞"; **depth,** 16¹¹⁄₁₆"; **capacity,** 1¹⁄₁₀ cubic feet. **Cavity dimensions: height,** 7⅞"; **width,** 14¹³⁄₁₆"; **depth,** 15⁹⁄₁₆". **Cooking power:** 800 watts. **Controls:** electronic. **Warranty: parts and labor,** one year; **magnetron tube,** five years.

Approx. retail price	Approx. low price
$250	$181

GENERAL ELECTRIC JE1423H

The General Electric JE1423H is a basic-featured, full-size countertop microwave oven with simple electronic controls. It has ten power levels, three-stage programming, and timed cooking with a 100-minute digital timer. The cabinet has a simulated woodgrain finish. A kit for built-in installation is optional.

Specifications: height, 14½"; **width**, 23⅝"; **depth**, 15¹⁵⁄₁₆"; **capacity:** 1⅖ cubic feet. **Cavity dimensions: height**, 10⅝"; **width**, 16"; **depth**, 13⅝". **Cooking power:** 700 watts. **Controls:** electronic. **Warranty: parts and labor**, one year, in home; **magnetron tube, parts**, ten years.

Approx. retail price	Approx. low price
$230	$209

SHARP R-4A82

The Sharp R-4A82 is a fully featured, full-size microwave oven with a glass turntable and electronic controls. It has timed cooking up to 100 minutes, automatic start, ten power levels, weight defrost, and four-stage memory. It has three special keys for popcorn, beverage, and dinner-plate functions with a single keystroke. The cabinet has a simulated woodgrain finish and a black door. It also comes in white as Model R-4A92. An optional built-in kit is available.

Specifications: height, 12¼"; **width**, 21⅝"; **depth**, 16¾"; **capacity**, 1¹⁄₁₀ cubic feet. **Cavity dimensions: height**, 8¼"; **width**, 15"; **depth**, 16⅛". **Cooking power:** 800 watts. **Controls:** electronic. **Warranty: parts and labor**, two years; **magnetron tube**, seven years.

Approx. retail price	Approx. low price
$300	$230

SAMSUNG MW8600T

The Samsung MW8600T is a value-priced, fully featured, full-size countertop microwave oven with electronic controls. It has a turntable, ten power levels, and automatic start. It offers several more advanced features, including four-stage cooking; weight defrost; three-recipe memory; popcorn pad; and single-touchpad cooking for one, three, and five minutes. It comes with a removable glass turntable and cookbook. The cabinet is simulated woodgrain with a black door.

Specifications: height, 14¾"; **width**, 22½"; **depth**, 17⅛"; **capacity**, 1⅖ cubic feet. **Cavity dimensions: height**, 10⅔";

width, 14¼"; depth, 14⅞". **Cooking power:** 700 watts. **Controls:** electronic. **Warranty: labor,** two years; **parts,** one year; **magnetron tube,** eight years.

Approx. retail price	Approx. low price
$270	$198

Medium-Size Microwave Ovens

GENERAL ELECTRIC
JVM14OG

The General Electric JVM14OG is a better-quality, fully featured, medium-size microwave oven in the manufacturer's Spacemaker II line. It has electronic controls, a digital timer for cooking up to 100 minutes, ten power levels, and a removable shelf. The advanced features include automatic defrost, automatic roast, five-stage programmed cooking, word prompts, and a temperature probe. This countertop model comes with an under-the-cabinet hanging kit; a built-in kit is optional. **Specifications: height,** 16"; **width,** 23½"; **depth,** 13"; **capacity,** 1 cubic foot. **Cavity dimensions: height,** 7½"; **width,** 18"; **depth,** 12½". **Cooking power:** 625 watts. **Controls:** electronic. **Warranty: parts and labor,** one year; **magnetron tube, parts,** ten years.

Approx. retail price	Approx. low price
not available	$224

QUASAR MQS0806W

The Quasar MQS0806W is a better-quality, medium-size microwave oven. It can accommodate most 8- by 12-inch, two-quart baking dishes. This brand new model offers a humidity sensor, which lets you reheat foods and heat frozen foods and vegetables without having to set the time and power level. It also has weight defrost, three-stage memory, automatic start, popcorn key, five power levels, and timed cooking up to 100 minutes. It comes in a simulated woodgrain cabinet. **Specifications: height,** 12"; **width,** 20⅛"; **depth,** 14½"; **capac-**

Prices are accurate at time of printing; subject to manufacturer's change.

ity, ⅘ cubic foot. **Cavity dimensions: height,** 8¹⁄₁₆"; **width, 13";
depth, 13". Cooking power:** 700 watts. **Controls:** electronic.
Warranty: parts and labor, one year; **magnetron tube,** five
years.

Approx. retail price	**Approx. low price**
$239	$178

PANASONIC NN-5360A

The Panasonic NN-5360A is a value-priced, medium-sized
microwave oven with simple-to-use electronic touch controls
and a turntable. It has two-stage memory and a digital LCD
(liquid crystal display) clock for timed cooking up to 100 minutes. Power levels range from 80 to 700 watts. It comes in a
simulated woodgrain cabinet with a black door.
Specifications: height, 12"; width, 20⅛"; **depth,** 14½"; **capacity,** ⅘ cubic foot. **Cavity dimensions: height,** 7⅞"; **width, 13";
depth, 13". Cooking power:** 700 watts. **Controls:** electronic.
Warranty: parts and labor, one year; **magnetron tube,** five
years.

Approx. retail price	**Approx. low price**
$180	$173

PANASONIC NN-5500A

The Panasonic NN-5500A is a medium-size, better-quality
microwave oven with some popular automatic functions and a
turntable. It has weight defrost, automatic start, three-stage
memory, memory recipe key, timed cooking up to 100 minutes,
and single-touch controls for popcorn, potatoes, and three
types of frozen convenience foods—dinners, entrees, and
vegetables.
Specifications: height, 12¹⁄₁₆"; **width,** 20¹⁄₁₆"; **depth,** 14³⁄₁₆"; **capacity,** ⅘ cubic foot. **Cavity dimensions: height,** 7⅞"; **width,
13"; depth, 13". Cooking power:** 700 watts. **Controls:** electronic. **Warranty: parts and labor,** one year; **magnetron tube,**
five years.

Approx. retail price	**Approx. low price**
$210	$159

Prices are accurate at time of printing; subject to manufacturer's change.

Compact Microwave Ovens

MAGIC CHEF M22-6

✓ **BEST BUY**

The Magic Chef M22-6 is a good-quality, fully featured, under-the-cabinet compact microwave oven big enough to accommodate most 9- by 12-inch baking dishes. It has automatic defrost and cook, ten power levels, and timed cooking up to 100 minutes. Its drop-down door provides a convenient, eye-level shelf for mixing, stirring, and serving. The oven has a black textured wraparound cabinet and a black door.

Specifications: height, 9½"; **width,** 22½"; **depth,** 11⅞"; **capacity,** ⅗ cubic foot. **Cavity dimensions:** not available. **Cooking power:** 600 watts. **Controls:** electronic. **Warranty: parts and labor,** one year; **magnetron tube,** five years.

Approx. retail price	Approx. low price
$229	$229

SAMSUNG MW3500T

RECOMMENDED

The Samsung MW3500T is a value-priced, fully featured compact microwave oven with electronic controls. It has a removable glass turntable and features weight defrost, automatic start, and four-stage memory. This model has timed cooking up to 100 minutes, ten power levels, and a simulated woodgrain cabinet with a black front.

Specifications: height, 10⅜"; **width,** 18⅝"; **depth,** 12½"; **capacity,** ⅗ cubic foot. **Cavity dimensions:** not available. **Cooking power:** 550 watts. **Controls:** electronic. **Warranty: parts and labor,** one year; **magnetron tube,** five years.

Approx. retail price	Approx. low price
$180	$135

Subcompact Microwave Ovens

SAMSUNG MW2170U

RECOMMENDED

The Samsung MW2170U is a handy, subcompact microwave oven ideal for heating leftovers and most single-portion frozen dishes. Its dial controls are easy to operate. This model has two power levels (high and defrost), timed cooking up to 35 minutes, a removable glass tray, and an optional bracket for under-the-cabinet mounting. It comes in polar white with a black door.

Specifications: height, 8⅞"; **width,** 17⁵⁄₁₆"; **depth,** 12¼"; **capacity,** ⅖ cubic foot. **Cavity dimensions: height,** 5½"; **width,** 11"; **depth,** 11". **Cooking power:** 500 watts. **Controls:** mechanical. **Warranty: labor,** one year; **parts,** two years; **magnetron tube,** eight years.

Approx. retail price	Approx. low price
$160	$100

SAMSUNG MW2570U   `RECOMMENDED`

The Samsung MW2570U is a handy, subcompact microwave oven ideal for heating leftovers and most single-portion frozen dishes. This model has electronic controls, ten power levels, timed cooking up to 100 minutes, a removable glass tray, an interior light, and an optional bracket for under-the-cabinet mounting. It comes in polar white with a black door.

Specifications: height, 8⅞"; **width,** 17¹⁵⁄₁₆"; **depth,** 12¼"; **capacity,** ⅖ cubic foot. **Cavity dimensions: height,** 5½"; **width,** 11"; **depth,** 11". **Cooking power:** 500 watts. **Controls:** electronic. **Warranty: labor,** one year; **parts,** two years; **magnetron tube,** eight years.

Approx. retail price	Approx. low price
$160	$116

Over-the-Range Microwave Oven

PANASONIC NN-2408   ✔ **BEST BUY**

The Panasonic NN-2408 is an over-the-range microwave oven with electronic controls. It has weight defrost, automatic start, automatic reheat, a three-stage memory, and timed cooking up to 100 minutes. This model also has a two-speed exhaust fan and cooktop light.

Specifications: height, 16⅜"; **width,** 29¹⁵⁄₁₆"; **depth,** 14³⁄₁₆"; **ca-**

Prices are accurate at time of printing; subject to manufacturer's change.

pacity, 1 cubic foot. **Cavity dimensions: height,** 8⅜₁₆"; **width,** 18⅝₁₆"; **depth,** 11". **Cooking power:** 700 watts. **Controls:** electronic. **Warranty: parts and labor,** one year; **magnetron tube,** five years.

Approx. retail price	Approx. low price
$500	$382

Microwave/Convection Oven

SHARP R-9H81

The Sharp R-9H81 is a full-size combination microwave/convection oven with a turntable and lots of advanced features. It broils, bakes, roasts, defrosts, and heats. Model R-9H81 has weight defrost, a humidity sensor, a probe, four-stage memory, timed cooking up to 100 minutes, five power levels, and automatic start. It has special keys for reheat, popcorn, and minute-plus functions. Model R-9H81 has a stainless steel interior, a broiling trivet, and a baking rack. Model R-9H81 comes in a charcoal pinstripe cabinet; model R-9H91 comes in white. A kit for built-in installation is optional.

Specifications: height, 14¾"; **width,** 24⅝"; **depth,** 18⅜"; **capacity,** 1½ cubic feet. **Cavity dimensions: height,** 9⅝"; **width,** 16⅛"; **depth,** 16⅛". **Cooking power:** 700 watts. **Controls:** electronic. **Warranty: parts and labor,** two years; **magnetron tube,** seven years.

Approx. retail price	Approx. low price
$600	$506

Ranges

When you shop for a new range, oven, or built-in cooktop, you will find many styles and options. Manufacturers have introduced many new designs and technologies, particularly in cooktops, which allow you to match your purchase with your cooking preferences and your budget.

Today's ranges, ovens, and cooktops may look very different from the cooking appliances you grew up with—and, in fact, they are. In the past, traditional electric-coil heating elements or gas burners were a cook's only choices. Now, however, you can select from a broad variety of cooking options, including solid-disc electric elements, sealed gas burners, and several types of smoothtop cooking surfaces. And the increased availability of convertible cooktops and ranges allows you to create a "custom" cooking center by mixing and matching optional cooking modules to suit your family's needs.

Gas or Electric

Your kitchen may dictate your choice of gas or electric, unless you plan to undertake a costly remodeling job. Electric ranges require a 208- or 240-volt line. Gas ranges need a gas line, as well as a 115-volt outlet for the lights, clock, and burner-ignition system.

Range Designs

Free-standing ranges have a cooktop and an oven (or two) and stand on the floor between two base cabinets or at the end of a line of cabinets. Free-standing ranges are usually 30 inches wide, but they are also made in other widths ranging from 21 to 40 inches.

Over-and-under ranges are also called double-decker, eye-level, or high-low ranges. This kind of range has two ovens: one above and one below the cooktop. Both ovens may be gas or electric, or one oven may be a microwave, convection, or a combination microwave/convection unit.

Slide-in and drop-in ranges fit between two cabinets or into a space in a cooking island. The sides of these ranges are usually unfinished. A slide-in range sits on the floor; a drop-in range may hang from the countertop or sit on a low base.

Built-in ovens and cooktops are ranges divided into separate units for flexibility in kitchen design. A built-in oven may have one or two oven cavities.

Cooktops

Traditional cooktops have four cooking elements. On most gas models, the burners are all the same size. Some gas cooktops offer higher power on one burner for faster heating. Most electric cooktops have two six-inch and two eight-inch coil elements. On both gas and electric cooktops, heating elements may be grouped together in a cluster, with no work space in the center, or they may have a divided configuration with burners grouped on either side of the cooktop, with a work space, griddle, or fifth burner in the middle. Some built-in cooktops have burners arranged in an inverted *U*.

A modular, or convertible, cooktop has plug-in, interchangeable optional accessories that may include extra burners, a grill, a griddle, a rotisserie, a wok, a deep-fat fryer, or a smooth glass-ceramic cooking surface. The electric heating elements under a smoothtop may be radiant or halogen. A solid-element electric cooktop has smooth discs, or hobs, rather than coil elements. These raised or flush-mounted discs take longer to heat up than coils, but they offer more uniform heating and more precise temperature control, especially at low settings.

Ovens

In addition to a conventional electric or gas oven, you may want a microwave or convection oven in your range. Convection ovens cook faster and cooler than regular ovens, because hot air is forced into the oven by a high-speed fan. The heated air goes to the food to start the cooking process immediately and makes preheating unnecessary. Food cooks faster and at a lower temperature. The drawbacks of a convection oven are the noise of the fan and the care you must take when you place food in the oven to prevent overcooking and drying. Microwave ovens cook with electromagnetic waves produced by a magnetron tube. For more information, see the chapter on microwave ovens.

Cleaning Your Oven

A self-cleaning oven uses intense heat (up to 800 degrees Fahrenheit) to burn spills to powdery ash that is easily wiped off after the cleaning cycle has finished. This feature can add $100 or more to the cost of a range, but it is relatively inexpensive to operate.

A continuous-cleaning oven has a special catalytic coating on the oven walls that partially absorbs and spreads the soil during normal baking. Major spills must be wiped up promptly, or they remain on the oven floor and burn. Racks and door parts must be cleaned by hand, but you cannot scrub the interior of a continuous-cleaning oven with abrasives or use conventional oven cleaners because they ruin the special finish.

Best Buys '91

Our Best Buy and Recommended ranges follow. They were selected on the basis of quality, efficiency, energy use, and value. The ranges are divided into gas and electric categories, each with several subcategories. Within each subcategory, models are arranged by quality. The best of the Best Buys is listed first, followed by our second choice, and so on. Remember that a Best Buy or Recommended designation refers only to the model listed and not necessarily to other models made by the same manufacturer. Approximate prices apply to models in basic white or the finish mentioned in the description.

GAS RANGES

Freestanding Gas Ranges

TAPPAN 30-2549

The Tappan 30-2549 is a moderately priced, basic, 30-inch gas range with important convenience features, but few expensive frills. This range has a continuous-cleaning oven. The broiler is located in a roll-out drawer below the oven, which has a black-glass door with a window. The 30-2549 has a clock with a four-hour timer and electronic pilotless ignition. The cooktop lifts up and locks to facilitate cleaning. This range comes in white or almond.

Specifications: overall dimensions, height, 45⁵⁄₃₂″; **width,** 29⅞″; **depth,** 25⅜″; **oven dimensions, height,** 15⅞″; **width,** 23″; **depth,** 19³⁄₁₆″. **Warranty: parts and labor,** one year.

Approx. retail price	Approx. low price
$439	$366

GENERAL ELECTRIC JGBP26GEJ

The General Electric JGBP26GEJ is particularly easy to clean because it has removable burners and a lift-up cooktop. The oven is self-cleaning, with a removable door and waist-high broiler. A removable storage drawer is below the oven. The JGBP26GEJ has an automatic oven timer and clock, as well as electronic pilotless ignition. This range has a black-glass oven door and almond cooktop and sides.

Specifications: overall dimensions, height, 47⁷⁄₁₆″; **width,** 29¹⁵⁄₁₆″; **depth,** 25⅜″; **oven dimensions, height,** 15⅞″; **width,** 23″; **depth,** 19³⁄₁₆″. **Warranty: parts and labor,** one year; 90-day replacement/refund if not satisfied.

Approx. retail price	Approx. low price
not available	$680

Prices are accurate at time of printing; subject to manufacturer's change.

FRIGIDAIRE GG32N

BEST BUY

The Frigidaire GG32N is a 30-inch gas range with an oven that must be cleaned manually. The cooktop lifts up and locks for cleaning; the oven door, oven bottom panels, and burner grates are removable. This range has a clock with a four-hour timer, electronic pilotless ignition, and an efficient broiler in a roll-out drawer below the oven.

Specifications: overall dimensions, height, 45½"; **width,** 30"; **depth,** 25"; **oven dimensions, height,** 15⅞"; **width,** 23"; **depth,** 19³⁄₁₆". **Warranty: parts and labor,** one year.

Approx. retail price	**Approx. low price**
$460	$452

MODERN MAID PHU185

RECOMMENDED

The Modern Maid PHU185 is a unique 30-inch modular gas range with many deluxe features. It has a downdraft ventilation system at the center of its cooktop that draws smoke and odors down and out of the house. You can program the self-cleaning oven to turn on at a preset time, using a digital clock/timer. A storage drawer is below the oven, and the broiler is waist high. The PHU185 has electronic pilotless ignition. Its modular cooktop comes with cartridges for two gas burners and a grill; cartridges for a griddle, a rotisserie, or additional burner are optional. The grill, optional griddle, filter, vent cover, splatter shield, and drips pans can all be cleaned in a dishwasher.

Specifications: overall dimensions, height, 36"; **width,** 30"; **depth,** 28"; **oven dimensions, height,** 16"; **width,** 23"; **depth,** 17". **Warranty: parts,** one year.

Approx. retail price	**Approx. low price**
$2,070	$1,497

Over-and-Under Gas Ranges

SEARS KENMORE 78509

BEST BUY

The Sears Kenmore 78509 is a reliable, sturdy gas range with a self-cleaning lower oven and an upper oven that must be

cleaned manually. A single eye-level panel controls both ovens and includes a programmable timer to preset the lower oven to turn on and off or to clean. The 78509 has electronic pilotless ignition. The lower oven has a waist-high broiler and a storage drawer underneath. The cooktop is brightly illuminated, and lifts up for cleaning. This range comes in black.
Specifications: overall dimensions, height, 66¾₁₆"; **width,** 29⅞"; depth, 28"; upper oven dimensions, height, 12⅜"; **width,** 20"; depth, 13"; lower oven dimensions, height, 15⅞"; **width,** 23"; depth, 19¾₁₆". **Warranty: parts and labor,** one year.

Approx. retail price	Approx. low price
$1,069	not available

CALORIC RMS-395

The Caloric RMS-395 is a well-constructed gas range with two continuous-clean ovens, both of which are controlled from an eye-level panel that has a clock/timer. The cooktop lifts off for cleaning, and it has raised edges to contain spills. The square burner grates are also removable. Both ovens have black-glass oven doors with windows; the door on the lower oven is removable for spot cleaning. The broiler is in a separate roll-out drawer below the lower oven. The RMS-395 has automatic pilotless ignition. It comes in almond, white, or harvest.
Specifications: overall dimensions, height, 65¾"; **width,** 30"; depth, 27⅜"; upper oven dimensions, height, 13"; width, 20"; depth, 13"; lower oven dimensions, height, 14½"; **width,** 24"; depth, 19". **Warranty: parts,** three years.

Approx. retail price	Approx. low price
$1,000	$586

Combination Gas/Microwave Over-and-Under Ranges

MAGIC CHEF 24-6CKXWV8

The Magic Chef 24-6CKXWV8 is a convenient cooking center that combines gas and microwave cooking. Its lower gas oven is self-cleaning, with a waist-high broiler and a storage drawer underneath. The one-cubic-foot microwave oven has ten power levels and touch controls with programmed cooking. This range has an automatic clock with one-hour timer and electronic pilotless ignition. The cooktop has sealed burners. **Specifications: overall dimensions, height,** 65¾"; **width,** 30"; **depth,** 12½"; **upper oven dimensions, height,** 8"; **width,** 18"; **depth,** 12½"; **lower oven dimensions, height,** 15"; **width,** 22"; **depth,** 18". **Warranty: parts and labor,** one year; **magnetron tube,** five years, **sealed burner parts,** five years.

Approx. retail price	Approx. low price
$1,549	$1,410

WHIRLPOOL SM988PES

The Whirlpool SM988PES combines an upper microwave oven with a lower self-clean gas oven. The spacious 1⁹⁄₁₀-cubic-foot microwave oven has touch controls for ten power levels, programmed cooking, and a probe. The lower oven is also programmable. This model has electronic pilotless ignition. Its well-lit cooktop lifts up for cleaning, and the burner grates and chrome reflector bowls are removable. The broiler is in a roll-out drawer under the lower oven.
Specifications: overall dimensions, height, 72"; **width,** 30⅛"; **depth,** 27⅞"; **upper oven dimensions, height,** 9⅞"; **width,** 16⁷⁄₁₆"; **depth,** 13⅞"; **lower oven dimensions, height,** 14½"; **width,** 24"; **depth,** 19". **Warranty: parts and labor,** one year; **magnetron tube,** five years; one-year replacement if not satisfied.

Approx. retail price	Approx. low price
not available	$1,579

Drop-in/Slide-in Gas Ranges

GENERAL ELECTRIC JGSP10GEK

The General Electric JGSP10GEK is a fully featured gas slide-in range with a self-cleaning oven. The oven is easy to program, using an electronic digital clock/timer. The JGSP10GEK has a waist-high broiler and electronic pilotless ignition. The cooktop lifts up for cleaning, and the burner grates, chrome drip pans, and oven door are removable. A storage drawer is below the oven. This range has a black-glass oven door with a window and a brushed-chrome cooktop. **Specifications: overall dimensions, height,** 37¼"; **width,** 29⅞"; **depth,** 27¾"; **oven dimensions, height,** 15³⁄₁₆"; **width,** 22¹¹⁄₁₆"; **depth,** 17¹⁄₁₆". **Warranty: parts and labor,** one year; 90-day replacement/refund if not satisfied.

Approx. retail price	Approx. low price
not available	$706

CALORIC RJR305

The Caloric RJR305 is a sleek, 30-inch gas range that drops into a space in the countertop. Its seamless, upswept cooktop design does a good job of containing spills, and its oven cavity is more spacious than those of many other drop-in models. The RJR305 has electronic pilotless ignition and a programmable, continuous-cleaning oven with a waist-high broiler. To facilitate cleaning, the oven door and burner grates are removable, and the cooktop lifts up. This range has a black-glass oven door with a window and a brushed-chrome cooktop. **Specifications: overall dimensions, height,** 27¾"; **width,** 29⅞"; **depth,** 27½"; **oven dimensions, height,** 15⅛"; **width,** 23¾"; **depth,** 19". **Warranty: parts,** three years.

Approx. retail price	Approx. low price
$1,000	$717

Built-in Gas Ovens

CALORIC RWS202 ✔BEST BUY

The Caloric RWS202 is a good choice for the family that does a lot of broiling. Its large, efficient broiler is in a separate roll-out drawer below the oven, which must be cleaned manually. The RWS202 has electronic pilotless ignition and a clock/timer. The oven door and oven bottom are removable for cleaning.

Both the oven and the broiler have black-glass doors. The oven door has a window.

Specifications: overall dimensions, height, 40"; **width,** 24"; **depth,** 23¼"; **oven dimensions, height,** 13¼"; **width,** 18"; **depth,** 20". **Warranty: parts,** three years.

Approx. retail price	Approx. low price
$620	$482

MAGIC CHEF 90-4KLX ✔BEST BUY

The Magic Chef 90-4KLX is a continuous-cleaning wall oven with a separate roll-out broiler. A digital clock/timer programs the oven, which has electronic pilotless ignition. The automatic controls are particularly easy to understand and operate. The oven door comes off for cleaning. Both doors are black glass, and the oven door has a large window.

Specifications: overall dimensions, height, 38"; **width,** 22½"; **depth,** 23¼"; **oven dimensions, height,** 14"; **width,** 18"; **depth,** 19¼". **Warranty: parts and labor,** one year.

Approx. retail price	Approx. low price
$479	not available

Gas Cooktop

WHIRLPOOL SC8536EX ✔BEST BUY

The Whirlpool SC8536EX is a 36-inch gas cooktop with a built-in griddle. The griddle has a removable cover to provide work space when it is not being used. The cooktop has a raised edge to contain spills, and the control knobs lift off for easy cleaning. The SC8536EX has electronic pilotless ignition. This cooktop comes in almond. Model SC8536EWW is the same product in white.

Specifications: dimensions, height, 5"; **width,** 36"; **depth,** 21". **Warranty: parts and labor,** one year; one-year replacement if not satisfied.

Approx. retail price	Approx. low price
$429	$399

Prices are accurate at time of printing; subject to manufacturer's change.

Modular Gas Cooktops

JENN-AIR CG206

The Jenn-Air CG206 is a 30-inch gas cooktop that comes with a grill module and two fixed gas burners. It can accept optional plug-in modules for a griddle, a wok, or two additional burners. The CG206 has a central downdraft venting system to draw smoke and odors from the kitchen. This cooktop has electronic pilotless ignition. It comes in black or stainless steel.

Specifications: dimensions, height, not available; **width**, 29⅞"; **depth**, 21½". **Warranty: parts**, two years; **labor**, one year.

Approx. retail price	Approx. low price
not available	$727

KITCHENAID KGCM860T

The KitchenAid KGCM860T is a 36-inch modular cooktop. It comes with modules for two gas burners and a nonstick grill/griddle, and can accept optional plug-in modules for an additional griddle and two additional burners. Downdraft ventilation pulls smoke and odors down and out of the kitchen. The KGCM860T has electronic pilotless ignition. It comes in brushed chrome with black trim.

Specifications: dimensions, height, 16½"; **width**, 36"; **depth**, 21". **Warranty: parts and labor**, one year; one-year replacement if not satisfied.

Approx. retail price	Approx. low price
$789	$769

ELECTRIC RANGES

Freestanding Electric Ranges

MAGIC CHEF 38-2CXW-ON

The Magic Chef 38-2CXW-ON is a 30-inch range engineered with many easy-clean features. It has a self-cleaning oven, re-

---

movable reflector pans and oven door, and a cooktop with seamless, raised edges to contain spills. The two six-inch and two eight-inch coil elements are also removable for cleaning. An easy-to-operate automatic clock/timer programs the oven. The 38-2CXW-ON has a waist-high broiler; a storage drawer is below the oven. This range comes in almond or white with a black-glass oven door that has a window.

Specifications: overall dimensions, height, 46"; **width**, 30"; **depth**, 25½"; **oven dimensions, height**, 15"; **width**, 22"; **depth**, 18". **Warranty: parts and labor**, one year.

Approx. retail price	**Approx. low price**
$529	$543

WHIRLPOOL RF317PXW

The Whirlpool RF317PXW is a high-quality, basic 30-inch range with several convenience features including easy-clean solid-disc heating elements. The oven must be cleaned manually, but its door comes off to make the job easier. The cooktop has two six-inch and two eight-inch solid elements, sealed to the surface so no spills can drip through. The upswept cooktop is smooth, with no cracks to collect debris. An automatic clock/timer programs the oven to turn on and off at preset times. The RF317PXW has a waist-high broiler and a storage drawer beneath the oven. It comes in almond or white with a black-glass oven door that has a window.

Specifications: overall dimensions, height, 45⁵⁄₁₆"; **width**, 30"; **depth**, 27¼"; **oven dimensions, height**, 16¾"; **width**, 22"; **depth**, 18¼". **Warranty: parts and labor**, one year; one-year replacement if not satisfied.

Approx. retail price	**Approx. low price**
$549	$538

GENERAL ELECTRIC JBC16GN

The General Electric JBC16GN is an efficient 30-inch range with few frills. It has a continuous-cleaning oven. The cooktop has three six-inch and one eight-inch coil elements that tilt up for cleaning. Also styled for easy cleaning are the aluminum

reflector pans and trim rings, all of which are removable. The JBC16GN includes a clock/timer, but not programmed cooking. A storage drawer is beneath the oven, and the broiler is waist high. The oven door is black glass with a window.
Specifications: overall dimensions, height, 45⅛"; width, 29⅞"; depth, 27¼"; oven dimensions, height, 16"; width, 23"; depth, 17¾". Warranty: parts and labor, one year; 90-day replacement/refund if not satisfied.

Approx. retail price	Approx. low price
not available	$559

JENN-AIR S136
RECOMMENDED

The Jenn-Air S136 is a 30-inch range with a modular cooktop that includes several deluxe features for the serious cook. This model comes with a plug-in grill module. Both sides of the S136 are convertible, so you can plug in optional modules on either side. These modules include coil or solid-disc elements, a glass-ceramic smooth cooktop, an induction cooktop, a wok, a grill, a canning element, a griddle, a rotisserie/kabob, or a cooker/steamer. An electronic clock/timer programs the oven, which is self-cleaning. The broiler is waist high. A downdraft venting system pulls smoke down and out of the kitchen. This range comes in black, with a windowed black-glass oven door.
Specifications: overall dimensions, height, 35½"; width, 29¹⁵⁄₁₆"; depth, 26⅜"; oven dimensions, height, 14¾"; width, 21"; depth, 18⁹⁄₁₆". Warranty: parts, two years; **labor,** one year.

Approx. retail price	Approx. low price
not available	$1,117

Over-and-Under Electric Range

HOTPOINT RH758GM
 ✓ BEST BUY

The Hotpoint RH758GM has a self-cleaning lower oven and a manually cleaned upper oven with removable panels that fit in the lower oven for cleaning during the cleaning cycle. Controls for both ovens are at eye level, and include a clock and automatic oven timer. The two six-inch and two eight-inch coil elements snap out for cleaning, and the reflector pans and trim rings are also removable. The one-piece cooktop design eliminates cracks and crevices. The cooktop is illuminated, and a vent is built in below the upper oven. Both black-glass oven doors have windows, and the lower door is removable for cleaning. The RH758GM has a waist-high broiler and a storage drawer underneath the lower oven.

Specifications: overall dimensions, height, 71⅝"; width, 30"; depth, 27⅞"; upper oven dimensions, height, 15"; width, 21"; depth, 12½"; lower oven dimensions, height, 16"; width, 23"; depth, 17¼". Warranty: parts and labor, one year; magnetron tube, five years; 90-day replacement/refund if not satisfied.

Approx. retail price	Approx. low price
not available	$899

Combination Electric/Microwave
Over-and-Under Electric Ranges

SEARS KENMORE 98711 ✔ BEST BUY

The Sears Kenmore 98711 combines the convenience of microwave cooking with a self-cleaning traditional oven. The lower electric oven is programmed with an automatic clock/timer. The lift-up cooktop is lighted and has two six-inch and two eight-inch coil elements. A range hood is built in below the upper oven to draw away smoke and cooking odors. The extra-large, 1⅖-cubic-foot microwave oven has touch controls for ten power levels, a digital timer, programmed cooking, and a shelf to cook several items at once. The 98711 has a waist-high broiler and a storage drawer. It comes in white with two black-glass oven doors, both with windows. Model 98718 is in almond.

Specifications: overall dimensions, height, 71⅝"; width, 30"; depth, 28⅛"; upper oven dimensions, height, 11⅞"; width, 16"; depth, 13⅜"; lower oven dimensions, height, 16"; width, 23"; depth, 17¼". Warranty: parts and labor, one year; magnetron tube, five years.

Approx. retail price
$1,310

Approx. low price
not available

WHIRLPOOL RM996PXV

The Whirlpool RM996PXV is a luxury range with a large upper microwave oven and a lower self-cleaning traditional electric oven. Its cooktop, which is brightly lit from behind, has two six-inch and two eight-inch plug-in coil elements. Both ovens offer programmed cooking. The spacious $1\frac{3}{10}$-cubic-foot microwave oven has touch controls for ten power levels, a temperature probe, a delay/start option, and a quick-defrost cycle. A storage drawer is below the lower oven, which has a waist-high broiler. Both have black-glass oven doors.

Specifications: overall dimensions, height, $71\frac{1}{2}$"; **width,** 30"; **depth,** $27\frac{5}{16}$"; **upper oven dimensions, height,** $9\frac{7}{8}$"; **width,** $16\frac{7}{16}$"; **depth,** $13\frac{7}{8}$"; **lower oven dimensions, height,** $16\frac{3}{4}$"; **width,** 22"; **depth,** $18\frac{1}{4}$". **Warranty: parts and labor,** one year; **magnetron tube,** five years; one year replacement if not satisfied.

Approx. retail price
not available

Approx. low price
$1,253

Drop-in/Slide-in Electric Ranges

CALORIC EST307

The Caloric EST307 is a reliable 30-inch slide-in range with a self-cleaning oven and automatic programmed cooking. Easy-clean features include a lift-up cooktop, removable chrome reflector pans, and a removable black-glass oven door. The two six-inch and two eight-inch coil elements are also removable for cleaning. The EST307 has a well-designed, highly efficient infrared broiler at waist height.

Specifications: overall dimensions, height, 36"; **width,** 30"; **depth,** $25\frac{1}{4}$"; **oven dimensions, height,** 16"; **width,** 23"; **depth,** $17\frac{1}{2}$". **Warranty: parts,** three years.

Approx. retail price
$800

Approx. low price
$598

Prices are accurate at time of printing; subject to manufacturer's change.

WHITE-WESTINGHOUSE KS540G

The White-Westinghouse KS540G is a high-quality 30-inch slide-in range with continuous-cleaning oven. An automatic clock/timer programs the oven. This range has two six-inch and two eight-inch plug-in coil heating elements, and its cooktop lifts up for cleaning. The black-glass, windowed oven door is also removable to make cleaning easier. The broiler is waist high, and a storage drawer is underneath the oven. The cooktop is available in stainless steel or almond.

Specifications: overall dimensions, height, 36"; width, 30"; depth, 29"; oven dimensions, height, 16"; width, 23"; depth, 18¾". Warranty: parts and labor, one year.

Approx. retail price	Approx. low price
$549	not available

WHIRLPOOL RS610PXV

The Whirlpool RS610PXV is a well-constructed, basic drop-in range with an oven that must be cleaned manually. It does offer programmed cooking with an automatic clock/timer. The seamless cooktop has two six-inch and two eight-inch plug-in coil elements. The cooktop lifts up for cleaning, and the oven door is removable. This range has a brushed-chrome cooktop and a black-glass oven door with a window.

Specifications: overall dimensions, height, 31⅞"; width, 30"; depth, 22¾"; oven dimensions, height, 16¾"; width, 22"; depth, 18¼". Warranty, parts and labor, one year; one-year replacement if not satisfied.

Approx. retail price	Approx. low price
$569	$533

Built-in Electric Ovens

GIBSON OE27S7ZY

The Gibson OE27S7ZY is a 27-inch, self-cleaning wall oven with an extra-wide broiler that broils food faster and more evenly. It also has a dual-radiant baking system, sending heat

---

Prices are accurate at time of printing; subject to manufacturer's change.

down from the eye-level broiling element and up from the baking element for browner, more even cooking.

Specifications: overall dimensions, height, 30¾"; **width**, 26⅞"; **depth**, 25⅜"; **oven dimensions, height**, 16"; **width**, 18½"; **depth**, 18½". **Warranty, parts and labor**, one year; five years on thermostat and oven elements.

Approx. retail price	Approx. low price
$629	$527

✔ **BEST BUY**

SEARS KENMORE 40189

The Sears Kenmore 40189 is a basic built-in electric oven that fits into a 24-inch cabinet. This oven must be cleaned manually, but it includes an automatic digital clock/timer for programmed cooking. A preheat signal sounds when the desired temperature is reached. The broiler is at the top of the oven. This model's black-glass oven door has a window.

Specifications: overall dimensions, height, 28⁹⁄₁₆"; **width**, 23¾"; **depth**, 26¾"; **oven dimensions, height**, 15"; **width**, 17"; **depth**, 18½". **Warranty: parts and labor**, one year.

Approx. retail price	Approx. low price
$440	not available

Built-in Electric/Microwave Ovens

GENERAL ELECTRIC JKP68GK

✔ **BEST BUY**

The General Electric JKP68GK is a sophisticated, double built-in oven with an extra-large microwave oven over a self-cleaning electric lower oven. Electronic touch controls provide programmed cooking for both ovens. The 1⅖-cubic-foot microwave oven offers time- or temperature-controlled cooking using an automatic sensor. It has ten power levels, a 99-minute timer, automatic defrost cycle, and a shelf for cooking several items at once. The lower oven has an electronic meat thermometer and an electronic timer. Both ovens have black-glass doors with windows, and the lower oven door lifts off for cleaning.

Prices are accurate at time of printing; subject to manufacturer's change.

Specifications: overall dimensions, height, 42"; **width,** 26"; **depth,** 24"; **upper oven dimensions, height,** 11⅛"; **width,** 16"; **depth,** 13⅜"; **lower oven dimensions, height,** 15"; **width,** 19"; **depth,** 18¼". **Warranty, parts and labor,** one year; **magnetron tube,** five years; 90-day replacement/refund if not satisfied.

Approx. retail price	Approx. low price
not available	$1,262

TAPPAN 57-2709

The Tappan 57-2709 combines a spacious microwave oven and a large self-cleaning electric lower oven. Separate touch controls provide programmed cooking for each oven. The 1³⁄₁₀-cubic-foot microwave oven has ten power levels, a browning element that works well, and a turntable. The lower oven has a digital clock/timer and a removable oven door. The broiler is at the top of the lower oven. Both ovens have black-glass doors with windows.

Specifications: overall dimensions, height, 48¹³⁄₁₆"; **width,** 26⅞"; **depth,** 27½"; **upper oven dimensions, height,** 9⅜"; **width,** 15½"; **depth,** 14½"; **lower oven dimensions, height,** 16"; **width,** 18½"; **depth,** 18½". **Warranty: parts and labor,** one year.

Approx. retail price	Approx. low price
$1,079	$951

Conventional Electric Cooktops

MAGIC CHEF 87F-1G

The Magic Chef 87F-1G is an easy-to-clean built-in cooktop with four coil heating elements. A nonstick griddle is built in between the elements. The 87F-1G has two six-inch and two eight-inch plug-in elements and removable reflector pans. The cooktop has raised, seamless edges to contain spills, and lifts up for cleaning. It comes in almond.

Specifications: dimensions, height, not available; **width,** 36"; **depth,** 21". **Warranty: parts and labor,** one year.

Approx. retail price	Approx. low price
$259	not available

Prices are accurate at time of printing; subject to manufacturer's change.

SEARS KENMORE 43589

The Sears Kenmore 43589 is a contemporary-looking, black-glass electric cooktop with two six-inch and one eight-inch solid-disc elements, plus one nine-inch, solid-disc element for extra-large pots. The nine-inch element has an automatic sensor to maintain a constant temperature. The sealed elements make this cooktop particularly easy to keep clean.

Specifications: dimensions, height, 3⅜"; **width**, 30"; **depth**, 21". **Warranty: parts and labor**, one year.

Approx. retail price	Approx. low price
$300	$239

Modular Electric Cooktops

JENN-AIR C203

The Jenn-Air C203 has one six-inch and one eight-inch coil element permanently installed on its right side; the left side is convertible. A grill module comes with this cooktop. Optional modules include solid-disc elements, additional coil elements, a glass-ceramic smooth cooktop, an induction cartridge, a wok, a griddle, a rotisserie/kabob, and a cooker/steamer. A downdraft vent in the center of the 30-inch cooktop draws smoke and odors down and out of the kitchen.

Specifications: dimensions, height, not available; **width**, 29⅞"; **depth**, 21½". **Warranty: parts**, two years; **labor**, one year.

Approx. retail price	Approx. low price
not available	$458

FRIGIDAIRE RBD139N

The Frigidaire RBD139N is a 36-inch modular cooktop that comes with two conventional coil elements and a grill module. Optional plug-in modules include a black-glass smoothtop with radiant heating elements, a black-glass solid element, a solid-disc module, and a griddle. A downdraft venting system pulls smoke and cooking odors down and out of the kitchen.

Specifications: dimensions, height, 16½"; **width**, 36"; **depth**,

Prices are accurate at time of printing; subject to manufacturer's change.

21". **Warranty: parts and labor,** one year.

Approx. retail price	Approx. low price
$669	$560

Smoothtop Electric Cooktops

AMANA AKH30

The Amana AKH30 is a glass-ceramic cooktop with heating elements that glow red from beneath the smooth black surface. This cooktop has two six-inch and one eight-inch electric elements below the smooth surface, plus one eight-inch quartz halogen element that heats up almost instantly. The AKH30 requires no special cookware. It is scratch- and stain-resistant, and its smooth surface can be used as extra counter space when the heating elements are not in use. It can be installed with the controls along the left or right side.

Specifications: dimensions, height, 3¾"; **width,** 29⁹⁄₁₆"; **depth,** 20¾". **Warranty: parts and labor,** one year; **glass-ceramic top,** five years; **heating elements,** four years.

Approx. retail price	Approx. low price
not available	$548

GENERAL ELECTRIC JP342L

The General Electric JP342L is a sleek, 30-inch smoothtop. Its four radiant heating elements, mounted below the surface, glow red when turned on. The JP342L has one six-inch and two eight-inch elements, plus one dual element that can change from six to nine inches in diameter, depending on the size of the pot you want to use. The black ceramic cooktop is easy to clean, since spills wipe easily from the smooth surface. Its controls provide infinite heat levels.

Specifications: dimensions, height, not available; **width,** 29⅜"; **depth,** 20½". **Warranty: parts and labor,** one year; 90-day replacement/refund if not satisfied.

Approx. retail price	Approx. low price
not available	$496

Prices are accurate at time of printing; subject to manufacturer's change.

Refrigerators

Energy costs over a refrigerator's 13-year life expectancy will exceed its purchase price. Therefore, you should shop for an energy-efficient model big enough to meet your needs for the next 13 years.

Compare the energy efficiency of each model by examining the bright yellow "EnergyGuide" label. You should also get a current *Consumer Selection Guide*, which lists the estimated energy cost of each model by sending a check for $1.50 to the Association of Home Appliance Manufacturers (AHAM), 20 North Wacker Drive, Chicago, Illinois 60606.

In addition to the manufacturer's warranty, there's a bit more consumer protection available to you if you should ever need it. Most of the models listed in this section of this publication under the protection of The Major Appliance Consumer Action Panel, or MACAP. You can appeal to this independent complaint resolution group if you take steps recommended by the manufacturer to resolve any problems and still feel the manufacturer has not backed the refrigerator you bought to your satisfaction. You can get more information about MACAP by contacting AHAM.

Matching Refrigerator Size to Your Needs

Buying a larger refrigerator than you need wastes money. Bigger units tend to be less energy efficient than small refrigerators, and you may end up cooling unused space inside your refrigerator. As a rule of thumb, plan for eight- to ten-cubic feet of cavity space for a family of two and add one-cubic foot for each additional family member. The freezer section should provide three-cubic feet for two people, with another cubic foot for each additional person.

Refrigerator Configurations

Single-door refrigerators range in storage capacity from 1½ to 19-cubic feet. Models under six-cubic feet are compacts. Single-door refrigerators are less expensive to buy and operate than other styles. Most models have a small interior freezer that may have to be defrosted manually.

Two-door bottom-mount refrigerators have a freezer compartment below the refrigerator section. This configuration is not widely available, but some people prefer to have the refrigerator compartment at eye level. Bottom-mounted freezers tend to be larger than top-mounted freezers.

Two-door side-by-side refrigerators are large capacity, free-standing units that have doors running their full length. Some models have a small door built into the refrigerator door to access frequently used beverages without opening the entire door.

Built-in refrigerators are often camouflaged with custom cabinet work. This kind of refrigerator is larger, more expensive, and more costly to operate than free-standing models.

Features and Terminology

Energy labels are mandated by federal law and state the expected annual operating cost of the appliance based on a power cost of 8.04 cents per kilowatt-hour. The actual cost of your power may be higher or lower, but this figure is useful when you compare different models.

Frostless, or **frost-free**, refrigerators automatically eliminate frost with heaters that melt the frost and evaporate the water. This is not an energy-efficient system, but it saves you time and effort by eliminating the need to defrost the refrigerator.

Energy-saving features are included in the design of many refrigerators. A **power-saver switch** saves energy by turning off the door heater (a loop or coil that carries hot refrigerant gas around the inside of the door to remove condensation during periods of high humidity). **Separate temperature controls** for the freezer and refrigerator also save energy.

Food shelves are adjustable in most refrigerators, so you can place the shelves to suit your needs. The freezer door should be able to hold small items. Glass shelves contain food spills and wipe clean easily.

Ice makers are either built in or optional. This convenience usually adds about $100 to the cost of the appliance. Installation may require a plumber.

Best Buys '91

Our Best Buy refrigerators follow. They are divided into these categories: single-door, two-door top-mount, two-door bottom-mount, side-by-side, and built-in refrigerators. Within each category, the refrigerators are listed in ascending order of size. Remember that a Best Buy or Recommended designation applies only to the model listed.

SINGLE-DOOR REFRIGERATORS

WELBILT W-1011 | RECOMMENDED

The Welbilt W-1011 is a value-priced, 10-cubic-foot, single-door refrigerator. It requires less energy to operate than larger refrigerators, so it is less expensive to own in the long run. It does not have automatic defrosting, which also saves energy. The W-1011 comes in white and has three wire shelves, a crisper, and two ice-cube trays. Like other single-door models, the freezer compartment is recommended only for short-term storage of frozen foods, and it will not keep ice cream solidly frozen.

Specifications: height, $55\frac{5}{16}$"; **width,** $24\frac{5}{8}$"; **depth,** $27\frac{1}{2}$"; **shelf capacity,** not available; **energy cost,** not available. **Warranty, parts and labor,** one year; **compressor,** five years.

Approx. retail price	**Approx. low price**
$300	$299

GENERAL ELECTRIC TA14SL | RECOMMENDED

The GE TA14SL has a small capacity and requires less energy to operate than larger models, so it is less expensive in the long run. The TA14SL does not have automatic defrosting, which also saves energy. This model has $11\frac{4}{5}$-cubic feet of refrigerator capacity and a $2\frac{1}{10}$-cubic-foot freezer compartment. This compartment is recommended only for short-term storage of frozen food, and, like other single-door models, it will not keep ice cream frozen solid. Available in white or almond, the TA14SL has dairy and vegetable/fruit bins, two ice-cube trays, two wire shelves, and three door shelves.

Specifications: height, 61"; **width**, 28"; **depth**, 27"; **shelf capacity**, $15\frac{3}{5}$ square feet; **energy cost**, $44 per year. **Warranty: parts and labor**, one year; **sealed system**, five years.

Approx. retail price	Approx. low price
not available	$364

TWO-DOOR BOTTOM-MOUNT REFRIGERATOR

AMANA BC20N

BEST BUY

The Amana BC20N provides access to its $13\frac{3}{5}$-cubic-foot refrigerator at eye level. Its $6\frac{3}{5}$-cubic-foot freezer is underneath. This model has three adjustable, half-width glass shelves; two large, humidity-controlled crispers; a sealed, adjustable-temperature meat keeper; a removable egg bucket; a dairy bin; and two microwave-safe leftover containers that fit in the door. Separate thermostats for the refrigerator and freezer maintain constant storage temperatures. The freezer's shelf and glide-out basket provide easy access to frozen foods. Shelf huggers, rollers, and a bottle rack are also included. It comes in white or almond. An ice maker is optional.

Specifications: height, 68"; **width**, 32"; **depth**, $32\frac{1}{2}$"; **shelf capacity**, $20\frac{1}{5}$ square feet; **energy cost**, $88 per year. **Warranty: parts and labor**, one year; **sealed system and food liner**, five years.

Approx. retail price	Approx. low price
not available	$820

Prices are accurate at time of printing; subject to manufacturer's change.

TWO-DOOR TOP-MOUNT REFRIGERATORS

BEST BUY

HOTPOINT CTX14EM

The Hotpoint CTX14EM is a deluxe, small, no-frost refrigerator with a freezer that maintains a near-zero temperature. The $10\frac{1}{2}$-cubic-foot fresh-foods section has two adjustable wire shelves; one fixed shelf; two vegetable/fruit bins; a utility pan; egg and dairy bins; and two door shelves. The $3\frac{4}{5}$-cubic-foot freezer has a split-level shelf and two door shelves. CTX14EM also has adjustable rollers. It comes in white or almond. An ice maker is optional.

Specifications: height, 61"; **width**, 28"; **depth**, $29\frac{9}{16}$"; **shelf capacity**, 20 square feet; **energy cost**, $89 per year. **Warranty: parts and labor**, one year; **sealed system**, five years.

Approx. retail price	Approx. low price
not available	$453

BEST BUY

FRIGIDAIRE FPD17TF

The Frigidaire FPD17TF is a value-priced, frost-free refrigerator that holds up to $16\frac{3}{5}$-cubic feet of food: $12\frac{4}{5}$-cubic feet in the fresh-foods section and $3\frac{4}{5}$-cubic feet in the top-mounted freezer. Model FPD17TF is very energy efficient. It has three, full-width wire shelves that slide out for cleaning and can be adjusted to several preset positions, plus a fourth fixed shelf and three door shelves. There are two, good-sized, sealed hydrators and a spreads compartment. An ice maker is optional. This model comes in white or almond.

Specifications: height, $64\frac{3}{16}$"; **width**, 28"; **depth**, $30\frac{5}{8}$"; **shelf capacity**, $20\frac{9}{10}$ square feet; **energy cost**, $62 per year. **Warranty: parts and labor**, one year; **refrigerating system and cabinet liner**, five years.

Approx. retail price	Approx. low price
$599	$516

Prices are accurate at time of printing; subject to manufacturer's change.

WHITE-WESTINGHOUSE RT176M

The White-Westinghouse RT176M is a frost-free refrigerator with a 16⅘-cubic-foot capacity: 13-cubic feet in the refrigerator section and 3⅘-cubic feet in the top-mounted freezer. It has three cantilevered, adjustable, full-width epoxy-coated wire shelves, one fixed shelf, and one full-width plus three half-width door shelves. RT176M has a sealed crisper, a deli tray, two dairy compartments, rollers, and an energy-saver switch. It comes in white, almond, harvest, coffee, or avocado. **Specifications: height,** 64³⁄₁₆"; **width,** 28"; **depth,** 30¾"; **shelf capacity,** 23³⁄₁₀ square feet; **energy cost,** $68 per year. **Warranty: parts and labor,** one year; **compressor,** five years.

Approx. retail price	Approx. low price
not available	$622

WHIRLPOOL ET18DKXW

The Whirlpool ET18DKXW is a deluxe, no-frost, 18¹⁄₁₀-cubic-foot top-mount refrigerator. The 13⅓-cubic-foot refrigerator section has two full-width glass shelves (one adjustable) and two half-width glass shelves (one adjustable). Four half-width, adjustable door shelves and one full-width door shelf provide ample door storage. The 4⅘-cubic-foot freezer has one shelf, four ice-cube trays, and an ice bucket. ET18DKXW has two sealed crispers, an adjustable meat pan, and door-mounted utility and dairy compartments. It comes in white or almond. An ice maker is optional.
Specifications: height, 66¼"; **width,** 29½"; **depth,** 29½"; **shelf capacity,** 25 square feet; **energy cost,** $71 per year. **Warranty: parts and labor,** one year; **sealed system,** five years.

Approx. retail price	Approx. low price
$679	$636

AMANA TXI20N

The Amana TXI20N is a deluxe, no-frost, 19⅘-cubic-foot top-mount refrigerator. The 14½-cubic-foot refrigerator section has a total of four glass shelves: three half-width adjustable and one full-width fixed. Ample storage space on the door consists of two half-width adjustable shelves, a removable egg bucket, two microwave-safe leftover storage containers, and a dairy compartment. It has an adjustable-temperature meat keeper, a bottle rack, and two humidity-controlled crispers. The freezer has an optional ice maker with a cube bin, an adjustable shelf, and adjustable door shelves. It comes in white or almond.

Specifications: height, 68"; **width**, 32"; **depth**, 31⅞"; **shelf capacity**, 26 7/10 square feet; **energy cost**, $72 per year. **Warranty: parts and labor**, one year; **sealed system and food liner**, five years.

Approx. retail price	Approx. low price
not available	$799

FRIGIDAIRE FPCI21TF

BEST BUY

The Frigidaire FPCI21TF is a value-priced, 20⅗-cubic-foot top-mount refrigerator. It has four white, epoxy-coated, adjustable wire shelves (one full-width and three half-width), plus a fixed shelf above its two hydrators (one sealed). The 15-cubic-foot fresh-foods section also has three door shelves, spreads and snack bins, and a removable egg tray. The 5⅗-cubic-foot freezer has a single white, epoxy-coated wire shelf; two door shelves; two cube trays; and a removable ice server. It comes in white or almond. An ice maker, a black panel kit, and a custom panel kit, which can be used to give it a built-in look, are optional.

Specifications: height, 66 11/16"; **width**, 31"; **depth**, 30⅝"; **shelf capacity**, 26⅖ square feet; **energy cost**, $76 per year. **Warranty: parts and labor**, one year; **sealed system and liner**, five years.

Approx. retail price	Approx. low price
$669	$624

GENERAL ELECTRIC TBX25RN

BEST BUY

General Electric TBX25RN is a well-designed, deluxe-featured frostless refrigerator. It is a top-mount with 17¼-cubic feet of refrigerator space and 7½-cubic feet of freezer space. Its five extra-deep, adjustable door shelves hold much more

Prices are accurate at time of printing; subject to manufacturer's change.

than door shelves in many other models. It has two full-width glass shelves (one adjustable) and two half-width glass shelves (one adjustable). Other features include an ice maker; cubes and crushed ice dispenser; two large, adjustable-humidity crispers; an adjustable-temperature meat pan; an egg bin; a utility bin; a tilt-out bin for storing hard-to-stack items; and four under-the-shelf, microwave-safe leftover storage containers. It comes in white or almond with black handles.

Specifications: height, 67"; **width**, 34½"; **depth**, 32¾"; **shelf capacity**, 30 square feet; **energy cost**, $93 per year. **Warranty: parts and labor**, one year; **sealed system**, five years.

Approx. retail price	Approx. low price
not available	$1,174

SIDE-BY-SIDE REFRIGERATORS

FRIGIDAIRE FPCI19VF

The Frigidaire FPCI19VF is an energy-efficient, value-priced, 19-cubic-foot, frost-free side-by-side refrigerator. Its 12⅕-cubic-foot refrigerator section has five shelves (four of which are adjustable); white, epoxy-coated, full-width wire shelves; five door shelves; a sealed hydrator; an adjustable-temperature chill drawer; removable egg tray; and spreads, utility, and snack bins. The 6⅘-cubic-foot freezer has five wire interior shelves, six door shelves, and a slide-out basket. It comes in white or almond. An ice maker is optional.

Specifications: height, 66"; **width**, 31"; **depth**, 30⅝"; **shelf capacity**, 23⁷⁄₁₀ square feet; **energy cost**, $91 per year. **Warranty: parts and labor**, one year; **sealed system and liner**, five years.

Approx. retail price	Approx. low price
$849	$750

WHIRLPOOL ED22DWXW

The Whirlpool ED22DWXW is a deluxe-featured, 21⅗-cubic-foot side-by-side refrigerator. Its four, adjustable, slide-out glass shelves have edges that will hold up to 12 ounces of spilled liquid. Its four, extra-deep, adjustable door shelves hold much more than door shelves in many other models. The 14½-cubic-foot refrigerator section also has two large humidity-controlled sealed crispers, an adjustable-temperature meat pan, and utility bin. The freezer has four slide-out baskets, a pizza rack, and five door shelves. This model has an ice maker, through-the-door cube and chilled water dispenser, rollers, and a wine rack. It comes in white or almond with a big variety of panel, handle, and trim kit options.

Specifications: height, 66½"; **width,** 32¾"; **depth,** 32⅜"; **shelf capacity,** 25 square feet; **energy cost,** $103. **Warranty: parts and labor,** one year; **sealed system,** five years.

Approx. retail price	**Approx. low price**
$1,369	**$1,213**

FRIGIDAIRE FPCE24VWF

The Frigidaire FPCE24VWF is a 24-cubic-foot, deluxe-featured, frost-free, energy-efficient, side-by-side refrigerator with an ice maker, and through-the-door cube and water dispenser. The 14⁷⁄₁₀-cubic-foot refrigerator section has glass shelves, three of which are adjustable. It also has one humidity-controlled and one sealed hydrator, an adjustable-temperature chill drawer, and a wine rack. The door holds three adjustable shelves, a beverage dispenser, spreads and egg bins, and three microwave-safe leftover storage containers. The freezer section has four wire shelves and five door shelves. It comes in white or almond. A black panel kit and custom-frame kit are optional.

Specifications: height, 66"; **width,** 35¾"; **depth,** 31⅝"; **shelf capacity,** 26⁹⁄₁₀ square feet; **energy cost,** $106 per year. **Warranty: parts and labor,** one year; **sealed system and liner,** five years.

Approx. retail price	**Approx. low price**
$1,339	**$1,301**

HOTPOINT CSX27DL

The Hotpoint CSX27DL is a 26⅘-cubic-foot, deluxe-featured, frost-free, side-by-side refrigerator with an ice maker and through-the-door ice and water dispenser. The 16⅔-cubic-

---

foot refrigerator section has three glass shelves, all of which are adjustable, a sealed snack pan, an adjustable-temperature meat pan, an egg storage bin, and two vegetable/fruit pans (one sealed). The door has five shelves, four of which are extra deep and adjustable; they hold much more than door shelves in many other models. The freezer has three interior shelves, a storage bin, and five door shelves. CSX27DL also has an enamel-on-steel cabinet liner, adjustable rollers and dairy compartment. It comes in white or almond. A custom trim kit and a black Lexan panel kit are optional.

Specifications: height, 68¾"; **width**, 35¾"; **depth**, 32½"; **shelf capacity**, 29⅖ square feet; **energy cost**, $110 per year. **Warranty: parts and labor**, one year; **sealed system**, five years.

Approx. retail price	Approx. low price
not available	$1,253

GENERAL ELECTRIC TFX27RL

✔BEST BUY

General Electric TFX27RL is a 26⅔-cubic-foot capacity, deluxe-featured, frost-free side-by-side refrigerator with ice maker and through-the-door cubes, crushed ice, and water dispenser. The 16⅔-cubic-foot refrigerator section has three adjustable glass shelves, a sealed crisper, an adjustable-temperature meat pan, a utility bin, and a sealed snack pan. The door has five shelves, four of which are extra deep, and adjustable shelves that hold a lot more than door shelves in many other models. The freezer has three adjustable white wire shelves, sliding storage bin, and five door shelves (three are removable). It comes in white or almond with black door handles. A custom trim kit and a black Lexan panel kit are optional.

Specifications: height, 68¾"; **width**, 35¾"; **depth**, 32½"; **shelf capacity**, 28⅘ square feet; **energy cost**, $110 per year. **Warranty: parts and labor**, one year; **sealed system**, five years.

Approx. retail price	Approx. low price
not available	$1,423

BUILT-IN REFRIGERATOR

SUB-ZERO 532

The Sub-Zero 532 is a true built-in refrigerator in a side-by-side design. Like most built-in models, it is available from custom kitchen dealers and appliance stores. It has separate compressors for the 18⅘-cubic-foot refrigerator and the 11⅕-cubic-foot freezer, both of which have an all-white interior. The fresh-foods section has five glass shelves, four of which are adjustable; four sealed, humidity-adjustable crispers; a utility drawer; an egg rack; two spreads bins; and three adjustable door shelves. The freezer has an ice maker and ice drawer, four pull-out baskets, three shelves, and five adjustable door shelves. As with most true built-in refrigerators, it requires custom panels.

Specifications: height, 84″; **width**, 48″; **depth**, 24″; **shelf capacity**, not available; **energy cost**, $109. **Warranty: labor**, one year; **parts**, three years; **sealed system**, five years; **sealed system parts**, twelve years.

Approx. retail price not available	**Approx. low price** $3,182

Freezers

Energy costs over a freezer's 13-year life expectancy will exceed its purchase price. Therefore, you should shop for an energy-efficient model big enough to meet your needs for the next 13 years.

Compare the energy efficiency of each model by examining the bright yellow "EnergyGuide" label. Or get a copy of the *Consumer Selection Guide* by writing to the Association of Home Appliance Manufacturers, 20 North Wacker Drive, Chicago, Illinois 60606.

In addition to the manufacturer's warranty, the association gives you a bit more consumer protection if you should ever need it for most name brands. If you take steps recommended by the manufacturer to resolve any problems and still feel the manufacturer has not backed the product to your satisfaction, you can appeal to the Major Appliance Consumer Action Panel. For details about this independent complaint resolution group, contact AHAM.

Upright or Chest?

The two styles of freezers, upright and chest, are equally popular. Each has its advantages and disadvantages.

Convenience: An upright offers the convenience of front-door loading. It also has shelves for easy access to foods. In a chest freezer, goods have to be stacked rather than shelved, and they are less accessible. Many chest freezers have pull-out baskets to make it easier to store and remove frozen food.

Expense: Compared to an upright model of comparable size, a chest freezer is less expensive to buy and operate.

Size: Upright freezers range in capacity from under one and a half cubic feet to about 30 cubic feet. Chest freezers have capacities from roughly four and seven-tenths to 28 cubic feet.

Space: An upright takes up less space than a chest unit. An upright is a good choice if you want a freezer in the kitchen because it is more convenient. A chest freezer is often preferred for a basement where floor space is not a problem.

How Large a Freezer Do You Need?

A freezer that is too large will be inefficient and costly to operate. But a freezer that is too small defeats its purpose and causes a lot of frustration. Allow about three cubic feet of freezer space for each family member. Add another two cubic feet for special purposes, such as impromptu dinner parties, and two to three cubic feet if you plan to freeze game or produce, or if you like to prepare meals in advance.

Features and Terminology

Baskets: For storing bulk items, baskets are useful. Chest freezers usually have one or more sliding baskets, combined with step dividers, which provide direct access to the total freezer space. Upright models usually have one basket or bin.

Controls: A freezer works best at 0° F or slightly below. Some models have a temperature control.

Defrost systems: Chest freezers and some upright models must be defrosted manually. A few upright models come with automatic defrost, which will add about $100 to the purchase price and 15 to 20 percent per year to the operating cost.

Energy efficiency: Since 1972, freezers have become over 65 percent more energy efficient because of improved condensers, evaporators, fan motors, door seals, and insulating techniques. The energy labels on freezers let you compare the energy use of comparable models. They show the estimated annual operating cost, based on an energy cost of 8.04 cents per kilowatt-hour.

Fast-freezing shelves: Some shelves have an extra cooling coil running through them to facilitate faster freezing. These may be called fast-freeze or refrigerated shelves.

Interior light: This can help you find what you're looking for, especially in a chest freezer located in a dark basement.

Lock: A lock on your freezer is very important if there are young children who might climb inside a freezer and get trapped. It is also useful if your freezer is in a garage or where the contents may not be secure without a lock.

Best Buys '91

Our Best Buys and Recommended upright and chest freezers follow. We have listed models in ascending order of total capacity: Those with the largest freezing space are listed first. Remember that a Best Buy or Recommended designation applies only to the model listed; it does not necessarily apply to other models made by the same manufacturer.

UPRIGHT FREEZERS

WHIRLPOOL EV110CXW

The Whirlpool EV110CXW is an 11-cubic foot upright freezer with very good energy efficiency for its size. Like most freezers, it requires defrosting from time to time. This model has three shelves, a bulk storage trivet, four door shelves, a power-saver switch, and leveling legs. **Specifications: height,** 57¼"; **width,** 24"; **depth,** 29"; **shelf capacity,** 10 square feet; **energy cost,** $51 per year. **Warranty: parts and labor,** one year; **sealed system,** ten years; **food spoilage,** up to $125 (cumulative total) in ten years.

Approx. retail price
$369

Approx. low price
not available

GENERAL ELECTRIC CA13DL

The General Electric CA13DL is a 13³/₁₀-cubic foot manually defrosted upright that has good energy efficiency for its size. This model has three fast-freezing shelves; a top cold plate; four door shelves; an audible alarm if the temperature rises above a safe level; an interior light; and a quality, baked enamel-on-steel cabinet liner. It comes with a very good food-

---

Prices are accurate at time of printing; subject to manufacturer's change.

FREEZERS

protection warranty. It is only available in white.
Specifications: height, 54½"; **width,** 28"; **depth,** 28³⁄₁₆"; **shelf capacity,** 14⅕ square feet; **energy cost,** $40 per year. **Warranty: parts and labor,** one year; **sealed system,** five years.

Approx. retail price
not available

Approx. low price
$379

MAGIC CHEF DF-15

The Magic Chef DF-15 is a well-made, 15⅕-cubic foot upright freezer. It has three fast-freezing cavity shelves, four door shelves, and a juice-can shelf. This manually defrosted model also has a lower storage gate for good access to bulky items, an automatic interior light, a door lock with pop-out key, and temperature controls.
Specifications: height, 60"; **width,** 30"; **depth,** 28⅜"; **shelf capacity,** 14⁷⁄₁₀ square feet; **energy cost,** $57. **Warranty: parts and labor,** one year; **refrigeration system,** five years.

Approx. retail price
$399

Approx. low price
$379

FRIGIDAIRE UFP-16N

The Frigidaire UFP-16N is a 15⁷⁄₁₀-cubic foot frost-free upright freezer. Automatic defrosting eliminates the need to periodically melt ice that typically builds up in a freezer. However, it subjects the contents to freezer burn. The UFP-16N has four shelves and one adjustable shelf, a sliding epoxy-coated basket, four door shelves, juice rack, interior light, and a lock with pop-out key. It comes in almond only.
Specifications: height, 61½"; **width,** 32"; **shelf capacity,** 18⅕ square feet; **energy cost,** $71 per year. **Warranty: parts and labor,** one year; **refrigeration system and liner,** five years.

Approx. retail price
$589

Approx. low price
$581

GIBSON FV19M2WX

The Gibson FV19M2WX is a no-frills, 19¹⁄₁₀-cubic foot manually defrosted upright freezer. It has three refrigerated

Prices are accurate at time of printing; subject to manufacturer's change.
CONSUMER GUIDE®

371

shelves and five molded door shelves, including two juice-can racks. Other features include a temperature control, leg levelers, and a lock with pop-out key. It comes in white only. **Specifications: height**, 67¾"; **width**, 32"; **depth**, 26⅜"; **shelf capacity**, 19⁷⁄₁₀ square feet; **energy cost**, $59 per year. **Warranty: parts and labor**, one year; **refrigeration system and liner**, five years.

Approx. retail price	Approx. low price
not available	$413

CHEST FREEZERS

GIBSON FH08M5DX

The Gibson FH08M5DX is a chest freezer with a capacity of 8⁹⁄₁₀ cubic feet. It has basic features and is economical. This manually defrosted unit has a sliding, epoxy-coated basket, a temperature control, and a textured-steel exterior. It is available only in almond with a brown lid. **Specifications: height**, 34¹¹⁄₁₆"; **width**, 35"; **depth**, 23"; **energy cost**, $33 per year. **Warranty: parts and labor**, one year; **refrigeration system and liner**, five years; **compressor (limited)**, ten years; **food loss**, three years.

Approx. retail price	Approx. low price
not available	$265

GENERAL ELECTRIC CB10DL

The General Electric CB10DL has many deluxe features and excellent energy efficiency. This 10-cubic foot chest freezer is defrosted manually, which means it consumes relatively little energy. It has an adjustable temperature control, a removable, sliding bulk storage basket, an interior light, a lock with pop-out key, and an up-front drain. Audible and visual indicators are activated if the cavity temperature rises above 20° F. It comes in white only. **Specifications: height**, 35"; **width**, 42⅛"; **depth**, 24¼"; **energy cost**, $32 per year. **Warranty: parts and labor**, one year; **sealed system**, five years; **food spoilage**, up to $100 (cumulative total)

Prices are accurate at time of printing; subject to manufacturer's change.

due to defects, one year; up to $100 (cumulative total) due to defects in the sealed system, five years.

Approx. retail price	Approx. low price
not available	$317

WHIRLPOOL EH150FXW ✔**BEST BUY**

The Whirlpool EH150FXW is a 15-cubic foot chest freezer with basic features and very good energy efficiency. It has a temperature control, a sliding basket, a lock with pop-out key, a power cord lock, and textured-steel exterior. It comes in almond only.

Specifications: height, 35″; **width**, 46⅛″; **depth**, 29¼″; **energy cost**, $37 per year. **Warranty: parts and labor**, one year; **sealed system**, ten years; **food spoilage**, up to $125 (cumulative total) in ten years.

Approx. retail price	Approx. low price
$369	not available

FRIGIDAIRE CFS18L ✔**BEST BUY**

The Frigidaire CFS18L is an 18-cubic foot chest freezer with basic features and very good energy efficiency. A large, sliding, epoxy-coated basket provides convenient storage for frequently used foods. This chest has a temperature control, a lock with pop-out key, a combination divider/drain pan, a power-cord retainer, a textured-steel exterior, and a baked enamel interior. It comes in almond only.

Specifications: height, 35″; **width**, 52¾″; **depth**, 29½″; **energy cost**, $49 per year. **Warranty: parts and labor**, one year; **refrigeration system and liner**, five years.

Approx. retail price	Approx. low price
$419	not available

Dishwashers

You can rely on a good dishwasher to produce sparkling clean dishes and save you four hours a week, the time the average homemaker spends washing dishes by hand. In fact, the machine's cleaning action removes more grease and germs than you could ever remove by hand.

Built-in dishwashers are permanently attached to water pipes, drains, and electrical lines. The main disadvantage of a built-in dishwasher is that it deprives you of kitchen cabinet space. There are a few compact built-in models, which are slimmer than the standard 24 inches.

Portable dishwashers roll on casters and connect to the sink faucet and drain with hoses. Most portables have a flow-through valve that lets you draw water from the faucet while the appliance is in operation. Some models can be converted to built-in units. If you are a renter who hopes to someday own a house or condominium where you will permanently install a dishwasher, a convertible model is a good choice.

Some dishwashers offer increased cleaning vigor, quiet operation, and many energy-saving features. All dishwashers have an air-dry feature that saves energy by turning off the heating element used in the regular heat-dry cycle. Some models have shorter, energy-efficient cycles for fine china and lightly soiled dishes. Others feature shorter rinse and dry cycles, built-in water softeners, and heating elements that quickly heat the wash and rinse water to 140° F. Except for cookware with burned-on food, dishes do not need to be rinsed before you put them in the dishwasher.

For most brand-name models and all of our selections, the Association of Home Appliance Manufacturers offers a bit of consumer protection in addition to the manufacturer's warranty. If you take steps recommended by the manufacturer to resolve any problems and still feel the manufacturer has not backed the product to your satisfaction, you can appeal to the Major Appliance Consumer Action Panel. For details about this independent complaint resolution group, write to AHAM, 20 N. Wacker Dr., Chicago, Illinois 60606.

Features and Terminology

Construction: The dishwasher tub must withstand continual contact with hot water and detergents. Stainless steel, used in a few high-quality models, is the most durable and the most expensive material. Porcelain enamel on steel is also durable. Most models have layers of insulation to muffle operating noise.

Controls: Push-button or dial controls are the most economical and reliable. Electronic touch controls add a bit more to the cost of the machine and give it a high-tech look.

Cycles: A dishwasher can have from two to nine-or-more cycles. Three basic cycles handle most chores: a light wash (called energy-saving wash by some manufacturers), a normal wash, and a heavy-duty cycle for pots and pans.

Spray-washing action: The best washing action comes from a three-level spray assembly that has arms at the top and bottom and a turret to help spray the upper rack. The problem with the three-level assembly is that the center turret takes up some of the washer's capacity. Units with two-level spray arms also do a good job, and sometimes the increased capacity of the unit is more important than three-level washing. One-level washing may not provide satisfactory cleaning.

Time delay: Many models now have a time-delay setting, which starts your dishwasher automatically at a preset time.

Water heating: A growing number of models feature an internal water-temperature booster system that ensures consistently hot water of about 140° F for the wash and rinse cycles. You can reduce the cost of operating your hot water heater by setting the thermostat as low as 120° F.

Best Buys '91

Our Best Buy and Recommended dishwashers follow, divided into the categories of built-in dishwashers and portable models. Within each category, the best of the Best Buys is listed first, followed by our second choice, and so on. Remember that a Best Buy designation applies only to the model listed; it doesn't necessarily apply to other models by the same manufacturer or to an entire product line.

BUILT-IN DISHWASHERS

IN-SINK-ERATOR CLASSIC SUPREME

The In-Sink-Erator Classic Supreme is an underrated built-in dishwasher of impressive quality. Its value is evident in the triple-coated porcelain-on-steel tank and inner door, the powerful ½-horsepower motor, and the multi-position upper rack. It has four cycles: pots and pans, normal, light, and rinse/hold. The Classic Supreme also has triple sound insulation, a self-cleaning, three-stage water filtration system, a built-in food disposer, an automatic intake water temperature booster, and a fan-driven heated air drying system.
Specifications: height, adjustable from 33¹¹⁄₁₆″ to 35″; **width**, 24″; **depth**, 26″; **heating element wattage**, 750 watts; **volts**, 115; **water use**, regular wash, 9¾ gallons. **Warranty: parts and labor**, one year; **motor**, five years; **tank and inner door**, ten years.

Approx. retail price $549	**Approx. low price** not available

HOTPOINT HDA950G

The Hotpoint HDA950G is a value-priced built-in dishwasher with many useful features, including a plate warmer, a water-temperature booster, and a porcelain-enamel interior finish. It has five cycles: pots and pans, normal, light wash, rinse/hold, and plate warmer. The HDA950G has very good, three-level washing action, extra-heavy sound insulation, a soft-food dis-

---

poser, and detergent and rinse-aid dispensers. It comes with door panels in white, almond, black, and harvest, or you may wish to install custom panels of up to ¼-inch thick.

Specifications: height, adjustable from 33⅞″ to 35″; **width**, 23⅞″; **depth**, 25¾″; **heating element wattage**, 700 watts; **volts**, 120; **water use**, regular wash, 11 gallons. **Warranty: parts and labor**, one year.

Approx. retail price	Approx. low price
not available	not available

KITCHENAID KUDS22OT

KitchenAid KUDS22OT, or Superba model, is a fully featured built-in dishwasher with quality and reliability that justify its price. This model has push-button controls, two-level washing action, a ½-horsepower motor, a triple filtration system, high-density sound insulation, and a porcelain-on-steel tub and inner door. It has five cycles: soak and scrub pots and pans, normal, light/china, quick glass, and rinse/hold. A built-in water temperature booster heats incoming water up to 140° F. Other features include a 16-position, adjustable upper rack, stainless-steel hard-food disposer, and detergent and rinse-aid dispensers. The standard trim package consists of white, almond, black, and harvest wheat panels. You can also use a special brushed stainless-steel panel or custom trim up to ¼-inch thick.

Specifications: height, adjustable from 33¹¹⁄₁₆″ to 35″; **width**, 24″; **depth**, 25″; **heating element wattage**, 1475 watts; **volts**, 115; **water use**, regular wash, 9¾ gallons. **Warranty: parts and labor**, one year; **racks**, three years; **motor (parts only)**, five years; **tub and inner door (parts only)**, ten years.

Approx. retail price	Approx. low price
$699	not available

FRIGIDAIRE DW-4500F

The Frigidaire DW-4500F is a full-featured built-in dishwasher made with fiberglass, foil and foam padding, and sound-dampening sheets to reduce operating noise levels. This model has three-way washing action, mechanical controls,

Prices are accurate at time of printing; subject to manufacturer's change.

and a ⅓-horsepower motor. Its cycles are pots and pans, heavy soil, short wash, normal soil, rinse/hold, rinse/dry, and Sani 150. This high-temperature cycle boosts water up to 150°F to clean heavily soiled dishes. The model's water temperature booster also heats intake water of a minimum of 120°F to the proper washing temperature. Other features include delay start, a soft-food disposer, a silverware basket, and an adjustable upper rack. The standard door panels are almond, black, and white. A custom trim kit and other panel colors are optional.

Specifications: height, adjustable from 34" to 35"; **width,** 23¹⁵⁄₁₆"; **depth,** 25⁵⁄₁₆"; **heating element wattage,** 760 watts; **volts,** 115; **water use,** regular wash, 9⅕ gallons. **Warranty: parts and labor,** one year; **water distribution system (parts),** two years; **tub and inner-door liner (parts),** ten years.

> **Approx. retail price**
> **not available**
>
> **Approx. low price**
> **not available**

MAYTAG WU504

✔ **BEST BUY**

The Maytag WU504 is a well-made built-in dishwasher that represents good value among comparably equipped models. It has a hard- and soft-food disposer and three-way washing action, which means you need to prerinse only dishes with burned-on foods. It has a ⅓-horsepower motor, a water temperature booster, and a smooth, double-coated porcelain-enamel interior. This model has mechanical controls and four cycles: regular, pots and pans, low energy, and rinse/hold. Model WU504 has forced-air drying and your choice of four front panels: white, almond, black, or harvest wheat.

Specifications: height, adjustable from 34" to 35½"; **width,** 24"; **depth,** 24¹⁄₁₆"; **heating element wattage,** not available; **volts,** 115; **water use,** regular wash, 11 gallons. **Warranty: parts and labor,** one year; **cabinet against rust (parts) and wash system (parts),** five years; **tub and inner-door liner (parts),** ten years.

> **Approx. retail price**
> $540
>
> **Approx. low price**
> **not available**

GENERAL ELECTRIC
GSD1100L

The General Electric GSD1100L is a fully equipped built-in dishwasher with push-button controls. It has excellent, three-level washing action, a soft-food disposer, and good sound insulation. The washing cycles are normal, light wash, pots and pans, and rinse/hold. Other features include delay start, a temperature sensor system, and a rinse-aid dispenser. Front panels come in two colors: almond or black, or you can use custom panels.

Specifications: height, adjustable from 34″ to 35″; **width**, 24″; **depth**, 24″; **heating element wattage**, not available; **volts**, 120; **water use**, regular wash, not available. **Warranty: parts and labor**, one year; **water distribution system (parts)**, two years; **tub and liner**, ten years.

Approx. retail price	Approx. low price
not available	not available

PORTABLE DISHWASHERS

WHITE-WESTINGHOUSE
SP560M

The White-Westinghouse SP560M is a value-priced, portable/convertible dishwasher. It has push-button and dial controls, three-way washing action, and detergent and rinse agent dispensers. Its five cycles are normal, light, pot scrub, plate warm, and rinse/hold. This model has a ⅓-horsepower motor, removable silverware basket, and self-cleaning water filter. The self-storing hose has a water-release button that lets you use the faucet when the hose is connected. The machine rolls on casters and can be installed as a built-in with an optional conversion kit.

Specifications: height, 37¼″; **width**, 24⅝″; **depth**, 26⅞″; **heating element wattage**, 800 watts; **volts**, 120; **water use**, regular wash, 12½ gallons; **Warranty: parts and labor**, one year; **water**

---

distribution system (parts), two years; **tub and door liner (parts)**, ten years.

Approx. retail price
not available

Approx. low price
not available

KITCHENAID KPDI620T

KitchenAid KPDI620T is a top-quality, portable/convertible dishwasher with push-button and dial controls. It has a two-level washing action, a ½-horsepower motor, a triple filtration system, and four cycles: pots and pans, normal, light/china, and rinse/hold. Model KPDI620T also has a water-temperature booster, a stainless-steel hard-food disposer, and a porcelain-on-steel tub and door liner. The unit moves on large casters and comes with a wood top and a black/almond reversible front panel.

Specifications: height, adjustable from 33¹¹⁄₁₆″ to 35″; **width,** 24″; **depth,** 25″; **heating element wattage,** 1360 watts; **volts,** 115; **water use,** regular wash, 9¾ gallons. **Warranty: parts and labor,** one year; **racks,** three years; **motor (parts),** five years; **tub and inner door (parts),** ten years.

Approx. retail price
$529

Approx. low price
not available

HOTPOINT HDB827G ✔BEST BUY

The Hotpoint HDB827G is a good-quality, portable/convertible dishwasher. It has three-level washing action and five cycles: pots and pans, normal, light, rinse/hold, and plate warmer. This model has a porcelain-enamel interior, built-in soft-food disposer, and detergent and rinse-agent dispensers. It has a wood veneer top and comes with a reversible door and access panels in white or almond.

Specifications: height, adjustable from 33⅞″ to 35″; **width,** 24″; **depth,** 25¾″; **heating element wattage,** not available; **volts,** 120; **water use,** regular wash, 9½ gallons. **Warranty: parts and labor,** one year.

Approx. retail price
not available

Approx. low price
not available

Food-Waste Disposers and Trash Compactors

Taking out the garbage rarely ranks as anyone's favorite household chore. But two specialized appliances—the food-waste disposer and the trash compactor—can make this kitchen cleanup task easier and more pleasant.

A disposer, installed under the kitchen sink, gets rid of everything—from eggshells to chicken bones to apple cores—by grinding them up and flushing them down the drain. A trash compactor, which may be built in under the counter or free-standing, tackles non-food wastes, such as cans, paper, and bottles, by compressing them into a neat, manageable bundle that can be easily carried out to the curb for pickup.

Food-Waste Disposers

You can pay as little as $50 for a food-waste disposer or as much as $300. The lowest price models, however, have smaller motors (less than $\frac{1}{2}$ horsepower) that are not as sturdy and more likely to jam. CONSUMER GUIDE® recommends buying a disposer with at least a $\frac{1}{2}$-hp motor for maximum efficiency and reliability. These more powerful (and more expensive) models also have better sound insulation (although no disposer is truly quiet during operation), and are more likely to resist corrosion.

You can probably install a disposer under the kitchen sink and hook it up yourself, especially if you are replacing an existing model. Before buying a unit, check your local building codes to make sure they allow installation of a disposer.

Continuous or Batch Feed?

Disposers are available in continuous-feed or batch-feed configurations. Both mount under the sink and grind up food wastes in the same way. The difference between the two is the way they are operated.

A continuous-feed disposer is activated by a remote switch (usually on the wall behind or next to the sink). With the disposer turned on and cold water running, waste can be fed into it continuously. Most continuous-feed disposers come with a safety cover or lid to keep waste from flying out.

A batch-feed disposer is activated only when its cover, or stopper, is in place; the cover is the switch that turns on the motor. You load the unit with about a quart of food waste, turn on the water, and insert the cover. You cannot add more waste without stopping the disposer.

Although continuous-feed units handle more waste more quickly, a batch-feed disposer may be a safer choice for households with small children. From a price standpoint, both types are about equal. Continuous-feed models usually cost less to buy but are more expensive to install because you need a wall switch. A batch-feed model costs more to buy but less to install. If you are replacing an existing disposer and installing the new one yourself, stick to the type you are replacing because the proper connections are already in place.

Disposer Features

Anti-jam systems: Better disposers have anti-jamming cycles that reverse the motor's direction to clear jams. Others clear jams by applying jolts of power to the machine. We prefer the reversing feature because the jolt-of-power system may stress the motor and grinding blades.

Corrosion resistance: CONSUMER GUIDE® recommends disposers made of stainless steel or corrosion-resistant metal alloys.

Dishwasher-drain access: If you have a dishwasher or plan to install one, make sure the disposer you select has a side opening to connect to a dishwasher-drain hose.

Mounting system: If you are planning to install the disposer yourself, look for a "quick-mount" system that requires no special tools.

Sound insulation: Good sound insulation, usually rubber or plastic foam, helps reduce noise and vibration while the disposer is in use.

Trash Compactors

A trash compactor, which is about half the size of a standard dishwasher, compresses dry trash—such as bottles, cans, and paper—into dense bundles. Since it only handles dry trash, a compactor will not replace your kitchen garbage can or food-waste disposer, but it will greatly reduce the volume of trash you have to deal with. All compactors have some kind of deodorizing system, but they are not equipped to deal with the strong odors that would result from storing compressed food wastes for several days. Also, certain other kinds of trash, such as aerosol cans, should not be compacted for safety or environmental reasons.

Trash Compactor Features

Operating Convenience: Several models have bars at the base so you can open the loading drawer with a touch of your toe if your hands are full. Others have special loading chutes so trash can be dropped inside without opening the drawer. Some compactors have indicator lights to let you know that they are operating or that they have jammed.

Price: Trash compactors cost from about $300 to $600, or more. Operating expenses, in addition to the purchase price, include the bags used for trash storage. Some models use ordinary plastic garbage bags or generic compactor bags that may be purchased at a supermarket or discount store, while others require special bags that must be bought from a dealer. You will also periodically need to replace the charcoal filters or the liquid or solid deodorant used in the deodorizing system.

Safety features: Safety features, such as key locks, prevent curious children from opening the trash drawer or operating the compactor accidentally. If you have children in the house, make sure the model you buy has a safety lock.

Sound insulation: Improved motor designs and increased insulation have reduced the operating noise of today's trash compactors. Also, faster operation and larger capacity mean the noise is emitted for shorter periods of time and less frequently.

Best Buys '91

Our Best Buy and Recommended food-waste disposers (divided into continuous-feed and batch-feed models) and trash compactors are listed below. The products are in descending order of quality within each category. Remember that a Best Buy or Recommended rating applies only to the model listed, not necessarily to other models built by the same manufacturer.

CONTINUOUS-FEED DISPOSERS

KITCHENAID KCDS250S

The KitchenAid KCDS250S is a well-made disposer with a powerful one-horsepower motor and an excellent warranty. Its full polystyrene insulation acts as a sound barrier to muffle operating noise, making this disposer extremely quiet. Its stainless-steel grinding chamber and shredder resist corrosion. Two 360-degree swivel impellers can reverse automatically to eliminate jams. This disposer has a dishwasher-drain connection.

Specifications: drain diameter, standard (1½"); **volts,** 120; **mounting,** quick mount. **Warranty: parts and labor,** seven years.

Approx. retail price	Approx. low price
$229	not available

IN-SINK-ERATOR CLASSIC

The In-Sink-Erator Classic has a strong one-horsepower motor and an excellent warranty. It includes automatic reversing action to prevent jams. If a jam occurs, it can be cleared manually with the small wrench that comes with the disposer. Thick polystyrene sound insulation deadens motor noise, making the Classic very quiet while in operation. This sturdy disposer has a corrosion-resistant stainless-steel grinding chamber, a tough nickel chrome shredder ring, and two 360-degree swivel impellers. The Classic has a dishwasher-drain connection.

Specifications: drain diameter, standard (1½"); **volts,** 120; **mounting,** quick mount. **Warranty: parts and labor,** seven years.

Approx. retail price	Approx. low price
$300	not available

SEARS KENMORE 6051

The Sears Kenmore 6051 is a continuous-feed disposer with a ¾-horsepower motor driving its stainless-steel impellers. It reverses automatically to resist jamming; if a jam does occur, a self-service wrench is included to clear the jam manually. The 6051 has a corrosion-resistant stainless-steel grinding chamber, shredder ring, and shredder plate. Full polystyrene sound insulation reduces operating noise. This disposer has a dishwasher-drain connection.

Specifications: drain diameter, standard (1½"); **volts,** 115; **mounting,** quick mount. **Warranty: parts and labor,** five years.

Approx. retail price	Approx. low price
$150	not available

Prices are accurate at time of printing; subject to manufacturer's change.

BATCH-FEED DISPOSERS

IN-SINK-ERATOR
CLASSIC L/C

The In-Sink-Erator Classic L/C is a heavy-duty disposer with a powerful one-horsepower motor that is activated when you turn the stopper. It is backed by a strong warranty. The Classic L/C includes automatic reversing action to prevent jams; if a jam does occur, you can clear it with the small wrench included with the disposer. This model has a very effective polystyrene sound barrier, reducing operating noise to a minimum. The Classic L/C has a stainless-steel grinding chamber and 360-degree swivel impellers, plus a polypropylene corrosion shield. It includes a dishwasher-drain connection.

Specifications: drain diameter, standard (1½"); **volts**, 115; **mounting**, quick mount. **Warranty: parts and labor**, seven years.

Approx. retail price	Approx. low price
$370	not available

GENERAL ELECTRIC
GFB1050G

The General Electric GFB1050G has a rugged ¾-horsepower motor with automatic reversing action to prevent jamming during the grinding operation. This batch-feed disposer has a drain housing made of corrosion-resistant glass-filled polyester, a nylon hopper, and stainless-steel impellers. The GFB1050G is activated by turning a stopper. It is fully insulated to muffle noise during operation.

Specifications: drain diameter, standard (1½"); **volts**, 115; **mounting**, quick mount. **Warranty: parts and labor**, one year.

Approx. retail price	Approx. low price
not available	$184

MAYTAG FB11   RECOMMENDED

The Maytag FB11 is a batch-feed disposer that is highly reliable. Its ½-horsepower motor does not have a full sound insulation shield, so it may be noisier than some other disposers. This model turns on automatically when its lid is dropped in place, and stops when the lid is removed. The FB11 has stainless-steel swivel impellers, which swing away from food wastes to prevent jamming. It has a dishwasher-drain connection.

Specifications: drain diameter, standard (1½"); **volts,** 115; **mounting,** quick mount. **Warranty: labor,** one year; **parts,** five years.

Approx. retail price	Approx. low price
not available	$234

TRASH COMPACTORS

BROAN 1050

The Broan 1050 is a slim compactor only 12 inches wide, so it takes up less space in the kitchen than some other models. This disposer can be installed under the counter or used as a free-standing unit anywhere in the kitchen. It delivers a powerful 5,000 pounds of compaction force. The door swings out to the side to remove trash bags, and has a toe release for hands-free loading. The entire drawer slides out for cleaning. The 1050 has a removable key lock and uses a solid deodorizer. A bag storage area is behind a flip-down door panel. This model comes with reversible almond/black and coffee/harvest front panels; a solid wood cutting-board top is optional.

Specifications: height, 34½"; **width,** 12"; **depth,** 20¼"; **volts,** 120. **Compaction force,** 5,000 pounds. **Warranty: parts and labor,** one year.

Approx. retail price	Approx. low price
$599	not available

WHIRLPOOL TF8600XT

The Whirlpool TF8600XT is a free-standing compactor with a special "Dense Pack" cycle that packs 20 percent more trash into a bag than the normal cycle. This unit is extremely quiet during operation, because of thick fiberglass insulation

Prices are accurate at time of printing; subject to manufacturer's change.

around the motor and gears and inside the cabinet. The TF8600XT delivers 2,300 pounds of compaction force. Its drawer opens with the touch of a toe for hands-free convenience, and a key lock insures safety. The TF8600XT includes a bag caddy, and uses a solid air freshener to deodorize. It comes with a reversible almond/black front panel. **Specifications: height**, 34¼"; **width**, 15"; **depth**, 24¼"; **volts**, 120. **Compaction force**, 2,300 pounds. **Warranty: parts and labor**, one year.

> **Approx. retail price**
> $449
>
> **Approx. low price**
> not available

KITCHENAID KUCS181T

✔BEST BUY

The KitchenAid KUCS181T is a high-quality convertible trash compactor providing 3,000 pounds of compaction force. A "litter bin" chute lets you load small items even while the compactor is operating. The trash basket tilts down for easy bag removal. The KUCS181T has a charcoal air filter and an odor-control fan. It includes a bag-storage compartment. This compactor comes with front panels in almond, white, black, or harvest wheat; a wood cutting-board top is optional.
Specifications: height, 34⅛"; **width**, 17¾"; **depth**, 24⅝"; **volts**, 115. **Compaction force:** 3,000 pounds. **Warranty, parts and labor**, one year; **motor**, five years.

> **Approx. retail price**
> $579
>
> **Approx. low price**
> not available

Vacuum Cleaners

Using a vacuum cleaner is not the back-breaking chore it was years ago. New models are lightweight, powerful, and easy to manipulate. They also have a greater range of features to clean a variety of surfaces including wall-to-wall carpeting, area rugs, vinyl tile, ceramic tile, marble, or hardwood. No matter what the type of flooring, regular cleaning is the best way to ensure beauty and longevity. Since today's vacuum cleaners tackle the task in less time and with less strain, proper floor care and maintenance is a breeze.

When shopping for a vacuum cleaner, keep your specific needs in mind. Your mother may have had an upright and you may have inherited a preference for this style, but be sure it's the best choice for your home and lifestyle. Don't be afraid to ask to actually sample some vacuum cleaners on the showroom floor. This is the only way to be sure you're making the perfect choice. Also, depending on the amount of space and stairs to be cleaned, you might want to throw away notions of a one-vacuum cleaner household (especially if children and/or pets are part of your family). Here's a descriptive breakdown explaining the advantages and disadvantages of each style to make vacuum cleaner selection simpler.

Upright and canister vacuum cleaners have different strengths and weaknesses. Your cleaning habits, as well as the size and type of the floors in your home, determine which kind of full-featured vacuum cleaner you should buy. Wet/dry and mini vacuum cleaners are useful for tackling spills.

Upright, Canister, or Powerhead Vacuum Cleaner?

An upright is best for rug and carpet cleaning. Its beater bar/brush digs up embedded dirt and grit from even high pile carpeting. Currently available uprights are more lightweight than other models, making them easier to handle on stairs, but they still cannot boast the maneuverability of a canister. The upright also generally loses to the canister in above-floor cleaning (like upholstery, window sills, etc.), since attachments to tackle these jobs are not as accessible and the upright doesn't roll along with the job as easily.

Canister vacuum cleaners are designed to make up for the shortcomings of uprights. The canister is usually quieter than the upright and does a fine job of cleaning bare floors and low-pile carpets. The nozzle's low-profile permits better access under furniture, into tight spaces, and on stair treads. The canister's easy-to-change attachments allow it to be used effectively to remove dust from walls, draperies, and lamp shades. Because it lacks the upright's beater bar/brush, the canister does not remove dirt that has sifted down into carpet pile as well. Most new canister models are extremely lightweight and maneuverable.

A strong canister vacuum cleaner with a powerhead combines the best of both the upright and the standard canister. It has a rolling tank (usually with a tool caddy), a hose, and a nozzle just like the canister, but it also has a powerhead, which is a beater/bar brush similar to those on uprights. When you shop for a powerhead, examine the brush roll carefully. Some have an independent motor that allows them to dig deeper into thick pile carpet, others have a turbo, or suction-driven, brush roll that has less strength but may still be adequate for your needs.

Mini Vacuum Cleaners

Compact vacuum cleaners come in many shapes and sizes. They are designed for quick spot cleanups of dry spills. These scaled-down units can be a great convenience, as long as you remember that compact vacuum cleaners are intended for small jobs. The motors on minis have limited power, and the dust bag or cup must be emptied often. Cordless minis are supremely portable and ideal for room-to-room touch-ups as well as car care. Corded models have greater strength and don't run out of juice, but you'll have to work with the same outlet area limitations that a regular vacuum cleaner has.

Wet/Dry Vacuum Cleaners

Wet/dry vacuum cleaners handle wet messes indoors and out. Full-size models quickly clean up a muddy garage or soapy washing machine overflow. Some feature a blower for added versatility. Cordless hand-held versions offer the ultimate convenience in quick clean-ups of spilled drinks or other small wet/dry spills.

Safety

As with any electrically powered product, you want to be sure that your vacuum cleaner will be safe to use. Look for the Underwriters Laboratories (UL) seal, which means the product meets their safety standards. Most major vacuum cleaner manufacturers will not introduce a vacuum cleaner to the public without this seal. All of the product selections in this chapter are UL listed.

Features and Terminology

Bag-full indicator: Some models have a signal light that lets you know when it is time to change the bag. This is an important feature because cleaning performance drops off considerably when the bag is full.

Cord reel: This feature provides for cord storage hidden within the vacuum body that automatically rewinds cord in a flash. Other vacuum cleaners require cording to be hand-wound around storage hooks on the outside of the cleaner.

Dust bag/cup: The dust bag should be large enough to avoid frequent changes but easy to change when necessary. Be sure the particular disposable bag size and style that your vacuum cleaner uses is readily available. Also check with the manufacturer to find out if your model has an optional reusable bag or a washable dust cup. Most new uprights have top-loading vacuum bags; this means that dust and dirt enter the bag from the top rather than being pushed up from the bottom. This takes stress off the motor and provides better/stronger vacuum cleaner performance.

Overall efficiency: You can get a good idea of a vacuum cleaner's efficiency by testing it on gritty, granular materials, such as sand or salt, which are difficult to pick up. Cotton fiber or fine powder may look bad on carpet, but they actually require very little suction to remove. After running the machine, examine the carpet pile to see if the substance was picked up or just pushed into the carpet.

Self-propulsion: Self-propelled machines glide easily over thick carpets with only gentle guidance from the user.

Suction selector: The control allows you to determine the amount of suction needed for cleaning jobs and is especially useful for cleaning draperies, upholstery, and delicate fibers. A concentration of suction can be used on areas with stubborn lint or pet hair.

Wattage, horsepower, or amps: Vacuum cleaner manufacturers rate the power of their product in different ways. To make it possible to compare the available models, ask your local dealer to convert horsepower or amps into watts. If he or she does not want to do this for you, contact the manufacturer directly. If you convert a cordless vacuum cleaner's power into watts, remember that the wattage only accounts for recharging. The vacuum cleaner itself is driven by a power cell battery, which runs at a higher rate of power than the wattage indicates.

Best Buys '91

Our Best Buy vacuum cleaners follow. They are arranged in the following categories: upright, canister, powerhead canister, mini, and wet/dry vacuum cleaners. These appliances have been selected on the basis of convenience, performance, and overall value. Within each category, the item we consider the best of the Best Buys is listed first, followed by our second choice, and so on. Remember that the Best Buy designation applies only to the model listed; it does not necessarily apply to other models made by the same manufacturer.

UPRIGHT VACUUM CLEANERS

HOOVER ELITE 600 (U4465-900)

✔ BEST BUY

The Hoover Elite 600 (U4465-900) is a powerful lightweight vacuum cleaner that delivers 705 watts and weighs about 12 pounds. A 12-inch brush roll; a cleaning nozzle with a brush on each side; top-fill, nine-quart bags; and quick-release extra-long, 31-foot cord are standard. An included five-piece attachment set has a six-foot hose, a wand, a crevice tool, a brush, and a converter.

Warranty: one year.

Approx. retail price	Approx. low price
$190	$156

PANASONIC DELUXE MC-6210

✔ BEST BUY

The Panasonic Deluxe MC-6210 is a well-designed upright that has an extra-wide (14-inch) metal agitator bar and 720 watts of power for heavy-duty cleaning. The MC-6210 weighs only 15⅗ pounds and has a 23-foot wraparound cord. It uses disposable dust bags with a ten-quart capacity and features a bag-full indicator. Optional attachment kits are available. A seven-piece kit (MC-670AS, $13) includes a hose, a two-piece extension wand, a dusting brush, a plastic wand, a crevice tool, and an upholstery nozzle. An eight-piece kit (MC-770AD, $30) includes the same items as kit MC-670, but the wands and the additional three-position floor nozzle are metal instead of plastic.

Warranty: one year.

Approx. retail price	Approx. low price
$215	$205

REGINA 7000

✔ BEST BUY

The Regina 7000 is quite a powerful vacuum cleaner. It also has one of the widest agitator bars on the market, measuring a full 16 inches. This model stores accessories and a hose right on board, making it almost as easy as a canister to clean with the permanently attached, exposed hose and the easy-to-reach attachments (two extension wands, upholstery brush, dusting brush, and crevice tool).

Warranty: one year.

Approx. retail price	Approx. low price
$139	not available

HOOVER U4581-910 LEGACY

The Hoover U4581-910 Legacy is a powerful vacuum cleaner, with a motor driven by 835 watts, but still comes in at a low price. The top-loading dust bag is generous at nine quarts, and the plastic agitator bar measures a standard 12 inches. The extra-long 35-foot cord is not automatically retractable, but it does feature a swiveling cord-release hook that releases the full coil of cord in one motion. The U4581-910 Legacy model is available in ultra blue deep and features a headlight and five-piece attachment set (including crevice tool, hose, extension wand, dusting brush, and furniture nozzle).

Warranty: one year.

Approx. retail price	Approx. low price
$270	$190

CANISTER VACUUM CLEANERS

ORECK SUPER BUSTER B (BB280D)

The Oreck Super Buster B (BB280D) weighs only 4 pounds, and still packs 550 watts of power. This good-looking canister is so compact, measuring only 12¼ inches by 4½ inches, that it can be carried around by a built-in canister handle. Attachments include a hose, bare floor and wall tool, utility tool with a 5-inch brush, crevice tool, three-piece wand set, and closet tool caddy. For added versatility, this vacuum cleaner also functions as a blower. The dust bags are disposable. In addi-

tion, the Super Buster B features a trouble indicator that alerts the user to obstructions or lets you know when the bag is full.
Warranty: motor, two years; **case**, ten years.

Approx. retail price	Approx. low price
$125	not available

SANYO SC27

The Sanyo SC27's a true bargain because of high wattage (850 watts). It even has a retractable cord, an unusual treat for a canister in this price range and at this low 6⅝-pound weight. It features a removable dust cup, eliminating the need for purchasing disposable paper bags. Attachments include a crevice tool and round brush. There's a storage hook on this attractive red-and-black vacuum cleaner.
Warranty: one year.

Approx. retail price	Approx. low price
$75	$71

SHARP EC-6310

The Sharp EC-6310 is easily portable because it weighs only seven pounds. This white canister has red accents and offers 800 watts of power. Its features include an 18-foot retractable cord. The attachments include a hose, a suction nozzle, an upholstery brush, a round brush, a crevice tool, and a three-piece extension wand.
Warranty: one year.

Approx. retail price	Approx. low price
$130	$119

POWERHEAD CANISTER VACUUM CLEANERS

METRO OMNIVAC OV3ABC

The Metro Omnivac OV3ABC pairs a powerful motor with compact design. It's a powerhead canister vacuum cleaner lightweight enough to tow with the included shoulder strap. It weighs only eight pounds, but the OV3ABC has an all-steel canister for durability. With 800 watts of power and an 11-inch-wide agitator bar, this vacuum cleaner can handle heavy-duty jobs. It also converts to a power blower for sweeping walkways and workshops as well as inflating toys and air mattresses. The permanent cloth bag holds two quarts, the cord measures 20 feet, and the hose measures 6½ feet. Attachments include the powerhead, two wands, nozzle, crevice tool, dusting brush, floor/wall brush, inflator, shoulder strap, and hose.

Warranty: motor, two years; **parts and labor**, one year.

Approx. retail price	Approx. low price
$215	$207

HOOVER SPECTRUM S3575

The Hoover Spectrum S3575 is a no-nonsense lifetime unit with proven durability, quality, and features. It boasts an impressive 1000 watts of power behind the suction, and the sturdy steel agitator bar length is generous at 14 inches. Features include a large seven-quart dust bag, six-foot hose, better-than-average 25-foot cord, and a bag-full indicator. A four-piece tool kit is included (dusting brush, furniture nozzle, crevice tool, and bare floor brush). This vacuum cleaner is manageable at about 24 pounds.

Warranty: one year.

Approx. retail price	Approx. low price
$400	$316

BLACK & DECKER CA1440

The Black & Decker CA1440 is a colorful (maroon and black), powerful vacuum cleaner with 1150 watts of strength. The agitator bar measures ten inches, the hose is 5½ feet long, and the retractable cord is a convenient 16⅖ feet long. The disposable dust bags hold five quarts of debris. This unit is not a lightweight at 29 pounds. Instead, its value is based on quality construction and durability. Attachments include a crevice tool, furniture brush, floor tool, and upholstery tool.

Warranty: two years.

Approx. retail price	Approx. low price
$240	not available

EUREKA IRONSIDES 1799

The Eureka Ironsides 1799—a sturdy, old reliable—has a headlight, a 20-foot retractable cord, and an eight-piece attached tool kit. The kit includes a 6½-foot hose, two chrome wands, a motorized powerhead, a dusting brush, an upholstery brush, a floor/wall brush, and a crevice tool. The disposable dust bag holds 4⅖ quarts.

Warranty: one year.

Approx. retail price	Approx. low price
$400	$244

MINI VACUUM CLEANERS

PANASONIC MC-1060 JET FLO

The Panasonic MC-1060 Jet Flo, a corded mini packed with power, surpasses cordless versions in strength and effectiveness. A rotating agitator bar, ample 25-foot cord, and headlight make it efficient and convenient. The Jet Flo also features a two-speed suction control, rubber furniture-guard bumper, and includes a dusting brush accessory.

Warranty: one year.

Approx. retail price	Approx. low price
$76	$68

METRO VAC 'N' BLO JR. VM-12-IDA

The Metro Vac 'N' Blo Jr. VM-12-IDA has as many attachments as a full-size vacuum cleaner, and it has the power to handle full-size jobs, too, thanks to corded operation. It's constructed of sturdy steel yet weighs less than three pounds. It has a one-pint dust cup, a 15-foot cord, and a three-foot hose attachment. Other attachments include a 20-inch extension wand, crevice tool, dusting brush, pick-all nozzle, inflator adaptor, and shoulder strap.

Warranty: one year.

Approx. retail price	Approx. low price
$60	$57

SANYO PC5L

The Sanyo PC5L is a no-nonsense hand vacuum cleaner. It's a compact wide-mouth cordless that has an attachment to convert the cleaner to a hand-held emergency searchlight. It also comes with a crevice tool and features a standard no-paper-filter dust cup. The PC5L weighs less than two pounds.

Warranty: one year.

Approx. retail price	Approx. low price
$35	not available

WET/DRY VACUUM CLEANERS

SHOP VAC WET/DRY WITH POWER BLOWER (333-40)

The Shop Vac Wet/Dry with Power Blower (333-40) is a full-size vacuum cleaner that's sturdy and simply designed. It cleans up messes indoors and out, and has an ample 10-gallon dry capacity (8 gallon wet). The vacuum cleaner is made of dent- and rust-resistant plastic, styled in orange and black. The unit can convert to a hand-held electric blower. It features automatic shutoff to prevent overflow. Its accessories include a seven-foot hose, two extension wands, a wet/dry nozzle with a squeegee insert, four caster wheels, foam filter sleeve and paper filter bag, and blower attachments. Hundreds of optional accessories are available from car cleaning tools to upholstery cleaning attachments.

Warranty: limited, two years.

Approx. retail price	Approx. low price
$130	$107

Prices are accurate at time of printing; subject to manufacturer's change.

BLACK & DECKER DB4000
POWERPRO DUSTBUSTER
PLUS

The Black & Decker DB4000 PowerPro Dustbuster Plus is a cordless, hand-held, wet/dry vacuum cleaner. This plastic vacuum cleaner is white with a gray see-through bowl. It weighs slightly under four pounds and comes with a crevice tool, a ceiling wand, and a furniture brush. The debris cup holds up to eight ounces.

Warranty: 30-day money-back guarantee; two years.

Approx. retail price	Approx. low price
$71	$53

ORECK WD69

The Oreck WD69 is a moderately sized wet/dry vac that holds up to five gallons of dry debris and three gallons of wet debris. It comes with an impressive array of 12 attachments that handle everything from draining water from a sink drain to dusting. A wider-than-average hose and the extension wands make it acceptable for cleaning bulky messes. It also functions as a power blower and rolls around on four caster wheels. It's made of high-impact plastic, styled in almond with brown accents, and weighs only 13 pounds.

Warranty: motor, one year; **five-gallon container**, five years.

Approx. retail price	Approx. low price
$98	not available

Clothes Washers

Clothes washers have become one of the American household's most indispensable timesavers. Once found only in utility rooms and basements, clothes washers are now also found in closets, hallways, and attics. Some of the new, innovatively designed models will fit in tight spaces in your home that you may never have considered before.

Modular Parts and Microelectronics

The use of modular internal parts is making washing machine repairs easier and less expensive. Modular snap-in and snap-out parts facilitate in-home maintenance. For this reason, be sure the washer you purchase has front access to its mechanical parts.

Electronic touch controls are now used in some washing machines. You program the machine to select a wash/rinse or drying cycle appropriate to the kind of load, and the washer cleans your clothes automatically.

Energy-Saving Features

Clothes washers can have many energy-saving features. Some machines automatically rinse with cold water. Rinsing a typical load of wash with cold instead of warm water reduces energy consumption by up to eight percent. Some machines use less water for a standard load. Mini baskets and small-load features also save on water consumption.

Federal law requires clothes washers to carry an energy label stating the expected annual operating cost of the appliance based on a power cost of 8.04 cents per kilowatt-hour. The actual cost of your power is likely to differ, but this figure is a standard that you can use when comparing the energy efficiency of different models.

Safety Factors

A washer is a potentially lethal combination of 220 volts of electricity and a tub of water. As with all electrical devices, look for the Underwriters Laboratories (UL) seal, which indicates the machine meets their stringent safety requirements.

If you have young children, look for a lid switch that stops the agitator or spin action when the lid is raised. Some washers have an automatic lock that will not allow the lid to be opened during the spin cycle.

For most brand-name models, the Association of Home Appliance Manufacturers offers you a bit of consumer protection in addition to the manufacturer's warranty. If you take steps recommended by the manufacturer to resolve any problems and still feel the manufacturer has not backed the product to your satisfaction, you can appeal to the Major Appliance Consumer Action Panel. For details about this independent complaint resolution group, write to AHAM, 20 N. Wacker Dr., Chicago, Illinois 60606.

Features and Terminology

Capacity: Tub sizes range from 1½ cubic feet to 3 cubic feet, but there is no standardized terminology for machine capacity. Some machines of standard capacity are labeled "large" capacity, which can be confusing. Large items such as queen and king-size bedding require the largest-capacity machines.

Cycles: Three wash cycles (regular, permanent press, and delicate) and a soak setting can handle most household laundry chores. Cycles can be preset prior to each load (semiprogrammed) or entirely automatic (fully programmed).

Lint filter: This mechanism filters lint out of the rinse water and keeps it from being deposited on your clothes. A lint filter should be easy to remove and clean if necessary. Many machines have self-cleaning filters.

Load-balance stabilizer: When a load becomes unbalanced, some washers buzz a warning, some shut off, and others slow down and compensate automatically for the imbalance. The buzzer system is generally the most effective, assuming you are within earshot and can redistribute the load.

Speed: Most machines offer two speeds, but there are other combinations. Normal agitate/normal spin and slow agitate/slow spin are the most common.

Water temperature: Several combinations of hot, warm, and cold water temperatures are available for wash and rinse cycles. A warm rather than hot rinse is kinder to clothes and more energy efficient; a warm-rinse cycle may add $40 to the cost of the machine. A cold-rinse cycle is often as effective as a warm one and more energy efficient.

Best Buys '91

Our Best Buy clothes washers follow, arranged in the following categories: large-capacity, standard-capacity, and compact washers, and over-and-under combination washers and dryers. The machines within a category are listed in order of quality. The best of the Best Buys is first, followed by our second choice, and so on. A Best Buy designation applies only to the model listed. It does not necessarily mean that other models by the same manufacturer are equally satisfactory.

LARGE-CAPACITY WASHERS

MAYTAG A412

The Maytag A412 is a well-made, large-capacity clothes washer. This single-speed washer has a ⅓-horsepower motor. It has two cycles (regular and permanent press), four water levels, and three temperature settings for wash and rinse, hot/cold, warm/cold, and cold/cold. Other features include a lint filter and fabric softener dispenser. It comes in white, almond, and harvest wheat.

Prices are accurate at time of printing; subject to manufacturer's change.

Specifications: height, 43⅝"; width, 25½"; depth, 27"; volts/amps, 120/15. Warranty: labor, one year; parts, two years; cabinet against rust (parts only) five years; transmission (parts only), ten years.

Approx. retail price
not available

Approx. low price
$580

WHITE-WESTINGHOUSE LA400M

✔ BEST BUY

The White-Westinghouse LA400M represents good value in a single-speed, large-capacity clothes washer. It has a ½-horsepower motor. It has three water levels, three temperature settings (all with cold rinse), and eight cycles: three timed regular cycles, three permanent press cycles, delicates, and soak/prewash. The LA400M has a self-cleaning lint filter and a water-saver control. It comes in white or almond.

Specifications: height, 43⅝"; width, 27"; depth, 27"; volts/amps, 115/15. Warranty: parts and labor, one year; transmission (parts only), five years; tub, parts and labor, 25 years.

Approx. retail price
not available

Approx. low price
$409

WHIRLPOOL LA5580XT

✔ BEST BUY

The Whirlpool LA5580XT is a good quality, two-speed, large-capacity clothes washer. This model has a ½-horsepower motor. It has seven cycles: super wash, regular/heavy, regular/normal, permanent press/normal, permanent press/light, knits/gentle normal, and knits/gentle light. The LA5580XT has four water-level settings and three wash/rinse water temperature settings—hot/cold, warm/cold, and cold/cold.

Specifications: height, 42⅜"; width, 26⅞"; depth, 25½"; volts/amps, 120/NA. Warranty: parts and labor, one year; gear case assembly and top against rust, five years; outer tub, ten years.

Approx. retail price
$449

Approx. low price
$409

Prices are accurate at time of printing; subject to manufacturer's change.

MAGIC CHEF W20H-2

The Magic Chef W20H-2 is a good quality, two-speed, large-capacity clothes washer. It has a powerful ¾-horsepower motor, dial controls, bleach dispenser, and self-cleaning lint filter. The W20H-2 has four wash/rinse water temperature settings—hot/warm, hot/cold, warm/cold, and cold/cold. It has four water-level settings and three cycles—cotton and linen, permanent press, and knits/delicates. This model comes in white or almond.

Specifications: height, 44"; **width**, 27"; **depth**, 27"; **volts/amps**, 120/15. **Warranty: parts and labor**, one year; **wash basket and outer tub (parts only)**, ten years; **transmission (parts only)**, ten years.

Approx. retail price	**Approx. low price**
$389	not available

STANDARD-CAPACITY WASHERS

MAYTAG A112

The Maytag A112 is a sturdy, standard-capacity, single-speed clothes washer. The tub, hoses, and other parts are well made and reliable. It has a ⅓-horsepower motor and two cycles, regular and permanent press. The A112 has three water-level settings and three wash/rinse temperature settings—hot/cold, warm/cold, and cold/cold. This unit has a lint filter and a bleach dispenser. It comes in white, almond, or harvest wheat.

Specifications: height, 43⅝"; **width**, 25½"; **depth**, 27"; **volts/amps**, 120/15. **Warranty: parts and labor**, one year; **parts**, two years; **cabinet against rust (parts only)**, five years; **transmission (parts only)**, ten years.

Approx. retail price	**Approx. low price**
$510	$495

WHIRLPOOL LA5700XT

The Whirlpool LA5700XT is a good quality, two-speed, standard-capacity clothes washer. It has a powerful ½-horsepower motor. Its eight wash cycles are super wash, regular/ heavy, regular/normal, permanent press/normal, permanent press/light, knits/gentle normal, knits/gentle light, and soak. The LA5700XT has easy-to-use dial controls, four wash/rinse water temperature selections, and four water-level settings. It has a self-cleaning lint filter, bleach dispenser, and comes in white or almond.

Specifications: height, 42⅜"; **width**, 26⅞"; **depth**, 25½"; **volts/ amps**, 120/NA. **Warranty: parts and labor**, one year; **gear case assembly and top against rust**, five years; **outer tub**, ten years.

Approx. retail price	**Approx. low price**
$470	$446

GENERAL ELECTRIC WWA5800M

✔**BEST BUY**

The General Electric WWA5800M is a standard-capacity, single-speed clothes washer that has the features most users need, including a mini-tub for delicates and small items. It has four water-level selections, three wash temperatures, all with cold rinse; and six cycles (regular heavy, regular normal, regular light, regular soak, permanent press normal, and permanent press light). It has a lint filter but no bleach or fabric softener dispenser. It comes in white or almond.

Specifications: height, 42½"; **width**, 27"; **depth**, 25"; **volts/ amps**, 115/15 or 20. **Warranty: parts and labor**, one year; **transmission (parts only)**, five years.

Approx. retail price	**Approx. low price**
not available	$385

HOTPOINT WLW2500B

✔**BEST BUY**

The Hotpoint WLW2500B is a sturdy, two-speed, standard-capacity clothes washer. It has three water-level settings and three wash/rinse temperature settings. Its six wash cycles are regular heavy, regular normal, regular light, regular soak, permanent press, and knits/delicates. It has a self-cleaning lint filter and bleach dispenser but no fabric softener dispenser. This model comes in white or almond.

Specifications: height, 42½"; **width**, 27"; **depth**, 25"; **volts/**

Prices are accurate at time of printing; subject to manufacturer's change.

CLOTHES WASHERS

amps, 115/15 or 20. **Warranty: parts and labor,** one year; **transmission (parts only),** five years.

Approx. retail price	Approx. low price
not available	$355

COMPACT WASHERS

WHITE-WESTINGHOUSE LT150L

The White-Westinghouse LT150L is a compact, front-loading clothes washer that can be stacked or installed under the counter with its matching dryer. Instead of an agitator, its two-directional tumbling action is said to require less water for a full load, and, as a result, less soap, bleach, and energy. The electronically controlled motor eliminates the need for a transmission, so you never have to pay for what is considered the most expensive part of a washer to repair. It has three water levels, three temperature settings (all with cold rinse), a lint filter, and four cycles—regular, permanent press, delicates, and prewash/soak. It comes in white or almond.
Specifications: height, 34⅝"; **width,** 27"; **depth,** 25½"; **volts/amps,** 120/15. **Warranty: parts and labor,** one year; **drive (parts only),** five years.

Approx. retail price	Approx. low price
not available	$646

WHIRLPOOL LC4900XT

The Whirlpool LC4900XT is a compact, portable/convertible, two-speed clothes washer that has many of the features found on full-size models, including a powerful ½-horsepower motor. Paired with its matching clothes dryer, the machines allow you to fit an entire laundry center into a tight space. This is a great advantage if space is a crucial problem, but the capacity of this machine is 1½ cubic feet compared to 2⅖ cubic feet in a standard-size machine. This model has six cycles: super wash, regular/heavy, permanent press, knits/gentle, soak, and prewash. It has four water levels and four wash/rinse

Prices are accurate at time of printing; subject to manufacturer's change.
406   CONSUMER GUIDE®

CLOTHES WASHERS

water temperature settings: hot/warm, hot/cold, warm/cold, and cold/cold. The LC4900XT comes with casters and a faucet attachment, or it can be permanently installed with an optional conversion kit. It comes in white or almond.

Specifications: height, 32½"; **width,** 23⅞"; **depth,** 23⅝"; **volts/amps,** not available. **Warranty: parts and labor,** one year; **gear assembly and top against rust,** five years; **outer tub,** ten years.

Approx. retail price	Approx. low price
$489	$461

OVER-AND-UNDER COMBINATIONS

MAYTAG SE1000/SG1000

The Maytag SE1000 (electric dryer) or SG1000 (gas dryer) is a full-size, top-loading washer with a stacked full-size electric or gas dryer. Both machines are controlled by a single set of electronic touch controls located at eye level. The single-speed, ⅓-horsepower washer has three wash/rinse water temperature settings: hot/warm, warm/warm, and cold/warm. It has three wash cycles: regular, permanent press, and delicates/knits. The washer also has bleach and fabric softener dispensers, a lint filter, and adjustable wash and soak times. The dryer has a sensor control that detects when clothes are dry and shuts off automatically. It has regular, permanent press, air fluff, and timed cycles and a delicate temperature setting. It is available in white or almond.

Specifications: height, 73"; **width,** 27½"; **depth,** 27½"; **volts/amps,** (washer) 115/15; (electric dryer) 240/30, (gas dryer) 115/30. **Warranty: parts and labor,** one year; **parts,** two years; **electronic controls and cabinets, stand and tumbler against rust (parts only),** five years; **transmission (parts only),** ten years.

Approx. retail price	Approx. low price
not available (SE1000)	$1,182
not available (SG1000)	$1,215

Prices are accurate at time of printing; subject to manufacturer's change.

FRIGIDAIRE LCE462L

✔ BEST BUY

The Frigidaire LCE462L, also called Skinny-Mini, is a compact, two-speed top-loading washer with a stacked compact dryer. It has three wash cycles: regular, permanent press, and knit/delicate. The LCE462L has three water level settings and four water temperature settings: hot/cold, warm/cold, warm/warm, and cold/cold. The washer has a ½-horsepower motor, a self-cleaning lint filter, and a bleach dispenser. The electric dryer has both timed and automatic cycles for regular, permanent press, knit/delicates, and air fluff cycles. It has four drying temperatures and an end-of-cycle signal. Available colors are white and almond.

Specifications: height, 65⅞"; **width,** 24"; **depth,** 27⅛"; **volts/amps,** 120-208 or 120-240/30. **Warranty: parts and labor,** one year; **washer transmission (parts only),** five years; **inner wash basket,** 25 years.

Approx. retail price	Approx. low price
$679	$678

Clothes Dryers

Different types of clothes and washable household items require different drying procedures for satisfactory results. Towels, for example, require high drying temperatures. For permanent press sportswear, on the other hand, you should use lower temperatures and a cycle that ends with a cooldown. If many of your clothes are permanent press, be sure your new dryer has a permanent press cycle.

Gas or Electric?

Natural gas clothes dryers generally cost $20 to $40 more than electric ones, but in most parts of the country, they cost about two-thirds as much to operate. Both gas and electric dryers come in full-size and compact models; you can also get small-capacity portable electric units. Gas dryers must be installed permanently because they are attached to the gas line and vented to the outside. Most gas models include an energy-saving electronic-ignition system; the burner ignites after the power has been turned on.

Features and Terminology

Air fluff: On this setting, the machine tumbles the load without heat; it is used for drying or freshening pillows, down jackets, and blankets.

Controls: Three kinds of controls are available. A timed control permits you to run the machine for a period of an hour or longer. An automatic control can be set for the desired degree of dryness. An electronic control senses when the load is dry and shuts off the dryer.

Drying cycles: Three basic cycles handle most kinds of fabric: regular, permanent press, and air fluff. A permanent press cycle has a cool-down period of about five minutes, during which the drum rotates with the heat off. This cycle minimizes heat-set wrinkles and should bring the load to room temperature. A delicate or gentle cycle runs on low heat.

Dryness sensor: This is a safeguard against overdrying; it detects the moisture content of the clothes or of the dryer's exhaust, and automatically shuts off the unit when the humidity reaches a certain level.

Lint filter: An effective lint filter is essential to the performance of a dryer. It should be accessible and easy to remove for cleaning. Some lint filters have audible alerts that signal when they are full.

Drying rack: If you frequently wash sneakers or other items that you would prefer to dry without tumbling, get a model that comes with a drying rack.

Wrinkle prevention: This fabric-care system is convenient if you are unable to unload your dryer as soon as it stops. The unit continues to tumble the load intermittently without heat for as long as two and a half hours. On some models a buzzer sounds at intervals during this period.

Consumer Protection

All our selections are backed with an extra bit of consumer protection if you should ever need it. If you have problems with any of most brand-name dryers, follow all of the manufacturer's recommendations to resolve them, and you still are not satisfied, you can appeal to the Major Appliance Consumer Action Panel. For details about this complaint resolution group, contact the Association of Home Appliance Manufacturers, 20 N. Wacker Dr., Chicago, Illinois 60606.

Best Buys '91

Our Best Buy and Recommended clothes dryers follow, divided into the following categories: large-capacity dryers, standard-capacity dryers, and compact dryers. Because gas and electric conversions of the same dryer are most often identical except for their model numbers and the power source they use, we give the two model numbers at the beginning of the product review and discuss the product features as they apply to both. If there are distinctions between the gas and electric versions of a model, these differences are itemized. If a particular model is unavailable in a gas or electric version, this is also stated.

Remember that a Best Buy or Recommended designation applies only to the model listed. It does not necessarily apply to other models made by the same manufacturer.

LARGE-CAPACITY CLOTHES DRYERS

MAYTAG DE512/DG512

✓**BEST BUY**

The Maytag DE512 (electric) or DG512 (gas) is a large-capacity clothes dryer equipped with a thermostat that measures exhaust air temperature and shuts the machine off automatically (after the cool-down period) when the load is dry. There are two heat settings: regular and delicate. You can also run an air fluff cycle for up to 20 minutes. The other cycles are timed drying for up to 60 minutes, automatic regular with adjustable degrees of dryness, and automatic permanent press with adjustable degrees of dryness. A buzzer alerts you when the cycle is done. A diagonal airflow pattern during operation is said to provide improved performance, even at low temperatures. The model is available in white, almond, or harvest wheat.

Specifications: height, 43⅝"; **width**, 28½"; **depth**, 27"; **volts/amps**, 240/30 (electric), 120/15 (gas); **venting**, two-way; **lint trap location**, front, in opening. **Warranty: parts and labor**, one year; **parts only**, two years; **cabinet against rust**, five years; **transmission**, ten years.

Approx. retail price	Approx. low price
$485	$460
(DE512)	
$530	$488
(DG512)	

Prices are accurate at time of printing; subject to manufacturer's change.

WHITE-WESTINGHOUSE
DE400K/DG400K

The White-Westinghouse DE400K (electric) or DG400K (gas) is a value-priced, large-capacity clothes dryer. It has a timer cycle with three temperature settings: regular, low, and air fluff. This model has four leveling legs and comes in white or almond.

Specifications: height, 43⅝"; **width**, 26⅞"; **depth**, 27"; **volts/ amps**, 120 or 240/30 or 120 or 208/30 (electric); 120/15 (gas); **venting**, four-way (electric); three-way (gas); **lint trap location**, front, bottom of access. **Warranty: parts and labor**, one year.

Approx. retail price	Approx. low price
not available (DE400K)	$319
not available (DG400K)	$352

MAGIC CHEF
YE20H-3/YG20H-3

The Magic Chef YE20H-3 (electric) or YG20H-3 (gas) is a good-quality, dial-controlled, large-capacity clothes dryer. It has two automatic drying cycles—cotton/linen and permanent press. The machine shuts off automatically when the load reaches the degree of dryness you select. It also has a timed cycle of up to 100 minutes. Other features are an end-of-cycle alert with nonvariable volume and an optional drying rack. It comes in white or almond.

Specifications: height, 44"; **width**, 27"; **depth**, 27"; **volts/amps**, 220 or 240/30 (electric), 120/15 (gas); **venting**, four-way (electric); three-way (gas); **lint trap location**, front, bottom of access. **Warranty: parts and labor**, one year.

Approx. retail price	Approx. low price
$349 (YE20H-3)	not available
$399 (YG20H-3)	not available

Prices are accurate at time of printing; subject to manufacturer's change.

STANDARD-CAPACITY CLOTHES DRYERS

HOTPOINT
DLB2650B/DLL2650B

The Hotpoint DLB2650B (electric) and DLL2650B (gas) is a fully featured, reliable, standard-capacity clothes dryer. It has a timed cycle of up to 50 minutes and four automatic cycles for heavy fabric, normal fabric, permanent press, and knits. The unit shuts off automatically after a humidity sensor detects the load has been dried to the preselected level. Other features are an adjustable-volume end-of-cycle signal, porcelain-enamel drum, wrinkle prevention, a drum light, and an air fluff setting. **Specifications: height,** 42½"; **width,** 27"; **depth,** 25"; **volts/amps,** 120 or 240/30 (electric), 120/15 or 20 (gas); **venting,** four-way (electric), three-way (gas); **lint trap location,** front, bottom of access. **Warranty: parts and labor,** one year.

Approx. retail price	Approx. low price
not available (DLB2650B)	$296
not available (DLL2650B)	$332

WHIRLPOOL
LE5800XS/LG5800XS

The Whirlpool LE5800XS (electric) or LG5800XS (gas) is a durable, energy-saving clothes dryer with multiple fabric-care selections. With the infinitely variable temperature control, you can choose the right amount of heat for the load. The six drying cycles are automatic regular, automatic permanent press (with cool-down cycle), timed drying up to 70 minutes, damp dry, air fluff, and tumble press. The full-width hamper door folds down to give you work space. There is an audible signal at the end of each cycle and when the lint filter needs cleaning. Available colors are white and almond.

Prices are accurate at time of printing; subject to manufacturer's change.

CLOTHES DRYERS

Specifications: height, 42⅜"; **width,** 29"; **depth,** 25¹³⁄₁₆" (electric), 26³⁄₁₆" (gas); **volts/amps,** 240/NA (electric), 110/NA (gas); **venting,** one-way; **lint trap location,** top rear, right. **Warranty: parts and labor,** one year.

Approx. retail price	Approx. low price
$349	not available
(LE5800XS)	
$399	not available
(LG5800XS)	

GENERAL ELECTRIC
DDE7500G/DDG7580G

✓ **BEST BUY**

The General Electric DDE7500G (electric) or DDG7580G (gas) is a reliable, standard-capacity clothes dryer. Two automatic cycles, regular and permanent press, dry the load until it reaches the degree of dryness you select. It also has a timed-drying cycle of up to 70 minutes. Temperature selections are high, medium, low, and air fluff. This model features an end-of-cycle alert with variable volume, wrinkle prevention, and a durable, porcelain enamel drum. It comes in white or almond. **Specifications: height,** 43½"; **width,** 27"; **depth,** 25"; **volts/amps,** 120 or 240/30 (electric), 120/15 or 20 (gas); **venting,** four-way (electric), three-way (gas); **lint trap location,** front, bottom of access. **Warranty: parts and labor,** one year.

Approx. retail price	Approx. low price
not available	$343
(DDE7500G)	
not available	$386
(DDG7580G)	

COMPACT CLOTHES DRYERS

WHITE-WESTINGHOUSE
DE250K/DG250K

✓ **BEST BUY**

The White-Westinghouse DE250K (electric) or DG250K (gas) is an economical, compact clothes dryer that can be stacked above the brand's LT250L Space Mates front-loading clothes washer. It has two automatic cycles—auto dry and auto permanent press—as well as timed dry. This model has four temperature settings, wrinkle prevention, and an end-of-cycle alert with variable volume.

Specifications: height, 34⅝"; **width**, 27"; **depth**, 25½"; **volts/amps**, 120/208 or 120/240/30 (electric), 120/15 (gas); **venting**, three-way (electric), two-way (gas); **lint trap location**, front, bottom of access. **Warranty: parts and labor**, one year.

Approx. retail price	Approx. low price
not available	$406
(DE250K)	
not available	$443
(DG250K)	

WHIRLPOOL
LE4930XT/LG4931XT

The Whirlpool LE4930XT (electric) or the LG4931XT (gas) is an economical, compact clothes dryer. It stacks neatly above a companion clothes washer and fits in tight spaces. This model has timed drying for regular/heavy, permanent press, and air fluff cycles, as well as an end-of-cycle signal. While its best feature is that it fits in tight spaces, its drawback is that it dries a load half the size handled by large-capacity dryers. It comes in white or almond.

Specifications: height, 32"; **width**, 23⅞"; **depth**, 21¹⁵⁄₁₆"; **volts/amps**, 120/15 (electric), 240/15 (gas); **venting**, one-way; **lint trap location**, inside, back of drum. **Warranty: parts and labor**, one year.

Approx. retail price	Approx. low price
$399	$333
(LE4930XT)	
$389	$366
(LG4931XT)	

Prices are accurate at time of printing; subject to manufacturer's change.

Air Conditioners

A room air conditioner can be a big help in escaping summer's heat and humidity. If you want the largest selection and the lowest prices, don't wait until the hot weather arrives to start shopping. Stores offer the broadest selection and preseason price specials in early spring. If you shop in the fall, prices will be even lower, but selection may be limited.

Room air conditioners are a good choice for many families because they are much less expensive to purchase and to operate than a central air conditioning system. If the air conditioner you select has sufficient cooling capacity, you can close off and cool a single room or a particular area of your home.

Energy Efficiency

Today's room air conditioners are more energy efficient than ever before. Under provisions of a federal law that took effect January 1, 1990, energy-efficiency standards for air conditioners have been made stricter. All room air conditioners manufactured after that date must now have an Energy Efficiency Rating (EER) of at least 8.0. (The EER is computed by dividing cooling capacity, measured in British thermal units per hour, or Btuh, by the watts of power used.) All the models listed here have very high ratings, making them particularly energy efficient.

The federal government requires all air conditioners to carry a bright-yellow energy label giving cost-of-operation information, including the EER. The higher the EER, the more efficient the air conditioner and the lower its operating cost. Even though a model with a high EER may carry a higher price tag, you will save money in the long run in lower electricity bills.

Your Cooling Needs

You want to buy a room air conditioner with enough cooling capacity for your needs. If a unit is too small, your room will never be sufficiently cool. If a unit is too large, it will not dehumidify properly, and the room will be uncomfortable and clammy. Also, large units tend to be noisier than smaller ones. Sometimes it is better to buy two or three smaller units than one large one. This allows you to cool the rooms you use most, only when you are using them.

Area to Be Cooled (in square feet)	Cooling Capacity (in Btuh)
Up to 150	4,000-5,000
150-250	5,000-6,000
250-450	6,000-8,500
450-600	8,500-11,000
600-900	11,000-15,000
900-1,200	15,000-19,000

Features and Terminology

Efficiency in both performance and energy should be your primary concern when you buy an air conditioner. But you should also consider moisture-removal rates. If the air is cool but humid, you will not feel comfortable. All the models listed here have good moisture-removal rates for their size.

Air movement: Look for fully adjustable louvers and vents that let you adjust air movement in different directions. Avoid units with motor-driven louvers.

Electrical requirements: Room air conditioners operate on 115-volt or 230-volt circuits. Most household outlets are 115 volts, 15 amps. The National Electrical Code allows a room air conditioner rated at 115 volts and 7½ amps or less to use this circuit. An appliance branch circuit (115 volts and 15 amps) is a special circuit provided only for the connection of a major appliance. The code allows a room air conditioner rated at 115 volts and 12 amps or less to use this circuit. Appliances requiring greater power are generally operated on a 230-volt circuit installed by an electrician.

Energy savers: Energy-efficient models usually have fans that turn on and off with the compressor instead of running continuously. This action can be automatic, or you may have to start it yourself.

Filters: The filter should be cleaned or replaced at the start of the cooling season and then cleaned once a month during the season. Some models have a visual signal that reminds you to clean the filter. Make sure that the air conditioner you choose has an easily accessible filter.

Thermostatic controls: This numbered dial or series of buttons alters the frequency with which the compressor turns on and off. Some thermostatic controls have one or more fan-only setting that run without the compressor.

Best Buys '91

Our Best Buy and Recommended air conditioners follow. They are arranged in three categories, according to their cooling capacity. The categories are 5,000 to 8,000 Btuh, 8,000 to 10,000 Btuh, and over 10,000 Btuh. Within each category, the units are listed in order of quality. The best of the Best Buys is first, followed by our second choice, and so on. A Best Buy or Recommended designation applies only to the model listed; it does not necessarily apply to other models made by the same manufacturer.

AIR CONDITIONERS FROM 5,000 TO 8,000 BTUH

GENERAL ELECTRIC AME06LA

The General Electric AME06LA (EER, 9.5) is a 6,000 Btuh model that offers efficient cooling and quiet operation. It includes a 12-hour delay start/stop timer to turn the unit on or off at a preset time. The AME06LA has a sliding electronic thermostat and three fan speeds, including an ultra-low setting for quiet nighttime use, plus a fan-only setting. This model also has an air exchanger and an energy-saver switch. Its louvers are fully adjustable to send cool air to every corner of the room. The AME06LA's washable filter is easily removed by snapping off the woodgrain front panel.

Specifications: height, 13⁷/₁₆"; **width,** 20¾"; **depth,** 19¹⁵/₁₆"; **weight,** 66 pounds; **maximum window width,** not available; **watts,** 630; **volts,** 115; **amps,** 5.6; **moisture removal rate,** 1³/₁₀ pints per hour; **air delivery,** 220 maximum cubic feet per minute. **Warranty: parts and labor,** one year; **sealed system,** five years.

Approx. retail price	Approx. low price
not available	$460

CARRIER ZMB7051

The Carrier ZMB7051 (EER, 9.0) is a compact air conditioner that provides 5,400 Btuh of cooling power and is quite efficient for its size. It has three fan speeds and an adjustable thermostat, plus a 24-hour programmable timer so you can set it to turn on or off at a specific time. Other convenience features are an energy-saver switch, an air exchanger, and a vent. The ZMB7051 also has four-way adjustable air-flow louvers and an easily accessible filter. It operates very quietly.

Specifications: height, 14⁷/₈"; **width,** 20¹/₁₆"; **depth,** 17⅛"; **weight,** 74 pounds; **maximum window width,** 40¹/₁₆"; **watts,** 600; **volts,** 115; **amps,** 5.6; **moisture removal rate,** 1⅘ pints per hour; **air delivery,** 175 maximum cubic feet per minute. **Warranty: parts and labor,** one year; limited warranty on all parts plus labor allowance, years two to five.

Approx. retail price	Approx. low price
$399	$332

FRIGIDAIRE A06LH5N

✔ **BEST BUY**

The Frigidaire A06LH5N (EER, 9.0) offers efficient cooling at a reasonable price. This 5,900-Btuh model includes an air exhaust and vent, plus eight-way adjustable louvers to direct cool air throughout the room. It has a two-speed fan; the lower speed doubles as a "quiet" button to reduce operating noise. **Specifications: height,** 12⁷⁄₁₆″; **width,** 19⅛″; **depth,** 18½″; **weight,** 71 pounds (shipping); **maximum window width,** 38″; **watts,** 655; **volts,** 115; **amps,** 6; **moisture removal rate,** 1⁹⁄₁₀ pints per hour; **air delivery,** 140 maximum cubic feet per minute. **Warranty: parts and labor,** one year; **sealed system,** five years.

Approx. retail price	**Approx. low price**
not available	$331

PANASONIC CW-601HU   RECOMMENDED

The Panasonic CW-601HU (EER, 9.1) is a 6,000-Btuh unit that costs a little more than other models its size, but its unique L-shaped design may appeal to people who are particularly concerned about operating noise. This air conditioner's compressor is installed outside the window, so very little sound enters the room. And since the front panel is only 6½″ high, you can easily see outside the window. The CW-601HU has two fan speeds, a ten-position adjustable thermostat, and four-way air louvers, but no energy-saver switch or exhaust.

Specifications: height, 13¹³⁄₃₂″ overall, 6½″ front panel; **width,** 22″; **depth,** 23⅝″; **weight,** 66 pounds; **maximum window width,** 40¹³⁄₁₆″; **watts,** 655; **volts,** 115; **amps,** 6; **moisture removal rate,** 1½ pints per hour; **air delivery,** 160 maximum cubic feet per minute. **Warranty: parts and labor,** one year; **sealed system,** five years.

Approx. retail price	**Approx. low price**
$490	$399

AIR CONDITIONERS FROM 8,000 TO 10,000 BTUH

AMANA 10C2MA ✔ BEST BUY

The Amana 10C2MA (EER, 9.6) is a highly efficient 10,000-Btuh model that is extremely sturdy and reliable. It has three fan speeds and eight cooling levels, plus exhaust and vent functions. Its push-button controls are easy to operate. The 10C2MA's filter is easily accessible, and its horizontal air louvers adjust up and down and from side to side to send cool air throughout the room.

Specifications, height, 15⅞"; **width,** 24½"; **depth,** 23⅞"; **weight,** 115 pounds (shipping); **maximum window width,** 42"; **watts,** 1,040; **volts,** 115; **amps,** 9⅕"; **moisture removal rate,** 2 pints per hour; **air delivery,** 340 maximum cubic feet per minute. **Warranty: parts and labor,** one year; **sealed system,** five years.

Approx. retail price
$479

Approx. low price
$463

SEARS KENMORE 78088

✓BEST BUY

The Sears Kenmore 78088 (EER, 9.7) is an energy-efficient 8,000-Btuh air conditioner with several convenient extras. It has three fan speeds and an adjustable thermostat, plus a "super thrust" setting for stronger air flow. Air louvers are adjustable in four directions. The 78088 has an energy-saver switch and exhaust and vent settings. The filter slides out easily.

Specifications, height, 15"; **width,** 22¹¹⁄₁₆"; **depth,** 23½"; **weight,** 84 pounds; **maximum window width,** 38"; **watts,** 825; **volts,** 115; **amps,** 7½; **moisture removal rate,** 2 pints per hour; **air delivery,** 163 maximum cubic feet per minute. **Warranty: parts and labor,** one year; **sealed system,** five years.

Approx. retail price
$450

Approx. low price
not available

FRIEDRICH SS09H10A

✓BEST BUY

The Friedrich SS09H10A (EER, 11.0) is one of the most energy-efficient air conditioners available; you will make up for its additional initial cost in reduced electricity bills. This 9,000-Btuh model offers five fan speeds and nine cooling speeds. It has an energy-saver switch, exhaust and vent functions, and six-way adjustable louvers to send cool air to every corner of the room. The SS09H10A is quiet, reliable, and well-con-

Prices are accurate at time of printing; subject to manufacturer's change.

structed. Its easily accessible, washable filter includes a mosquito trap and a special germicidal treatment.

Specifications: height, 15^{11}/$_{16}$"; **width,** 25^{15}/$_{16}$"; **depth,** 27$\frac{1}{4}$"; **weight,** 111 pounds; **maximum window width,** 42"; **watts,** 820; **volts,** 115; **amps,** 7$\frac{2}{5}$; **moisture removal rate,** 1$\frac{1}{2}$ pints per hour; **air delivery;** 300 maximum cubic feet per minute. **Warranty: parts and labor,** one year; **sealed system,** five years.

Approx. retail price	Approx. low price
$769	$696

WHIRLPOOL ACQO82XW

✔ BEST BUY

The Whirlpool ACQO82XW (EER, 9.0) is a sleek, compact 8,000-Btuh air conditioner with an angled control panel, so controls are easy to see and use. It has three fan speeds and an adjustable thermostat. Twelve-way adjustable louvers disperse cool air throughout the room. The ACQO82XW has a exhaust feature that does a good job of removing stale air and smoke, and its slide-out filter is easy to remove and clean.

Specifications: height, 15$\frac{3}{4}$"; **width,** 25$\frac{1}{4}$"; **depth,** 24$\frac{1}{8}$"; **weight,** 90 pounds; **maximum window width,** 54"; **watts,** 890; **volts,** 115; **amps,** 8$\frac{1}{2}$; **moisture removal rate,** 1^{7}/$_{10}$ pints per hour; **air delivery,** 255 maximum cubic feet per minute. **Warranty: parts and labor,** one year; **sealed system,** five years.

Approx. retail price	Approx. low price
$439	$429

AIR CONDITIONERS OVER 10,000 BTUH

WHITE-WESTINGHOUSE AS147N1A

✔ BEST BUY

The White-Westinghouse AS147N1A (EER, 9.5) is an extremely efficient 14,000-Btuh unit that can cool a large area quietly and efficiently. This heavy-duty model has two fan speeds and an adjustable thermostat. Exhaust and vent settings draw smoke, odors, or stale air outside and bring in fresh air. An

automatic energy-saver control is also included. The AS147N1A's filter can easily be removed for cleaning by tilting out the front panel. It's a good value at a reasonable price.
Specifications: height, 18½"; **width,** 26½"; **depth,** 27"; **weight,** 158 pounds (shipping); **maximum window width,** 47"; **watts,** 1,475; **volts,** 115; **amps,** 12; **moisture removal rate,** 3⅕ pints per hour; **air delivery,** 475 maximum cubic feet per minute. **Warranty: parts and labor,** one year; **sealed system,** five years.

Approx. retail price	**Approx. low price**
$799	$623

EMERSON QUIET KOOL 12DM13

✔ **BEST BUY**

The Emerson Quiet Kool 12DM13 (EER, 9.0) provides 11,800 Btuh of cooling and does a good job of removing moisture from the air. This model has three fan speeds, including a special "quiet" setting, and an adjustable thermostat including a fan-only setting. The 12DM13 has an energy-saver switch and an exhaust setting, plus eight-way adjustable air louvers to send cool air to each corner of the room. The washable filter slides in and out with the front grille in place.
Specifications: height, 13¾"; **width,** 25"; **depth,** 18½"; **weight,** 93 pounds; **maximum window width,** 46"; **watts,** not available; **volts,** 115; **amps,** 11½; **moisture removal rate,** 3½ pints per hour; **air delivery,** 320 maximum cubic feet per minute. **Warranty: parts and labor,** one year.

Approx. retail price	**Approx. low price**
$710	$572

Air Cleaners

The two basic methods of cleaning the air in the home are filtration and precipitation. Filtration makes use of a medium that "catches" airborne particles by trapping them in an area open enough for air to pass through but too small for the particle to penetrate. As particles flow by, they are "caught" through the use of an adhesive coating or "hairy" fiber.

The precipitator or electrostatic filter uses a high-voltage electrical source to give each particle flowing across it a negative charge. When this negatively charged particle passes across the positively charged collector, it is attracted to the coil and retained.

Whichever type of air cleaner you use, place it where it will benefit from maximum air flow in the area you are trying to condition. An air filter, no matter how efficient, can remove impurities only from the air that passes across it. Don't believe any salesperson that tells you that it will end the necessity for dusting your home. Most such visible particles are so large that they fall out of the air stream before it reaches the filter. A good air filter does much more by removing the almost invisible (and often much more harmful) particles that fill the air that we breathe.

Under certain circumstances, when prescribed by a doctor, an air cleaner may be a tax-deductible medical expense.

Best Buys '91

Our Best Buy and Recommended air cleaners follow. They have been selected on the basis of overall value and efficient performance. The air cleaners are presented in the following order: table-top air cleaners and built-in cleaners. Within each category, air cleaners are listed in order of quality. Remember that a Best Buy designation applies only to the model listed, and not necessarily to other models made by the same manufacturer.

TABLE-TOP AIR CLEANERS

Table-top air cleaners are intended for small areas and light loads. They can be beneficial in helping remove smoke and/or pollen from a room. Their air flow is limited to the room in which they are located.

BIONAIRE F-150

 ✔BEST BUY

The Bionaire F-150 has a 3-speed high-efficiency fan that, based on laboratory testing, cleans a 100-square-foot room in 5 minutes. A dirty filter indicator tells you when it's time to clean it. Four two-stage electronically charged filters provide a large cleaning surface. An "on/off" ionizing switch allows the fan to be operated independently of the filter section.
Specifications: height, 13⅝"; **width,** 6¼"; **depth,** 8"; **weight;** 7⅘ pounds. **Warranty:** one year.

Approx. retail price	Approx. low price
$221	$139

POLLENEX PURE AIR 99 MODEL 1850 R

✔BEST BUY

The Pollenex Pure Air 99 Model 1850 R has a multi-stage electrostatic filter. A 5-position push-button power control adjusts the fan speed, and a separate ionizer switch turns the filter section on or off independently of the fan.
Specifications: height, 10⅜"; **width,** 8⅞"; **depth,** 12¼"; **weight,** 7⅘ pounds. **Warranty:** 90 days.

Approx. retail price	Approx. low price
$130	$68

Prices are accurate at time of printing; subject to manufacturer's change.

BUILT-IN AIR CLEANERS

Many larger built-in models can be installed in a "free-standing" manner that requires a lot of floor room. They are most often incorporated into the heating or cooling air duct system, even though some can also be installed in a wall or other area independently from the ducts. Most heating and cooling manufacturers have their own brand of filters; since it is designed to fit their equipment without modification, use of the original manufacturer's product is worth checking out.

SPACE-GARD

✓**BEST BUY**

The Space-Gard air filter attaches to a warm air furnace or air conditioner. The replaceable pleated paper element is nearly as efficient as HEPA ultra-high-efficiency clean room filters. The medium generally lasts twelve months, and replacement is relatively easy and clean.

Warranty: lifetime.

Approx. retail price	Approx. low price
not available	$400
(with installation)	

EMERSON SST14/SST20

✓**BEST BUY**

The Emerson SST14 and SST20 electronic air cleaners are available in two sizes to match the air flow of a particular furnace, and to keep size and installation costs at a minimum. An optional charcoal filter is available to absorb odors. This unit is installed by heating/air conditioning dealers.

Warranty: parts, two years.

Approx. retail price	Approx. low price
$300	not available
(SST/14)	
$450	not available
(SST/20)	

Ceiling Fans

Ceiling fans add a pleasant atmosphere to any room. In today's homes you are likely to find them anywhere—from the porch to the dining room to the bedroom. Prices range from $29.95 to more than $600, depending on features and the type of construction. While all the fans hanging in the store display may look very similar, there are important differences in their construction that correlate directly with their performance.

What To Look For

The type, finish, and size of the fan you choose will depend on the location and the use for which it's intended. Beyond that, noise level is the most important consideration, especially when a fan is being used in a bedroom. As a rule, the larger fans are quieter than small fans in terms of air noise because they can move more air at lower fan speeds. Choose a 52-inch blade unless the size is restricted by the available ceiling space.

Poorly balanced motors and blades, poor bearing tolerance, and even loose motor windings are responsible for high noise levels in many fans. When making your selection, listen closely to the display unit in the store and try it on each of the speeds provided. Usually the background noise in most stores limits your ability to detect an inherent problem unless the fan is exceedingly noisy, and noise levels can vary greatly between individual fans. For this reason, always insist on a return or exchange privilege if the fan proves to be noisy, even though it may operate perfectly well otherwise.

With most ceiling fans, you get what you pay for. Inexpensive models may look good when new, but the brass plating may be thin and the wood and mounting fixtures may be less sturdy. The motor unit itself may be noisy or out of balance. There are some good fans to be found in the lower-priced lines, though, so don't overlook them entirely if they suit your needs. As a rule, higher-priced fans are more likely to be quieter and sturdier.

Why Go Remote?

Infrared remote controls are the latest innovation in ceiling fans. When would you use them? They are a real luxury in a dining room or a den, allowing you to adjust the fan speed and turn the fan and light on and off from the comfort of your easy chair. They are almost a necessity for very tall or otherwise inaccessible ceilings where it may not be practical to install a wall switch.

Fan Installation

If you are using a ceiling fan to replace an existing ceiling light fixture, you can probably install it yourself without any difficulty by following the manufacturer's instructions. Check this out in advance; because of its greater weight and the "torque rebound" when the motor is started, a ceiling fan requires more support than a conventional ceiling light. If the room has no ceiling light in the area where you would like to mount the fan, you may have to call in an electrician or use a surface wiring material such as Wiremold to install a fixture box in the area where you want to install the fan. If it is necessary to call in an electrician, be sure to take this cost into consideration in your planning; since installation costs vary widely, get an estimate first before you finalize your purchase. If you plan to use a multi-position wall-mounted speed control, choose the one recommended by the manufacturer for easiest installation and best results, especially again in terms of noise level. If you use an independent control, be sure that it is the type that prevents motor hum.

Most top-line fans are reversible, allowing you to change the direction of the rotation in winter. The premise is that you can pull air up from the center of the room and force it out along the ceiling and down along the walls, thereby circulating the hot room air that tends to gather near the ceiling. In real life, we have never found that to be much of an advantage. Usually the fan operating in its normal mode accomplishes this same goal, and is particularly useful with cathedral ceilings. We have not been able to measure any significant difference in heat distribution between the reversible and normal mode; we would therefore consider a reversing switch a marginal feature in making your choice.

Best Buys '91

Our Best Buys were chosen on performance and estimated overall value. Within each category, products are listed in order of estimated overall quality. Remember that a Best Buy or Recommended designation applies only to that model; it does not necessarily apply to other models by the same manufacturer or to an entire product line.

HUNTER STUDIO 25634

The Hunter Studio 25634 (also available as 25630 in antique brass finish) features Hunter's new "Comfort Monitor" multifunction remote control, which turns the fan "on/off" and controls speed, reverses rotation, and controls "on/off" and brightness of the optional fan light. The remote transmitter mounts in a wall holder when not in use.
Warranty: five years.

Approx. retail price	**Approx. low price**
$225	$166

HUNTER ORIGINAL 25750

The Hunter Original 25750 (and companion "Original" series fans, model suffix denotes finish) has a permanent oil bath bearing reservoir and a solid cast-iron housing with a 28-pole motor for quietness and durability. The motor on this model is extremely durable.
Warranty: motor, lifetime.

Approx. retail price	**Approx. low price**
$380	$245

Prices are accurate at time of printing; subject to manufacturer's change.

NUTONE ELEGANCE

✓ BEST BUY

The Nutone Elegance (and traditionally styled Verandah II series) is a contemporary paddle fan with four or five (depending on model) 52-inch blades and a very quiet, powerful motor with programmable remote control.

Warranty: as long as you own your home.

Approx. retail price	Approx. low price
$190	not available
(3-speed)	
$285	$210
(computerized remote)	

EQUINOX FILIGREE CLASSIC 50525-2

✓ BEST BUY

The Equinox Filigree Classic 50525-2, together with all "F" series models, are low-cost fans with good durability and performance records. This model has electronically balanced blades and a sealed-bearing housing.

Warranty: five years; motor, lifetime.

Approx. retail price	Approx. low price
$80	$79

BROAN VANTAGE 525R

✓ BEST BUY

The Broan Vantage 525R is a good-quality, 52-inch, 4-blade fan with high-quality optional light kits. Both the housing and trim are heavy-gauge material that can hold up to extreme use.

Warranty: motor, five years.

Approx. retail price	Approx. low price
$198	$155

Portable Space Heaters

Portable space heaters as we know them have been common since the turn of the century. In those times when central heating was found only in the finest homes, they were used as a basic heat source in otherwise frigid areas such as bathrooms and dining areas. With the open, unguarded elements of electric heaters and the dense emissions from the "pot-type" kerosene heaters, the typical heater of that time could never pass today's stringent standards.

Modern space heaters found a rebirth in the mid-1970s as a means of reducing energy consumption by heating only one or two rooms rather than the entire house. Such "zoning" is still the primary reason for their continuing popularity, but many people like the level of comfort they produce as well.

Heaters have also improved. The double-clean burners of the best, modern, high-tech kerosene heaters keep emission levels below the recommended maximums under normal operation. Unless it's a vented model, you should still provide adequate ventilation by cracking a window in accordance with the manufacturer's instructions. Both kerosene and electric heaters are equipped with elaborate guards to prevent contact with flammable materials, and tip-over switches turn them off if they are accidentally overturned.

Advantages and Disadvantages

Electric space heaters have no emissions, but the cost of operation is significantly higher than that of kerosene heaters (up to 3 times as much depending on the relative cost of electrical power and high-grade kerosene where you live). They are not as portable, since an outlet is required in the vicinity, and they are not useful for emergency heat during a power outage. However, they produce no odors and no need for replenishing fuel. With a kerosene heater, this can be a messy chore. The heater (or removable tank) must be carried outdoors, and you must use extreme care to avoid spilling kerosene when refilling the tank. Otherwise, you may be faced with a safety hazard or transport that odor back into the house.

Both electric and kerosene heaters come in two basic types—convection and radiant. Convection-type heaters warm the air in the room and are omni-directional. Radiant heaters are usually identified by their reflective shield and brightly glowing heat sources. Radiant energy travels through the air and does not generate heat until it strikes an object, which may be a person, a wall, or furnishings in the room. (Radiant heat will also travel through glass, so don't waste energy by directing it toward a patio door or window.) The big advantage of radiant heaters is that they allow you to enter a cold room, turn them on, and feel a very pleasant warmth almost immediately, while convective heaters require some time to warm all the air within the room. The radiant heater's coverage is usually limited to about a 30 degree angle from the face of the heater, so it should be properly placed.

Ceramic Heaters

Ceramic element electric heaters are a new type of heater. A ceramic thermistor (or electrical resistor) varies resistance according to temperature. This thermistor is housed in a small box, usually about the size of an 8-inch cube, complete with a fan and an element. This type of heater is self-limiting in that the resistance increases in proportion to temperature so that it provides a constantly modulating heat surface. This allows it to discharge a relatively large volume of heated air over a large surface area of element surface, making it particularly safe. Be cautious when making your purchase; some inexpensive heaters are packaged to look like ceramic heaters, but in reality they contain a conventional nichrome element that does not possess the safety characteristics of a true ceramic element.

The Efficiency Game

Kerosene heaters have relatively high efficiency ratings. All those that we recommend have double-clean systems that cost a little more, but their high efficiency and very low emissions still make them the best value. Don't let anybody sell you an electric heater on the basis that it's more efficient than others. All electric resistance heaters are 100 percent efficient because they deliver 3.412 Btus of heat for every watt of power consumed. The biggest difference among them is in the manner in which they distribute heat, the sturdiness of their construction, and their inherent safety characteristics.

Best Buys '91

Our Best Buys were chosen on performance, estimated overall value, and safety. Within each category products are listed in order of estimated overall quality. Remember that a Best Buy or Recommended designation applies only to that model; it does not necessarily apply to other models.

ELECTRIC SPACE HEATERS

TOASTMASTER COMFORT SENSOR DELUXE 2539

✓ **BEST BUY**

The Toastmaster Comfort Sensor Deluxe 2539 forced-air heater has two fan speeds and two heat levels (1500 and 1200 watts) that shift automatically with thermostat setting, providing quiet air circulation. This convection-type model has a woodgrain metal case and a plastic top with a built-in carrying handle. The unit remains cool to the touch while in operation. **Specifications: height,** 6″; **width,** 25″; **depth,** 6″; **weight,** 3¾ pounds. **Warranty:** one year.

Approx. retail price	**Approx. low price**
$66	$50

Prices are accurate at time of printing; subject to manufacturer's change.

PRESTO VERTICAL QUARTZ
07892

The Presto Vertical Quartz 07892 is a twin-tube quartz heater for the many applications where radiant heat is preferred to convective. The tube switches on and off depending on the control setting, and the wide base prevents accidental tipping. This model provides approximately a 30-degree angle of reflection for radiant heat output.

Specifications: height, 28"; width, 14¼"; depth, 16"; weight, 9¹/₁₀ pounds (shipping). **Warranty:** two years.

Approx. retail price	Approx. low price
$73	$55

PELONIS DISC FURNACE
1500-II

> RECOMMENDED

The Pelonis Disc Furnace 1500-II is an ultra-safe ceramic disc heater, superior to its many imitators. The ceramic disc has a 1500-watt honeycomb element. This model has a built-in carrying handle and a washable filter. It tends to be somewhat noisy on high speeds.

Specifications: height, 8¾"; width, 6¼"; depth, 6¼"; weight, 7 pounds. **Warranty:** five years.

Approx. retail price	Approx. low price
$90	not available

SOUNDESIGN CERAMIC
FURNACE MODEL CH-5200

> RECOMMENDED

The Soundesign Ceramic Furnace Model CH-5200 uses ceramic wafers and a washable filter. Both the timed cycle and thermostatic controls provide comfort levels for varying conditions.

Specifications: height, 7½"; width, 6"; depth, 5⅜"; weight, 5⅗ pounds. **Warranty:** one year.

Approx. retail price	Approx. low price
$119	$97

PORTABLE KEROSENE HEATER

TOYOSTOVE DC100

✓**BEST BUY**

The Toyostove DC100 and the identical Kerosun DC90 Double-Clean model (Toyotomi U.S.A. has owned Kerosun since 1985) are the only top-ranked kerosene heaters. The reason is the double-clean burner that keeps emissions at levels far below those of conventional kerosene heaters. They are of excellent quality and incorporate the usual safety devices plus a wick-stop to prevent overextending the wick.

Specifications: height, 24⅜"; **width,** 18⅝"; **depth,** 18⅝"; **weight,** 26⁹⁄₁₀ pounds. **Warranty:** one year.

Approx. retail price	Approx. low price
$240	not available

Baby Equipment

Safety has to be your first consideration when you purchase baby equipment. Despite strict federal safety regulations regarding manufacture, accidents still occur. No matter how safe a product is, it can be hazardous if it is used incorrectly. Make sure to read all manufacturer's directions for use and closely follow all recommendations for safe assembly. And from a practical as well as safety point of view, ask yourself if a particular product suits your needs before purchasing.

Product Safety

How do you know if a product is really safe for your baby? In addition to making sure that it passes all federal safety regulations (this should be listed with the product's packaging), here are a few checks you can make right in the store.

Run your hands over the equipment. Put them everywhere your inquisitive baby may reach. Is the surface rough or sharp to the touch? Check any hinges, springs, or moving parts, and note whether there are places where your baby's hands or fingers could get caught or pinched.

Are all small parts fastened securely? Make sure nothing can come loose that your baby might swallow.

If the product is designed to hold a child, determine if it is easy to use. For example, will the seatbelt prove difficult to latch? Is it easy to adjust for a baby's comfort? Any kind of belt or harness should hold the baby securely and comfortably. Use your imagination. Make sure there is no way your baby can climb or wiggle out. Be sure carriers and seats are sturdy and will not tip over or fall sideways.

Product Design

Consider the ways in which you plan to use a particular product and whether its design will help or hinder you. For example, if you are looking at a stroller/carriage, try folding it a few times. Lift it in the folded position to see if it will be easy for you to put in your car trunk.

Remember that extras add to price. If you have an extra baby blanket or comforter, you don't need a stroller that comes with one. If you plan to put the crib against a wall, you may not need one with two drop sides. Consider whether or not materials are easy to clean and whether pads are removable.

Look for equipment that conforms to standards established by the Juvenile Products Manufacturers Association. These standards are voluntary, but some items—such as cribs and car seats—must meet federal regulations.

Best Buys '91

Our Best Buy and Recommended baby equipment follows. We reviewed products in the following categories: cribs, strollers, car seats, baby carriers, and nursery monitors. Within each category, products are listed in order of quality. The item we consider the best of the Best Buys is listed first, followed by our second choice, and so on. Remember that a Best Buy or Recommended rating applies only to the model listed; it does not necessarily apply to other models made by the same manufacturer.

CRIBS

Functional, well-designed cribs are available at moderate prices. Cribs made of fine hardwoods are more expensive. Federal standards in effect since 1974 ensure that most cribs on the market are fairly safe. However, some are safer than others. For example, stay away from cribs with decorative open spaces in the ends in which a baby can become trapped. Also, avoid designs that feature horizontal parts that could be used by your baby as a ladder. Look for a crib with evenly spaced bars on all four sides. Lift and shake the crib to see if it is sturdy. Look for a metal bar, which adds stability, under the crib; two bars are ideal. Be sure the drop side(s) operate(s) smoothly and easily; a double-release mechanism prevents accidental release. Make sure the finish is smooth with no jutting hardware to hurt your baby.

SIMMONS TURIN 1403

The Simmons Turin 1403 has an elegant, sturdy design and is constructed of solid Northern hard maple and veneers. The brass-ball casters offer easy mobility when desired. The double drop sides feature a handy foot-operated release. The mattress adjusts to four heights as a child grows. This model is available in a natural wood or painted white finish.
Warranty: return to the store if there is a defect in manufacturing.

Approx. retail price	**Approx. low price**
$340	$271

SIMMONS CABRI 1213

The Simmons Cabri 1213 crib is a brand-new model with a very elegant design. Made of Northern hard maple and ash, it comes in two finishes: white and natural maple. The classic Windsor-style spindles, arch head, and foot ends impart an old-world quality to its craftsmanship. Heavy-duty hardware with rounded corners and strong steel stabilizing bars secure the crib. Extra-deep dropsides help prevent a child from climbing out and various-position mattress springs adjust to a baby's growth.
Warranty: return to the store if there is a defect in manufacturing process.

Approx. retail price	**Approx. low price**
$300	$277

Prices are accurate at time of printing; subject to manufacturer's change.

STROLLERS

There are several types of strollers: regular strollers; umbrella strollers, which are lightweight, collapsible, and good for travel or occasional use; tandem strollers, which carry more than one child; and stroller/carriages, which act as both a stroller and carriage. We have reviewed strollers that perform several functions well. They are all heavy enough to withstand everyday use, but lightweight enough to be packed into the car. They offer upright, semi-upright, and prone seat positions, and have canopies that can be removed or pushed back.

The best strollers are designed with meticulous attention to safety. They maneuver easily, have solid wheels, and are equipped with shock absorbers at least on the rear wheels. Seats are comfortable and covered with soft, absorbent fabric, and belts are securely attached. Though they collapse easily, they employ safety features that lock them into the open position.

GRACO STROLL-A-BED 7215

The Graco Stroll-A-Bed 7215 is a safe and easy-to-use stroller. The padded reversible handle and guard rail are practical features. This stroller converts effortlessly into an infant bed, making it great for travel. Plastic and vinyl parts are wipe-off clean; the seat pad is machine washable. You can open this relatively lightweight, yet sturdy stroller with one hand. It collapses conveniently to store in the car trunk. The rear wheels are secured with dual parking brakes.
Warranty: one year.

Approx. retail price
$79

Approx. low price
not available

CENTURY ULTIMA 11-168-PML

The Century Ultima 11-168-PML is a medium-priced stroller that has all the looks and many of the features of more expen-

---

sive models. The unique posture-pivot handle adjusts to fit most heights and strides, and it reverses for forward- or rear-facing positions. The new Euro-canopy with its peek-a-boo window coordinates with the liner and lets you watch your baby. The extra-wide body has a removable napper bar. Other features include a reversible comfort pad, a full-quilted boot (machine washable) for all-weather protection, a two-position molded footrest, and a deep parcel basket.

Warranty: one year.

Approx. retail price	Approx. low price
$119	$118

FISHER-PRICE 9121 [RECOMMENDED]

The Fisher-Price 9121 is a convertible carriage/stroller. You just press down on the handle to open the stroller. It converts or folds flat with the push of a button. The comfortable pad is reversible and machine washable, and the tray snaps off and stores behind the seat. This stroller also features a large, fully enclosed removable storage basket, a three-point restraint belt, and convenient one-step brakes. The large wheels and soft suspension make riding easy, even over uneven surfaces.

Warranty: three years.

Approx. retail price	Approx. low price
$140	$124

CAR SEATS

Most states have laws mandating the use of car seats for infants and small children. All car seats are required to conform to Federal Motor Vehicle Safety Standards. Infants under 20 pounds must be belted in the seat, facing the rear, and in a reclining position. Larger children may sit upright facing forward. Except for infant seats, most car seats convert from a reclining position to an upright one and can be used for children up to 40 pounds.

Incorrect use of car seats can be dangerous. If they are confusing to operate, they may be used in an improper manner. In

Prices are accurate at time of printing; subject to manufacturer's change.

evaluating car seats, our primary consideration was ease of use. We also looked for comfort and special features. Price differences were largely due to quality of upholstery.

EVENFLO 205145 TRAVEL TANDEM

The Evenflo 205145 Travel Tandem car seat/carrier offers convenience and safety. You can use it in a second car by simply lifting it out of its base. It also locks into most shopping carts and can be used as a rocker. Features include an up-front easy belt release, a rear storage compartment, a multi-position handle/stand, and removable, washable cloth padding. It is recommended for infants up to 20 pounds and meets all federal motor vehicle safety standards.
Warranty: one year.

Approx. retail price	**Approx. low price**
$60	not available

FISHER-PRICE 9101 ·····RECOMMENDED·····

The Fisher-Price 9101 car seat is very easy to handle. The exclusive auto-restraint safety system locks and unlocks with the press of a thumb. When locked, the belt automatically adjusts to the right fit. When unlocked, restraint belts move freely to provide more slack. The machine-washable pad is easily removed for cleaning. The seat installs quickly with standard automotive belt systems, and offers three comfortable recline positions. This model meets all federal motor vehicle safety standards for automobiles and aircraft. In the rear-facing position, it holds infants up to 20 pounds; the forward-facing position accommodates older children up to 40 pounds.
Warranty: three years; **pad**, one year.

Approx. retail price	**Approx. low price**
$79	$69

CENTURY STE4365 ·····RECOMMENDED·····

The Century STE4365 is the only car seat that is adjustable with six unique growth combinations through three shoulder and two crotch positions, which is ideal for heavy winter snowsuits. Made with machine-washable fabric, this car seat features quick-change harness positions with a simple pull-front lever. The dashboard decals help keep your baby amused. Its smooth, gray-blue molded plastic shell has armrests and supports your baby comfortably. This seat accommodates children from infancy up to 40 pounds.

Warranty: one year.

Approx. retail price	**Approx. low price**
$70	$70

BABY CARRIERS

Baby carriers are not car seats, but they are convenient seats for infants up to about 18 pounds. Constructed of smooth, molded plastic, they provide gentle support for young babies when you can't hold them or when you are not in a room with a playpen or crib. They are great for traveling, usually offering a convenient seat for your baby while he or she is being fed. Many are rockers, so your baby can nap in one, too. Although our selections are lightweight, they won't tip over as long as a baby is not over the recommended weight. Many fit right into a shopping cart.

Before purchasing a baby carrier, make sure the surface is smooth all over and that the safety belt is easy to use and secure.

COSCO 06-520-BEO ROCKING BABY CARRIER

The Cosco 06-520-BEO Rocking Baby Carrier offers gentle rocking motion, a rear storage compartment, and a carry handle that rotates to any position. Side handles make lifting easy. The vinyl pad is easy to clean with a sponge. This carrier is suitable for infants up to 18 pounds.

Warranty: one year.

Approx. retail price	**Approx. low price**
$25	$17

Prices are accurate at time of printing; subject to manufacturer's change.

CENTURY KANGA-ROCKA-ROO 1592

✓ **BEST BUY**

The Century Kanga-Rocka-Roo 1592 is a baby carrier suitable for infants from birth up to 18 pounds. It adjusts for rocking, carrying, feeding, and napping, and boasts a unique, lidded storage pouch in the back that's removable for cleaning. It also features a four-position carry handle and a quick-lock buckle on a three-point safety strap for easy entry and exit. The molded plastic base accommodates a machine-washable fabric pad.

Warranty: one year.

Approx. retail price	Approx. low price
$35	$20

GRACO 5500-81 SOFT 'N SENSIBLE

RECOMMENDED

The Graco 5500-81 Soft 'n Sensible molded plastic baby carrier features a soft pad that is easy to remove, machine washable, and replaceable. For babies up to 20 pounds, this comfortable carrier features a front tray of sponge-washable molded plastic that makes it perfect for feeding time or holding small toys. The adjustable sure-grip handle is padded for comfortable carrying.

Warranty: one year.

Approx. retail price	Approx. low price
$30	not available

NURSERY MONITORS

You can't always be in the room with your baby, but you can keep in touch, via sounds, with a nursery monitor. This devise uses a transmitter in a baby's room to relay noises—even soft cooing sounds—to a receiver, which remains with you in another part of the house or even outdoors. Most transmitters pick up sounds within a 10-foot radius. Receivers are battery powered, and most have belt clips so you are free to move around.

Prices are accurate at time of printing; subject to manufacturer's change.

Nursery monitors operate on public airways, so extraneous factors, including another nursery monitor in the area or a portable phone, may cause interference, although many units let you switch between two channels.

FISHER-PRICE 1510

✓ BEST BUY

The Fisher-Price 1510 is a nursery monitor that lights up with even the tiniest baby sounds. A light indicator lets you know if your baby is cooing or crying—even when you're in a noisy room. The louder your baby's sound, the more lights. The portable transmitter permits the monitor to go wherever the baby goes. You can use the handy receiver belt clip to move around easily. Two AC adapters are included. You can also operate the transmitter with four C-size batteries; the receiver takes one 9-volt battery. Features also include a low battery indicator, a channel selector, and a rotary "on/off" volume control. This model is listed with Underwriters Laboratories.

Warranty: one year.

Approx. retail price	Approx. low price
$60	$45

SONY NTM-1

RECOMMENDED

The Sony NTM-1 baby monitor is a great-looking device with sleek European-looking design. The transmitter plugs into a wall outlet; the receiver plugs into a wall outlet (an adapter is included) or can be operated with one 9-volt alkaline battery. The transmitter picks up a baby's sounds from as far away as 10 feet. The monitor light blinks when picking up loud sounds; volume is adjustable. The monitor has a rounded antenna with no sharp points and can be mounted on the wall or set on a table. The receiver has a handy belt clip. A two-channel selection and a power light to indicate a low battery offer added convenience.

Warranty: one year.

Approx. retail price	Approx. low price
$60	$48

Prices are accurate at time of printing; subject to manufacturer's change.

Index